DISCARDED

D1433057

6134386 70

DISCARD

The Logic of Practice

The Logic of Practice

Pierre Bourdieu

Translated by Richard Nice

Stanford University Press
Stanford, California

Stanford University Press
Stanford, California
© 1980 Les Éditions de Minuit
English translation © 1990 Polity Press, Cambridge
    in association with Blackwell Publishers, Oxford
Originally published in French 1980 by
    Les Éditions de Minuit as *Le sens pratique*
Originating publisher of English edition:
    Polity Press, Cambridge
First published in the U.S.A. by
Stanford University Press, 1990
Cloth ISBN 0-8047-1727-3
Paper ISBN 0-8047-2011-8

Original Printing 1990
Last figure below indicates year of this printing:
15 14 13 12 11 10
This book is printed on acid-free paper.

Contents

Preface

What special affinities appeared to him to exist between the moon and woman?

Her antiquity in preceding and surviving successive tellurian generations: her nocturnal predominance: her satellitic dependence: her luminary reflection: her constancy under all her phases, rising and setting by her appointed times, waxing and waning: the forced invariability of her aspect: her indeterminate response to inaffirmative interrogation: her potency over effluent and refluent waters: her power to enamour, to mortify, to invest with beauty, to render insane, to incite to and aid delinquency: the tranquil inscrutability of her visage: the terribility of her isolated dominant implacable resplendent propinquity: her omens of tempest and of calm: the stimulation of her light, her motion and her presence: the admonition of her craters, her arid seas, her silence: her splendour, when visible: her attraction, when invisible.

James Joyce, *Ulysses*

In the social sciences, the progress of knowledge presupposes progress in our knowledge of the conditions of knowledge. That is why it requires one to return persistently to the same objects (here, those examined in *Outline of a Theory of Practice* and, secondarily, in *Distinction*); each doubling-back is another opportunity to objectify more completely one's objective and subjective relation to the object.[1] One has to endeavour to reconstruct retrospectively the successive stages of the relationship, because this labour, which is first exerted on the person who performs it (and which some authors have tried to write into the texture of their 'work in progress', as Joyce put it), tends to remove its own traces. The essential point I try to put over in this book, a point which is in no way personal, would be liable to lose its meaning and its effectiveness if, by letting it be dissociated from the practice from which it started and to which it ought to return, I were to leave it in the unreal, neutralized mode of existence which is that of theoretical 'theses' of epistemological essays.

It is not easy to communicate the social effects that the work of Claude Lévi-Strauss produced in the French intellectual field, or the concrete mediations through which a whole generation was led to adopt a new way of conceiving intellectual activity that was opposed in a thoroughly dialectical fashion to the figure of the politically committed 'total' intellectual represented by Jean-Paul Sartre. This exemplary confrontation probably played a significant part in encouraging a number of those who were then turning towards the social sciences, to conceive the ambition of reconciling theoretical and practical intentions, bringing together the scientific and the ethical or political vocation – which are so often forced to remain separate – in a humbler and more responsible way of performing their task as researchers, a kind of militant craftmanship, as remote from pure science as from exemplary prophecy.

In the Algeria of the late fifties and early sixties, then struggling for its independence, to work towards a scientific analysis of Algerian society meant trying to understand and explain the real foundations and objectives of that struggle, objectives which, beyond the strategically necessary unity, were clearly socially differentiated and even antagonistic; and so endeavouring, not, of course, to influence the outcome of the struggle, but to render the probable deviations predictable and therefore more difficult. For that reason I cannot disown even the naiveties of writings (1961, 1962a) which, though they then seemed to me to achieve the desired reconciliation of the practical and the scientific intention, owe much to the emotional context in which they were written. Still less can I repudiate the predictions, or rather warnings, which concluded my two empirical studies of Algerian society, *Travail et travailleurs en Algérie* (1963) and *Le Déracinement* (1964), even if (especially the latter) they were subsequently used to justify some of the probable deviations which they strove in advance to prevent.

Needless to say, in such a context, in which the problem of racism arose, at every moment, as a question of life or death, a book like Lévi-Strauss's *Race and History* (1952) was much more than an intellectual argument against evolutionism. But it is harder to communicate the intellectual and emotional impact of seeing American Indian mythologies analysed as a language containing its own reason and *raison d'être*. The impact was all the greater because in the course of my research I had been reading some of the innumerable collections of ritual data, recorded without order or method and seeming to have no rhyme or reason, which abound in the libraries and bibliographies devoted to North Africa. The respectful patience and attention to detail with which, in his seminars at the Collège de France, Lévi-Strauss dismantled and reassembled the – at first sight – meaningless sequences of these tales, could not fail to be seen as the model of a kind of scientific humanism. I use that phrase, however derisory it may appear, because it seems to me to express fairly exactly the kind of meta-scientific enthusiasm for science with which I undertook the study of Kabyle ritual, an object which I had initially excluded from my research for reasons similar to those which lead some people, especially in the formerly colonialized countries, to see ethnology as a kind of essentialism, focusing on those aspects of practice most likely to reinforce racist representations. And indeed, virtually all the works partially or totally devoted to ritual which were available when I was writing my *Sociologie de l'Algérie* (1958) seemed to me guilty, at least as regards their objective intention and their social effects, of a particularly scandalous form of ethnocentrism which, with no other justification than a vague Frazerian evolutionism, tending to justify the colonial order, described practices which could only be seen as unjustifiable. That is why I first turned my attention in quite other directions, signposted by some exemplary writings. The book by Jacques Berque, *Les Structures sociales du Haut Atlas* (1955), a model of materialist methodology, particularly valuable in this area, and his admirable articles 'Qu'est-ce qu'une tribu nord-africaine?' (1954) and 'Cent vingt-ans de sociologie maghrébine' (1956), gave me countless starting-points and invaluable points of reference; André Nouschi's studies in agrarian history (1961, 1962) led me to seek the principle of the transformations undergone by peasant economy and society, even in the regions apparently least affected by colonialism, in the history of colonial policy and the major laws on land ownership; and the works of Émile Dermenghem and Charles-André Julien, in their different areas, guided my first steps.

I would never have come to study ritual traditions if the same concern to 'rehabilitate' which had first led me to exclude ritual from the universe of legitimate objects and to distrust all the works which made room for it had not persuaded me, from 1958, to try to retrieve it from the false solicitude of primitivism and to challenge the racist contempt which, through the self-contempt it induces in its victims, helps to deny them knowledge and recognition of their own tradition. For, however great the effect of respectability and encouragement that can be induced, unconsciously rather than consciously, by the fact that a problem or a method comes to be constituted as highly legitimate in the scientific field, this could not completely obscure for me the incongruity and even absurdity of a study of ritual practices conducted in the tragic circumstances of war. This was brought home to me again recently when I rediscovered some photographs of stone jars, decorated with snakes and intended to store seed-corn; I took those photographs in the course of field-work in the Collo region, and their high quality, although I had no flash-gun, was due to the fact that the roof of the house into which they were built had been destroyed when the occupants were expelled by the French army. There was no need to have exceptional epistemological lucidity or outstanding ethical or political vigilance in order to question the deep-rooted determinants of a so obviously 'misplaced' *libido sciendi*. My inevitable disquiet was relieved to some extent by the *interest* my informants always manifested in my research whenever it became theirs too, in other words a striving to recover a meaning that was both their own and alien to them. All the same, it was undoubtedly an awareness of the 'gratuitous' nature of purely ethnographic inquiry that led me to undertake, at the Algiers Institute of Statistics, along with Alain Darbel, Jean-Paul Rivet, Claude Seibel and a whole group of Algerian students, the two projects which later underpinned my two books analysing the social structure of the colonized society and its transformations, *Travail et travailleurs en Algérie* and *Le Déracinement*, as well as various more ethnographic articles in which I aimed to analyse the attitudes towards time which are the basis of pre-capitalist economic behaviour.

The philosophical glosses which, for a time, surrounded structuralism have neglected and concealed what really constituted its essential novelty – the introduction into the social sciences of the structural method or, more simply, of the relational mode of thought which, by breaking with the substantialist mode of thought, leads one to characterize each element by the relationships which unite it with all the others in a system and from which it derives its meaning and function. What is both difficult and rare is not the fact of having what are called 'personal ideas', but of helping in some degree to produce and impose those impersonal modes of thought which enable the most diverse people to think previously unthinkable thoughts. When one realizes how laboriously and slowly the relational (or structural) mode of thought caught on even in mathematics or physics, and when one considers the specific obstacles which hinder its implementation in the social sciences, one can appreciate what an achievement it was to extend the scope of this mode of thought to the 'natural' symbolic systems of language, myth, religion or art. It presupposed, *inter alia*, as Ernst Cassirer pointed out, the practical overcoming of the distinction, established by Leibniz, between truths of reason and truths of fact, in order to treat historical facts as systems of intelligible relations, and to do so in scientific practice and not only in discourse as had been done since Hegel.[2]

In fact, as much as the appearance of absurdity or incoherence, what protects myths or rites from relational interpretation is the fact that they sometimes offer an apparent meaning to partial or selective readings which expect to derive the sense of each element from a special revelation rather than a systematic interrelating with all the elements of the same class. Thus comparative mythology, which pays more attention to the vocabulary of myth or ritual than to its syntax and which identifies translation with word-for-word decoding, ultimately tends only to produce a kind of immense dictionary of all the symbols of all possible traditions, constituted as essences capable of being defined in themselves, and thus gives a concrete image of the libraries imagined by Borges which contain 'everything that can be expressed in all languages'.[3] Those who take the short cut which leads directly from each signifier to the corresponding signified, who dispense with the long detour through the complete system of signifiers within which the relational value of each of them is defined (which has nothing to do with an intuitively grasped 'meaning'), are inevitably limited to an approximate discourse which, at best, only stumbles on to the most apparent significations (for example, the correspondence between ploughing and copulation) by the light of a kind of Jungian-style anthropological intuition backed up by a Frazerian comparative culture which picks out decontextualized themes from the universe of mythical systems and universal religions.[4]

Isolated in this way, these themes offer no further resistance to the recontextualizations which their inspired interpreters inevitably foist on them when, preaching 'spiritual renewal' by a return to the common sources of the great traditions, they rummage in the history of religions or the ethnology of archaic civilizations for the basis of a learned religiosity and an edifying science, obtained by a respiritualization of despiritualizing science. It was also to Lévi-Strauss's credit that he provided the means of completing the abandonment of recourse to the mythological mode of thought in the science of mythologies (a break initiated by Durkheim and Marcel Mauss), by resolutely taking this mode of thought as his object instead of setting it to work, as native mythologists always do, in order to provide a mythological solution to mythological problems. As can be seen clearly when the mythologies studied are powers at stake in social struggles, and particularly in the case of the so-called universal religions, this scientific break is inseparable from a social break with the equivocal readings of 'mythophile' philologists who, by a sort of conscious or unconscious duplicity, transform the comparative science of myths into a quest for the invariants of the great Traditions, endeavouring thereby to combine the profits of scientific lucidity with the profits of religious orthodoxy. Not to mention those who play on the inevitable ambiguity of a learned discourse which borrows from religious experience the words used to describe that experience, in order to produce the appearances of sympathetic participation and enthusiastic proximity and to use the exaltation of primitive mysteries as the pretext for a regressive, irrationalist cult of origins.

In other words, there is hardly any need to point to the colonial situation and the dispositions it favours in order to explain the nature of the ethnology of the Maghreb countries around 1960, particularly as regards the ritual traditions. Those who nowadays set themselves up as judges and distribute praise and blame among the sociologists and ethnologists of the colonial past would be better occupied in trying to understand what it was that prevented the most lucid and the best intentioned of those they condemn from understanding things which are now self-evident for even the least lucid and sometimes the least well-intentioned observers: in what is unthinkable at a given time, there is not only everything that cannot be thought for lack of the ethical or political dispositions which tend to bring it into consideration, but also everything that cannot be thought for lack of instruments of thought such as problematics, concepts, methods and techniques (which explains why good intentions so often make bad sociology – cf. Bourdieu 1976).[5]

The fact remains that I was confronted with a mass of collections of data that were generally incomplete and technically deficient, all the more so when their authors had no specific training and therefore lacked both methods of recording and hypotheses capable of orienting their research and their inquiries (although it sometimes happens that amateurs – or professionals from another discipline, such as linguists – provide rigorously recorded material which is not stripped of everything that the expectations constituting an 'informed' problematic tend to define as insignificant). Against a background of imperfect or incomplete collections of agrarian calendars, marriage rituals or tales, mostly assembled and interpreted in accordance with a vaguely Frazerian logic, a few works of great quality stood out. In particular: a number of works published in the Fichier de documentation berbère (especially the excellent studies by Dallet – 'Le verbe kabyle' (1953) – and Genevois – on the house, weaving, and many other matters – by Yamina Aït Amar ou Saïd and Sister Louis de Vincennes – on marriage and the turn of the year), without which most of the work published since the War would not have existed or would have been very different; the Berber texts published by linguists (in particular, Laoust and Picard); and various monographs such as Germaine Chantréaux's indispensable study (1941–2) of weaving at Aït Hichem, which interested me in both Aït Hichem and weaving; Slimane Rahmani's work on the populations of Cape Aokas and especially his writings on archery, the month of May and rites connected with cows and milking; and those of Reverend Father Devulder (whose warm hospitality provided me with one of the refuges I needed in order to conduct my fieldwork) on wall paintings and magical practices among the Ouadhias (Devulder 1951, 1957).

Alongside these ethnographic contributions there appeared, after I had started to work on ritual, three attempts at anthropological interpretation which deserve a special mention. Paulette Galand-Pernet's article on 'the days of the old woman' (1958) endeavours to extract the meaning of a long-observed and very widespread tradition, by means of a compilation and a 'Dumézilian' analysis of the variants, aimed at establishing the invariant features (transitional period, ugliness, cruelty, whirlwind, rock, evil forces, etc.); it is remarkable that this form of methodological comparativism, which relocates the cultural feature in question in the universe of the geographical variants, arrives at interpretations very close to those which are obtained by reinserting it in the cultural system in which it functions. Among the very many publications devoted to the cycle of the farming year among the Berber-speaking populations, and more specifically, to the opposition between ploughing and harvesting, the two works by Jean Servier, *Les Portes de l'année* (1962) and *L'Homme et l'invisible* (1964), stand out inasmuch as they seek to show, on the basis of very rich ethnographic material, that all the actions of everyday life conform to the symbol of each season, thus setting up a correspondence between the symbolism of the farming rites and the symbolism of the rites of passage. But the limits of the interpretation proposed are no doubt due to the fact that it looks for the principle of the correspondences observed among the different areas of practice in the universal symbolism of the cycle of life and death rather than in the very logic of the ritual practices and objects, seen in terms of their relations to one another. Although folk tales, which are generally fairly free variations on fundamental themes of the tradition, lead one less directly to the deep-rooted schemes of the *habitus* than do ritual practices themselves or, at the level of discourse, riddles, sayings or proverbs, Camille Lacoste's *Le Conte kabyle* (1970) brings together some interesting ethnographic information, particularly on the world of women, and it has the virtue of refusing the easy solutions of comparativism inasmuch as it seeks the key to a historical discourse within the discourse itself. But it is not sufficient to note that the universal logic of myth can never be apprehended outside of its particular actualization, in order to move beyond a dictionary of the fundamental features of a particular culture, a contribution which is in itself extremely valuable (as can be seen simply from the index of *Le Conte kabyle*).

It is only too clear that mythic signs, which are more 'motivated' in their tangible exterior and their psychological resonance, lay themselves open to all the forms of intuitionism which seek to extract directly from them the meaning (as opposed to the value) of the cultural features, taken individually or fused in the felt unity of an overall vision; the more so since so-called intuitive understanding is the inevitable product of the learning through familiarization that is implied in any extended work of inquiry and analysis. But it is less obvious that one does not have to choose between evocation of the whole set of intuitively intelligible features and the endless compilation of scattered elements or the (apparently) impeccable analysis of some well-defined and unassailable domain which could really only be accounted for by replacing it in the complete network of the relationships constituting the system. To apprehend the elements of a corpus as themes capable of being interpreted in isolation or at the level of partial sets, is to forget that, as Saussure (1974: 118) put it, '*arbitrary* and *differential* are two correlative qualities'; that each of these features only means what the others do not mean and that, being in itself (partially) indeterminate, it only receives its full determination from its relationship to the set of other features, i.e. as a difference in a system of differences. For example, if the ethnologist's trained intuition immediately sees a crossroads – a dangerous place, haunted by spirits and often marked by heaps of stones, like places where blood has been spilt – as the point where two opposing direcitons, the male, dry East and the female, wet West, intersect, mingle and couple, this is obviously because it implicitly connects it with all the places or acts of crossing, like the point where the threads cross in weaving, or the dangerous assembly of the weaving loom, or the quenching water and the act of quenching iron, or ploughing or the sexual act. But in fact the relationship of this feature with fertility or, more precisely, with male fertility, confirmed by certain rites,[6] can only be fully understood by reconstructing the set of differences which, step by step, determine it. Thus, by opposition to the *fork* which, as an informant put it, 'is the place where ways divide, separate' (*anidha itsamfaragen ibardhan*), in other words an empty place (like *thigejdith*, the central fork in the house which has to be filled by *asalas*, the main beam), it is constituted as a 'place where ways meet' (*anidha itsamyagaran ibardhan*), that is, as full; in opposition to the house, that is, to the female-full (*laâmara*) and the fields and the forest, the male-full (*lakhla*), it is defined as the male-empty, etc. To give a complete account of the slightest rite, to rescue it completely from the absurdity of an unmotivated sequence of unmotivated acts and symbols, one would thus have to reinsert each of the acts and symbols which it brings into play into the system of differences which determines it most directly, and eventually into the whole mythico-ritual system; and also, simultaneously, into the syntagmatic sequence which defines it in its singularity which, as the intersection of all the sets of differences (crossroads, daybreak, quenching water, etc.), limits the arbitrariness of its own elements. Thus one can describe the advance of any structural research in the very same words that Duhem (1974: 204–5) uses to describe the advance of physical science: 'a symbolic painting in which continual retouching gives greater comprehensiveness and unity . . . whereas each detail of this picture, cut off and isolated from the whole, loses all meaning and no longer represents anything'.

Duhem's description accurately describes the countless, always minor, adjustments which lead from the first rough outline of the system to the provisionally final table which contains many more facts in a much denser network of relationships. Because I cannot relate here, as only a research journal could, all the successive small steps forward, the countless *trouvailles* which would have escaped eyes less prepared to spot them, or the many restructurings each time leading to a redefinition of the meaning of the elements already integrated into the model, I shall simply reproduce a provisional synopsis which I presented to a conference on Mediterranean ethnology held at Burg Wartenstein in 1959 and which, with a few modifications, could still serve as a 'summary' of the final analysis – except that the essential feature of such an analysis is that it cannot be summarized:

'Autumn and winter are opposed to spring and summer as wet is opposed to dry, up to down, cold to hot, left to right, west and north to east and south, or night to day. The organizing principle of the temporal succession is the same one which determines the division of labour between the sexes, the distinction between the moist foods of the wet season and the dry foods of the dry season, the alternations of social life between feasts, rites, games and work, and the organization of space. The same principle underlies certain structural features of the group, such as the opposition between the "moieties" (*s'uff*) and determines the internal spatial organization of the house and the fundamental opposition in the system of values (*nif*, point of honour, vs. *h'urma*, honour). Thus, corresponding to the opposition between the wet season, associated with fertility and germination, and the dry season, associated with the death of cultivated nature, is the opposition between ploughing and weaving, associated with the sexual act, on the one hand, and harvesting, associated with death, on the other, and also the opposition between the ploughshare which gives life and the sickle which destroys it. All these oppositions take their place in a broader system in which life is opposed to death, water to fire, the powers of nature, which have to be placated, to the techniques of culture, which have to be handled with precaution.' (1964b: 56–7; see also 1965 for a similar exposition)

To move beyond this provisional construction, which sketched the first outline of a network of relations of opposition which still needed to be completed and complicated, in 1962 I started to record on punched cards (some 1,500 of them) all the published data that I had been able to confirm by inquiry together with the data I had myself collected, either by endeavouring to observe and question more systematically in areas of practice already much studied, such as the agrarian calendar, weddings or weaving, or by bringing to light, in response to a different problematic (in other words, a different theoretical culture), whole areas of practice which previous authors had more or less systematically ignored (although one can always find scattered observations), such as the structure and orientation of time (divisions of the year, the day, human life), the structure and orientation of space (especially inside the house), children's games and movements of the body, the rituals of infancy and the parts of the body, values (*nif* and *h'urma*) and the sexual division of labour, colours and the traditional interpretation of dreams, etc. To which must be added the information I derived, in the last stage of my work, from a questioning of informants and of texts systematically oriented not towards 'symbols' but towards symbolic practices such as going in and coming out, filling and emptying, opening and closing, tying and untying, etc. All these new data were important in my eyes not so much because they were 'new' (so long as there is a generative *habitus* somewhere at work, one will never cease to 'discover' new data) but rather because of their strategic role as 'intermediate terms', as Wittgenstein calls them, which made it possible to discover new correlations. I am thinking, for example, of the link between the ploughshare and lightning which, beyond the folk etymology of the two words, reveals the fact that the ploughshare can be used as a euphemism to mean lightning; the belief that lightning leaves a mark in the soil identical to that of the ploughshare; the legend that an ancestor of the family assigned to 'go out for the first ploughing' saw lightning strike one of his plots, dug in the earth at that spot, and found a piece of metal which he 'grafted' on to his ploughshare; the link, marked by the verb *qabel*, between the values of honour and spatial and temporal orientations; the link, established through the loom and the properties associated with its differential position in the space of the house, between the orientation of space, the division of labour between the sexes, and the values of honour; or, finally, all the links which, through the opposition between the paternal uncle and the maternal uncle, are set up between the official system of kinship relations and the mythico-ritual system.

The establishment of a file with which all the possible cross-tabulations could be carried out made it possible to draw up, for each of the fundamental acts or symbols, the network of relations of opposition or equivalence which determine it, by means of a simple coding enabling the co-occurrences and mutual exclusions to be located manually. In parallel to this, I had overcome the practical antinomies arising from the aim of establishing a systematic synthesis of all the details observed, by limiting myself to analysis of the internal space of the house which, as a miniature version of the cosmos, constituted an object that was both complete and circumscribed. In fact, my article on the Kabyle house (1970), written in 1963 and published in the collection of texts edited by Jean Pouillon and Pierre Maranda in honour of Claude Lévi-Strauss, is perhaps the last work I wrote as a blissful structuralist. For it was becoming apparent to me that to account for the quasi-miraculous and therefore somewhat incredible necessity, without any organizing intention, that was revealed by analysis, one had to look to the incorporated dispositions, or more precisely the body schema, to find the ordering principle (*principium importans ordinem ad actum*, as the Scholastics put it) capable of orienting practices in a way that is at once unconscious and systematic. I had been struck by the fact that the rules of transformation making it possible to move from the space inside the house to the space outside can be brought back to movements of the body, such as a half-turn, which play a well-known role in rites, where objects, animals or clothing are constantly turned upside down or back to front, to the left or the right, etc.

But above all, it was the ambiguities and contradictions which the very effort to push the application of the structural method to its furthermost conclusions constantly raised, that led me to question not so much the method itself as the anthropological theses tacitly posited in the very fact of consistently applying it to practices. To fix the various oppositions or equivalences which analysis enabled me to identify, I had constructed diagrams, for the various areas of practice – agrarian rites, cooking, women's activities, periods of the life-cycle, moments of the day, etc. – which, taking practical advantage of the virtue of the synoptic diagram according to Wittgenstein, 'of making possible that understanding which consists just in the fact that we "see the connections"' (1979: 9), gave visible form to the relations of homology or opposition while restoring the linear order of temporal succession. The 'grouping of factual material' performed by the diagram is in itself an act of construction, indeed an act of interpretation, inasmuch as it brings to light the whole system of relationships and removes the advantage one has when manipulating separate relationships, as and when they occur to intuition, by forcing one to relate each opposition to all the others.

It was this very property of the synoptic diagram that led me to discover the limits of the logic immanent in the practices which it sought to make manifest, in the form of the contradictions manifested by the synchronization effect which it performs. Trying to combine all the available information about the 'agrarian calendar' in a single circular diagram, I encountered countless contradictions as soon as I endeavoured to fix simultaneously more than a certain number of fundamental oppositions, of whatever kind. Similar difficulties arose whenever I tried to superimpose the diagrams corresponding to the various areas of practice: if I established one set of equivalences, then another one, indubitably observed, became impossible, and so on. If I mention the hours I passed, with Abdelmalek Sayad (who has helped me greatly in my analysis of ritual and with whom I undertook similar work on variants of the marriage ritual – with the same result), trying to resolve these contradictions instead of noting them immediately and seeing in them the effect of the limits inherent in practical logic, which is only ever coherent roughly, up to a point, I do so mainly to show how difficult it is to escape from the social demand, reinforced by the structuralist vulgate, which led me to seek perfect coherence in the system.[7] Quite apart from the fact that the very intention of understanding practical logics presupposes a conversion of all one's acquired dispositions, in particular a renunciation of everything that is normally associated with reflexion, logic and theory – 'noble' activities entirely raised against 'common' modes of thought – the difficulty was made all the greater by the fact that interpretation cannot put forward any other proof of its truth than its capacity to account for the totality of the facts in a completely coherent way. This explains, it seems to me, why it was so hard to accept and really take into account in my analysis the objective ambiguity (even in terms of the system of classification) of a whole set of symbols or practices (cinders, the ladle, the doll used in some rites, etc.), to classify them as unclassifiable and to write this inability to classify everything into the very logic of the system of classification.

It also took me a long time to understand that the logic of practice can only be grasped through constructs which destroy it as such, so long as one fails to consider the nature, or rather the effects, of instruments of objectification such as genealogies, diagrams, synoptic tables, maps, etc., among which, thanks to the recent work of Jack Goody (1977), I would now include mere transcription in writing. Probably because this inquiry was never inspired by a pure theoretical concern for epistemological clarification, I never thought of moving, as is commonly done nowadays, from critical analysis of the social and technical conditions of the objectification and definition of the limits of validity of the products obtained in these conditons, to a 'radical' critique of all objectification and thereby of science itself. If it is to be more than the projection of personal feelings, social science necessarily presupposes the stage of objectification, and once again the necessary breakthrough is achieved with the aid of the tools provided by structuralist objectification.

Having said this, it is not so easy to understand and to make it practically understood that, as the model of a practice which does not have this model as its principle, the diagram and all the oppositions, equivalences and analogies that it displays at a glance are only valid so long as they are taken for what they are, logical models giving an account of the observed facts in the most coherent and most economical way; and that they become false and dangerous as soon as they are treated as the real principles of practices, which amounts to simultaneously overestimating the logic of practices and losing sight of what constitutes their real principle. One of the practical contradictions of scientific analysis of a practical logic lies in the paradoxical fact that the most coherent and also most economical model, giving the simplest and most economical account of the whole set of facts observed, is not the principle of the practices which it explains better than any other construct; or – which amounts to the same thing – that practice does not imply – or rather excludes – mastery of the logic that is expressed within it.

An example will make this clearer. We know that the homology between the agrarian cycle and the cycle of weaving, the principle of which was stated long ago by Basset,[8] is paralleled by a homology, which has often been noted, between the cycle of weaving and the cycle of human life – so long, of course, as one does not go beyond the lowest common denominator of the three cycles whose 'correspondences' are evoked, piecemeal, in terms of the logic of the situation in question, both by informants and by interpreters who unwittingly reproduce the logic of practical understanding of the mythico-ritual system. In other words, in this particular case, the complete model could be summed up in the following formula: the loom is to weaving, the product of a dangerous uniting of contraries which is torn from it by a violent cutting, as the field (or the earth) is to the corn and as woman (or the womb) is to the child. This construct, which the users would no doubt accept, and which makes it possible to account for the quasi-totality of the relevant facts (or those produced by observation or questioning armed with this model), or, rather, to recreate them (theoretically) without being obliged to undertake an interminable narrative, is not as such the principle of agents' practice. The generative formula which enables one to reproduce the essential features of the practices treated as an *opus operatum* is not the generative principle of the practices, the *modus operandi*. If the opposite were the case, and if practices had as their principle the generative principle which has to be constructed in order to account for them, that is, a set of independent and coherent axioms, then the practices produced according to perfectly conscious generative rules would be stripped of everything that defines them distinctively as practices, that is, the uncertainty and 'fuzziness' resulting from the fact that they have as their principle not a set of conscious, constant rules, but practical schemes, opaque to their possessors, varying according to the logic of the situation, the almost invariably partial viewpoint which it imposes, etc. Thus, the procedures of practical logic are rarely entirely coherent and rarely entirely incoherent.

To demonstrate this, at the risk of wearying the reader, one would have to recite pell-mell all the facts collected, without imposing on them even the basic level of construction represented by chronological order (inasmuch as it evokes practically the correspondence between the cycles and in particular with the agrarian cycle): the woman who starts the weaving abstains from all dry food and on the evening when the loom is assembled the whole family eats a meal of couscous and fritters; the loom is assembled in autumn and most of the weaving is done in winter; the art of decorating cloth was taught by Titem Tahittust, who found a fragment of wonderful woven cloth in a dunghill; the empty or full triangles which decorate the weaving represent a star when they are attached by their base (or, if they are larger, the moon), and are called *thanslith*, a symbol which, as its name indicates, 'is at the origin of all design', when they are attached by their apex; maidens must not step across the weaving; the point where the threads cross is called *erruh'*, the soul; when rain is wanted, the carding-comb is placed on the threshold and sprinkled with water, etc. (To avoid a facile effect of disparateness, I mention here only those pertinent facts which have been collected by the same observer (Chantréaux 1941–2), in the same place (the village of Aït Hichem) and which I have been able to verify, completing them on some points.)

Above all, one would have to show how, guided by a sort of sense of compatibilities and incompatibilities which leaves many things indeterminate, ritual practices can apprehend the same object in very different ways, within the limits defined by the most flagrant incompatibilities (and also, of course, by technical constraints) or define different objects in identical ways, treating the loom in practice sometimes as a person who is born, grows up and dies, sometimes as a field which is sown and then stripped of its product, or as a woman, in which case weaving is seen as a delivery, or again, in another of its social uses, as a guest – like the guest it is placed with its back to the 'wall of light' – who is welcomed, or as a sacred refuge or a symbol of 'uprightness' and dignity.[9] In short, the practices observed stand in relation to practices explicitly governed by the principles that the analyst has to produce in order to account for them – if indeed this were possible and desirable in practice, where perfect coherence is never an advantage – as old houses, with their successive annexes and all the objects, partially discordant but fundamentally in harmony with them, that have accumulated in them in the course of time, to apartments designed from end to end in accordance with an aesthetic concept imposed all at once and from outside by an interior designer. The coherence without apparent intention and the unity without an immediately visible unifying principle of all the cultural realities that are informed by a quasi-natural logic (is this not what makes the 'eternal charm of Greek art' that Marx refers to?) are the product of the age-old application of the same schemes of action and perception which, never having been constituted as explicit principles, can only produce an unwilled necessity which is therefore necessarily imperfect but also a little miraculous, and very close in this respect to a work of art. The ambiguity of many symbols and ritual acts and the contradictions which, although they are practically compatible, set them against each other on one point or another, and the impossibility of bringing them all into a single system that can be simply deduced from a small number of principles, all result from the fact that, without needing to establish the homology explicitly, but led by a practical understanding of the overall equivalence between a moment in the agrarian cycle and a moment in weaving (for example, the assembly of the loom and the opening of ploughing), agents apply the same schemes of perception and action to either situation or transfer the same ritualized sequences from one to another (as happens, for example, with funeral chants which may be sung by men at harvest time and by women when the woven cloth is being cut). This practical sense is, on reflexion, no more and no less mysterious than the one that confers stylistic unity on all the choices that the same person, that is, the same taste, may make in the most varied areas of practice, or the sense that enables a scheme of appreciation such as the opposition between bland and bold, dull and lively, insipid and piquant, to be applied to a dish, a colour, a person (more precisely, their eyes, their features, their beauty) and also to remarks, jokes, a style, a play or a painting. It is the basis of those realities, overdetermined and at the same time under-determined, which, even when their principle has been understood, remain very difficult to master completely, except in a kind of lyrical paraphrase that is as inadequate and sterile as ordinary discourse about works of art. I am thinking, for example, of the countless consonances and dissonances that result from the superimposition of approximate applications of the same schemes of thought: thus, the loom, which is a world in itself, with its up and down, its east and west, its heaven and earth, its fields and harvests, and its crossroads, dangerous encounters of contrary principles, derives some of its properties and its uses (for example, in oaths) from its position, determined according to the very principle of its internal divisions, within the space of the house, which itself stands in the same relation, as microcosm to macrocosm, to the world as a whole. Real mastery of this logic is only possible for someone who is completely mastered by it, who possesses it, but so much so that he is totally possessed by it, in other words depossessed. And this is because there can only be practical learning of the schemes of perception, appreciation and action which are the precondition of all 'sensible' thought and practice, and which, being continually reinforced by actions and discourses produced according to the same schemes, are excluded from the universe of objects of thought.

As I have constantly suggested by frequent use of deliberately ethnocentric comparisons, I would probably have been less inclined to make a critical re-examination of the elementary acts of anthropology if I had not felt ill at ease with the definition of the object that structuralism offered when, with a confidence to which I could not aspire, it asserted the epistemological privilege of the observer. In opposition to intuitionism, which fictitiously denies the distance between the observer and the observed, I kept on the side of the objectivism that is concerned to understand the logic of practices, at the cost of a methodical break with primary experience; but I never ceased to think that it was also necessary to understand the specific logic of that form of 'understanding' without experience that comes from mastery of the principles of experience – that what had to be done was not to sweep away the distance magically through spurious primitivist participation, but to objectify the objectifying distance and the social conditions that make it possible, such as the externality of the observer, the objectifying techniques that he uses, etc. Perhaps because I had a less abstract idea than some people of what it is to be a mountain peasant, I was also, and precisely to that extent, more aware that the distance is insurmountable, irremovable, except through self-deception. Because theory – the word itself says so – is a spectacle, which can only be understood from a viewpoint away from the stage on which the action is played out, the distance lies perhaps not so much where it is usually looked for, in the gap between cultural traditions, as in the gulf between two relations to the world, one theoretical, the other practical. It is consequently associated in reality with a social distance, which has to be recognized as such and whose true principle, a difference in distance from necessity, has to be understood, failing which one is liable to attribute to a gap between 'cultures' or 'mentalities' what is in fact an effect of the gap between social conditions (also arising in the anthropologist's native experience in the form of class differences). Familiarity, which books cannot give, with the practical mode of existence of those who do not have the freedom to distance the world can thus be the basis both of a more acute awareness of distance and of a real proximity, a kind of solidarity beyond cultural differences.

Thus I was forced constantly to question both the generic and the particular aspects of my relationship to the object (without, I believe, introducing any self-indulgence). And it may be that the objectification of the generic relationship of the observer to the observed which I endeavoured to perform, through a series of 'tests' that increasingly tended to become experiments, is the most significant product of my whole undertaking, not for its own sake, as a theoretical contribution to the theory of practice, but as the principle of a more rigorous definition, less dependent on individual dispositions, of the proper relation to the object which is one of the most decisive conditions of truly scientific practice in the social sciences.

The scientific effects of this work of objectification of the relationship to the object seem to me particularly clear in the case of my research on Kabyle marriage. On the basis of genealogies drawn up in various villages, first in Kabylia, then in the Collo valley, and finally in Ouarsenis, Abdelmayek Sayad and I had tried to calculate the frequency, within the universe of possible forms of marriage, of marriage with the parallel cousin, which the ethnographic tradition regarded as the local 'norm'. We found that the proportions that emerged were quite meaningless because they depended on the extent of the social unit in relation to which the calculation was made, which could not be objectively determined but was at stake in strategies within social reality itself. After I had abandoned a project yielding only negative information in order to concentrate my efforts on analysis of marriage ritual, it became clear to me that the variations observed in the unfolding of the ceremonies, far from being simple variants seemingly predisposed to serve the structuralist interpretation, in fact corresponded to variations in the genealogical, economic and social relations between the spouses and consequently in the social significance and function of the unions sanctioned by the ritual. One only had to observe that the ritual that is deployed on its full scale for marriages between great families from different tribes is reduced to its simplest expression for marriages between parallel cousins, to see that each of the forms of the ritual that accompanies each form of marriage is not a simple variant, arising from a kind of semiological game, but a dimension of a strategy which takes on its meaning within the space of possible strategies. Since this strategy is the product, not of obedience to a norm explicitly posited and obeyed or of regulation exerted by an unconscious 'model', it became clear that it cannot be explained without taking into account not only the purely genealogical relationship between the spouses (which can itself undergo strategic manipulation) but a whole range of information about the families united by the marriage, such as their relative positions within their groups, the history of their past exchanges and the balance-sheet of these transactions at the moment in question, about the spouses (age, previous marriages, physical appearance, etc.), the history of the negotiation and the associated exchanges which led up to the union, etc.

'One only had to observe that the ritual . . . to see . . .' Rhetoric takes short cuts which almost make one forget that scientific practice never takes the form of an inevitable sequence of miraculous intellectual acts, except in methodology manuals and academic epistemology. It is not easy, without self-congratulation or reconstruction by hindsight, to describe the long effort applied to oneself which little by little leads to the *conversion* of one's whole view of action and the social world that is presupposed by 'observation' of facts that are totally new because they were totally invisible to the previous view: marriage ritual conceived no longer simply as a set of ritual acts signifying by their difference in a system of differences (which it also is) but as a social strategy defined by its position in a system of strategies oriented towards the maximizing of material and symbolic profit; 'preferential' marriage treated no longer as the product of obedience to a norm or conformity to an unconscious model but as a reproduction strategy, taking on its meaning in a system of strategies generated by the *habitus* and oriented towards realization of the same social function; the conducts of honour, seen no longer as the product of obedience to rules or submission to values (which they also are, since they are experienced as such), but as the product of a more or less conscious pursuit of the accumulation of symbolic capital.

It was, I think, no accident that between the time when I had to abandon the problem of Kabyle marriage and the time when I was able to return to it, in the early 1970s, I had attempted to revise a study I had carried out in 1960 in a village in Béarn (south-west France), which I had consciously conceived as a kind of reverse test of my experience, as an anthropologist, of familiarization with an alien world (see Bourdieu 1962b; 1972). Alerted by a simple sentence uttered in a real situation ('The A's are much more kith-and-kin with the B's now there's a *polytechnicien* in the family'), I was able to see what all societies and all theories of kinship strive to repress by proceeding as if the real relations between kin were deducible from kinship relations as defined by the genealogical model. One is more or less 'kith and kin', at equivalent genealogical distances, depending on how much interest one has in it and how 'interesting' the kinsmen in question are. To observe that kinship relations are also relations of interest, that the socially exalted relationship between brothers can, in the case of Kabylia, conceal structural conflicts of interest, or in Béarn, serve as a mask and a justification for economic exploitation, with a younger brother often being an acknowledged 'unpaid servant', often condemned to celibacy; to observe that the domestic unit, the site of competition for the economic and symbolic capital (land, a name, etc.) of which it has exclusive ownership, is divided by struggles for the appropriation of this capital, in which each person's strength depends on the economic and symbolic capital he possesses in his own right according to his genealogical and economic position and the extent to which he is able to get the group on his side by conforming to the rules officially governing kin relations; to see that the matrimonial exchanges of the structuralist tradition are only one aspect of an economy of exchanges between the sexes and between the generations which always obeys the logic of costs and benefits, including the costs of transgressing the official norm and the gains in respectability accruing from respect for the rule; and to see all this, not within one of the highly neutralized social relationships which the anthropologist usually experiences (if indeed this were possible, for everywhere there are things that are not said or not done in the presence of an outsider), but within an observing relationship which was itself a kind of kinship – was to perform nothing less than a conversion of the whole relationship to the object and to oneself and a practical break with the naive humanism which is perhaps simply a form of indulgence towards an indulgent self-image and which, combined with the desire to rehabilitate (a natural reaction against the prevailing contempt), had sometimes led me to write about the Kabyle sense of honour in terms redolent of essays on the heroes of Corneille. (I must say that, on this decisive point, my reading of Max Weber – who, far from opposing Marx, as is generally thought, with a spiritualist theory of history, in fact carries the materialist mode of thought into areas which Marxist materialism effectively abandons to spiritualism – helped me greatly in arriving at this kind of generalized materialism; this will be a paradox only to those who have an over-simple view of Weber's thought, owing to the combined effect of the rarity of translations, the one-sidedness of the early French and American interpretations, and the perfunctory anathemas pronounced by 'Marxist' orthodoxy.)

The distance the anthropologist puts between himself and his object – institutionalized in the division between anthropology and sociology – is also what enables him to stand outside the game, along with everything he really shares with the logic of his object. Probably the clearest example of this separation, which prevents social scientists from putting into their scientific practice the practical understanding they have of the logic of practice, is what Voloshinov calls philologism, the propensity to treat words and texts as if they had no other *raison d'être* than to be decoded by scholars. Nothing is more paradoxical, for example, than the fact that people whose whole life is spent fighting over words should strive at all costs to fix what seems to them to be the one true meaning of objectively ambiguous, overdetermined or indeterminate symbols, words, texts or events which often survive and generate interest just because they have always been at stake in struggles aimed precisely at fixing their 'true' meaning. This is true of all sacred texts, which, being invested with a collective authority, like sayings, maxims or gnomic poems in pre-literate societies, can be used as the tools of a recognized power over the social world, a power which one can appropriate by appropriating them through interpretation.[10]

Is it really sufficient to account for practices by a 'grouping of the factual material' which enables one to 'see the correlations'? And when one tacitly reduces them to the semiological juggling which the interpreter's discourse makes of them, is this not another way of abandoning them to absurdity? I have no polemical axe to grind in pointing out that the anthropologist would probably give a better account of rituals or kinship relations if he introduced into his theory the 'understanding' – in Wittgenstein's sense of the ability to use them correctly – that is evident in his relations with the founding fathers of the discipline or his skill at performing the social rituals of academic life. To analyse a ritual with complete immunity from the ethnocentrism of the observer, without relapsing into the spurious intuitive participation of those who hanker for patriarchal origins or the neo-Frazerian cult of vestiges, it is necessary and sufficient to understand this practical understanding, the same one with which, when faced with a rite whose reason escapes us, we at least understand that we are dealing with a rite; and to understand what distinguishes it from the interpretation which one can only arrive at by placing oneself outside the practice.[11] In other words, one has to reintegrate into the theory of rituals the theory of the practical understanding of all the ritual acts and discourses which we ourselves perform, not only in churches and cemeteries, the particularity of which lies precisely in the fact that it does not occur to anyone to experience them as absurd, arbitrary or unmotivated, although they have no other *raison d'être* than that they exist or are socially recognized as worthy of existing (sociological analysis must also establish the conditions of possibility and validity of this understanding and these acts: see Bourdieu 1975b; Bourdieu and Delsaut 1975). Rites are practices that are ends in themselves, that are justified by their very performance; things that one does because they are 'the done thing', 'the right thing to do', but also because one cannot do otherwise, without needing to know why or for whom one does them, or what they mean, such as acts of funeral piety. This is what the work of interpretation, which seeks to restore their meaning, to grasp their logic, makes one forget: they may have, strictly speaking, neither meaning nor function, other than the function implied in their very existence, and the meaning objectively inscribed in the logic of actions or words that are done or said in order to 'do or say something' (when there is 'nothing else to be done'), or more precisely in the generative structures of which these words or actions are the product – or even in the oriented space within which they are performed.

Just as one cannot speak adequately of ritual unless one understands that ritual is essentially behaviour that is both 'sensible' and devoid of sense intention and that the scientific intention is essentially the project of discovering sense, so too one cannot really account for the social uses of kinsmen and kinship unless one has objectified the objectifying relationship and seen what it hides: agents (and the observer too as soon as he ceases to be an observer) do not have with their kinsmen and their kinship the relationship that is set up in observation and which presupposes no practical use of kin or kinship. In short, one has quite simply to bring into scientific work and into the theory of practices that it seeks to produce, a theory –

which cannot be found through theoretical experience alone – of what it is to be 'native', that is, to be in that relationship of 'learned ignorance', of immediate but unselfconscious understanding which defines the practical relationship to the world. (This procedure is, needless to say, the exact opposite of the one that consists in founding historical or sociological understanding either on a 'psychic participation' or a 'psychic reproduction', in Dilthey's terms, or on an 'intentional modification' or an 'intentional transposition into the Other', as Husserl puts it – sophisticated versions of the spontaneous theory of understanding as 'putting oneself in somebody else's place.')

The representation generally accepted of the opposition between the 'primitive' and the 'civilized' derives from ignoring the fact that the relationship that is set up, here as elsewhere, between the observer and the observed is a particular case of the relationship between knowing and doing, interpreting and using, symbolic mastery and practical mastery, between logical logic, armed with all the accumulated instruments of objectification, and the universally pre-logical logic of practice.[12] And this difference, which is inherent in intellectual activity and the intellectual condition, is no doubt what intellectual discourse has least chance of accurately expressing. What is at stake is how far the objectifier is willing to be caught up in his work of objectification. The objectivist relation to the object is a way of keeping one's distance, a refusal to take oneself as an object, to be caught up in the object. For example, I am not sure that I would have come near to what I now see as the meaning of ritual experience and the function of the generative schemes which it implements, if I had been content to push the anamnesis of what is socially repressed far enough to remember that, just as the Kabyles condense their whole system of values into the word *qabel*, to face, to face the east, the future, so the older peasants in Béarn would say *capbat* (literally, head down) to mean not only 'down, below' but also 'northwards', and *capsus* or *catsus* (head up), meaning 'up' and also 'southwards' (likewise, *cap-aban*, head forward, for 'east' and *cap-arre*, head backward, for 'west'), and that words like *capbacha*, 'to bow the forehead', or *capbach* were associated with the idea of shame, humiliation, dishonour or affront; or even to realize that the most legitimate guarantors of my most legitimate culture sometimes succumbed to this so-called pre-logical logic – that Plato, in Book X of *The Republic*, associates the just with the right hand, with upward, forward movement towards the sky, and the wicked with the left hand, with going down, the earth and the rear;[13] or that Montesquieu's theory of climates is based on mythic oppositions, the principle of which is exactly what we put into the antithesis between 'cold blood' and 'hot blood' and through this into the antithesis between north and south.[14] I also had to turn to more everyday usages, closer to home, with the analysis of taste, a system of generative and classificatory schemes (manifested in pairs of antagonistic adjectives such as 'unique' and 'common', 'brilliant' and 'dull', 'heavy' and 'light', etc.) which function in the most varied fields of practice and are the basis of the ultimate, undisputed and ineffable values, exalted by all social rituals and especially in the cult of the work of art (see Bourdieu and Saint-Martin 1975; Bourdieu 1975, 1984).

But I would probably not have overcome the last obstacles that prevented me from recognizing the forms of thought most characteristic of pre-logical logic in the logic of practice if I had not, somewhat accidentally, encountered this 'primitive' logic in the very heart of the familiar world, in the responses to a public opinion survey by a polling organization in 1975, in which the respondents were asked to associate French political leaders with a variety of objects. (For a full description of this 'test', in which the interviewer presented the respondents with lists of six objects – colours, trees, classical heroes, etc. – and invited them to assign just one of each to one of six politicians, and for an analysis of the logic underlying the attributions, see Bourdieu 1984: 546–59). Having a native's full command of the system of schemes which inclined them to identify the Communist leader Georges Marchais with the pine tree, the colour black and the crow, or Valéry Giscard d'Estaing with the oak, the colour white or the lily of the valley, I was able to hold together my native experience of the lazy familiarity with a symbolism that is neither entirely logical nor entirely illogical, neither entirely controlled nor entirely unconscious; my theoretical knowledge of the logic which emerges from the whole set of attributions and can be surprising for native experience; and my quasi-experimental observation of the functioning of this 'thinking in couples' which leaves indeterminate the principles of its distinctions or assimilations and never specifies in what respect the things it contrasts or assembles in fact contrast or resemble each other. It could be seen that in many of its operations, guided by a simple 'sense of the opposite', ordinary thought, like all 'pre-logical' (or practical) thought, proceeds by oppositions, an elementary form of specification that leads it, for example, to give to the same term as many opposites as there are practical relations it can entertain with what is not itself. This discovery was a concrete demonstration that the reification of the object of science in the essential otherness of a 'mentality' presupposes triumphant adherence to a non-objectified subject. Distance is not abolished by bringing the outsider fictitiously closer to an imaginary native, as is generally attempted; it is by distancing, through objectification, the native who is in every outside observer that the native is brought closer to the outsider.

This last example, like the others, is not put forward to exhibit the particular (and very real) difficulties of sociology or the particular merits of the sociologist, but to try to give a practical understanding of the fact that every genuine sociological undertaking is, inseparably, a socio-analysis, and so to help its product to become in turn the means of a socio-analysis.[15] It is not simply a question of using analysis of the social position from which discourses on the social world are produced – starting with discourses claiming scientificity – as one of the most potent weapons in the scientific and political critique of scientific and political discourse, and especially of the political uses of scientific 'legitimacy'. In contrast to the personalist denial which refuses scientific objectification and can only construct a fantasized person, sociological analysis, particularly when it places itself in the anthropological tradition of exploration of forms of classification, makes a self-reappropriation possible, by objectifying the objectivity that runs through the supposed site of subjectivity, such as the social categories of thought, perception and appreciation which are the unthought principle of all representation of the 'objective' world. By forcing one to discover externality at the heart of internality, banality in the illusion of rarity, the common in the pursuit of the unique, sociology does more than denounce all the impostures of egoistic narcissism; it offers perhaps the only means of contributing, if only through awareness of determinations, to the construction, otherwise abandoned to the forces of the world, of something like a subject.

BOOK I

Critique of Theoretical Reason

EBERLY LIBRARY
WAYNESBURG UNIVERSITY
WAYNESBURG, PA 15370

EBERLY LIBRARY
WAYNESBURG UNIVERSITY
WAYNESBURG, PA. 15370

Introduction

'How am I able to follow a rule?' – if this is not a question about causes, then it is about the justification for my following a rule in the way I do.

If I have exhausted the justifications I have reached bedrock, and my spade is turned. Then I am inclined to say: 'This is simply what I do.'

L. Wittgenstein, *Philosophical Investigations*

Man . . . is the most imitative (*mimetikotaton*) of all animals and he learns his first lessons through mimicry (*dia mimesos*).

Aristotle, *Poetics*

Of all the oppositions that artificially divide social science, the most fundamental, and the most ruinous, is the one that is set up between subjectivism and objectivism. The very fact that this division constantly reappears in virtually the same form would suffice to indicate that the modes of knowledge which it distinguishes are equally indispensable to a science of the social world that cannot be reduced either to a social phenomenology or to a social physics. To move beyond the antagonism between these two modes of knowledge, while preserving the gains from each of them (including what is produced by self-interested lucidity about the opposing position), it is necessary to make explicit the presuppositions that they have in common as theoretical modes of knowledge, both equally opposed to the practical mode of knowledge which is the basis of ordinary experience of the social world. This presupposes a critical objectification of the epistemological and social conditions that make possible both a reflexive return to the subjective experience of the world and also the objectification of the objective conditions of that experience.

The mode of knowledge that can be called 'phenomenological' sets out to reflect an experience which, by definition, does not reflect itself, the primary relationship of familiarity with the familiar environment, and thereby to bring to light the truth of that experience which, however illusory it may appear from the 'objective' viewpoint, remains perfectly certain, *qua* experience.[1] But it cannot go beyond a description of what specifically characterizes 'lived' experience of the social world, that is, apprehension of the world as self-evident, 'taken for granted'. This is because it excludes the question of the conditions of possibility of this experience, namely the coincidence of the objective structures and the internalized structures which provides the illusion of immediate understanding, characteristic of practical experience of the familiar universe, and which at the same time excludes from that experience any inquiry as to its own conditions of possibility. At a deeper level, it is also because, like the practical knowledge it takes for its object, it excludes any inquiry as to its own social conditions of possibility and more precisely as to the social meaning of the practical *epochè* that is necessary in order to conceive the intention of understanding primary understanding, or, to put it another way, as to the quite paradoxical social relationship presupposed by a reflexive turning back on to doxic experience.

Objectivism, which sets out to establish objective regularities (structures, laws, systems of relationships, etc.) independent of individual consciousnesses and wills, introduces a radical discontinuity between theoretical knowledge and practical knowledge, rejecting the more or less explicit representations with which the latter arms itself as 'rationalizations', 'prenotions' or 'ideologies'. It thus challenges the project of identifying the science of the social world with scientific description of pre-scientific experience or, more precisely, of reducing social science, as the phenomenologists do, to 'constructs of the second degree, i.e. constructs of the constructs made by the actors on the social scene' (Schutz 1962: 59), or, as Garfinkel and the ethnomethodologists do, to 'accounts of the accounts which agents produce and through which they produce the meaning of the world' (Garfinkel 1967). It raises, objectively at least, the forgotten question of the particular conditions which make doxic experience of the social world possible. For example, Saussurian semiology (or its derivatives, such as structuralist anthropology) emphasizes that immediate understanding is possible only if the agents are objectively attuned so as to associate the same meaning with the same sign, whether this be a word, a practice or a work, and the same sign with the same signifying intention; or, to put it another way, so that in their encoding and decoding operations they refer to one and the same system of constant relations, independent of individual consciousnesses and wills and irreducible to their execution in practices or works (for example, language as a code or cipher). In so doing, it does not strictly speaking contradict phenomenological analysis of primary experience of the social world as immediate understanding; but it defines the scope of its validity by establishing the particular conditions in which it is possible (that is, perfect coincidence of the ciphers used in encoding and decoding), which phenomenological analysis ignores.

The fact remains that, in all these operations, objectivism takes no account of what is inscribed in the distance and externality with respect to primary experience that are both the condition and the product of its objectifying operations. Forgetting what is emphasized by phenomenological analysis of experience of the familiar world, namely the appearance of immediacy with which the meaning of that world presents itself, it fails to objectify the objectifying relationship, that is, the epistemological break which is also a social discontinuity. And, because it ignores the relationship between the experiential meaning which social phenomenology makes explicit and the objective meaning that is constructed by social physics or objectivist semiology, it is unable to analyse the conditions of the production and functioning of the feel for the social game that makes it possible to take for granted the meaning objectified in institutions.

Thus one cannot move beyond the apparent antinomy between the two modes of knowledge and integrate their gains without subordinating one's scientific practice to a knowledge of the 'knowing subject', an essentially critical knowledge of the limits inherent in all theoretical knowledge, both subjectivist and objectivist. This would have all the appearances of a negative theory were it not for the specifically scientific effects it produces by forcing one to address the questions that are concealed by all theoretical knowledge. Social science must not only, as objectivism would have it, break with native experience and the native representation of that experience, but also, by a second break, call into question the presuppositions inherent in the position of the 'objective' observer who, seeking to interpret practices, tends to bring into the object the principles of his relation to the object, as is shown for example by the privileged status he gives to communicative and epistemic functions, which inclines him to reduce exchanges to pure symbolic exchanges. Knowledge does not only depend, as an elementary relativism suggests, on the particular viewpoint that a 'situated and dated' observer takes up vis-à-vis the object. A much more fundamental alteration – and a much more pernicious one, because, being constitutive of the operation of knowing, it inevitably remains unnoticed – is performed on practice by the sheer fact of taking up a 'viewpoint' on it and so constituting it as an object (of observation and analysis). And it goes without saying that this sovereign viewpoint is most easily adopted in elevated positions in the social space, where the social world presents itself as a spectacle seen from afar and from above, as a representation.

This critical reflexion on the limits of theoretical understanding is not intended to discredit theoretical knowledge in one or another of its forms and, as is often attempted, to set in its place a more or less idealized practical knowledge; but rather to give it a solid basis by freeing it from the distortions arising from the epistemological and social conditions of its production. It has nothing in common with the aim of rehabilitation, which has misled most discourses on practice; it aims simply to bring to light the theory of practice which theoretical knowledge implicitly applies and so to make possible a truly scientific knowledge of practice and of the practical mode of knowledge.

Analysis of the logic of practice would no doubt have advanced further if the academic tradition had not always posed the question of the relations between theory and practice in terms of value. Thus, in a famous passage of the *Theaetetus* Plato tips the balance from the very beginning when, through an entirely negative description of the logic of practice,[2] which is simply the reverse side of an exaltation of *skholè*, a freedom from the constraints and urgencies of practice which is presented as the *sine qua non* of access to truth ('our words are like servants to us'), he offers

intellectuals a 'theodicy of their own privilege'. To this justificatory
discourse which, in its most extreme forms, defines action as the 'inability
to contemplate', philosophy (even the *philosophia plebeia* which Platonic
elitism constitutes negatively) has only ever been able to respond with an
inversion of signs, a reversal of the table of values, as in this ideal-typical
text in which Nietzsche (1969: 119) concludes the most perceptive critique
of 'pure' knowledge by ascribing the very virtues it claims, such as
objectivity, to the mode of knowledge which he prefers:

'Henceforth, my dear philosophers, let us be on guard against the
dangerous old conceptual fiction that posited a "pure, will-less, painless,
timeless knowing subject"; let us guard against the snares of such
contradictory concepts as "pure reason", "absolute spirituality", "knowledge in itself": these always demand that we should think of an eye that
is completely unimaginable, an eye turned in no particular direction, in
which the active and interpreting forces, through which alone seeing becomes
seeing *something*, are supposed to be lacking; these always demand of the
eye an absurdity and a nonsense. There is *only* a perspective seeing, *only* a
perspective "knowing"; and the more affects we allow to speak about one
thing, the *more* eyes, different eyes, we use to observe one thing, the more
complete will our "concept" of this thing, our "objectivity", be.'

The problem is no doubt that one cannot escape from the play of
inverted preferences, in order to produce a genuine description of the logic
of practice, without bringing into play the theoretical, contemplative,
scholastic situation from which all discourses arise, including those that
are most determined to valorize practice.

But the most formidable barrier to the construction of an adequate
science of practice no doubt lies in the fact that the solidarity that binds
scientists to their science (and to the social privilege which makes it possible
and which it justifies or procures) predisposes them to profess the
superiority of their knowledge, often won through enormous efforts,
against common sense, and even to find in that superiority a justification
for their privilege, rather than to produce a scientific knowledge of the
practical mode of knowledge and of the limits that scientific knowledge
owes to the fact that it is based on a privilege. To take just one example:
in his classic text on economics, Samuelson (1951: 6–10) evokes the specific
logic of practice and of common sense only to reject it as unworthy.
Denying the pretension of economic agents to possess adequate knowledge
of economic mechanisms, the academic economist claims for himself a
monopoly on the total point of view and declares himself capable of
transcending the partial, particular viewpoints of particular groups and
avoiding the errors that spring from the 'fallacy of composition'. All
objectivist knowledge contains a claim to legitimate domination. Just as,
in *Troilus and Cressida*, the general ideas of the General reduce the
criticisms which Thersites, the private soldier, makes of his strategic grand
designs to a blinkered self-interest, so too the theoretician's claim to an
absolute viewpoint, the 'perspectiveless view of all perspectives' as Leibniz
would have put it, contains the claim to a power, founded in reason, over

particular individuals, who are condemned to error by the partisan partiality of their individual viewpoints.

The unanalysed element in every theoretical analysis (whether subjectivist or objectivist) is the theorist's subjective relation to the social world and the objective (social) relation presupposed by this subjective relation.[3] Intellectualism is, so to speak, an 'intellectualocentrism' in which the observer's relation to the social world, and therefore the social relation which makes observation possible, is made the basis of the practice analysed, through the representations constructed to account for it (rules, models, etc.). This projection of a non-objectified theoretical relationship into the practice that one is trying to objectify is at the root of a set of interlinked scientific errors (so that it would already be a considerable step forward if all would-be scientific discourse on the social world were preceded by a sign meaning 'everything takes place as if . . . ', which, functioning in the same way as quantifiers in logic, would constantly recall the epistemological status of such discourse). So it is not in order to satisfy some gratuitous taste for theoretical prolegomena, but in order to meet the most practical requirements of scientific practice, that we must make an analysis of the specific logic and the social conditions of possibility of scientific knowledge in the social sciences (and more especially of the theories of practice that it implicitly implements). This will also be, inseparably, an analysis of the specific logic of practical knowledge.

1

Objectification Objectified

There is perhaps no better way of grasping the epistemological and sociological presuppositions of objectivism than to return to the inaugural operations through which Saussure constructed the specific object of linguistics. These operations, ignored and masked by all the mechanical borrowings from the then dominant discipline and by all the literal translations of an autonomized lexicon on which the new 'structural' sciences were hastily founded, have become the epistemological unconscious of structuralism.[1]

To posit, as Saussure does, that the true medium of communication is not speech (*parole*), a datum immediately considered in its observable materiality, but language (*langue*), a system of objective relations which makes possible both the production and the decoding of discourse, is to perform a complete reversal of appearances by subordinating the very substance of communication, which presents itself as the most visible and real aspect, to a pure construct of which there is no sense experience.[2] Conscious of the paradoxical break with doxic experience that is implied in the fundamental thesis of the primacy of the language (in favour of which he none the less invokes the existence of dead languages or dumbness in old age as proof that one can lose speech while preserving a language, or the linguistic errors that point to the language as the objective norm of speech), Saussure indeed notes that everything tends to suggest that speech is 'the precondition of a language': a language cannot be apprehended outside the speech, a language is learned through speech and speech is the origin of innovations and transformations in language. But he immediately observes that the two processes mentioned have only chronological priority and that the relationship is reversed as soon as one leaves the domain of individual or collective history in order to inquire into the logical conditions for decoding. From this point of view, the language, as the medium ensuring the identity of the sound–sense associations performed by the speakers, and therefore their mutual understanding, comes first as the condition of the intelligibility of speech (1974: 17–20). Saussure, who elsewhere proclaims that 'the point of view creates the object', here clearly indicates the viewpoint one has to adopt in order to produce the 'specific object' of the new structural science: to make speech the product of the language one has to situate oneself in the logical order of intelligibility.

It would no doubt be worthwhile to try to set out the whole set of theoretical postulates implied in adopting this viewpoint, such as the primacy of logic and structure, apprehended synchronically, over individual and collective history (that is, the learning of the language and, as Marx might have said, 'the historical movement which gave birth to it') or the privilege granted to internal and specific relations, amenable to 'tautegorical' (to use Schelling's term) or structural analysis, over external economic and social determinations. However, not only has this already been done, partially at least, but it seems more important to concentrate on the viewpoint itself, the relationship to the object that it asserts and all that follows from this, starting with a particular theory of practice. This presupposes that one momentarily relinquishes, and then tries to objectify, the place designated in advance as that of the objective and objectifying observer who, like a stage manager playing at will with the possibilities offered by the objectifying instruments in order to bring the object closer or move it further away, to enlarge or reduce it, imposes on the object his own norms of construction, as if in a dream of power.

To locate oneself in the order of intelligibility, as Saussure does, is to adopt the viewpoint of an 'impartial spectator' who seeks to understand for the sake of understanding and who tends to assign this hermeneutic intention to the agents' practice and to proceed as if they were asking themselves the questions he asks himself about them. Unlike the orator, the grammarian has nothing to do with language except to study it in order to codify it. By the very treatment he applies to it, taking it as an object of analysis instead of using it to think and speak, he constitutes it as a *logos* opposed to *praxis* (and also, of course, to practical language). Does it need to be pointed out that this typically scholastic opposition is a product of the scholastic situation, in the strong sense of *skholè*, *otium*, inactivity, which is unlikely to be perceived as such by minds shaped by the academic institution? For lack of a theory of the difference between the purely theoretical relation to language of someone who, like himself, has nothing to do with language except understand it, and the practical relation to language of someone who seeks to understand in order to act and who uses language for practical purposes, just enough for the needs of practice and within the limits allowed by the urgency of practice, the grammarian is tacitly inclined to treat language as an autonomous, self-sufficient object, that is, a purposefulness without purpose – without any other purpose, at any rate, than that of being interpreted, like a work of art. The principle of the grammarians' errors lies therefore not so much in the fact that, as the sociolinguists complain, they take as their object a scholastic or formal language, but rather that they unwittingly adopt a scholastic or formal relation towards all language, whether popular or formal.

The most constant tendencies of the formal grammar which linguistics is and always has been, are inscribed in the scholastic situation which, through the relation to language that it encourages and its neutralization of the functions embedded in the ordinary use of language, governs in many ways the academic treatment of language. One only has to think of the inimitable examples generated by the grammarian's imagination, from bald kings of France to Wittgenstein doing the washing-up, which, like the paradoxes cherished by all formalisms, are able to deploy all their ambiguities and enigmas only because the scholastic *epochè* has isolated them from any practical situation. The 'condition of felicity' of scholastic discourse is the scholastic institution and all that it implies, such as the speakers' and the receivers' disposition to accept and indeed believe in what is said. This did not escape Paul Valéry (1960: 696): '*Quia nominor Leo* does not mean *For my name is Lion* but: *I am an example of grammar.*' The chain of commentary unleashed by J. L. Austin's analysis of illocutionary acts has no reason to stop so long as ignorance of the conditions of production and circulation of commentary allows and encourages people to search solely in the discourse in question for the 'conditions of felicity' which, though theoretically and practically inseparable from the institutional conditions of the functioning of the discourse, have been assigned to the domain of external linguistics, that is, abandoned to sociology.

Language as conceived by Saussure, an intellectual instrument and an object of analysis, is indeed the dead, written, foreign language referred to by Mikhail Bakhtin, a self-sufficient system, detached from real usage and totally stripped of its functions, inviting a purely passive understanding (the extreme form of which is pure semantics as practised by Fodor and Katz). The illusion of the autonomy of the purely linguistic order that is asserted in the privilege accorded to the internal logic of language at the expense of the social conditions of its opportune use,[3] opened the way to all the subsequent research that proceeds as if mastery of the code were sufficient to confer mastery of the appropriate usages, or as if one could infer the usage and meaning of linguistic expressions from analysis of their formal structure, as if grammaticality were the necessary and sufficient condition of the production of meaning, in short, as if it had been forgotten that language is made to be spoken and spoken pertinently. It is not surprising that the aporias of Chomskian linguistics, which have taken the presuppositions of all grammars to their ultimate conclusions, are now forcing linguists to rediscover, as Jacques Bouveresse puts it, that the problem is not the possibility of producing an infinite number of 'grammatical' sentences but the possibility of producing an infinite number of sentences really appropriate to an infinite number of situations.

The independence of discourse with respect to the situation in which it functions and the bracketing of all its functions are implied in the initial operation which produces the language by reducing the speech act to a simple execution. And it would not be difficult to show that all the presuppositions, and all the consequent difficulties, of all forms of structuralism derive from this fundamental division between the language and its realization in speech, that is, in practice, and also in history, and from the inability to understand the relationship between these two entities other than as that between the model and its execution, essence and existence – which amounts to placing the linguist, the possessor of the model, in the position of a Leibnizian God possessing *in actu* the objective meaning of practices.

To delimit, within the range of linguistic phenomena, the 'terrain of the language', Saussure sets aside 'the physical part of communication', that is, speech as a pre-constructed object. Then, within the 'speech circuit', he isolates what he calls 'the executive side', that is, speech as a constructed object defined in opposition to language as the actualization of a certain sense in a particular combination of sounds, which he also eliminates on the grounds that 'execution is never the work of the mass' but 'always individual'. The word *execution*, used of an order or a muscial score and more generally of a programme or an artisitic project, condenses the whole philosophy of practice and history of semiology, a paradigmatic form of objectivism which, by privileging the *constructum* over the materiality of the practical realization, reduces individual practice, skill, everything that is determined practically by reference to practical ends, that is, style, manner, and ultimately the agents themselves, to the actualization of a kind of ahistorical essence, in short, nothing.[4]

But it is undoubtedly anthropology which, being predisposed by its identical viewpoint on the object to reckless borrowing of concepts, exhibits in a magnified form all the implications of the question-begging of objectivism. Charles Bally pointed out that linguistic research takes diffferent directions when dealing with the linguist's mother tongue or with a foreign language, and he emphasized in particular the tendency towards intellectualism entailed by apprehending language from the standpoint of the listening rather than the speaking subject, that is, as a means of decoding rather than a 'means of action and expression': 'The listener is on the side of the language, it is with the language that he interprets speech' (Bally 1965: 58, 78, 102). The practical relation the anthropologist has with his object, that of the outsider, excluded from the real play of social practices by the fact that he has no place (except by choice or by way of a game) in the space observed, is the extreme case and the ultimate truth of the relationship that the observer, willy-nilly, consciously or not, has with his object. The status of an observer who withdraws from the situation to observe implies an epistemological, but also a social break, which most subtly governs scientific activity when it ceases to be seen as such, leading to an implicit theory of practices that is linked to forgetfulness of the social conditions of scientific activity. The anthropologist's situation reminds us of the truth of the relationship that every observer has with the action he states and analyses, namely the insurmountable break with action and the world, with the imminent ends of collective action, with the self-evidence of the familiar world, that is presupposed in the very intention of talking about practice and especially of understanding it and seeking to make it understood other than by producing and reproducing it practically. If words have any meaning, then there cannot be a discourse (or a novel) of action: there is only a discourse which states action and which, unless it is to fall into incoherence or imposture, must never stop stating that it is only stating action. Undue participation of the subject in the object is never more evident than in the case of the primitivist participation of the bewitched or mystic anthropologist, which, like populist immersion, still plays on the objective distance from the object to play the game as a game while waiting to leave it in order to tell it. This means that participant observation is, in a sense, a contradiction in terms (as anyone who has tried to do it will have confirmed in practice); and that the critique of objectivism and its inability to apprehend practice as such in no way implies the rehabilitation of immersion in practice. The participationist option is simply another way of avoiding the question of the real relationship of the observer to the observed and its critical consequences for scientific practice.

In this respect, there is no better example than that of art history, which finds in the sacred character of its object every pretext for a hagiographic hermeneutics more concerned with the *opus operatum* than the *modus operandi*, and treats the work of art as a discourse to be decoded by reference to a transcendent code, analogous to Saussure's *langue*. It forgets that artistic production is also – to various degrees depending on the art and on the historically variable ways of practising it – the product of an 'art', as Durkheim (1956: 101) says, or, to put it another way, a *mimesis*, a sort of symbolic gymnastics, like ritual or dance; and that it always contains something 'ineffable', not through excess, as the celebrants would have it, but through absence. Here too, the inadequacy of scholarly discourse derives from its ignorance of all that its theory of the object owes to its theoretical relation to the object, as Nietzsche (1969: 103–4) suggested: 'Kant, like all philosophers, instead of envisaging the aesthetic problem from the point of view of the artist (the creator), considered art and the beautiful purely from that of the "spectator", and unconsciously introduced the "spectator" into the concept "beautiful".'

Intellectualism is inscribed in the fact of introducing into the object the intellectual relation to the object, of substituting the observer's relation to practice for the practical relation to practice. Anthropologists would be able to escape from all their metaphysical questioning about the ontological status or even the 'site' of culture only if they were to objectify their relation to the object, that of the outsider who has to procure a substitute for practical mastery in the form of an objectified model. Genealogies and other models are to the social orientation which makes possible the relation of immediate immanence to the familiar world, as a map, an abstract model of all possible routes, is to the practical sense of space, a 'system of axes linked unalterably to our bodies, which we carry about with us wherever we go', as Poincaré put it.

There are few areas in which the effect of the outsider's situation is so directly visible as in analysis of kinship. Having only cognitive uses for the kinship and the kin of others which he takes for his object, the anthropologist can treat the native terminology of kinship as a closed, coherent system of logically necessary relations, defined once and for all as if by construction in and by the implicit axiomatics of a cultural tradition. Failing to inquire into the epistemological status of his practice and of the neutralization of practical functions which it presupposes and consecrates, he considers only the symbolic effect of collective categorization, which shows and which creates belief, imposing obligations and prohibitions whose intensity varies in inverse ratio to distance in the space arbitrarily produced in this way. In doing so, he unwittingly brackets the different uses which may be made in practice of sociologically identical kinship relations. The logical relations he constructs are to 'practical' relations – practical because continuously practised, kept up and cultivated – as the geometrical space of a map, a representation of all possible routes for all possible subjects, is to the network of pathways that are really maintained and used, 'beaten tracks' that are really practicable for a particular agent. The family tree, a spatial diagram that can be taken in at a glance, *uno intuitu* and scanned indifferently in any direction from any point, causes the complete network of kinship relations over several generations to exist in the mode of temporal existence which is that of theoretical objects, that is, *tota simul*, as a totality in simultaneity. It puts on the same footing official relationships, which, for lack of regular maintenance, tend to become what they are for the genealogist, that is, theoretical relationships, like abandoned roads on an old map; and practical relationships which really function because they fulfil practical functions. It thereby tends to conceal the fact that the logical relations of kinship, which the structuralist tradition almost completely autonomizes with respect to economic determinants, exist in practice only through and for the official and unofficial uses made of them by agents whose inclination to keep them in working order and to make them work more intensively – hence, through constant use, ever more smoothly – rises with the degree to which they actually or potentially fulfil useful functions, satisfying vital material or symbolic interests.

To make completely explicit the implicit demand which lies behind genealogical inquiry (as in all forms of inquiry), one would first have to establish the social history of the genealogical tool, paying particular attention to the functions which, in the tradition of which anthropologists are the product, have produced and reproduced the need for this instrument, that is, the problems of inheritance and succession and, inseparably from these, the concern to maintain and preserve social capital, understood as effective possession of a network of kinship (or other) relations capable of being mobilized or at least manifested. This social genealogy of genealogy would have to extend into a social history of the relationship between the 'scientific' and social uses of the instrument. But the most important thing would be to bring to light the epistemological implications of the mode of investigation which is the precondition for the production of the genealogical diagram. This would aim to determine the full significance of the ontological transmutation that the researcher's questions bring about simply by demanding a quasi-theoretical relationship towards kinship, implying a break with the practical relation directly oriented towards functions.

In fact, projection into the object of a non-objectified objectifying relation produces different effects each time, albeit arising from the same principle, in the different areas of practice. Sometimes the anthropologist presents as the objective principle of practice that which is obtained and constructed through the work of objectification, projecting into reality what only exists on paper; sometimes he interprets actions which, like rites and myths, aim to *act* on the natural world and the social world, as if they were operations designed to interpret them.[5] Here too, the so-called objective relation to the object, which implies distance and externality, comes into contradiction in a quite practical way with the practical relationship which it has to deny in order to constitute itself and by the same token to constitute the objective representation of practice:

'His vision [that of a simple participant in a rite] is circumscribed by his occupancy of a particular position, or even of a set of situationally conflicting positions, both in the persisting structure of his society, and also in the rôle structure of the given ritual. Moreover, the participant is likely to be governed in his actions by a number of interests, purposes, and sentiments, dependent upon his specific position, which impair his understanding of the total situation. An even more serious obstacle against his achieving objectivity is the fact that he tends to regard as axiomatic and primary the ideals, values, and norms that are overtly expressed or symbolized in the ritual. . . . What is meaningless for an actor playing a specific rôle may well be highly significant for an observer and analyst of the total system' (V. Turner 1967: 67).

Only by means of a break with the theoretical vision, which is experienced as a break with ordinary vision, can the observer take account, in his description of ritual practice, of the fact of *participation* (and consequently of his own separation from this); only a critical awareness of the limits implied in the conditions of production of theory can enable him to include in the complete theory of ritual practice properties as essential to it as the partial, self-interested character of practical knowledge or the discrepancy between the practically experienced reasons and the 'objective' reasons of practice. But the triumphalism of theoretical reason is paid for in its inability, from the very beginning, to move beyond simple recording of the duality of the paths of knowledge, the path of appearances and the path of truth, doxa and episteme, common sense and science, and its incapacity to win for science the truth of what science is constructed *against*.

Projecting into the perception of the social world the unthought content inherent in his position in that world, that is, the monopoly of 'thought' which he is granted *de facto* by the social division of labour and which leads him to identify the work of thought with an effort of expression and verbalization in speech or writing – 'thought and expression are constituted simultaneously', said Merleau-Ponty – the 'thinker' betrays his secret conviction that action is fully performed only when it is understood, interpreted, expressed, by identifying the implicit with the unthought and by denying the status of authentic thought to the tacit and practical thought that is inherent in all 'sensible' action.[6] Language spontaneously becomes the accomplice of this hermeneutic philosophy which leads one to conceive action as something to be deciphered, when it leads one to say, for example, that a gesture or ritual act *expresses* something, rather than saying, quite simply, that it is 'sensible' (*sensé*) or, as in English, that it 'makes' sense. No doubt because they know and recognize no other thought than the thought of the 'thinker', and cannot grant human dignity without granting what seems to be constitutive of that dignity, anthropologists have never known how to rescue the people they were studying from the barbarism of pre-logic except by identifying them with the most prestigious of their colleagues – logicians or philosophers (I am thinking of the famous title, 'The primitive as philosopher'). As Hocart (1970, 32) puts it, 'Long ago [man] ceased merely to live and started to think how he lived; he ceased merely to feel life: he conceived it. Out of all the phenomena contributing to life he formed a concept of life, fertility, prosperity, and vitality.' Claude Lévi-Strauss does just the same when he confers on myth the task of resolving *logical* problems, of expressing, mediating and masking social contradictions – mainly in some earlier analyses, such 'La geste d'Asdiwal' (1958) – or when he makes it one of the sites where, like Reason in history according to Hegel, the universal Mind thinks itself,[7] thereby offering for observation 'the universal laws which govern the unconscious activities of the mind' (1951).

The indeterminacy surrounding the relationship between the observer's viewpoint and that of the agents is reflected in the indeterminacy of the relationship between the constructs (diagrams or discourses) that the observer produces to account for practices, and these practices themselves. This uncertainty is intensified by the interferences of the native discourse aimed at expressing or regulating practice – customary rules, official theories, sayings, proverbs, etc. – and by the effects of the mode of thought that is expressed in it. Simply by leaving untouched the question of the principle of production of the regularities that he records and giving free rein to the 'mythopoeic' power of language, which, as Wittgenstein pointed out, constantly slips from the substantive to the substance, objectivist discourse tends to constitute the model constructed to account for practices as a power really capable of determining them. Reifying abstractions (in sentences like 'culture determines the age of weaning'), it treats its constructions – 'culture', 'structures', 'social classes' or 'modes of produc-tion' – as realities endowed with a social efficacy. Alternatively, giving concepts the power to act in history as the words that designate them act in the sentences of historical narrative, it personifies collectives and makes them subjects responsible for historical actions (in sentences like 'the bourgeoisie thinks that . . . ' or 'the working class refuses to accept . . . ').[8] And, when the question cannot be avoided, it preserves appearances by resorting to systematically ambiguous notions, as linguists say of sentences whose representative content varies systematically with the context of use.

Thus the notion of the *rule* which can refer indifferently to the regularity immanent in practices (a statistical correlation, for example), the *model* constructed by science to account for it, or the *norm* consciously posited and respected by the agents, allows a fictitious reconciliation of mutually contradictory theories of action. I am thinking, of course, of Chomsky, who (in different contexts) describes grammatical rules as instruments of description of language; as systems of norms of which speakers have a certain knowledge; and finally as neuro-physiological mechanisms ('A person who knows a language has represented in his brain some very abstract system of underlying structures along with an abstract system of rules that determine, by free iteration, an infinite range of sound–meaning correspondences' (1967)). But it is also instructive to re-read a paragraph from the preface to the second edition of *The Elementary Structures of Kinship*, in which one may assume that particular care has been taken with the vocabulary of norms, models or rules, since the passage deals with the distinction between 'preferential systems' and 'prescriptive systems':

'Conversely, a system which *recommends* marriage with the mother's brother's daughter may be called prescriptive even if the *rule* is seldom observed, since it says what *must* be done. The question of how far and in what proportion the members of a given society *respect the norm* is very interesting, but a different question to that of where this society should properly be placed in a typology. It is sufficient to acknowledge the likelihood that *awareness* of the *rule* inflects *choices* ever so little in the *prescribed* directions, and that the percentage of *conventional* marriages is higher than would be the case if marriages were made *at random*, to be able to recognize what might be called a matrilateral *operator* at work in this society and acting as a pilot: certain alliances at least follow the path which it charts out for them, and this suffices to imprint a specific curve in the genealogical space. No doubt there will be not just one curve but a great number of local curves, merely incipient for the most part, however, and forming closed cycles only in rare and exceptional cases. But the *structural* outlines which emerge here and there will be enough for the system to be used in making a *probabilistic version* of more rigid systems, the *notion* of which is completely *theoretical* and in which marriage would conform rigorously to *any rule the social group pleases to enunciate*' (Lévi-Strauss 1969: 33, my italics).

The dominant tonality in this passage, as in the whole preface, is that of the norm, whereas *Structural Anthropology* is written in the language of the model or structure; not that such terms are entirely absent here, since the metaphors organizing the central passage ('operator', 'curve' in 'genealogical space', 'structural outlines') imply the logic of the theoretical model and the equivalence (which is both professed and repudiated) of the model and the norm: 'A preferential system is prescriptive when envisaged at the level of the model, a prescriptive system can only be preferential when envisaged at the level of reality' (1969: 33).

But for the reader who remembers the passages in *Structural Anthropology* on the relationship between language and kinship (for example, '"Kinship systems", like "phonemic systems", are built up by the mind on the level of unconscious thought' [Lévi-Strauss 1968: 34]) and the imperious way in which 'cultural norms' and all the 'rationalizations' or 'secondary arguments' produced by the natives were rejected in favour of the 'unconscious structures', not to mention the texts asserting the universality of the fundamental rule of exogamy, the concessions made here to 'awareness of the rule' and the dissociation from rigid systems 'the notion of which is entirely theoretical', may come as a surprise, as may this further passage from the same preface: 'It is nonetheless true that the empirical reality of so-called prescriptive systems only takes on its full meaning when related to a *theoretical model worked out by the natives themselves* prior to ethnologists' (1969: 32, my italics); or again:

'Those who practise them *know full well* that the spirit of such systems cannot be reduced to the tautological proposition that each group obtains its women from 'givers' and gives its women to 'takers'. They are also *aware* that marriage with the matrilateral cross cousin (mother's brother's daughter) provides the simplest illustration of the *rule*, the form most likely to *guarantee its survival*. On the other hand, marriage with the patrilateral cross cousin (father's sister's daughter) would violate it irrevocably' (1969: 32, my italics).

It is tempting to quote in reply a passage in which Wittgenstein effortlessly brings together all the questions evaded by structural anthropology and, no doubt, more generally by all intellectualism, which transfers the objective truth established by science into a practice that by its very essence rules out the theoretical stance which makes it possible to establish that truth:

'What do I call 'the rule by which he proceeds'? – The hypothesis that satifactorily describes his use of words, which we observe; or the rule which he looks up when he uses signs; or the one which he gives us in reply when we ask what his rule is? – But if observation does not enable us to see any clear rule, and the question brings none to light? – For he did indeed give me a definition when I asked him what he understood by 'N', but he was prepared to withdraw and alter it. So how am I to determine the rule according to which he is playing? He does not know it himself. – Or, to ask a better question: What meaning is the expression 'the rule by which he proceeds' supposed to have left to it here?' (1963: 38–9).

To slip from *regularity*, i.e. from what recurs with a certain statistically measurable frequency and from the formula which describes it, to a consciously laid down and consciously respected *ruling (règlement)*, or to unconscious *regulating* by a mysterious cerebral or social mechanism, are the two commonest ways of sliding from the model of reality to the reality of the model. In the first case, one moves from a rule which, to take up Quine's distinction (1972) between *to fit* and *to guide*, fits the observed regularity in a purely descriptive way, to a rule that governs, directs or orients behaviour – which presupposes that it is known and recognized, and can therefore be stated – thereby succumbing to the most elementary form of legalism, that variety of finalism which is perhaps the most widespread of the spontaneous theories of practice and which consists in proceeding as if practices had as their principle conscious obedience to consciously devised and sanctioned rules. As Ziff puts it:

'Consider the difference between saying "The train is *regularly* two minutes late" and "*As a rule*, the train is two minutes late" . . . There is the suggestion in the latter case that that the train be two minutes late is as it were in accordance with some policy or plan . . . Rules connect with plans or policies in a way that regularities do not . . . To argue that there must be rules in the natural language is like arguing that roads must be red if they correspond to red lines on a map' (1960: 38).

In the second case, one acquires the means of proceeding as if the principle (if not the end) of the action were the theoretical model one has to construct in order to account for it, without however falling into the most flagrant naiveties of legalism, by setting up as the principle of practices or institutions objectively governed by rules unknown to the agents – significations without a signifying intention, finalities without consciously posited ends, which are so many challenges to the old dilemma of mechanism and finalism – an unconscious defined as a mechanical operator of finality. Thus, discussing Durkheim's attempts to 'explain the genesis of symbolic thought', Lévi-Strauss writes:

'Modern sociologists and psychologists resolve such problems by appealing to the unconscious activity of the mind; but when Durkheim was writing, psychology and modern linguistics had not yet reached their main conclusions. This explains why Durkheim foundered in what he regarded as an irreducible antinomy (in itself a considerable progress over late nineteenth-century thought as exemplified by Spencer): the blindness of history and the finalism of consciousness. Between the two there is *of course the unconscious finality of the mind*' (1947: 527, my italics).

It is easy to imagine how minds trained to reject the naivety of finalist explanations and the triviality of causal explanations (particularly 'vulgar' when they invoke economic and social factors) could be fascinated by all the mysterious teleological mechanisms, meaningful and apparently willed products without a producer, which structuralism brought into being by sweeping away the social conditions of production, reproduction and use of symbolic objects in the very process in which it revealed immanent logic. And it is also easy to understand the credit given in advance to Lévi-Strauss's attempt to move beyond the antinomy of action consciously oriented towards rational ends and mechanical reaction to determinations by locating finality in mechanism, with the notion of the unconscious, a kind of *Deus ex machina* which is also a God in the machine. The naturalization of finality implied in forgetting historical action, which leads one to inscribe the ends of history in the mysteries of a Nature, through the notion of the unconscious, no doubt enabled structural anthropology to appear as the most natural of the social sciences and the most scientific of the metaphysics of nature. 'As the mind *is* also *a thing*, the functioning of this thing teaches us something about the nature of things; even pure reflexion is in the last analysis an internalization of the cosmos' (Lévi-Strauss 1966: 248, my italics).

One sees the oscillation, in the same sentence, between two contradictory explanations of the postulated identity of mind and nature: an essential identity – the mind is a thing – or an identity acquired through learning – the mind is the internalization of the cosmos. The two theses, which are merged with the help of the ambiguity of another formulation, 'an image of the world inscribed in the architecture of the mind' (1964: 346), in any case both exclude individual and collective history. Beneath its air of radical materialism, this philosophy of nature is a philosophy of mind which amounts to a form of idealism. Asserting the universality and eternity of the logical categories that govern 'the unconscious activity of the mind', it ignores the dialectic of social structures and structured, structuring dispositions through which schemes of thought are formed and transformed. These schemes – either logical categories, principles of division which, through the principles of the division of labour, correspond to the structure of the social world (and not the natural world), or temporal structures, imperceptibly inculcated by 'the dull pressure of economic relations' as Marx puts it, that is, by the system of economic and symbolic sanctions associated with a particular position in the economic structures – are one of the mediations through which the objective structures ultimately structure all experience, starting with economic experience, without following the paths of either mechanical determination or adequate consciousness.

If the dialectic of objective structures and incorporated structures which operates in every practical action is ignored, then one necessarily falls into the canonical dilemma, endlessly recurring in new forms in the history of social thought, which condemns those who seek to reject subjectivism, like the present-day structuralist readers of Marx, to fall into the fetishism of social laws. To make transcendent entities, which are to practices as essence to existence, out of the constructions that science resorts to in order to give an account of the structure and meaningful products of the accumulation of innumerable historical actions, is to reduce history to a 'process without a subject', simply replacing the 'creative subject' of subjectivism with an automaton driven by the dead laws of a history of nature. This emanatist vision, which makes a structure – Capital or a Mode of production – into an entelechy developing itself in a process of self-realization, reduces historical agents to the role of 'supports' (*Träger*) of the structure and reduces their actions to mere epiphenomenal manifestations of the structure's own power to develop itself and to determine and overdetermine other structures.

2

The Imaginary Anthropology of Subjectivism

Jean-Paul Sartre deserves credit for having given an ultra-consistent formulation of the philosophy of action that is accepted, usually implicitly, by those who describe practices as strategies explicitly oriented by reference to ends explicitly defined by a free project or even, with some interactionists, by reference to the anticipated reactions of other agents. Thus, refusing to recognize anything resembling durable dispositions or probable eventualities, Sartre makes each action a kind of antecedent-less confrontation between the subject and the world. This is seen clearly in the passages in *Being and Nothingness* where he confers on the awakening of revolutionary consciousness – a 'conversion' of consciousness produced by a sort of imaginary variation – the power to create the sense of the present by creating the revolutionary future that denies it:

'It is necessary to reverse the common opinion and acknowledge that it is not the harshness of a situation or the sufferings it imposes that lead people to conceive of another state of affairs in which things would be better for everybody. It is on the day that we are able to conceive of another state of affairs, that a new light is cast on our trouble and our suffering and we *decide* that they are unbearable' (1957: 434–5, my italics; cf. also 1953).

If the world of action is nothing other than this imaginary universe of interchangeable possibles, entirely dependent on the decrees of the consciousness that creates it, and therefore entirely devoid of objectivity, if it is moving because the subject chooses to be moved, revolting because he chooses to be revolted, then emotions, passions, and also actions, are merely games of bad faith:

'It is no accident that materialism is serious; it is no accident that it is found at all times and places as the favourite doctrine of the revolutionary. This is because revolutionaries are serious. They come to know themselves first in terms of the world which oppresses them . . . The serious man is 'of the world' and has no resource in himself. He does not even imagine any longer the possibility of getting out of the world . . . he is in bad faith' (1957: 580).

The same incapacity to encounter 'seriousness' other than in the disapproved form of the 'spirit of seriousness' can be seen in an analysis of emotion which, significantly, is separated by *The Psychology of the Imagination* from the less radically subjectivist descriptions in *Sketch for a Theory of the Emotions*:

'What will decide me to choose the magical aspect or the technical aspect of the world? It cannot be the world itself, for this in order to be manifested waits to be discovered. Therefore it is necessary that the for-itself in its project must choose to be the one by whom the world is revealed as magical or rational; that is, the for-itself must as a free project of itself give to itself rational or magical existence. It is responsible for either one, for the for-itself can *be* only if it has chosen itself. Therefore the for-itself appears as the free foundation of its emotions as of its volitions. My fear is free and manifests my freedom' (1957: 445).

Like Descartes's God, whose freedom is limited only by a free decision, such as the one which is the source of the continuity of creation, and in particular of the constancy of truths and values, the Sartrian subject, whether an individual or collective subject, can break out of the absolute discontinuity of choices without past or future only by the free resolution of a pledge and self-loyalty or by the free abdication of bad faith, the sole foundations of the only two conceivable forms, authentic and inauthentic, of *constantia sibi*.[1]

No doubt one could counterpose to this analysis of Sartre's anthropology the numerous texts (especially in his earliest and last works) in which he recognizes, for example, the 'passive syntheses' of a universe of already constituted significations – such as the passage (1957: 465) in which he seeks to distinguish his position from the instantaneist philosophy of Descartes, or another (1960: 161) in which he announces the study of 'actions without agents, productions without a totalizer, counter-finalities, infernal circularities'. The fact remains that Sartre rejects with visceral repugnance 'those gelatinous realities, more or less vaguely haunted by a supra-individual consciousness, which a shame-faced organicism still seeks to retrieve, against all likelihood, in the harsh, complex, but clear-cut field of passive activity in which there are individual organisms and inorganic material realities' (1960: 305); and that he leaves no room, either on the side of the things of the world or on that of the agents, for anything that might seem to blur the sharp line his rigorous dualism seeks to maintain between the pure transparency of the subject and the mineral opacity of the thing.

The social world, the site of the 'hybrid' compromises between thing and meaning that define 'objective meaning' as meaning-made-thing and dispositions as meaning-made-body, is a real challenge for someone who can breathe only in the pure universe of consciousness and 'praxis'. And Sartre protests, not without reason, against the 'objective' (I would say objectivist) sociology which can only grasp a 'sociality of inertia'. His active voluntarism, impatient of all transcendent necessities, leads him to refuse class defined as a class of conditions and conditionings, and therefore of durable dispositions and life-styles, which he sees as class reduced to a thing, 'congealed' in an essence, reduced to inertia and impotence, and to which he contrasts 'the group totalizing in a praxis', arising from, but against, the class as a thing.[2] All 'objective' descriptions of this 'objective' class seem to him to be inspired by an insidiously demobilizing pessimism designed to contain, even push back, the working class into what it is and so distance it from what it has to be, the mobilized class, of which it might be said, as of the Sartrian subject, that it is what it makes itself.

Such a theory of individual and collective action naturally leads to the desperate project of a transcendental genesis of society and history (the *Critique of Dialectical Reason*), which Durkheim might almost have had in mind when he wrote in *The Rules of Sociological Method* (1982a: 62): 'It is because this imagined world offers no resistance that the mind, feeling completely unchecked, gives rein to limitless ambitions, believing it possible to construct – or rather reconstruct – the world through its own power and according to its wishes.' And one might continue with Nietzsche (1966: 16): 'Philosophy is this tyrannical desire itself, the most spiritual will to power, to the "creation of the world", to the *causa prima*.' Seeing 'in the social organization combinations which are artificial and to some degree arbitrary', as Durkheim (1982a: 63) puts it, without a second thought he subordinates the transcendence of the social – reduced to 'the reciprocity of constraints and autonomies' – to the 'transcendence of the ego', as the early Sartre put it:

'In the course of this action, the individual discovers the dialectic as rational transparency inasmuch as he produces it, and as absolute necessity inasmuch as it escapes him, in other words, *quite simply*, inasmuch as others produce it; finally, precisely in so far as he recognizes himself in overcoming his needs, he recognizes the law that others impose on him in overcoming their own (he recognizes it: this does not mean that he submits to it), he recognizes his own autonomy (inasmuch as it can be used by another and daily is, in bluffs, manoeuvres, etc.) as a foreign power and the autonomy of others as the inexorable law that allows him to coerce them' (1960: 133).

The transcendence of the social can only be the effect of 'recurrence', that is to say, in the last analysis, of number (hence the importance given to the 'series') or of the 'materialization of recurrence' in cultural objects (1960: 234 and 281); alienation consists in the free abdication of freedom in favour of the demands of 'worked-upon matter':

'The nineteenth-century worker *makes himself what he is*, that is, he practically and rationally determines the order of his expenditure – hence he decides in his free praxis – and by his freedom he makes himself what he is, what he was, what he must be: a machine whose wages represent no more than its running costs . . . Class being as the practico-inert comes to men by men through the passive syntheses of worked-upon matter' (1960: 294).

The assertion of the 'logical' primacy of 'individual praxis', constituent Reason, over History, constituted Reason, leads Sartre to pose the problem of the genesis of society in the same terms as those used by the theoreticians of the social contract:

'History determines the content of human relationships in its totality and these relationships . . . relate back to everything. But it is not history that *causes* there to be human relationships in general. It is not the problems of the organization and division of labour that have caused relationships to be set up among those *initially separate* objects, men' (1960: 179, my italics).

Just as for Descartes, God is invested with the ever-renewed task of creating *ex nihilo*, by a free decree of his will, a world which does not contain within itself the power of subsisting, so Sartre's typically Cartesian refusal of the viscous opacity of 'objective potentialities' and of objective meaning leads him to entrust the endless task of tearing the social whole, or the class, from the inertia of the 'practico-inert', to the absolute initiative of individual or collective 'historical agents' such as 'the Party', the hypostasis of the Sartrian subject. At the end of his immense imaginary novel of the death and resurrection of freedom, with its twofold movement, the 'externalization of internality' – which leads from freedom to alienation, from consciousness to the materialization of consciousness, or, as the title puts it, 'from praxis to the practico-inert' – and the 'internalization of externality' – which , through the abrupt short-cuts of the awakening of consciousness and the 'fusion of consciousnesses', leads 'from the group to history' from the reified state of the alienated group to the authentic existence of the historical agent – consciousness and thing are as irremediably separate as at the beginning, without anything resembling an institution or a socially constituted agent (the very choice of examples bears witness to this) ever having been observed or constructed. The appearances of dialectical discourse cannot mask the endless oscillation between the in-itself and the for-itself, or in the new language, between materiality and praxis, between the inertia of the group reduced to its 'essence', that is, its superseded past and its necessity (abandoned to sociologists), and the continuous creation of the collective free project, seen as an endless series of acts of commitment that are indispensable for saving the group from annihilation in pure materiality.

It is difficult not to see the inertia of a *habitus* in the persistence with which the objective intention of the Sartrian philosophy asserts itself (whatever the change in language) against the subjective intentions of its author, that is, against a permanent project of 'conversion' that is never more manifest, and manifestly sincere, than in some of his anathemas, which would perhaps be less violent if they did not have an undertone of conscious or unconscious self-critique. For example, one has to bear in mind the famous analysis of the café waiter to appreciate fully a sentence such as this: 'To all those who take themselves for angels, their neighbour's activities seem absurd because these people presume to transcend the human enterprise by refusing to take part in it' (1960: 182–3). The example of Sartre, the intellectual *par excellence*, who was capable of undergoing, as he describes them, 'experiences' that were produced by and for analysis, that is, things that deserve to be lived through because they deserve to be told, shows that just as objectivism universalizes the theorist's relation to the object of science, so subjectivism universalizes the experience that the subject of theoretical discourse has of himself as a subject. A professional exponent of consciousness committed to the illusion of 'consciousness without inertia', without a past and without an exterior, he endows all the subjects with whom he decides to identify – that is, almost exclusively the projective 'populace' (*le peuple*) born of this 'generous' identification – with his own experience as a pure, free-floating subject.

Analysis of Sartre's anthropology makes it clear that the principle and the point at stake in the struggle between objectivism and subjectivism is the idea that the science of man forms of man, who is the object and also the subject of this science (which we may assume to tend more towards subjectivism or objectivism depending on the subject's greater or lesser distance from the object of his science). It forces us to pose explicitly the anthropological questions which, out of a mixture of theoretical indifference and unawareness, economists (like anthropologists or linguists) answer without having posed them – that is, often incoherently – and which correspond very exactly to those that the philosophers raised, in the period of the rise of the bourgeoisie, in the sublimated form of the question of the relations between divine freedom and essences. The historical analogy helps us to see that the theory of action and, more precisely, of the relations between agents and objective conditions (or structures) that is implemented by economics constantly oscillates, from one text to another and sometimes from one page to another, between an objectivist vision that subjects freedoms and wills to an external, mechanical determinism or an internal, intellectual determinism and a subjectivist, finalist vision that substitutes the future ends of the project and of intentional action, or, to put it another way, the expectation of future profits, for the antecedents of causal explanation.

Thus the so-called 'rational actor' theory oscillates between the ultra-finalist subjectivism of a consciousness 'without inertia'[3] which creates the meaning of the world *de novo*, at every moment, and which can find continuity and constancy only in the faithfulness to oneself whereby it 'binds itself', like Ulysses sailing past the Sirens, and an intellectual determinism which, though it often defines itself in opposition to it, is separated only by a few differences in phrasing from a mechanistic determinism that reduces action to a mechanical reaction to mechanical determinations and reduces economic agents to indiscernible particles subjected to the laws of a mechanical equilibrium. For if choices are made to depend, on the one hand, on the structural constraints (technical, economic or legal) that delimit the range of possible actions and, on the other hand, on preferences presumed to be universal and conscious – or subject to universal principles – then the agents, constrained by the self-evidence of the reasons and the logical necessity of 'rational calculus', are left no other freedom than adherence to the truth – that is, to the objective chances – or the error of subjective thought, which is 'partial' in both senses.[4]

Sartre's ultra-subjectivist imagination has been outdone by the voluntarism of the anthropological fictions to which the 'rational actor' theorists have to resort (when they actually raise the question, which they usually avoid) in order to make rational decision-making the sole basis of the rational conduct of the 'rational actor', and more especially of the constancy and coherence of his preferences over time. For example, when they invoke strategies that consist in 'binding oneself' – in a variant of the Sartrian pledge which is described as the 'privileged way of resolving the problem of weakness of will' (Elster 1979: 37) – they are able to give the appearance of accounting for rational conduct, of explaining it, with the aid of numerous theoretical models; but in fact, by refusing to recognize any other way of founding it in reason than by giving reason as its foundation, they simply introduce a being of reason, an ought-to-be, as a *vis dormativa*, in the form of an agent all of whose practices have reason as their principle.[5] This is because, by definition, by the simple fact of accepting the idea of an economic subject who is economically unconditioned – especially in his preferences – they exclude inquiry into the economic and social conditions of economic dispositions that the sanctions of a particular state of a particular economy designate as more or less reasonable (rather than rational) depending on their degree of adjustment to its objective demands. Formal models most completely reveal their perhaps most indisputable virtue, their power to reveal *a contrario* the complexity of the reality that they simplify, when they caricature the imaginary anthropology of liberal subjectivism. This they do by striving at all costs to dissolve the arbitrariness of instituted reality in an inaugural *fiat* and to establish the free decision of a conscious, rational subject as the principle of the – at least seemingly – least rational practices, such as customary beliefs or preferences in matters of taste.[6]

The truth of the formal constructions that abound in economics (I am thinking for example of the long debate generated by C. C. Weiszacker's article (1971) on endogenous changes of taste, which subsequent authors like to describe as 'seminal') is revealed in the poverty and unreality of the propositions to which they apply. Thus Weiszacker himself first assumes that current preferences depend only upon consumption in the immediately preceding period, rejecting the idea of a genesis of preferences co-extensive with the whole history of consumption as too complex and therefore too difficult to formalize; and then, for the same reason, he assumes that the consumer's income is to be allocated over two goods only. And what can be said about all the fictitious examples, so obviously invented for the purposes of demonstration that they cannot demonstrate anything, except that one can demonstrate anything with the aid of arbitrary quantifications and calculations applied to 'imaginary groups' such as 20 pilots, 5 promoted, 15 failing, or 20 students, 6 scoring 200, 8 scoring 100 and 6 scoring 0 (Boudon 1977: 39). But to spare ourselves a long enumeration of all the 'mathematical re-creations' that present themselves very seriously as anthropological analyses, such as the 'prisoner's dilemma' and other puzzles designed for circular circulation, it will suffice to cite one example which is the limiting case of all smokers who decide to stop smoking and fat people who decide to fast:

'Let us take a nineteenth-century Russian who, in several years, should inherit vast estates. Because he has socialist ideals, he intends, now, to give the land to the peasants. But he knows that in time his ideals may fade. To guard against this possibility, he does two things. He first signs a legal document, which will automatically give away the land, and which can only be revoked with his wife's consent. He then says to his wife, "If I ever change my mind, and ask you to revoke the documents, promise me that you will not consent." He might add, "I regard my ideals as essential to me. If I lose these ideals, I want you to think that *I* cease to exist. I want you to regard your husband, then, not as me, the man who asks you for this promise, but only as his later self. Promise me that you will not do what he asks"' (Parfit 1973, quoted by Elster [1979: 109]).

It scarcely needs to be pointed out that the production and acceptance of this kind of example and, more generally, of some 'absurdly reasonable' exercises, as Nietzsche (1954) puts it, of formal thought which, dealing with indifferent objects, makes it possible to speak of the social world as if one were not speaking of it, presuppose and encourage denial of the social world.

Thus Pascal's analysis of the most unusual and most unlikely, in a word the least sociological, of all rational decisions, the decision to believe, which is the logical outcome of the argument of the wager (and quite naturally attracts the interest of Jon Elster [1979: 47–54]), can be made to work as a heuristic model *a contrario*. Given, Pascal says, that a man who gambles on the existence of God is staking a finite investment to win infinite gains, belief presents itself without dispute as the only rational strategy; so long, of course, as one believes sufficiently in reason – Pascal points this out, but Jon Elster and all those who, like him, have grown used to living in the pure world of logic resolutely forget it – to be susceptible to these reasons. The fact remains that one cannot rationally pursue the project of founding belief on a rational decision without being led to ask reason to collaborate in its own annihilation in belief, a 'disavowal of reason' that is supremely 'in accordance with reason'. To move from the decision to believe, which reason can induce, to a durable belief that can withstand the intermittences of consciousness and will, one has to invoke other powers than those of reason. This is because reason, which we are supposed to believe capable of leading to the decision to believe, can in no way durably sustain belief:

'For we must make no mistake about ourselves: we are as much automaton as mind. As a result, demonstration is not the only instrument for convincing us. How few things can be demonstrated! Proofs only convince the mind; habit provides the strongest proofs and those that are most believed. It inclines the automaton, which leads the mind unconsciously along with it. Who ever proved that it will dawn tomorrow, and that we shall die? And what is more widely believed? It is, then, habit that convinces us and makes so many Christians. It is habit that makes Turks, heathen, trades, soldiers, etc. . . . . In short, we must resort to habit once the mind has seen where the truth lies, in order to steep and stain ourselves in that belief which constantly eludes us, for it is too much trouble to have the proofs always present before us. We must acquire an easier belief, which is that of habit. With no violence, art or argument it makes us believe things, and so inclines all our faculties to this belief that our soul falls naturally into it. When we believe only by the strength of our conviction and the automaton is inclined to believe the opposite, that is not enough. We must therefore make both parts of us believe: the mind by reasons, which need to be seen only once in a lifetime, and the automaton by habit, and not allowing it any inclination to the contrary' (1966: 274).

This extraordinary analysis of the foundations of belief, which might be meditated upon by all those who insist on seeing belief in terms of representations, did not prevent Pascal from falling into the usual error of professional exponents of logos and logic who always tend, as Marx put it, to take the things of logic for the logic of things. Starting out from the realistic concern to conceive the voluntary decision to believe along the lines of ordinary acquisition of ordinary beliefs, he ends up by presenting the voluntary decision of the subject of practice as the principle of the original practice which generates the durable inclination to practice:

'You want to find faith and you do not know the road. You want to be cured of unbelief and you ask for the remedy; learn from those who were once bound like you and who now wager all they have . . . Follow the way by which they began. They behaved just as if they did believe, taking holy water, having masses said, and so on. That will make you believe quite naturally, and will make you more docile' (1966: 152).

By proceeding as if will and consciousness were the basis of the disposition which 'with no violence, art or argument makes us believe', Pascal leaves intact the mystery of the first beginning, carried away by the infinite regression of the decision to decide; by making belief the product of a free but self-destructive decision to free himself from freedom, he falls into the antinomy of voluntary arbitrary belief, which has naturally been seized on by connoisseurs of logical paradoxes. As Bernard Williams (1973, quoted by Elster [1979: 50–1]) points out, even if it is possible to decide to believe p, one cannot both believe p and believe that the belief that p stems from a decision to believe p; if the decision to believe p is to be carried out successfully, it must also obliterate itself from the memory of the believer.[7]

Needless to say, all these antinomies flow from the will to think practice in terms of the logic of decisions of the will. In fact, it is understandable that Anglo-American philosophers should be forced to admit that they can find no basis for the distinction between *omission* and *commission* that is so vital to a voluntarist theory. Acts of commission, that is, conscious, voluntary commitments, generally do no more than sanction the progressive slippages of omission, the innumerable, infinitesimal non-decisions that can be described with hindsight as 'destiny' or 'vocation' (and it is no accident that the examples of 'decision' most often given are almost always *breaks*). But, at a deeper level, how can one fail to see that decision, if decision there is, and the 'system of preferences' which underlies it, depend not only on all the previous choices of the decider but also on the conditions in which his 'choices' have been made, which include all the choices of those who have chosen for him, in his place, pre-judging his judgements and so shaping his judgement. The paradoxes encountered by the endeavour to conceive belief in terms of the logic of decision show that the real acquisition of belief is defined by the fact that it resolves these antinomies in practice. Genesis implies amnesia of genesis. The logic of the acquisition of belief, that of the continuous, unconscious conditioning that is exerted through conditions of existence as much as through explicit encouragements or warnings, implies the forgetting of acquisition, the illusion of innateness. There is therefore no need to invoke that last refuge of freedom and the dignity of the person, 'bad faith' in the sense of a decision to forget decision and a lie to oneself, in order to account for the fact that belief, or any other form of cultural acquirement, can be experienced simultaneously as logically necessary and sociologically unconditioned.[8]

Thus, the anthropological constructs to which 'rational actor' theorists have to resort in order to deal with the consequences of the theoretical postulate that rational action can have no other principle than the intention of rationality and the free, informed calculation of a rational subject, constitute a refutation *per absurdum* of the postulate. The principle of practices has to be sought instead in the relationship between external constraints which leave a very variable margin for choice, and dispositions which are the product of economic and social processes that are more or less completely reducible to these constraints, as defined at a particular moment.[9] The 'rational actor' theory, which seeks the 'origin' of acts, strictly economic or not, in an 'intention' of 'consciousness', is often associated with a narrow conception of the 'rationality' of practices, an economism which regards as rational (or, which amounts to the same thing in this logic, as economic) those practices that are consciously oriented by the pursuit of maximum (economic) profit at minimum (economic) cost. Finalist economism explains practices by relating them directly and exclusively to economic interests, treated as consciously posited ends; mechanistic economism relates them no less directly and exclusively to economic interests, defined just as narrowly but treated as causes. Both are unaware that practices can have other principles than mechanical causes or conscious ends and can obey an economic logic without obeying narrowly economic interests. There is an economy of practices, a reason immanent in practices, whose 'origin' lies neither in the 'decisions' of reason understood as rational calculation nor in the determinations of mechanisms external to and superior to the agents. Being constitutive of the structure of rational practice, that is, the practice most appropriate to achieve the objectives inscribed in the logic of a particular field at the lowest cost, this economy can be defined in relation to all kinds of functions, one of which, among others, is the maximization of monetary profit, the only one recognized by economism.[10] In other words, if one fails to recognize any form of action other than rational action or mechanical reaction, it is impossible to understand the logic of all the actions that are reasonable without being the product of a reasoned design, still less of rational calculation; informed by a kind of objective finality without being consciously organized in relation to an explicitly constituted end; intelligible and coherent without springing from an intention of coherence and a deliberate decision; adjusted to the future without being the product of a project or a plan. And, if one fails to see that the economy described by economic theory is a particular case of a whole universe of economies, that is, of fields of struggle differing both in the stakes and scarcities that are generated within them and in the forms of capital deployed in them, it is impossible to account for the specific forms, contents and leverage points thus imposed on the pursuit of maximum specific profits and on the very general optimizing strategies (of which economic strategies in the narrow sense are one form among others).[11]

3

Structures, *Habitus*, Practices

Objectivism constitutes the social world as a spectacle offered to an observer who takes up a 'point of view' on the action and who, putting into the object the principles of his relation to the object, proceeds as if it were intended solely for knowledge and as if all the interactions within it were purely symbolic exchanges. This viewpoint is the one taken from high positions in the social structure, from which the social world is seen as a representation (as the word is used in idealist philosophy, but also as in painting) or a performance (in the theatrical or musical sense), and practices are seen as no more than the acting-out of roles, the playing of scores or the implementation of plans. The theory of practice as practice insists, contrary to positivist materialism, that the objects of knowledge are constructed, not passively recorded, and, contrary to intellectualist idealism, that the principle of this construction is the system of structured, structuring dispositions, the *habitus*, which is constituted in practice and is always oriented towards practical functions. It is possible to step down from the sovereign viewpoint from which objectivist idealism orders the world, as Marx demands in the *Theses on Feuerbach*, but without having to abandon to it the 'active aspect' of apprehension of the world by reducing knowledge to a mere recording. To do this, one has to situate oneself *within* 'real activity as such', that is, in the practical relation to the world, the pre-occupied, active presence in the world through which the world imposes its presence, with its urgencies, its things to be done and said, things made to be said, which directly govern words and deeds without ever unfolding as a spectacle. One has to escape from the realism of the structure, to which objectivism, a necessary stage in breaking with primary experience and constructing the objective relationships, necessarily leads when it hypostatizes these relations by treating them as realities already constituted outside of the history of the group – without falling back into subjectivism, which is quite incapable of giving an account of the necessity of the social world. To do this, one has to return to practice, the site of the dialectic of the *opus operatum* and the *modus operandi*; of the objectified products and the incorporated products of historical practice; of structures and *habitus*.

The bringing to light of the presuppositions inherent in objectivist construction has paradoxically been delayed by the efforts of all those who, in linguistics as in anthropology, have sought to 'correct' the structuralist model by appealing to 'context' or 'situation' to account for variations, exceptions and accidents (instead of making them simple variants, absorbed into the structure, as the structuralists do). They have thus avoided a radical questioning of the objectivist mode of thought, when, that is, they have not simply fallen back on to the free choice of a rootless, unattached, pure subject. Thus, the method known as 'situational analysis', which consists of 'observing people in a variety of social situations' in order to determine 'the way in which individuals are able to exercise choices within the limits of a specified social structure' (Gluckman 1961; cf. also Van Velsen 1964), remains locked within the framework of the rule and the exception, which Edmund Leach (often invoked by the exponents of this method) spells out explicitly: 'I postulate that structural systems in which all avenues of social action are narrowly institutionalized are impossible. In all viable systems, there must be an area where the individual is free to make choices so as to manipulate the system to his advantage' (Leach 1962: 133).

The conditionings associated with a particular class of conditions of existence produce *habitus*, systems of durable, transposable dispositions, structured structures predisposed to function as structuring structures, that is, as principles which generate and organize practices and representations that can be objectively adapted to their outcomes without presupposing a conscious aiming at ends or an express mastery of the operations necessary in order to attain them. Objectively 'regulated' and 'regular' without being in any way the product of obedience to rules, they can be collectively orchestrated without being the product of the organizing action of a conductor.[1]

It is, of course, never ruled out that the responses of the *habitus* may be accompanied by a strategic calculation tending to perform in a conscious mode the operation that the *habitus* performs quite differently, namely an estimation of chances presupposing transformation of the past effect into an expected objective. But these responses are first defined, without any calculation, in relation to objective potentialities, immediately inscribed in the present, things to do or not to do, things to say or not to say, in relation to a probable, 'upcoming' future (*un à venir*), which – in contrast to the future seen as 'absolute possibility' (*absolute Möglichkeit*) in Hegel's (or Sartre's) sense, projected by the pure project of a 'negative freedom' – puts itself forward with an urgency and a claim to existence that excludes all deliberation. Stimuli do not exist for practice in their objective truth, as conditional, conventional triggers, acting only on condition that they encounter agents conditioned to recognize them.[2] The practical world that is constituted in the relationship with the *habitus*, acting as a system of cognitive and motivating structures, is a world of already realized ends – procedures to follow, paths to take – and of objects endowed with a 'permanent teleological character', in Husserl's phrase, tools or institutions. This is because the regularities inherent in an arbitrary condition ('arbitrary' in Saussure's and Mauss's sense) tend to appear as necessary, even natural, since they are the basis of the schemes of perception and appreciation through which they are apprehended.

If a very close correlation is regularly observed between the scientifically constructed objective probabilities (for example, the chances of access to a particular good) and agents' subjective aspirations ('motivations' and 'needs'), this is not because agents consciously adjust their aspirations to an exact evaluation of their chances of success, like a gambler organizing his stakes on the basis of perfect information about his chances of winning. In reality, the dispositions durably inculcated by the possibilities and impossibilities, freedoms and necessities, opportunities and prohibitions inscribed in the objective conditions (which science apprehends through statistical regularities such as the probabilities objectively attached to a group or class) generate dispositions objectively compatible with these conditions and in a sense pre-adapted to their demands. The most improbable practices are therefore excluded, as unthinkable, by a kind of immediate submission to order that inclines agents to make a virtue of necessity, that is, to refuse what is anyway denied and to will the inevitable. The very conditions of production of the *habitus*, a virtue made of necessity, mean that the anticipations it generates tend to ignore the restriction to which the validity of calculation of probabilities is subordinated, namely that the experimental conditions should not have been modified. Unlike scientific estimations, which are corrected after each experiment according to rigorous rules of calculation, the anticipations of the *habitus*, practical hypotheses based on past experience, give disproportionate weight to early experiences. Through the economic and social necessity that they bring to bear on the relatively autonomous world of the domestic economy and family relations, or more precisely, through the specifically familial manifestations of this external necessity (forms of the division of labour between the sexes, household objects, modes of consumption, parent–child relations, etc.), the structures characterizing a determinate class of conditions of existence produce the structures of the *habitus*, which in their turn are the basis of the perception and appreciation of all subsequent experiences.

The *habitus*, a product of history, produces individual and collective practices – more history – in accordance with the schemes generated by history. It ensures the active presence of past experiences, which, deposited in each organism in the form of schemes of perception, thought and action, tend to guarantee the 'correctness' of practices and their constancy over time, more reliably than all formal rules and explicit norms.[3] This system of dispositions – a present past that tends to perpetuate itself into the future by reactivation in similarly structured practices, an internal law through which the law of external necessities, irreducible to immediate constraints, is constantly exerted – is the principle of the continuity and regularity which objectivism sees in social practices without being able to account for it; and also of the regulated transformations that cannot be explained either by the extrinsic, instantaneous determinisms of mechanistic sociologism or by the purely internal but equally instantaneous determination of spontaneist subjectivism. Overriding the spurious opposition between the forces inscribed in an earlier state of the system, outside the body, and the internal forces arising instantaneously as motivations springing from free will, the internal dispositions – the internalization of externality – enable the external forces to exert themselves, but in accordance with the specific logic of the organisms in which they are incorporated, i.e. in a durable, systematic and non-mechanical way. As an acquired system of generative schemes, the *habitus* makes possible the free production of all the thoughts, perceptions and actions inherent in the particular conditions of its production – and only those. Through the *habitus*, the structure of which it is the product governs practice, not along the paths of a mechanical determinism, but within the constraints and limits initially set on its inventions. This infinite yet strictly limited generative capacity is difficult to understand only so long as one remains locked in the usual antinomies – which the concept of the *habitus* aims to transcend – of determinism and freedom, conditioning and creativity, consciousness and the unconscious, or the individual and society. Because the *habitus* is an infinite capacity for generating products – thoughts, perceptions, expressions and actions – whose limits are set by the historically and socially situated conditions of its production, the conditioned and conditional freedom it provides is as remote from creation of unpredictable novelty as it is from simple mechanical reproduction of the original conditioning.

Nothing is more misleading than the illusion created by hindsight in which all the traces of a life, such as the works of an artist or the events at a biography, appear as the realization of an essence that seems to pre-exist them. Just as a mature artistic style is not contained, like a seed, in an original inspiration but is continuously defined and redefined in the dialectic between the objectifying intention and the already objectified intention, so too the unity of meaning which, after the event, may seem to have preceded the acts and works announcing the final significance, retrospectively transforming the various stages of the temporal series into mere preparatory sketches, is constituted through the confrontation between questions that only exist in and for a mind armed with a particular type of schemes and the solutions obtained through application of these same schemes. The genesis of a system of works or practices generated by the same *habitus* (or homologous *habitus*, such as those that underlie the unity of the life-style of a group or a class) cannot be described either as the autonomous development of a unique and always self-identical essence, or as a continuous creation of novelty, because it arises from the necessary yet unpredictable confrontation between the *habitus* and an event that can exercise a pertinent incitement on the *habitus* only if the latter snatches it from the contingency of the accidental and constitutes it as a problem by applying to it the very principles of its solution; and also because the *habitus*, like every 'art of inventing', is what makes it possible to produce an infinite number of practices that are relatively unpredictable (like the corresponding situations) but also limited in their diversity. In short, being the product of a particular class of objective regularities, the *habitus* tends to generate all the 'reasonable', 'common-sense',[4] behaviours (and only these) which are possible within the limits of these regularities, and which are likely to be positively sanctioned because they are objectively adjusted to the logic characteristic of a particular field, whose objective future they anticipate. At the same time, 'without violence, art or argument', it tends to exclude all 'extravagances' ('not for the likes of us'), that is, all the behaviours that would be negatively sanctioned because they are incompatible with the objective conditions.

Because they tend to reproduce the regularities immanent in the conditions in which their generative principle was produced while adjusting to the demands inscribed as objective potentialities in the situation as defined by the cognitive and motivating structures that constitute the *habitus*, practices cannot be deduced either from the present conditions which may seem to have provoked them or from the past conditions which have produced the *habitus*, the durable principle of their production. They can therefore only be accounted for by relating the social conditions in which the *habitus* that generated them was constituted, to the social conditions in which it is implemented, that is, through the scientific work of performing the interrelationship of these two states of the social world that the *habitus* performs, while concealing it, in and through practice. The 'unconscious', which enables one to dispense with this interrelating, is never anything other than the forgetting of history which history itself produces by realizing the objective structures that it generates in the quasi-natures of *habitus*. As Durkheim (1977: 11) puts it:

'In each one of us, in differing degrees, is contained the person we were yesterday, and indeed, in the nature of things it is even true that our past *personae* predominate in us, since the present is necessarily insignificant when compared with the long period of the past because of which we have emerged in the form we have today. It is just that we don't directly feel the influence of these past selves precisely because they are so deeply rooted within us. They constitute the unconscious part of ourselves. Consequently we have a strong tendency not to recognize their existence and to ignore their legitimate demands. By contrast, with the most recent acquisitions of civilization we are vividly aware of them just because they are recent and consequently have not had time to be assimilated into our collective unconscious.'

The *habitus* – embodied history, internalized as a second nature and so forgotten as history – is the active presence of the whole past of which it is the product. As such, it is what gives practices their relative autonomy with respect to external determinations of the immediate present. This autonomy is that of the past, enacted and acting, which, functioning as accumulated capital, produces history on the basis of history and so ensures the permanence in change that makes the individual agent a world within the world. The *habitus* is a spontaneity without consciousness or will, opposed as much to the mechanical necessity of things without history in mechanistic theories as it is to the reflexive freedom of subjects 'without inertia' in rationalist theories.

Thus the dualistic vision that recognizes only the self-transparent act of consciousness or the externally determined thing has to give way to the real logic of action, which brings together two objectifications of history, objectification in bodies and objectification in institutions or, which amounts to the same thing, two states of capital, objectified and incorporated, through which a distance is set up from necessity and its urgencies. This logic is seen in paradigmatic form in the dialectic of expressive dispositions and instituted means of expression (morphological, syntactic and lexical instruments, literary genres, etc.) which is observed in the intentionless invention of regulated improvisation. Endlessly overtaken by his own words, with which he maintains a relation of 'carry and be carried', as Nicolai Hartmann put it, the virtuoso finds in his discourse the triggers for his discourse, which goes along like a train laying its own rails (Ruyer 1966: 136). In other words, being produced by a *modus operandi* which is not consciously mastered, the discourse contains an 'objective intention', as the Scholastics put it, which outruns the conscious intentions of its apparent author and constantly offers new pertinent stimuli to the *modus operandi* of which it is the product and which functions as a kind of 'spiritual automaton'. If witticisms strike as much by their unpredictability as by their retrospective necessity, the reason is that the *trouvaille* that brings to light long buried resources presupposes a *habitus* that so perfectly possesses the objectively available means of expression that it is possessed by them, so much so that it asserts its freedom from them by realizing the rarest of the possibilities that they necessarily imply. The dialectic of the meaning of the language and the 'sayings of the tribe' is a particular and particularly significant case of the dialectic between *habitus* and institutions, that is, between two modes of objectification of past history, in which there is constantly created a history that inevitably appears, like witticisms, as both original and inevitable.

This durably installed generative principle of regulated improvisations is a practical sense which reactivates the sense objectified in institutions. Produced by the work of inculcation and appropriation that is needed in order for objective structures, the products of collective history, to be reproduced in the form of the durable, adjusted dispositions that are the condition of their functioning, the *habitus*, which is constituted in the course of an individual history, imposing its particular logic on incorporation, and through which agents partake of the history objectified in institutions, is what makes it possible to inhabit institutions, to appropriate them practically, and so to keep them in activity, continuously pulling them from the state of dead letters, reviving the sense deposited in them, but at the same time imposing the revisions and transformations that reactivation entails. Or rather, the *habitus* is what enables the institution to attain full realization: it is through the capacity for incorporation, which exploits the body's readiness to take seriously the performative magic of the social, that the king, the banker or the priest are hereditary monarchy, financial capitalism or the Church made flesh. Property appropriates its owner, embodying itself in the form of a structure generating practices perfectly conforming with its logic and its demands. If one is justified in saying, with Marx, that 'the lord of an entailed estate, the first-born son, belongs to the land', that 'it inherits him', or that the 'persons' of capitalists are the 'personification' of capital, this is because the purely social and quasi-magical process of socialization, which is inaugurated by the act of marking that institutes an individual as an eldest son, an heir, a successor, a Christian, or simply as a man (as opposed to a woman), with all the corresponding privileges and obligations, and which is prolonged, strengthened and confirmed by social treatments that tend to transform instituted difference into natural distinction, produces quite real effects, durably inscribed in the body and in belief. An institution, even an economy, is complete and fully viable only if it is durably objectified not only in things, that is, in the logic, transcending individual agents, of a particular field, but also in bodies, in durable dispositions to recognize and comply with the demands immanent in the field.

In so far – and only in so far – as *habitus* are the incorporation of the same history, or more concretely, of the same history objectified in *habitus* and structures, the practices they generate are mutually intelligible and immediately adjusted to the structures, and also objectively concerted and endowed with an objective meaning that is at once unitary and systematic, transcending subjective intentions and conscious projects, whether individual or collective. One of the fundamental effects of the harmony between practical sense and objectified meaning (*sens*) is the production of a common-sense world, whose immediate self-evidence is accompanied by the objectivity provided by consensus on the meaning of practices and the world, in other words the harmonization of the agents' experiences and the constant reinforcement each of them receives from expression – individual or collective (in festivals, for example), improvised or programmed (commonplaces, sayings) – of similar or identical experiences.

The homogeneity of *habitus* that is observed within the limits of a class of conditions of existence and social conditionings is what causes practices and works to be immediately intelligible and foreseeable, and hence taken for granted. The *habitus* makes questions of intention superfluous, not only in the production but also in the deciphering of practices and works.[5] Automatic and impersonal, significant without a signifying intention, ordinary practices lend themselves to an understanding that is no less automatic and impersonal. The picking up of the objective intention they express requires neither 'reactivation' of the 'lived' intention of their originator, nor the 'intentional transfer into the Other' cherished by the phenomenologists and all advocates of a 'participationist' conception of history or sociology, nor tacit or explicit inquiry ('What do you *mean*?') as to other people's intentions. 'Communciation of consciousnesses' presupposes community of 'unconsciouses' (that is, of linguistic and cultural competences). Deciphering the objective intention of practices and works has nothing to do with 'reproduction' (*Nachbildung*, as the early Dilthey puts it) of lived experiences and the unnecessary and uncertain reconstitution of an 'intention' which is not their real origin.

The objective homogenizing of group or class *habitus* that results from homogeneity of conditions of existence is what enables practices to be objectively harmonized without any calculation or conscious reference to a norm and mutually adjusted in the absence of any direct interaction or, *a fortiori*, explicit co-ordination. The interaction itself owes its form to the objective structures that have produced the dispositions of the interacting agents, which continue to assign them their relative positions in the interaction and elsewhere.[6] 'Imagine', Leibniz suggests (1866c: 548), 'two clocks or watches in perfect agreement as to the time. This may occur in one of three ways. The first consists in mutual influence; the second is to appoint a skilful workman to correct them and synchronize constantly; the third is to construct these two clocks with such art and precision that one can be assured of their subsequent agreement.' So long as one ignores the true principle of the conductorless orchestration which gives regularity, unity and systematicity to practices even in the absence of any spontaneous or imposed organization of individual projects, one is condemned to the naive artificialism that recognizes no other unifying principle than conscious co-ordination.[7] The practices of the members of the same group or, in a differentiated society, the same class, are always more and better harmonized than the agents know or wish, because, as Leibniz again says, 'following only (his) own laws', each 'nonetheless agrees with the other'. The habitus is precisely this immanent law, *lex insita*, inscribed in bodies by identical histories, which is the precondition not only for the co-ordination of practices but also for practices of co-ordination.[8] The corrections and adjustments the agents themselves consciously carry out presuppose mastery of a common code; and undertakings of collective mobilization cannot succeed without a minimum of concordance between the *habitus* of the mobilizing agents (prophet, leader, etc.) and the dispositions of those who recognize themselves in their practices or words, and, above all, without the inclination towards grouping that springs from the spontaneous orchestration of dispositions.

It is certain that every effort at mobilization aimed at organizing collective action has to reckon with the dialectic of dispositions and occasions that takes place in every agent, whether he mobilizes or is mobilized (the hysteresis of *habitus* is doubtless one explanation of the structural lag between opportunities and the dispositions to grasp them which is the cause of missed opportunities and, in particular, of the frequently observed incapacity to think historical crises in categories of perception and thought other than those of the past, however revolutionary). It is also certain that it must take account of the objective orchestration established among dispositions that are objectively co-ordinated because they are ordered by more or less identical objective necessities. It is, however, extremely dangerous to conceive collective action by analogy with individual action, ignoring all that the former owes to the relatively autonomous logic of the institutions of mobilization (with their own history, their specific organization, etc.) and to the situations, institutionalized or not, in which it occurs.

Sociology treats as identical all biological individuals who, being the products of the same objective conditions, have the same *habitus*. A social class (in-itself) – a class of identical or similar conditions of existence and conditionings – is at the same time a class of biological individuals having the same *habitus*, understood as a system of dispositions common to all products of the same conditionings. Though it is impossible for all (or even two) members of the same class to have had the same experiences, in the same order, it is certain that each member of the same class is more likely than any member of another class to have been confronted with the situations most frequent for members of that class. Through the always convergent experiences that give a social environment its physiognomy, with its 'closed doors', 'dead ends' and 'limited prospects', the objective structures that sociology apprehends in the form of probabilities of access to goods, services and powers, inculcate the 'art of assessing likelihoods', as Leibniz put it, of anticipating the objective future, in short, the 'sense of reality', or realities, which is perhaps the best-concealed principle of their efficacy.

To define the relationship between class *habitus* and individual *habitus* (which is inseparable from the organic individuality that is immediately given to immediate perception – *intuitus personae* – and socially designated and recognized – name, legal identity, etc.), class (or group) *habitus*, that is, the individual habitus in so far as it expresses or reflects the class (or group), could be regarded as a subjective but non-individual system of internalized structures, common schemes of perception, conception and action, which are the precondition of all objectification and apperception; and the objective co-ordination of practices and the sharing of a world-view could be founded on the perfect impersonality and interchangeability of singular practices and views. But this would amount to regarding all the practices or representations produced in accordance with identical schemes as impersonal and interchangeable, like individual intuitions of space which, according to Kant, reflect none of the particularities of the empirical ego. In fact, the singular *habitus* of members of the same class are united in a relationship of homology, that is, of diversity within homogeneity reflecting the diversity within homogeneity characteristic of their social conditions of production. Each individual system of dispositions is a structural variant of the others, expressing the singularity of its position within the class and its trajectory. 'Personal' style, the particular stamp marking all the products of the same *habitus*, whether practices or works, is never more than a deviation in relation to the style of a period or class, so that it relates back to the common style not only by its conformity – like Phidias, who, for Hegel, had no 'manner' – but also by the difference that makes the 'manner'.

The principle of the differences between individual *habitus* lies in the singularity of their social trajectories, to which there correspond series of chronologically ordered determinations that are mutually irreducible to one another. The *habitus* which, at every moment, structures new experiences in accordance with the structures produced by past experiences, which are modified by the new experiences within the limits defined by their power of selection, brings about a unique integration, dominated by the earliest experiences, of the experiences statistically common to members of the same class.[9] Early experiences have particular weight because the *habitus* tends to ensure its own constancy and its defence against change through the selection it makes within new information by rejecting information capable of calling into question its accumulated information, if exposed to it accidentally or by force, and especially by avoiding exposure to such information. One only has to think, for example, of homogamy, the paradigm of all the 'choices' through which the *habitus* tends to favour experiences likely to reinforce it (or the empirically confirmed fact that people tend to talk about politics with those who have the same opinions). Through the systematic 'choices' it makes among the places, events and people that might be frequented, the *habitus* tends to protect itself from crises and critical challenges by providing itself with a milieu to which it is as pre-adapted as possible, that is, a relatively constant universe of situations tending to reinforce its dispositions by offering the market most favourable to its products. And once again it is the most paradoxical property of the *habitus*, the unchosen principle of all 'choices', that yields the solution to the paradox of the information needed in order to avoid information. The schemes of perception and appreciation of the *habitus* which are the basis of all the avoidance strategies are largely the product of a non-conscious, unwilled avoidance, whether it results automatically from the conditions of existence (for example, spatial segregation) or has been produced by a strategic intention (such as avoidance of 'bad company' or 'unsuitable books') originating from adults themselves formed in the same conditions.

Even when they look like the realization of explicit ends, the strategies produced by the *habitus* and enabling agents to cope with unforeseen and constantly changing situations are only apparently determined by the future. If they seem to be oriented by anticipation of their own consequences, thereby encouraging the finalist illusion, this is because, always tending to reproduce the objective structures that produced them, they are determined by the past conditions of production of their principle of production, that is, by the already realized outcome of identical or interchangeable past practices, which coincides with their own outcome only to the extent that the structures within which they function are identical to or homologous with the objective structures of which they are the product. Thus, for example, in the interaction between two agents or groups of agents endowed with the same *habitus* (say A and B), everything takes place as if the actions of each of them (say a_1 for A) were organized by reference to the reactions which they call forth from any agent possessing the same *habitus* (say b_1 for B). They therefore objectively imply anticipation of the reaction which these reactions in turn call forth (a_2, A's reaction to b_1). But the teleological description, the only one appropriate to a 'rational actor' possessing perfect information as to the preferences and competences of the other actors, in which each action has the purpose of making possible the reaction to the reaction it induces (individual A performs an action a_1, a gift for example, in order to make individual B produce action b_1, so that he can then perform action a_1, a stepped-up gift), is quite as naive as the mechanistic description that presents the action and the riposte as so many steps in a sequence of programmed actions produced by a mechanical apparatus.

To have an idea of the difficulties that would be encountered by a mechanistic theory of practice as mechanical reaction, directly determined by the antecedent conditions and entirely reducible to the mechanical functioning of pre-established devices – which would have to be assumed to exist in infinite number, like the chance configurations of stimuli capable of triggering them from outside – one only has to mention the grandiose, desperate undertaking of the anthropologist, fired with positivist ardour, who recorded 480 elementary units of behaviour in 20 minutes' observation of his wife in the kitchen: 'Here we confront the distressing fact that the sample episode chain under analysis is a fragment of a larger segment of behavior which in the complete record contains some 480 separate episodes. Moreover, it took only twenty minutes for these 480 behavior stream events to occur. If my wife's rate of behavior is roughly representative of that of other actors, we must be prepared to deal with an inventory of episodes produced at the rate of some 20,000 per sixteen-hour day per actor ... In a population consisting of several hundred actor-types, the number of different episodes in the total repertory must amount to many millions in the course of an annual cycle' (Harris 1964: 74–5).

The *habitus* contains the solution to the paradoxes of objective meaning without subjective intention. It is the source of these strings of 'moves' which are objectively organized as strategies without being the product of a genuine strategic intention – which would presuppose at least that they be apprehended as one among other possible strategies.[10] If each stage in the sequence of ordered and oriented actions that constitute objective strategies can appear to be determined by anticipation of the future, and in particular, of its own consequences (which is what justifies the use of the concept of strategy), it is because the practices that are generated by the *habitus* and are governed by the past conditions of production of their generative principle are adapted in advance to the objective conditions whenever the conditions in which the *habitus* functions have remained identical, or similar, to the conditions in which it was constituted. Perfectly and immediately successful adjustment to the objective conditions provides the most complete illusion of finality, or – which amounts to the same thing – of self-regulating mechanism.

The presence of the past in this kind of false anticipation of the future performed by the *habitus* is, paradoxically, most clearly seen when the sense of the probable future is belied and when dispositions ill-adjusted to the objective chances because of a hysteresis effect (Marx's favourite example of this was Don Quixote) are negatively sanctioned because the environment they actually encounter is too different from the one to which they are objectively adjusted.[11] In fact the persistence of the effects of primary conditioning, in the form of the *habitus*, accounts equally well for cases in which dispositions function out of phase and practices are objectively ill-adapted to the present conditions because they are objectively adjusted to conditions that no longer obtain. The tendency of groups to persist in their ways, due *inter alia* to the fact that they are composed of individuals with durable dispositions that can outlive the economic and social conditions in which they were produced, can be the source of misadaptation as well as adaptation, revolt as well as resignation.

One only has to consider other possible forms of the relationship between dispositions and conditions to see that the pre-adjustment of the *habitus* to the objective conditions is a 'particular case of the possible' and so avoid unconsciously universalizing the model of the near-circular relationship of near-perfect reproduction, which is completely valid only when the conditions of production of the *habitus* and the conditions of its functioning are identical or homothetic. In this particular case, the dispositions durably inculcated by the objective conditions and by a pedagogic action that is tendentially adjusted to these conditions, tend to generate practices objectively compatible with these conditions and expectations pre-adapted to their objective demands (*amor fati*) (for some psychologists' attempts at direct verification of this relationship, see Brunswik 1949; Preston and Barrata 1948; Attneave 1953). As a consequence, they tend, without any rational calculation or conscious estimation of the chances of success, to ensure immediate correspondence between the *a priori* or *ex ante* probability conferred on an event (whether or not accompanied by subjective experiences such as hopes, expectation, fears, etc.) and the *a posteriori* or *ex post* probability that can be established on the basis of past experience. They thus make it possible to understand why economic models based on the (tacit) premise of a 'relationship of intelligible causality', as Max Weber (1922) calls it, between generic ('typical') chances 'objectively existing as an average' and 'subjective expectations', or, for example, between investment or the propensity to invest and the rate of return expected or really obtained in the past, fairly exactly account for practices which do not arise from knowledge of the objective chances.

By pointing out that rational action, 'judiciously' oriented according to what is 'objectively valid' (1922), is what 'would have happened if the actors had had knowledge of all the circumstances and all the participants' intentions' (1968: 6), that is, of what is 'valid in the eyes of the scientist', who alone is able to calculate the system of objective chances to which perfectly informed action would have to be adjusted, Weber shows clearly that the pure model of rational action cannot be regarded as an anthropological description of practice. This is not only because real agents only very exceptionally possess the complete information, and the skill to appreciate it, that rational action would presuppose. Apart from rare cases which bring together the economic and cultural conditions for rational action oriented by knowledge of the profits that can be obtained in the different markets, practices depend not on the average chances of profit, an abstract and unreal notion, but on the specific chances that a singular agent or class of agents possesses by virtue of its capital, this being understood, in this respect, as a means of appropriation of the chances theoretically available to all.

Economic theory which acknowledges only the rational 'responses' of an indeterminate, interchangeable agent to 'potential opportunities', or more precisely to average chances (like the 'average rates of profit' offered by the different markets), converts the immanent law of the economy into a universal norm of proper economic behaviour. In so doing, it conceals the fact that the 'rational' *habitus* which is the precondition for appropriate economic behaviour is the product of particular economic condition, the one defined by possession of the economic and cultural capital required in order to seize the 'potential opportunities' theoretically available to all; and also that the same dispositions, by adapting the economically most deprived to the specific condition of which they are the product and thereby helping to make their adaptation to the generic demands of the economic cosmos (as regards calculation, forecasting, etc.) lead them to accept the negative sanctions resulting from this lack of adaptation, that is, their deprivation. In short, the art of estimating and seizing chances, the capacity to anticipate the future by a kind of practical induction or even to take a calculated gamble on the possible against the probable, are dispositions that can only be acquired in certain social conditions, that is, certain social conditions. Like the entrepreneurial spirit or the propensity to invest, economic information is a function of one's power over the economy. This is, on the one hand, because the propensity to acquire it depends on the chances of using it successfully, and the chances of acquiring it depend on the chances of successfully using it; and also because economic competence, like all competence (linguistic, political, etc.), far from being a simple technical capacity acquired in certain conditions, is a power tacitly conferred on those who have power over the economy or (as the very ambiguity of the word 'competence' indicates) an attribute of status.

Only in imaginary experience (in the folk tale, for example), which neutralizes the sense of social realities, does the social world take the form of a universe of possibles equally possible for any possible subject. Agents shape their aspirations according to concrete indices of the accessible and the inaccessible, of what is and is not 'for us', a division as fundamental and as fundamentally recognized as that between the sacred and the profane. The pre-emptive rights on the future that are defined by law and by the monopolistic right to certain possibles that it confers are merely the explicitly guaranteed form of the whole set of appropriated chances through which the power relations of the present project themselves into the future, from where they govern present dispositions, especially those towards the future. In fact, a given agent's practical relation to the future, which governs his present practice, is defined in the relationship between, on the one hand, his *habitus* with its temporal structures and dispositions towards the future, constituted in the course of a particular relationship to a particular universe of probabilities, and on the other hand a certain state of the chances objectively offered to him by the social world. The relation to what is possible is a relation to power; and the sense of the probable future is constituted in the prolonged relationship with a world structured according to the categories of the possible (for us) and the impossible (for us), of what is appropriated in advance by and for others and what one can reasonably expect for oneself. The *habitus* is the principle of a selective perception of the indices tending to confirm and reinforce it rather than transform it, a matrix generating responses adapted in advance to all objective conditions identical to or homologous with the (past) conditions of its production; it adjusts itself to a probable future which it anticipates and helps to bring about because it reads it directly in the present of the presumed world, the only one it can ever know.[12] It is thus the basis of what Marx (1975: 378) calls 'effective demand' (as opposed to 'demand without effect', based on need and desire), a realistic relation to what is possible, founded on and therefore limited by power. This disposition, always marked by its (social) conditions of acquisition and realization, tends to adjust to the objective chances of satisfying need or desire, inclining agents to 'cut their coats according to their cloth', and so to become the accomplices of the processes that tend to make the probable a reality.

4

Belief and the Body

Practical sense is a quasi-bodily involvement in the world which presupposes no representation either of the body or of the world, still less of their relationship. It is an immanence in the world through which the world imposes its imminence, things to be done or said, which directly govern speech and action. It orients 'choices' which, though not deliberate, are no less systematic, and which, without being ordered and organized in relation to an end, are none the less charged with a kind of retrospective finality. A particularly clear example of practical sense as a proleptic adjustment to the demands of a field is what is called, in the language of sport, a 'feel for the game'. This phrase (like 'investment sense', the art of 'anticipating' events, etc.) gives a fairly accurate idea of the almost miraculous encounter between the *habitus* and a field, between incorporated history and an objectified history, which makes possible the near-perfect anticipation of the future inscribed in all the concrete configurations on the pitch or board. Produced by experience of the game, and therefore of the objective structures within which it is played out, the 'feel for the game' is what gives the game a subjective sense – a meaning and a *raison d'être*, but also a direction, an orientation, an impending outcome, for those who take part and therefore acknowledge what is at stake (this is *illusio* in the sense of investment in the game and the outcome, interest in the game, commitment to the presuppositions – *doxa* – of the game). And it also gives the game an objective sense, because the sense of the probable outcome that is given by practical mastery of the specific regularities that constitute the economy of a field is the basis of 'sensible' practices, linked intelligibly to the conditions of their enactment, and also among themselves, and therefore immediately filled with sense and rationality for every individual who has the feel for the game (hence the effect of consensual validation which is the basis of collective belief in the game and its fetishes). Because native membership in a field implies a feel for the game in the sense of a capacity for practical anticipation of the 'upcoming' future contained in the present, everything that takes place in it seems *sensible*: full of sense and objectively directed in a judicious direction. Indeed, one only has to suspend the commitment to the game that is implied in the feel for the game in order to reduce the world, and the actions performed in it, to absurdity, and to bring up questions about the meaning of the world and existence which people never ask when they are caught up in the game – the questions of an aesthete trapped in the instant, or an idle spectator. This is exactly the effect produced by the novel when, aiming to be a mirror, pure contemplation, it breaks down action into a series of snapshots, destroying the design, the intention, which, like the thread of discourse, would unify the representation, and reduces the acts and the actors to absurdity, like the dancers observed silently gesticulating behind a glass door in one of Virginia Woolf's novels (cf. Chastaing 1951: 157–9).

In a game, the field (the pitch or board on which it is played, the rules, the outcome at stake, etc.) is clearly seen for what it is, an arbitrary social construct, an artefact whose arbitrariness and artificiality are underlined by everthing that defines its autonomy – explicit and specific rules, strictly delimited and extra-ordinary time and space. Entry into the game takes the form of a quasi-contract, which is sometimes made explicit (the Olympic oath, appeals to 'fair play', and, above all, the presence of a referee or umpire) or recalled to those who get so 'carried away by the game' that they forget it is 'only a game'. By contrast, in the social fields, which are the products of a long, slow process of autonomization, and are therefore, so to speak, games 'in themselves' and not 'for themselves', one does not embark on the game by a conscious act, one is born into the game, with the game; and the relation of investment, *illusio*, investment, is made more total and unconditional by the fact that it is unaware of what it is. As Claudel put it, 'connaître, c'est naître avec', to know is to be born with, and the long dialectical process, often described as 'vocation', through which the various fields provide themselves with agents equipped with the *habitus* needed to make them work, is to the learning of a game very much as the acquisition of the mother tongue is to the learning of a foreign language. In the latter case, an already constituted disposition confronts a language that is perceived as such, that is, as an arbitrary game, explicitly constituted as such in the form of grammar, rules and exercises, expressly taught by institutions expressly designed for that purpose. In the case of primary learning, the child learns at the same time to speak the language (which is only ever presented in action, in his own or other people's speech) and to think *in* (rather than with) the language. The earlier a player enters the game and the less he is aware of the associated learning (the limiting case being, of course, that of someone born into, born with the game), the greater is his ignorance of all that is tacitly granted through his investment in the field and his interest in its very existence and perpetuation and in everything that is played for in it, and his unawareness of the unthought presuppositions that the game produces and endlessly reproduces, thereby reproducing the conditions of its own perpetuation.

Belief is thus an inherent part of belonging to a field. In its most accomplished form – that is, the most naive form, that of native membership – it is diametrically opposed to what Kant, in the *Critique of Pure Reason*, calls 'pragmatic faith', the arbitrary acceptance, for the purposes of action, of an uncertain proposition (as in Descartes's paradigm of the travellers lost in a forest who stick to an arbitrary choice of direction). Practical faith is the condition of entry that every field tacitly imposes, not only by sanctioning and debarring those who would destroy the game, but by so arranging things, in practice, that the operations of selecting and shaping new entrants (rites of passage, examinations, etc.) are such as to obtain from them that undisputed, pre-reflexive, naive, native compliance with the fundamental presuppositions of the field which is the very definition of doxa.[1] The countless acts of recognition which are the small change of the compliance inseparable from belonging to the field, and in which collective misrecognition is ceaselessly generated, are both the precondition and the product of the functioning of the field. They thus constitute investments in the collective enterprise of creating symbolic capital, which can only be performed on condition that the logic of the functioning of the field remains misrecognized. That is why one cannot enter this magic circle by an instantaneous decision of the will, but only by birth or by a slow process of co-option and initiation which is equivalent to a second birth.

One cannot really *live* the belief associated with profoundly different conditions of existence, that is, with other games and other stakes, still less give others the means of reliving it by the sheer power of discourse. It is correct to say in this case, as people sometimes do when faced with the self-evidence of successful adjustment to conditions of existence that are perceived as intolerable: 'You have to be born in it.' All the attempts by anthropologists to bewitch themselves with the witchcraft or mythologies of others have no other interest, however generous they may sometimes be, than that they realize, in their voluntarism, all the antinomies of the decision to believe, which make arbitrary faith a continuous creation of bad faith. Those who want to believe with the beliefs of others grasp neither the objective truth nor the subjective experience of belief. They cannot exploit their exclusion in order to construct the field in which belief is constituted and which membership makes it impossible to objectify; nor can they use their membership of other fields, such as the field of science, to objectify the games in which their own beliefs and investments are generated, in order to appropriate, through this participant objectification, the equivalent experiences of those they seek to describe and so obtain the means of accurately describing both.[2]

Practical belief is not a 'state of mind', still less a kind of arbitrary adherence to a set of instituted dogmas and doctrines ('beliefs'), but rather a state of the body. Doxa is the relationship of immediate adherence that is established in practice between a *habitus* and the field to which it is attuned, the pre-verbal taking-for-granted of the world that flows from practical sense. Enacted belief, instilled by the childhood learning that treats the body as a living memory pad, an automaton that 'leads the mind unconsciously along with it', and as a repository for the most precious values, is the form *par excellence* of the 'blind or symbolic thought' (*cogitatio caeca vel symbolica*) which Leibniz (1939b: 3) refers to, thinking initially of algebra, and which is the product of quasi-bodily dispositions, operational schemes, analogous to the rhythm of a line of verse whose words have been forgotten, or the thread of a discourse that is being improvised, transposable procedures, tricks, rules of thumb which generate through transferance countless practical metaphors that are probably as 'devoid of perception and feeling' as the algebraist's 'dull thoughts' (Leibniz 1866b: 163).[3] Practical sense, social necessity turned into nature, converted into motor schemes and body automatisms, is what causes practices, in and through what makes them obscure to the eyes of their producers, to be *sensible*, that is, informed by a common sense. It is because agents never know completely what they are doing that what they do has more sense than they know.

Every social order systematically takes advantage of the disposition of the body and language to function as depositories of deferred thoughts that can be triggered off at a distance in space and time by the simple effect of re-placing the body in an overall posture which *recalls* the associated thoughts and feelings, in one of the inductive states of the body which, as actors know, give rise to states of mind. Thus the attention paid to staging in great collective ceremonies derives not only from the concern to give a solemn representation of the group (manifest in the splendour of baroque festivals) but also, as many uses of singing and dancing show, from the less visible intention of ordering thoughts and suggesting feelings through the rigorous marshalling of practices and the orderly disposition of bodies, in particular the bodily expression of emotion, in laughter or tears. Symbolic power works partly through the control of other people's bodies and belief that is given by the collectively recognized capacity to act in various ways on deep-rooted linguistic and muscular patterns of behaviour, either by neutralizing them or by reactivating them to function mimetically.

Adapting a phrase of Proust's, one might say that arms and legs are full of numb imperatives. One could endlessly enumerate the values given body, *made* body, by the hidden persuasion of an implicit pedagogy which can instil a whole cosmology, through injunctions as insignificant as 'sit up straight' or 'don't hold your knife in your left hand', and inscribe the most fundamental principles of the arbitrary content of a culture in seemingly innocuous details of bearing or physical and verbal manners, so putting them beyond the reach of consciousness and explicit statement. The logic of scheme transfer which makes each technique of the body a kind of *pars totalis*, predisposed to function in accordance with the fallacy of *pars pro toto*, and hence to recall the whole system to which it belongs, gives a general scope to the apparently most circumscribed and circumstancial observances. The cunning of pedagogic reason lies precisely in the fact that it manages to extort what is essential while seeming to demand the insignificant, such as the respect for forms and forms of respect which are the most visible and most 'natural' manifestation of respect for the established order, or the concessions of politeness, which always contain political concessions.[4]

Bodily hexis is political mythology realized, *em-bodied*, turned into a permanent disposition, a durable way of standing, speaking, walking, and thereby of feeling and thinking. The opposition between male and female is realized in posture, in the gestures and movements of the body, in the form of the opposition between the straight and the bent, between firmness, uprightness and directness (a man faces forward, looking and striking directly at his adversary), and restraint, reserve and flexibility. As is shown by the fact that most of the words that refer to bodily postures evoke virtues and states of mind, these two relations to the body are charged with two relations to other people, time and the world, and through these, to two systems of values. 'The Kabyle is like the heather, he would rather break than bend.' The man of honour walks at a steady, determined pace. His walk, that of a man who knows where he is going and knows he will get there on time, whatever the obstacles, expresses strength and resolution, as opposed to the hesitant gait (*thikli thamahmahth*) announcing indecision, half-hearted promises (*awal amahmah*), the fear of commitments and inability to fulfil them. It is a measured pace, contrasting as much with the haste of the man who 'walks with great strides', like a 'dancer', as with the sluggishness of the man who 'trails along'.

The same oppositions reappear in ways of eating. First, in the use of the mouth: a man should eat with his whole mouth, wholeheartedly, and not, like women, just with the lips, that is, halfheartedly, with reservation and restraint, but also with dissimulation, hypocritically (all the dominated 'virtues' are ambiguous, like the very words that designate them; both can always turn to evil). Then in rhythm: a man of honour must eat neither too quickly, with greed or gluttony, nor too slowly – either way is a concession to nature.

The manly man who goes straight to his target, without detours, is also a man who refuses twisted and devious looks, words, gestures and blows. He stands up straight and looks straight into the face of the person he approaches or wishes to welcome. Ever on the alert, because ever threatened, he misses nothing of what happens around him. A gaze that is up in the clouds or fixed on the ground is that of an irresponsible man, who has nothing to fear because he has no responsibilities in his group. Conversely, a well brought-up woman, who will do nothing indecorous 'with her head, her hands or her feet' is expected to walk with a slight stoop, avoiding every misplaced movement of her body, her head or her arms, looking down, keeping her eyes on the spot where she will next put her foot, especially if she happens to have to walk past the men's assembly. She must avoid the excessive swing of the hips that comes from a heavy stride; she must always be girdled with the *thimeh'remth*, a rectangular piece of cloth with yellow, red and black stripes worn over her dress, and take care that her headscarf does not come unknotted, uncovering her hair. In short, the specifically feminine virtue, *lah'ia*, modesty, restraint, reserve, orients the whole female body downwards, towards the ground, the inside, the house, whereas male excellence, *nif*, is asserted in movement upwards, outwards, towards other men.

A complete account of this one dimension of the male and female uses of the body would require a full analysis of the division of labour between the sexes and also of the division of sexual labour. But a single example, that of the division of tasks in olive gathering, will suffice to show that the systems of oppositions, which it would be wrong to describe as value systems (informants always give them the performative self-evidence of naturalized arbitrariness: a man does this – he ties up animals – a woman does that . . .) derive their symbolic efficacy from their practical translation into actions that go without saying, like that of the woman who offers a man a stool or walks a few paces behind him. Here, the opposition between the straight and the bent, the stiff and the supple, takes the form of the distinction between the man who stands and knocks down the olives (with a pole) and the woman who stoops to pick them up. This practical, that is, simultaneously logical and axiological, principle, which is often stated explicitly – 'woman gathers up what man casts to the ground' – combines with the opposition between big and small to assign to women the tasks that are low and inferior, demanding submissiveness and suppleness, and minute, but also petty ('the lion does not pick up ants'), such as picking up the splinters of wood cut by men (who are responsible for everything that is discontinuous or produces discontinuity). It can be seen, incidentally, how such a logic tends to produce its own confirmation, by inducing a 'vocation' for the tasks to which one is assigned, an *amor fati* which reinforces belief in the prevailing system of classification by making it appear to be grounded in reality – which it actually is, since it helps to produce that reality and since incorporated social relations present themselves with every appearance of nature – and not only in the eyes of those whose interests are served by the prevailing system of classification.

When the properties and movements of the body are socially qualified, the most fundamental social choices are naturalized and the body, with its properties and its movements, is constituted as an analogical operator establishing all kinds of practical equivalences among the different divisions of the social world – divisions between the sexes, between the age groups and between the social classes – or, more precisely, among the meanings and values associated with the individuals occupying practically equivalent positions in the spaces defined by these divisions. In particular, there is every reason to think that the social determinations attached to a determinate position in the social space tend, through the relationship to one's own body, to shape the dispositions constituting social identity (ways of walking, speaking, etc.) and probably also the sexual dispositions themselves.[5]

In other words, when the elementary acts of bodily gymnastics (going up or down, forwards or backwards, etc.) and, most importantly, the specifically sexual, and therefore biologically preconstructed, aspect of this gymnastics (penetrating or being penetrated, being on top or below, etc.) are highly charged with social meanings and values, socialization instils a sense of the equivalences between physical space and social space and between movements (rising, falling, etc.) in the two spaces and thereby roots the most fundamental structures of the group in the primary experiences of the body which, as is clearly seen in emotion, takes metaphors seriously.[6] For example, the opposition between the straight and the bent, whose function in the incorporated division of labour between the sexes has been indicated, is central to most of the marks of respect or contempt that politeness uses in many societies to symbolize relations of domination. On the one hand, lowering or bending the head or forehead as a sign of confusion or timidity, lowering the eyes in humility or timidity, and also shame or modesty, looking down or underneath, kneeling, curtseying, prostration (before a superior or a god); on the other hand, looking up, looking someone in the eyes, refusing to bow the head, standing up to someone, getting the upper hand ... Male, upward movements and female, downward movements, uprightness versus bending, the will to be on top, to overcome, versus submission – the fundamental oppositions of the social order, whether between the dominant and the dominated or between the dominant-dominant and the dominated-dominant – are always sexually overdetermined, as if the body language of sexual domination and submission had provided the fundamental principles of both the body language and the verbal language of social domination and submission.[7]

Because the classificatory schemes through which the body is practically apprehended and appreciated are always grounded twofold, both in the social division of labour and in the sexual division of labour, the relation to the body is specified according to sex and according to the form that the division of labour between the sexes takes depending on the position occupied in the social division of labour. Thus, the value of the opposition between the big and the small, which, as a number of. experiments have shown, is one of the fundamental principles of the perception that agents have of their body and also of their whole relation to the body, varies between the sexes, which are themselves conceived in terms of this opposition (the dominant representation of the division of labour between the sexes gives the man the dominant position, that of the protector who embraces, encompasses, envelops, oversees, etc.); and the opposition thus specified receives in turn different values depending on the class, that is, depending on how strongly the opposition between the sexes is asserted within it, in practices or in discourses (ranging from clear-cut alternatives – 'macho' (*mec*) or 'fairy' (*tante*) – to a continuum) and depending on the forms that the inevitable compromise between the real body and the ideal, legitimate body (with the sexual characteristics that each social class assigns to it) has to take in order to adjust to the necessities inscribed in each class condition.

The relation to the body is a fundamental dimension of the *habitus* that is inseparable from a relation to language and to time. It cannot be reduced to a 'body image' or even 'body concept' (the two terms are used almost interchangeably by some psychologists), a subjective representation largely based on the representation of one's own body produced and returned by others. Social psychology is mistaken when it locates the dialectic of incorporation at the level of *representations*, with body image, the descriptive and normative 'feed-back' supplied by the group (family, peers, etc.) engendering self-image (or the 'looking-glass self'), that is, an agent's own representation of his/her social 'effects' (seduction, charm, etc.). This is firstly because all the schemes of perception and appreciation in which a group deposits its fundamental structures, and the schemes of expression through which it provides them with the beginnings of objectification and therefore of reinforcement, intervene between the individual and his/her body. Application of the fundamental schemes to one's own body, and more especially to those parts of the body that are most pertinent in terms of these schemes, is doubtless one of the privileged occasions for the incorporation of the schemes, because of the heavy investments placed in the body.[8] But secondly, and more importantly, the process of acquisition – a practical *mimesis* (or mimeticism) which implies an overall relation of identification and has nothing in common with an *imitation* that would presuppose a conscious effort to reproduce a gesture, an utterance or an object explicitly constituted as a model – and the process of reproduction – a practical reactivation which is opposed to both memory and knowledge – tend to take place below the level of consciousness, expression and the reflexive distance which these presuppose. The body believes in what it plays at: it weeps if it mimes grief. It does not represent what it performs, it does not memorize the past, it *enacts* the past, bringing it back to life. What is 'learned by body' is not something that one has, like knowledge that can be brandished, but something that one is. This is particularly clear in non-literate societies, where inherited knowledge can only survive in the incorporated state. It is never detached from the body that bears it and can be reconstituted only by means of a kind of gymnastics designed to evoke it, a *mimesis* which, as Plato observed, implies total investment and deep emotional identification. As Eric Havelock (1963), from whom this argument is borrowed, points out, the body is thus constantly mingled with all the knowledge it reproduces, and this knowledge never has the objectivity it derives from objectification in writing and the consequent freedom with respect to the body.

And it could be shown that the shift from a mode of conserving the tradition based solely on oral discourse to a mode of accumulation based on writing, and, beyond this, the whole process of rationalization that is made possible by (*inter alia*) objectification in writing, are accompanied by a far-reaching transformation of the whole relationship to the body, or more precisely of the use made of the body in the production and reproduction of cultural artefacts. This is particularly clear in the case of music, where the process of rationalization as described by Weber has as its corollary a 'disincarnation' of musical production or reproduction (which generally are not distinct), a 'disengagement' of the body which most ancient musical systems use as a complete instrument.

So long as the work of education is not clearly institutionalized as a specific, autonomous practice, so long as it is the whole group and a whole symbolically structured environment, without specialized agents or specific occasions, that exerts an anonymous, diffuse pedagogic action, the essential part of the *modus operandi* that defines practical mastery is transmitted through practice, in the practical state, without rising to the level of discourse. The child mimics other people's actions rather than 'models'. Body hexis speaks directly to the motor function, in the form of a pattern of postures that is both individual and systematic, being bound up with a whole system of objects, and charged with a host of special meanings and values. But the fact that schemes are able to pass directly from practice to practice without moving through discourse and consciousness does not mean that the acquisition of *habitus* is no more than a mechanical learning through trial and error. In contrast to an incoherent sequence of numbers which can only be learnt gradually, through repeated attempts and continuous, predictable progress, a numerical series is mastered more easily because it contains a structure that makes it unnecessary to memorize all the numbers mechanically one by one. Whether in verbal products such as proverbs, sayings, gnomic poems, songs or riddles, or in objects such as tools, the house or the village, or in practices such as games, contests of honour, gift exchange or rites, the material that the Kabyle child has to learn is the product of the systematic application of a small number of principles coherent in practice, and, in its infinite redundance, it supplies the key to all the tangible series, their *ratio*, which will be appropriated in the form of a principle generating practices that are organized in accordance with the same rationality.[9]

Experimental analyses of learning which establish that 'neither the formation nor the application of a concept requires conscious recognition of the common elements or relationship involved in the specific instances' (Berelson and Steiner 1964: 193) enable us to understand the dialectic of objectification and incorporation whereby practices and artefacts, systematic objectifications of systematic dispositions, tend in turn to engender systematic dispositions. When presented with a series of symbols – Chinese characters (in Hull's experiments) or pictures in which the colour, nature and number of the objects represented vary simultaneously (Heidbreder) – distributed into classes that were given arbitrary but objectively grounded names, subjects who were unable to state the principle of classification none the less achieved higher scores than they would if they were guessing at random. They thereby demonstrated that they had attained a practical mastery of the classificatory schemes that in no way implied symbolic mastery, that is, consciousness and verbal expression, of the procedures actually applied. These experimental findings are entirely confirmed by Albert B. Lord's analysis of the acquisition of structured material in the natural environment, based on his study of the training of the *guslar*, the Yugoslav bard. Practical mastery of what he calls the 'formula method', that is, the ability to improvise by combining 'formulae', sequences of words 'regularly employed under the same metrical conditions to express a given idea', is acquired through sheer familiarization, simply 'by hearing the poems', without the learner having 'the sense of learning and subsequently manipulating this or that formula or any set of formulae' (1960: 30–4). The constraints of rhythm or metre are internalized at the same time as melody and meaning, without ever being perceived in their own right.

Between learning through sheer familiarization, in which the learner insensibly and unconsciously acquires the principles of an 'art' and an art of living, including those that are not known to the producer of the practices or artefacts that are imitated, and explicit and express transmission by precept and prescription, every society provides structural exercises which tend to transmit a particular form of practical mastery. In Kabylia, there are the riddles and ritual contests that test the 'sense of ritual language' and all the games, often structured according to the logic of the wager, the challenge or the combat (duels, group battles, target-shooting, etc.), which require the boys to apply the generative schemes of the conduct of honour, in the 'let's pretend' mode;[10] there is daily participation in gift exchanges and their subtleties, in which small boys play the role of messengers, and particularly of intermediaries between the world of women and that of men. There is silent observation of discussions in the men's assembly, with their effects of eloquence, their rituals, their strategies, their ritual strategies and their strategic uses of ritual. There are interactions with kinsmen in which objective relationships are explored in all directions, by means of reversals requiring the same person who in one context behaved as a nephew to behave in another as a paternal uncle, so acquiring practical mastery of the transformational schemes that allow the shift from the dispositions associated with one position to those appropriate to the other. There are lexical and grammatical commutations ('I' and 'you' designating the same person according to the relation to the speaker) which teach the sense of the interchangeability and reciprocity of positions and the limits of both. At a deeper level, there are relations with the father and the mother which, through their asymmetry in antagonistic complementarity, constitute one of the occasions for internalizing inseparably the schemes of the sexual division of labour and the division of sexual labour.

But in fact all the actions performed in a structured space and time are immediately qualified symbolically and function as structural exercises through which practical mastery of the fundamental schemes is constituted. Social disciplines take the form of temporal disciplines and the whole social order imposes itself at the deepest level of the bodily dispositions through a particular way of regulating the use of time, the temporal distribution of collective and individual activities and the appropriate rhythm with which to perform them.

'Don't we all eat the same wheatcake (or the same barley)?' 'Don't we all get up at the same time?' These formulae, commonly used to reassert solidarity, contain an implicit definition of the fundamental virtue of conformity, the opposite of which is the desire to stand apart from others. Working when others are resting, lurking at home when others are working in the fields, travelling on deserted roads, loitering in the streets of the village when others are asleep or at the market – these are all suspicious forms of behaviour. 'There is a time for every thing' and it is important to do 'each thing in its time' (*kul waqth salwaqth-is* – 'each time in its time'). Thus a responsible man must be an early riser: 'He who does not finish his business early in the morning will never finish it.'[11] Getting up early to take out the livestock, to go to Koran school or simply to be outdoors with the men, at the same time as the men, is a duty of honour that boys are taught to respect from a young age. A man who leaves on time will arrive at the right place at the right time, without having to rush. There is mockery for the man who hurries, who runs to catch up with someone, who works so hastily that he is likely to 'maltreat the earth'. The tasks of farming, *horia erga* as the Greeks called them, are defined as much in their rhythm as in their moment.[12] The vital tasks, like ploughing and sowing, fall to those who are capable of treating the land with the respect it deserves, of approaching it (*qabel*) with the measured pace of a man meeting a partner whom he wants to greet and honour. This is underlined by the legend (told by a *t'aleb* of the Matmata tribe) of the origin of wheat and barley. Adam was sowing wheat; Eve brought him some wheatcake. She saw Adam sowing grain by grain, 'covering each seed with earth' and invoking God each time. She accused him of wasting his time. While he was busy eating, she started to broadcast the grain, without invoking the name of God. When the crop came up, Adam found his field full of strange ears of corn that were delicate and fragile, like woman. He called this plant (barley) *châir*, 'weak'.[13] To control the moment, and especially the tempo, of practices, is to inscribe durably in the body, in the form of the rhythm of actions or words, a whole relationship to time, which is experienced as part of the person (like the *gravitas* of Roman senators). It helps, for example, to discourage all forms of racing, seen as competititve ambition (*thah'raymith*), which would tend to transform circular time into linear time, simple reproduction into endless accumulation.

In a universe such as this, people never deal with 'nature' as science understands it – a cultural construct which is the historical product of a long process of 'disenchantment'. Between the child and the world, the whole group intervenes, not just with the warnings that inculcate a fear of supernatural dangers (cf. Whiting 1941: 215), but with a whole universe of ritual practices and utterances, which people it with meanings structured in accordance with the principles of the corresponding *habitus*. Inhabited space – starting with the house – is the privileged site of the objectification of the generative schemes, and, through the divisions and hierarchies it establishes between things, between people and between practices, this materialized system of classification inculcates and constantly reinforces the principles of the classification which constitutes the arbitrariness of a culture. Thus, the opposition between the sacred of the right hand and the sacred of the left hand, between *nif* and *h'aram*, between man, invested with protective and fertilizing powers, and woman, who is both sacred and invested with maleficent powers, is materialized in the division between masculine space, with the assembly place, the market or the fields, and female space, the house and the garden, the sanctuaries of *h'aram*; and, secondarily, in the opposition which, within the house itself, assigns regions of space, objects and activities either to the male universe of the dry, fire, the high, the cooked, the day, or the female universe of the moist, water, the low, the raw, the night. The world of objects, a kind of book in which each thing speaks metaphorically of all others and from which children learn to read the world, is read with the whole body, in and through the movements and displacements which define the space of objects as much as they are defined by it.[14] The structures that help to construct the world of objects are constructed in the practice of a world of objects constructed in accordance with the same structures. The 'subject' born of the world of objects does not arise as a subjectivity facing an objectivity: the objective universe is made up of objects which are the product of objectifying operations structured according to the same structures that the *habitus* applies to them. The *habitus* is a metaphor of the world of objects, which is itself an endless circle of metaphors that mirror each other *ad infinitum*.

All the symbolic manipulations of body experience, starting with displacements within a symbolically structured space, tend to impose the integration of body space with cosmic space and social space, by applying the same categories (naturally at the price of great laxity in logic) both to the relationship between man and the natural world and to the complementary and opposed states and actions of the two sexes in the division of sexual labour and the sexual division of labour, and therefore in the labour of biological and social reproduction. For example, the opposition between movement outwards, towards the field or the market, towards the production and circulation of goods, and movement inwards, towards the accumulation and consumption of the products of labour, corresponds symbolically to the opposition between the male body, self-enclosed and directed towards the outside world, and the female body, which is akin to the dark, damp house full of food, utensils and children, entered and left by the same, inevitably soiled opening.[15]

The opposition between the centrifugal male orientation and the centripetal female orientation, which is the principle of the organization of the internal space of the house, no doubt also underlies the relationship that the two sexes have to their own bodies, and more specifically to their sexuality. As in every society dominated by male values – and European societies, which assign men to politics, history or war, and women to the hearth, the novel and psychology, are no exception to this – the specifically male relationship to the body and sexuality is that of sublimation. The symbolism of honour tends both to refuse any direct expression of nature and sexuality and to encourage its transfigured manifestation in the form of manly prowess. Kabyle men, who are neither aware of nor concerned with the female orgasm, but who seek the confirmation of their potency in repetition rather than prolongation of intercourse, cannot forget that, through the female gossip that they both fear and despise, the eyes of the group always threaten their privacy. As for the women, it is true to say, as Erikson (1945) does, that male domination 'tends to restrict their verbal consciousness', only so long as this is taken to mean, not that they are denied all talk of sex, but that their discourse is dominated by the male values of virility, so that any reference to specifically female sexual 'interests' is excluded from this aggressive and shame-filled cult of male potency.

Psychoanalysis, a disenchanting product of the disenchantment of the world, which tends to constitute *as such* a mythically overdetermined area of signification, too easily obscures the fact that one's own body and other people's bodies are always perceived through categories of perception which it would be naive to treat as sexual, even if, as is confirmed by the women's suppressed laughter during conversations and the interpretations they give of graphic symbols in wall paintings, pottery or carpet motifs, etc., these categories always relate back, sometimes very concretely, to the opposition between the biologically defined properties of the two sexes. This would be as naive as it would be to reduce to their strictly sexual dimension the countless acts of diffuse inculcation through which the body and the world tend to be set in order, by means of a symbolic manipulation of the relation to the body and the world aimed at imposing what has to be called, in Melanie Klein's term (1948), a 'body geography', a particular case of geography, or rather of cosmology. The child's initial relation to its father and mother, or, to put it another way, to the paternal body and the maternal body, which provides the most dramatic opportunity to experience all the fundamental oppositions of mythopoeic practice, cannot be identified as the basis of the acquisition of the principles of the structuring of the self and the world, and in particular of every homosexual and heterosexual relationship, except in so far as that primary relationship is understood as being set up with objects whose sex is defined symbolically and not biologically. The child constructs its sexual identity, a central aspect of its social identity, at the same time as it constructs its representation of the division of labour between the sexes, on the basis of the same socially defined set of indissolubly biological and social indices. In other words, the growth of awareness of sexual identity and the incorporation of the dispositions associated with a particular social definition of the social functions assigned to men and women come hand in hand with the adoption of a socially defined vision of the sexual division of labour.

Psychologists' work on the perception of sexual differences makes it clear that children establish clear-cut distinctions very early (about age five) between male and female tasks, assigning domestic tasks to women and mothers and economic activities to men and fathers. (See, for example, Mott 1954. Hartley [1960] shows that when the father performs 'female' tasks or the mother 'male' tasks, they are seen as 'helping'.) Everything suggests that the awareness of sexual differences and the distinction between paternal and maternal functions are constituted simultaneously (see Dubin and Dubin 1965; Kohlberg 1967). The numerous analyses of the differential perception of father and mother indicate that the father is generally seen as more competent and more severe than the mother, who is regarded as 'gentler' and more affectionate than the father and is the object of a more emotionally charged and more agreeable relationship (see Dubin and Dubin 1965 for references). In fact, as Emmerich (1959, 1961) points out, underlying all these differences is the fact that children attribute more power to the father than to the mother.

It is not hard to imagine the weight that the opposition between masculinity and femininity must bring to bear on the construction of self-image and world-image when this opposition constitutes the fundamental principle of division of the social and the symbolic world. As is underlined by the twofold meaning of the word *nif*, physical potency inseparable from social potency, what is imposed through a certain social definition of maleness (and, consequently, of femaleness) is a political mythology, which governs all bodily experiences, not least sexual experiences themselves. Thus, the opposition between male sexuality – public and sublimated – and female sexuality – secret and, so to speak, 'alienated' (with respect to

Erikson's 'utopia of universal genitality', the 'utopia of full orgasmic reciprocity') is no more than a specific form taken by the opposition between the extraversion of politics or public religion and the introversion of private magic, the secret, hidden weapon of the dominated, made up for the most part of rites aimed at domesticating the male partners.

Everything takes place as if the *habitus* forged coherence and necessity out of accident and contingency; as if it managed to unify the effects of the social necessity undergone from childhood, through the material conditions of existence, the primary relational experiences and the practice of structured actions, objects, spaces and times, and the effects of biological necessity, whether the influence of hormone balances or the weight of the visible characteristics of physique; as if it produced a biological (and especially sexual) reading of social properties and a social reading of sexual properties, thus leading to a social re-use of biological properties and a biological re-use of social properties. This is seen very clearly in the equivalences it establishes between position in the division of labour and position in the division of the sexes. These equivalences are probably not peculiar to societies in which the divisions produced by these two principles coincide almost exactly. In a society divided into classes, all the products of a given agent, by an essential overdetermination, speak inseparably and simultaneously of his/her class – or, more precisely, his/her position and rising or falling trajectory within the social structure – and of his/her body – or, more precisely, of all the properties, always socially qualified, of which he/she is the bearer: sexual ones, of course, but also physical properties that are praised, like strength or beauty, or stigmatized.

5

The Logic of Practice

It is not easy to speak of practice other than negatively – especially those aspects of practice that are seemingly most mechanical, most opposed to the logic of thought and discourse. All the automatic reflexes of 'thinking in couples' tend to exclude the idea that the pursuit of conscious goals, in whatever area, can presuppose a permanent dialectic between an organizing consciousness and automatic behaviours. The usual obligatory choice between the language of consciousness and the language of the mechanical model would perhaps be less compelling if it did not correspond to a fundamental division in the dominant world-view. Those who have the monopoly on discourse about the social world think differently when they are thinking about themselves and about others (that is, the other classes): they are readily spiritualist as regards themselves, materialist towards others, liberal for themselves and dirigiste for others, and, with equal logic, teleological and intellectualist for themselves and mechanist for others. This is seen in economics, where writers oscillate between the tendency to credit economic agents, or rather the 'entrepreneur', with the capacity to assess objective chances rationally, and the tendency to credit the self-regulating mechanisms of the market with the absolute power to determine preferences.[1] As for the anthropologists, they would have been less inclined to use the language of the mechanical model if, when considering exchange, they had thought not only of *potlatch* or *kula*, but also of the games they themselves play in social life, which are expressed in the language of tact, skill, dexterity, delicacy or *savoir-faire*, all names for practical sense; and if they had set aside the exchange of gifts and words and considered exchanges in which hermeneutic errors are paid for instantly, such as the exchange of blows, discussed by George H. Mead (1962: 42–3), in which each stance of the opponent's body contains cues which the fighter has to grasp while they are still incipient, reading in the hint of a blow or a sidestep the future it contains, that is, the blow or a 'dummy'. Returning to the seemingly most mechanical and ritualized of exchanges, such as polite conversation, a stereotyped linking of stereotypes, they would have discovered the unceasing vigilance that is needed to manage this interlocking of prepared gestures and words; the attention to every sign that is indispensable, in the use of the most ritual pleasantries, in order to be carried along by the game without getting carried away by the game beyond the game, as happens when simulated combat gets the better of the combatants; the art of playing on the equivocations, innuendoes and unspoken implications of gestural or verbal symbolism that is required, whenever the right objective distance is in question, in order to produce ambiguous conduct that can be disowned at the slightest sign of withdrawal or refusal, and to maintain uncertainty about intentions that always hesitate between recklessness and distance, eagerness and indifference. One thus only has to go back to one's own games, one's own playing of the social game, to realize that the sense of the game is at once the realization of the theory of the game and its negation *qua* theory.

When one discovers the theoretical error that consists in presenting the theoretical view of practice as the practical relation to practice, and more precisely in setting up the model that has to be constructed to give an account of practice as the principle of practice, then simultaneously one sees that at the root of this error is the antinomy between the time of science and time of action, which tends to destroy practice by imposing on it the intemporal time of science. The shift from the practical scheme to the theoretical schema, constructed after the event, from practical sense to the theoretical model, which can be read either as a project, plan or method, or as a mechanical programme, a mysterious ordering mysteriously reconstructed by the analyst, lets slip everything that makes the temporal reality of practice in process. Practice unfolds in time and it has all the correlative properties, such as irreversibility, that synchronization destroys. Its temporal structure, that is, its rhythm, its tempo, and above all its directionality, is constitutive of its meaning. As with music, any manipulation of this structure, even a simple change in tempo, either acceleration or slowing down, subjects it to a destructuration that is irreducible to a simple change in an axis of reference. In short, because it is entirely immersed in the current of time, practice is inseparable from temporality, not only because it is played out in time, but also because it plays strategically with time and especially with tempo.

Science has a time which is not that of practice. For the analyst, time disappears: not only because, as has often been repeated since Max Weber pointed it out, arriving after the battle, the analyst cannot have any uncertainty as to what can happen, but also because he has the time to totalize, that is, to overcome the effects of time. Scientific practice is so detemporalized that it tends to exclude even the idea of what it excludes. Because science is only possible in a relation to time which is the opposite of that of practice, it tends to ignore time and so to detemporalize practice. A player who is involved and caught up in the game adjusts not to what he sees but to what he fore-sees, sees in advance in the directly perceived present; he passes the ball not to the spot where his team-mate is but to the spot he will reach – before his opponent – a moment later, anticipating the anticipations of the others and, as when 'selling a dummy', seeking to confound them. He decides in terms of objective probabilities, that is, in response to an overall, instantaneous assessment of the whole set of his opponents and the whole set of his team-mates, seen not as they are but in their impending positions. And he does so 'on the spot', 'in the twinkling of an eye', 'in the heat of the moment', that is, in conditions which exclude distance, perspective, detachment and reflexion. He is launched into the impending future, present in the imminent moment, and, abdicating the possibility of suspending at every moment the ecstasis that projects him into the probable, he identifies himself with the imminent future of the world, postulating the continuity of time. He thereby excludes the supremely real and quite theoretical possibility of sudden reduction to the present, that is, to the past, the abrupt severing of the commitments and attachments to the future which, like death, casts the anticipations of interrupted practice into the absurdity of the unfinished. Urgency, which is rightly seen as one of the essential properties of practice, is the product of playing in the game and the presence in the future that it implies. One only has to stand outside the game, as the observer does, in order to sweep away the urgency, the appeals, the threats, the steps to be taken, which make up the real, really lived-in, world. Only for someone who withdraws from the game completely, who totally breaks the spell, the *illusio*, renouncing all the stakes, that is, all the gambles on the future, can the temporal succession be seen as a pure discontinuity and the world appear in the absurdity of a future-less, and therefore senseless, present, like the Surrealists' staircases opening on to the void. The 'feel' (*sens*) for the game is the sense of the imminent future of the game, the sense of the direction (*sens*) of the history of the game that gives the game its sense.

Thus one has no chance of giving a scientific account of practice – and in particular of the properties it derives from the fact that it unfolds in time – unless one is aware of the effects that scientific practice produces by mere totalization. One only has to think of the synoptic diagram, which owes its scientific efficacy precisely to the synchronizing effect it produces (after much labour and *time*) by giving an instantaneous view of facts which only exist in succession and so bringing to light relationships (including contradictions) that would otherwise go unnoticed. As is seen in the case of ritual practices, the cumulation and juxtaposition of relations of opposition and equivalence which are not and cannot be mastered by any one informant, never in any case at the same time, and which can only be produced by reference to different situations, that is, in different universes of discourse and with different functions, is what provides the analyst with the privilege of totalization, that is, the capacity to possess and put forward the synoptic view of the totality and the unity of the relationships that is the precondition of adequate decoding. Because he has every likelihood of ignoring the social and logical conditions of the change in nature that he imposes on practice and its products and therefore the nature of the logical transformations he imposes on the information that has been gathered, the analyst is liable to fall into all the errors that flow from the tendency to confuse the actor's point of view with the spectator's point of view, for example looking for answers to a spectator's questions that practice never asks because it has no need to ask them, instead of wondering if the essence of practice is not precisely that it excludes such questions.

The paradigm of this fundamental epistemological error can be found in the 'perversity' of those writers who, according to T. E. Lawrence, attribute the viewpoint of 'a man sitting in an armchair' to 'a man entirely taken up by his task'. Maxime Chastaing, who quotes this text, continues: 'Ramuz converts the peasants' toil into apparent movements of the landscape. When the digger painfully stoops, it is not the earth that rises: either he is digging and he does not see the earth rising; or the earth seems to rise, and it is no longer the peasant who is looking but the cine camera of some vacationing artist that is mysteriously substituted for his eyes. Ramuz confuses work and leisure' (Chastaing 1951: 86). It is no accident that the novel oscillates between these two poles, with which social science is also familiar: on the one hand, the absolute viewpoint of an omnipresent and omniscient God who possesses the truth about his characters (denouncing their lies, explaining their silences) and who, like the objectivist anthropologist, interprets and explains; on the other, the viewpoint, presented as such, of a Berkeleyan spectator.

The privilege of totalization presupposes on the one hand the practical (and therefore implicit) neutralization of practical functions – that is, in the case in point, the bracketing of the practical use of temporal reference-points – a neutralization that the inquiry relationship itself produces, by setting up a situation of 'theoretical' questioning which presupposes the suspension of practical investments; and on the other hand, recourse to instruments of eternization – writing and all the other techniques for recording and analysing, theories, methods, diagrams, etc. – that have been accumulated in the course of history and take time to acquire and to implement. In the diagram of the calendar, the complete series of the temporal oppositions which are deployed successively by different agents in different situations, and which can never be practically mobilized together because the necessities of practice never require such a synoptic apprehension but rather discourage it through their urgent demands, are juxtaposed in the simultaneity of a single space. The calendar thus creates *ex nihilo* a whole host of relations (of simultaneity, succession or symmetry, for example) between reference-points at different levels, which, never being brought face to face in practice, are practically compatible even if they are logically contradictory.

In contrast to practice – 'an essentially linear series', like discourse, whose 'mode of construction obliges us to use a successive, linear series of signs to express relationships which the mind perceives or ought to perceive simultaneously and in a different order' – scientific schemas or diagrams, 'synoptic tables, trees, historical atlases, kinds of double-entry tables', makes it possible, as Cournot (1922: 364) points out, 'to use the surface area more or less successfully to represent systematic relations and links that would be difficult to make out in the sequence of discourse'. In other words, the synoptic diagram enables one to apprehend simultaneously and in a single glance, *uno intuitu et tota simul*, as Descartes put it, 'monothetically', as Husserl (1931: 335–6) put it, meanings that are produced and used polythetically, that is, not only one after another, but one by one, step by step. Furthermore, the sine-wave diagram which makes it possible to show the relations of opposition or equivalence among the elements by distributing them (as in a calendar) according to the laws of succession (that is, (1) 'y follows x' excludes 'x follows y'; (2) if y follows x and z follows y, then z follows x; (3) either y follows x or x follows y), while presenting in a simple way the fundamental oppositions between up and down, right and left, makes it possible to verify the relations between the successive reference-points and divisions, giving rise to all kinds of relations (some of them violating the laws of succession) which are excluded from practice because the different divisions or subdivisions that the observer may combine are not systematically conceived and used as moments in a succession but enter, according to the context, into oppositions at different levels (from the broadest, between the culminating points of summer and winter, to the narrowest, between two points in a subdivision of one of these periods).

Like genealogy, which substitutes a space of univocal, homogeneous relationships, established once and for all, for a spatially and temporally discontinuous set of strands of kinship, that are valued and organized in accordance with the needs of the moment and brought spasmodically into existence, or like the map which substitutes the homogeneous, continuous space of geometry for the discontinuous, patchy space of practical pathways, the calendar substitutes a linear, homogeneous, continuous time for practical time, which is made up of islands of incommensurable duration, each with its own rhythm, a time that races or drags, depending on what one is doing, that is, on the functions assigned to it by the actions that are performed in it. By distributing the reference-points of ceremonies or tasks along a continuous line, the calendar turns them into points of division, artificially creating the question of the intervals and correspondences between points that are metrically and no longer topologically equivalent.

Depending on how precisely an event has to be situated, on the nature of the event, and on the social status of the agent concerned, practice will draw on different systems of oppositions. For example, the 'period' known as *eliali*, far from being defined, as in a perfectly ordinate series, in relation to the moment that precedes it and the moment that follows it, and only in relation to them, can be opposed to *esmaïm* as well as to *el h'usum* or *thimgharine*; it can also be opposed, as '*eliali* of December', to '*eliali* of January', or again, by a different logic, be opposed as 'the great nights' to the 'lesser nights of *furar*' and the 'lesser nights of *maghres*'. One sees the artificiality and even unreality of the calendar which assimilates and aligns units of different levels and very unequal importance. Since all the divisions and subdivisions that the observer may record and cumulate are produced and used in different situations, separated in time, the question of how each of them relates to the unit at a higher level or, *a fortiori*, to the divisions or subdivisions of the 'periods' to which it is opposed, never arises in practice. The relationship between the series of moments distributed according to the laws of succession that is constructed by the observer, unconsciously guided by the model of the calendar, and the temporal oppositions successively put into practice, is similar to the relationship between the continuous, homogeneous political space of graduated scales of opinion and practical political positions. The latter are always taken up in response to a particular situation and to particular interlocutors or adversaries, and they activate oppositions at different levels depending on the political distance between the interlocutors (left : right :: left of the left : right of the left :: left of the left of the left : right of the left of the left :: etc.) in such a way that the same agent may find himself successively on his own right and on his own left in the 'absolute' space of geometry, contradicting the third law of succession.

The same analysis can be applied to the terminologies serving to designate social units. Ignorance of the uncertainties and ambiguities that these products of a practical logic owe to their functions and to the conditions in which they are used leads to the production of artefacts as impeccable as they are unreal. Nothing is more suspect than the ostentatious rigour of so many diagrams of social organization offered by anthropologists. Thus, the pure, perfect model of Berber society as a series of interlocking units, which ethnologists from Hanoteau to Jeanne Favret, and including Durkheim, have put forward, cannot be accepted unless one ignores, first, the arbitrariness of all the divisions (varying, in any case, from one place to another) that are made in the continuum of kinship relations (a continuity that is manifested for example by the imperceptible gradation of obligations in the case of bereavement) beyond the extended family (*akham*) and below the level of the clan (*adhrum* or *thakharubth*); then, the unceasing dynamics of units that are constantly made and unmade in history, in accordance with the logic of annexations and fusions (thus at Aït Hichem, the Aït Isaad combine several diminished clans – *thakharubth* – in a single clan) or scissions (in the same place, the Aït Mendil, originally united, have divided into two clans); and, finally, the fuzziness that is inseparable from native notions in their practical use (as opposed to the semi-academic artefacts that the situation of inquiry, here as elsewhere, invariably produces), because it is both the condition and the product of their functioning. Even more than with the temporal taxonomies of the agrarian calendar, the use of words or oppositions that serve to classify, that is, to produce groups, depends on the situation and, more precisely, on the function pursued through the production of classes, whether mobilization or division, annexation or exclusion.

Without entering into a detailed discussion of the schematic presentation that Jeanne Favret gives of the terminology collected by Hanoteau (Favret 1966, 1968), it can be pointed out that in the case of the village of Aït Hichem (see Bourdieu 1962c: 14–20) and in many other places, the hierarchy of the fundamental social units, those designated by the words *thakharubth* and *adhrum*, is the opposite of what Favret, following Hanoteau, puts forward. A few cases can indeed be found in which, as Hanoteau maintains, *thakharubth* encompasses *adhrum*, probably because terminologies collected at particular places and times designate the outcome of different histories, marked by the splitting up, the (no doubt frequent) disappearance and the annexation of lineages. It also often happens that the words are used indifferently to designate the same social division. This is the case in the Sidi Aïch region, in which the following units, starting with the most restricted, are distinguished: (a) *el h'ara*, the undivided family (called *akham*, the house, at

Aït Hichem, e.g. *akham n'Aït Ali*); (b) *akham*, the extended family, covering all the people bearing the name of the same ancestor (to the third or fourth generation) – *Ali ou X*, sometimes also designated by a term that is probably suggested by topography, since the path bends as one passes from one *akham* to another: *thaghamurth*, the elbow; (c) *adhrum*, *akharub* (or *thakharubth*) or *aharum*, bringing together the people whose common origin goes back beyond the fourth generation; (d) the *s'uff*, or more simply 'those above' and 'those below'; (e) the village, a purely local unit, here grouping the two leagues. The synonyms, to which must be added *thaârifth* (from *âarf*, to know one another), a group of acquaintances, equivalent to *akham* or *adhrum* (elsewhere, *thakharubth*), may not have been used haphazardly, since they emphasize either integration and internal cohesion (*akham*, *adhrum*) or opposition between groups (*taghamurth*, *aharum*). *S'uff*, used to suggest an 'arbitrary' unit, a conventional alliance as opposed to the other terms which denote individuals bearing a common name (Aït . . .), is often distinguished from *adhrum*, with which it coincides at Aît Hichem and in other places.

Practice has a logic which is not that of the logician. This has to be acknowledged in order to avoid asking of it more logic than it can give, thereby condemning oneself either to wring incoherences out of it or to thrust a forced coherence upon it. Analysis of the various but highly interdependent aspects of what might be called the theorization effect (forced synchronization of the successive, fictitious totalization, neutralization of functions, substitution of the system of products for the system of principles of production, etc.) brings out, in negative form, certain properties of the logic of practice which by definition escape theoretical apprehension. This practical logic – practical in both senses – is able to organize all thoughts, perceptions and actions by means of a few generative principles, which are closely interrelated and constitute a practically integrated whole, only because its whole economy, based on the principle of the economy of logic, presupposes a sacrifice of rigour for the sake of simplicity and generality and because it finds in 'polythesis' the conditions required for successful use of polysemy. In other words, symbolic systems owe their practical coherence – that is, on the one hand, their unity and their regularities, and on the other, their 'fuzziness' and their irregularities and even incoherences, which are both equally necessary, being inscribed in the logic of their genesis and functioning – to the fact that they are the product of practices that can fulfil their practical functions only in so far as they implement, in the practical state, principles that are not only coherent – that is, capable of generating practices that are both intrinsically coherent and compatible with the objective conditions – but also practical, in the sense of convenient, that is, easy to master and use, because they obey a 'poor' and economical logic.

Because of the successive apprehension of practices that are only performed in succession, the 'confusion of spheres', as the logicians call it, resulting from the highly economical but necessarily approximate application of the same schemes to different logical universes, is able to pass unnoticed. No one takes the trouble to systematically record and compare the successive products of the application of the generative schemes.

These discrete, self-sufficient units owe their immediate transparency not only to the schemes that are realized in them but also to the situation apprehended through these schemes in a practical relationship. The principle of the economy of logic, whereby no more logic is mobilized than is required by the needs of practice, means that the universe of discourse in relation to which a given class (and therefore the complementary class) is constituted can remain implicit, because it is implicitly defined in each case in and by the practical relationship to the situation. Since it is very unlikely that two contradictory applications of the same schemes will be brought face to face in what we must call a universe of practice (rather than a universe of discourse), the same thing may, in different universes of practice, have different things as its complementary term and may therefore receive different, even opposed, properties depending on the universe of practice.[2] Thus, as has been seen, the house as a whole is defined as female, damp, etc., when considered from outside, from the male point of view, that is, in opposition to the external world, but can be divided into a male-female part and a female-female part when it ceases to be seen by reference to a universe of practices co-extensive with *the* universe, and is treated instead as a universe (of practice as well as discourse) in its own right, which for the women it indeed is, especially in winter.[3]

The universes of meaning corresponding to different universes of practice are both self-enclosed – and therefore protected against logical control through systematization – and objectively adjusted to all the others in so far as they are loosely systematic products of a system of practically integrated generative principles that function in the most diverse fields of practice. In the approximate, 'fuzzy' logic which immediately accepts as equivalents the adjectives 'flat', 'dull' and 'bland', favourite terms in aesthetic or professorial judgement, or, in the Kabyle tradition, 'full', 'closed', 'inside', and 'below', the generative schemes are interchangeable in practice. This is why they can only generate systematic products, but with an approximate, fuzzy coherence that cannot withstand the test of logical criticism. *Sympatheia tôn holôn*, as the Stoics called it, the affinity among all the objects of a universe in which meaning is everywhere, and everywhere superabundant, has as its basis, or its price, the indeterminacy or overdetermination of each of the elements and each of the relationships among them: logic can be everywhere only because it is truly present nowhere.

Ritual practice performs an uncertain abstraction which brings the same symbol into different relationships by apprehending it through different aspects, or which brings different aspects of the same referent into the same relationship of opposition. In other words, it excludes the Socratic question of the respect in which the referent is apprehended (shape, colour, function, etc.), thereby obviating the need to define in each case the criterion governing the choice of the aspect selected and, *a fortiori*, the need to keep to that criterion at all times. Because the principle opposing the terms that have been related (for example, the sun and the moon) is not defined and usually comes down to a simple contrariety, analogy (which, when it does not function purely in the practical state, is always expressed elliptically – 'woman is the moon') establishes a relation of homology between relations of opposition (man : woman :: sun : moon), which are themselves indeterminate and overdetermined (hot : cold :: male : female :: day : night :: etc.), applying generative schemes different from those that can be used to generate other homologies into which one or another of the terms in question might enter (man : woman :: east : west, or sun : moon :: dry : wet).

This uncertain abstraction is also a false abstraction which sets up relationships based on what Jean Nicod calls 'overall resemblance' (Nicod 1961: 43–4). This mode of apprehension never explicitly limits itself to any one aspect of the terms it links, but takes each one, each time, as a whole, exploiting to the full the fact that two 'realities' are never entirely alike in all respects but are always alike in some respect, at least indirectly (that is, through the mediation of some common term). This explains, first, why among the different aspects of the indeterminate yet overdetermined symbols it manipulates, ritual practice never clearly opposes aspects symbolizing something to aspects symbolizing nothing, which might therefore be disregarded (such as colour or size in the case of letters of the alphabet). For example, while one of the different aspects through which a 'reality' like gall can be connected with other (equally equivocal) 'realities' – viz. bitterness (it is equivalent to oleander, wormwood or tar, and opposed to honey), greenness (it is associated with lizards and the colour green) and hostility (inherent in the two previous qualities) – necessarily comes to the forefront, it does not cease to be attached, like the keynote to the other sounds in a chord, to the other aspects which persist as undertones, through which it can be opposed to other aspects of another referent in other relationships. Without wishing to push the musical metaphor too far, one might suggest that a number of ritual sequences could be seen as modulations. Occurring with particular frequency because the specific principle of ritual action, the concern to stack all the odds on one's own side, favours the logic of development, with its variations against a background of redundancy, these modulations play on the harmonic properties of ritual symbols, whether duplicating one of the themes with a strict equivalent in all respects (gall evoking wormwood, which similarly combines bitterness with greenness), or modulating into remoter tonalities by playing on the associations of the secondary harmonics (lizard → toad) (for similar observations see Granet, 1929 passim, esp. p. 352).

Another modulation technique is association by assonance, which can lead to connections without mythico-ritual significance (*aman d laman*, water is trust) or, on the other hand, to symbolically overdetermined connections (*azka d azqa*, tomorrow is the grave). The double link, through sound and sense, creates a crossroads, a choice between two rival paths, either of which may be taken without contradiction at different moments, in different contexts. Ritual practice makes maximum possible use of the polysemy of the fundamental actions, mythic 'roots' that the linguistic roots partially reflect. Although imperfect, the correspondence between linguistic roots and mythic roots is sufficiently strong to provide the analogical sense with one of its most powerful supports, through the verbal associations, sometimes sanctioned and exploited by sayings and maxims, which, in their most successful forms, reinforce the necessity of a mythical connection with the necessity of a linguistic connection.[4] Thus the scheme open–close finds partial expression in the root *FTH'* which can equally well mean, figuratively as well as literally, *to open* (transitive) a door or a path (in ritual and extra-ordinary contexts), the heart ('opening one's heart'), a speech (for example, with a ritual formula), an assembly meeting, an action, a day, etc., *to be open*, applied to a 'door' in the sense of the beginning of any series, the heart (that is, the appetite), a bud, the sky, or a knot, *to open* (intransitive), applied to a bud, a face, a shoot, an egg, and therefore, more generally, to inaugurate, bless, make easy, place under good auspices ('May God open the doors'), – a cluster of senses covering virtually all the meanings attached to spring. But the mythical root is broader and vaguer than the linguistic root and lends itself to richer and more varied play: the scheme of opening–being opened makes it possible to set up associations among a whole set of verbs and nouns that go far beyond simple morphological affinity. Thus it can evoke the roots *FSU*, to unbind, untie, resolve, open, appear (used of young shoots, hence the name *thafsuth* given to spring); *FRKh*, to blossom, give birth (hence *asafrurakh*, blossoming, and *lafrakh*, the shoots that appear on trees in spring, and more generally, offspring, the outcome of any undertaking), to proliferate, multiply; *FRY*, to form, be formed (applied to figs), to begin to grow (applied to wheat or a baby), to multiply (a nestful of birds: *ifruri el âach*, the nest is full of fledglings), to shell or be shelled (peas and beans), and thus, to enter the period when fresh beans can be picked (*lah'lal usafruri*); and *FLQ*, to break, burst, split, deflower, to be split open like the egg or pomegranate broken at the time of marriage or ploughing.

One would only have to let oneself be carried along by the logic of associations in order to reconstruct the whole network of synonyms and antonyms, synonyms of synonyms and antonyms of antonyms. The same term could thus enter an infinity of relationships if the number of ways of relating to what is not itself were not limited to a few fundamental oppositions linked by relations of practical equivalence. At the degree of precision (that is, imprecision) at which they are defined, the different principles that practice applies successively or simultaneously in relating objects and selecting the relevant aspects are practically equivalent, so that this taxonomy can classify the same realities from several different viewpoints without ever classifying them in a totally different way.

But the language of overall resemblance and uncertain abstraction is still too intellectualist to be able to express a logic that is performed directly in bodily gymnastics, without passing through explicit apprehension of the 'aspects' chosen or rejected, the similar or dissimilar 'profiles'. By inducing an identity of reaction in a diversity of situations, impressing the same posture on the body in different contexts, the practical schemes can produce the equivalent of an act of generalization that cannot be accounted for without recourse to concepts – and this despite the fact that the enacted, unrepresented generality that arises from acting in a similar way in similar circumstances, but without 'thinking the similarity independently of the similar', as Piaget puts it, dispenses with all the operations required by the construction of a concept. Practical sense 'selects' certain objects or actions, and consequently certain of their aspects, in relation to 'the matter in hand', an implicit and practical principle of pertinence; and, by fixing on those with which there is something to be done or those that determine what is to be done in the given situation, or by treating different objects or situations as equivalent, it distinguishes properties that are pertinent from those that are not. Just as one has difficulty in apprehending simultaneously, as dictionaries do, the different meanings of a word that one can easily mobilize in the succession of particular utterances produced in particular situations, so the concepts that the analyst is forced to use (for example, the idea of 'resurrection' or 'swelling') to give an account of the practical identifications that ritual acts perform, are quite alien to practice, which knows nothing of such groupings or partial enactments of the same scheme and is concerned not with relationships such as up and down or dry and wet, nor even with concepts, but with tangible things, considered absolutely even as regards the properties that seem most typically relational.

To be persuaded that the different meanings produced by the same scheme exist in the practical state only in their relationship with particular situations, one only has to assemble, as in a dictionary, some applications of the opposition between 'in front' and 'behind'. Behind is where things one wants to get rid of are sent. For example, in one of the rites associated with the loom, these words are used: 'May the angels be before me and the Devil behind me'; in another rite, to protect against the evil eye, a child is rubbed behind the ear so that he will send evil 'behind his ear'. (To cast behind is also, at a more superficial level, to neglect, despise – 'to put behind one's ear' – or, more simply, not to face, not to confront). Behind is where ill fortune comes from: a woman on her way to market to sell a product of her labour, a blanket, yarn, etc., or of her husbandry, hens, eggs, etc., must not look behind her or the sale will go badly; according to a legend recorded by Galand-Pernet, the whirlwind attacks from behind the man who prays facing the *qibla*. 'Behind' is naturally associated with 'inside', with the female, (the eastern, front door is male, the back door is female), with all that is private, secret and hidden; but it is thereby also associated with that which follows, trailing behind on the earth, the source of fertility, *abruâ*, the train of a garment, a good-luck charm, happiness: the bride entering her new house strews fruit, eggs and wheat behind her, symbolizing prosperity. These meanings are defined by opposition to all those that are associated with 'in front', going forward, confronting (*qabel*), going towards the future, eastward, towards the light.

The logicism inherent in the objectivist viewpoint inclines one to ignore the fact that scientific construction cannot grasp the principles of practical logic without forcibly changing their nature. Objectification converts a practical succession into a represented succession, an action oriented in relation to a space objectively constituted as a structure of demands (things 'to be done') into a reversible operation performed in a continuous, homogeneous space. This inevitable transformation is inscribed in the fact that agents can adequately master the *modus operandi* that enables them to generate correctly formed ritual practices, only by making it work practically, in a real situation, in relation to practical functions. An agent who possesses a practical mastery, an art, whatever it may be, is capable of applying in his action the disposition which appears to him only in action, in the relationship with a situation (he can repeat the feint which strikes him as the only thing to do, as often as the situation requires). But he is no better placed to perceive what really governs his practice and to bring it to the order of discourse, than the observer, who has the advantage over him of being able to see the action from outside, as an object, and especially of being able to totalize the successive realizations of the *habitus* (without necessarily having the practical mastery that underlies these realizations or the adequate theory of this mastery). And there is every reason to think that as soon as he reflects on his practice, adopting a quasi-theoretical posture, the agent loses any chance of expressing the truth of his practice, and especially the truth of the practical relation to the practice. Academic interrogation inclines him to take up a point of view on his own practice that is no longer that of action, without being that of science, encouraging him to shape his explanations in terms of a theory of practice that meshes with the juridical, ethical or grammatical legalism to which the observer is inclined by his own situation. Simply because he is questioned, and questions himself, about the reasons and the *raison d'être* of his practice, he cannot communicate the essential point, which is that the very nature of practice is that it excludes this question. His remarks convey this primary truth of primary experience only by omission, through the silences and ellipses of self-evidence. And even this occurs only in the most favourable cases, when by skilful questioning the questioner persuades the informant to give free rein to the language of familiarity. This language, which recognizes only particular cases and details of practical interest or anecdotal curiosity, which always uses the proper names of people and places, which minimizes the vague generalities and *ad hoc* explanations appropriate for strangers, leaves unsaid all that goes without saying. It is akin to the discourse of Hegel's 'original historians' who, living 'in the spirit of the event', take for granted the presuppositions of those whose story they tell. Through its very obscurity and the absence of the spurious clarity of semi-enlightened remarks for the benefit of outsiders, it gives some chance of discovering the truth of practice as a blindness to its own truth.[5]

In contrast to logic, a mode of thought that works by making explicit the work of thought, practice excludes all formal concerns. Reflexive attention to action itself, when it occurs (almost invariably only when the automatisms have broken down), remains subordinate to the pursuit of the result and to the search (not necessarily perceived in this way) for maximum effectiveness of the effort expended. So it has nothing in common with the aim of explaining how the result has been achieved, still less of seeking to understand (for understanding's sake) the logic of practice, which flouts logical logic. Scientific analysis thus encounters and has to surmount a practical antinomy when it breaks with every form of operationalism that tacitly accepts but cannot objectify the most fundamental presuppositions of practical logic, and when it seeks to understand, in and for itself, and not to improve it or reform it, the logic of practice which understands only in order to act.

The idea of practical logic, a 'logic in itself', without conscious reflexion or logical control, is a contradiction in terms, which defies logical logic. This paradoxical logic is that of all practice, or rather of all practical sense. Caught up in 'the matter in hand', totally present in the present and in the practical functions that it finds there in the form of objective potentialities, practice excludes attention to itself (that is, to the past). It is unaware of the principles that govern it and the possibilities they contain; it can only discover them by enacting them, unfolding them in time.[6] Rites, even more than most practices, might almost be designed to demonstrate the fallacy of seeking to contain in concepts a logic that is made to do without concepts; of treating practical manipulations and bodily movements as logical operations; of speaking of analogies and homologies (as one has to in order to understand and explain) when it is simply a matter of practical transfers of incorporated, quasi-postural schemes.[7] A rite, a performative practice that strives to bring about what it acts or says, is often simply a practical *mimesis* of the natural process that is to be facilitated.[8] As opposed to metaphor and analogy, mimetic representation links phenomena as different as the swelling of grain in the cooking-pot, the swelling of a pregnant woman's belly and the sprouting of wheat in the ground, in a relationship that implies no spelling-out of the properties of the terms thus related or the principles applied in relating them. The most characteristic operations of its 'logic' – inverting, transferring, uniting, separating, etc. – take the form of bodily movements, turning to right or left, putting upside down, going in or coming out, tying or cutting, etc.

This logic which, like all practical logics, can only be grasped in action, in the temporal movement that disguises it by detemporalizing it, sets the analyst a difficult problem, which can only be solved by recourse to a theory of theoretical logic and practical logic. The professional dealers in *logos* want practice to express something that can be expressed in discourse, preferably logical. They find it hard to conceive that one can rescue a practice from absurdity and identify its logic other than by making it say what goes without saying and projecting on to it an explicit thought that it excludes by definition. One can imagine the philosophical or poetic effects that a mind trained by a whole educational tradition to cultivate Swedenborgian 'correspondences' would not fail to draw from the fact that ritual practice treats adolescence and springtime, with their advances towards maturity followed by sudden regressions, as equivalents, or that it counterposes male and female roles in production and reproduction as the discontinuous and the continuous.[9]

Probably the only way to give an account of the practical coherence of practices and works is to construct generative models which reproduce in their own terms the logic from which that coherence is generated; and to devise diagrams which, through their synoptic power of synchronization and totalization, quietly and directly manifest the objective systematicity of practice and which, when they make adequate use of the properties of space (up/down, right/left), may even have the merit of speaking directly to the body schema (as all those who have to transmit motor skills are well aware). At the same time, one has to be aware that these theoretical replications transform the logic of practice simply by making it explicit. Just as, in the time of Lévy-Bruhl, there would have been less amazement at the oddities of the 'primitive mentality' if it had been possible to conceive that the logic of magic and 'participation' might have some connection with the most ordinary experience of emotion or passion (anger, jealousy, hatred, etc.), so nowadays there would be less astonishment at the 'logical' feats of the Australian aborigines if the 'savage mind' were not unconsciously credited, in a kind of inverted ethnocentrism, with the relationship to the world that intellectualism attributes to every 'consciousness', and if anthropologists had not kept silent about the transformations leading from operations mastered in the practical state to the formal operations isomorphic with them and failed, by the same token, to inquire into the social conditions of that transformation.

The science of myth is entitled to describe the syntax of myth in the language of group theory, but only so long as it is not forgotten that, when it ceases to be seen as a convenient translation, this language destroys the truth that it makes accessible. One can say that gymnastics is geometry so long as this is not taken to mean that the gymnast is a geometer. There would be less temptation to treat agents implicitly or explicitly as logicians if one went back from the mythic logos to the ritual praxis which enacts, in the form of real actions, that is, body movements, the operations that theoretical analysis discovers in mythic discourse, an *opus operatum* that masks the constituting moment of 'mythopœic' practice under its reified significations. So long as mythico-ritual space is seen as an *opus operatum*, as an order of coexistent things, it is never more than a theoretical space, in which the only landmarks are the reference-points provided by relations of opposition (up/down, east/west, etc.) and where only theoretical operations can be effected, that is, logical displacements and transformations, which are as remote from really performed movements and actions, like falling or rising, as a celestial hound from a real, barking dog. Having established, for example, that the space inside the Kabyle house receives a symmetrically opposite meaning when it is re-placed in the total space outside, one is justified in saying that each of these two spaces, inside and outside, can be derived from the other by means of a semi-rotation, but only on condition that the language of mathematics is brought back to its basis in practice, so that terms like displacement and rotation are given their practical senses as movements of the body, such as walking forwards or backwards, or turning on one's heels. If this 'geometry in the tangible world', as Jean Nicod puts it, a practical geometry, or rather, geometric practice, makes so much use of inversion, it is surely because, like a mirror bringing to light the paradoxes of bilateral symmetry, the human body functions as a practical operator which reaches to the left to meet the right hand it has to shake, puts its left arm in the sleeve which was on the right until the garment was picked up, or reverses right and left, east and west, simply by turning about to 'face' someone' or 'turn its back' on him, or turns 'upside down' things that were 'the right way up' – all movements which the mythic view of the world charges with social significance and which rites exploit intensively. 'I find myself defining threshold / As the geometrical place / Of the comings and goings / In my Father's House' (quoted by Bachelard 1969: 223).

The poet immediately identifies the principle of the relationship between the internal space of the house and external space in the opposing movements (opposed in both direction and meaning) of going in and coming out. As a belated small-scale producer of private mythologies, it is easier for him to cut through dead metaphors and go straight to the principle of mythopœic practice, that is, to the movements and actions which, as in a sentence of Albert the Great's, picked up by René Char, can reveal the duality underlying the seeming unity of the object: 'In Germany, there once lived twins, one of whom opened doors by touching them with his right arm, and the other who closed them by touching them with his left arm' (quoted by Bachelard 1969: 224).

Thus one has to move from *ergon* to *energeia* (in accordance with the opposition established by Wilhelm von Humboldt), from objects or actions to the principle of their production, or, more precisely, from the *fait accompli* and dead letter of already effected analogy or metaphor ($a : b :: c : d$) that objectivist hermeneutics considers, to analogical practice understood as a transfer of schemes that the *habitus* performs on the basis of acquired equivalences, facilitating the substitutability of one reaction for another and enabling the agent to master all problems of a similar form that may arise in new situations, by a kind of practical generalization. To grasp the mythopœic act as the constituting moment, through myth understood as the constituted reality, does not mean, as idealists suppose, looking in consciousness for the universal categories of what Cassirer calls a 'mythopœic subjectivity' or, in Lévi-Strauss's terms, 'the fundamental structures of the human mind', which are supposed to govern all the empirical configurations realized, regardless of social conditions. Rather, it means reconstructing the socially constituted system of inseparably cognitive and evaluative structures that organizes perception of the world and action in the world in accordance with the objective structures of a given state of the social world. If ritual practices and representations are practically coherent, this is because they arise from the combinatorial functioning of a small number of generative schemes that are linked by relations of practical substitutability, that is, capable of producing results that are equivalent in terms of the 'logical' requirements of practice. This systematicity remains loose and approximate because the schemes can receive the quasi-universal application they are given only in so far as they function in the practical state, below the level of explicit statement and therefore outside the control of logic, and in relation to practical purposes which require of them and give them a necessity which is not that of logic.

The discussions that have developed about systems of classification, both among ethnologists (ethnoscience) and sociologists (ethnomethodology), have one thing in common: they forget that these cognitive instruments fulfil, as such, functions that are not purely cognitive. Produced by the practice of the successive generations, in a particular type of conditions of existence, these schemes of perception, appreciation and action, which are acquired through practice and implemented in the practical state without attaining explicit representation, function as practical operators through which the objective structures of which they are the product tend to be reproduced in practices. Practical taxonomies, cognitive and communicative instruments which are the precondition of the constitution of meaning and consensus on meaning, exert their structuring efficacy only in so far as they are themselves structured. This does not mean that they are amenable to a purely internal ('structural', 'componential', etc.) analysis which artificially isolates them from their conditions of production and use and so cannot understand their social functions.[10] The coherence that is observed in all the products of the application of the same *habitus* has no other basis than the coherence that the generative principles constituting that *habitus* derive from the social structures (the structure of relations between the groups, the sexes or the generations, or between the social classes) of which they are the product and which they tend to reproduce in a transformed, misrecognizable form, by inserting them into the structure of a system of symbolic relations.[11]

To react, as Lévi-Strauss (1968: 207) does, against external readings that cast myth into 'primitive stupidity' (*Urdummheit*) by directly relating the structure of symbolic systems to social structures, must not lead one to forget that magical or religious actions are fundamentally 'this-worldly' (*diesseitig*), as Weber puts it; being entirely dominated by the concern to ensure the success of production and reproduction, in a word, survival, they are oriented towards the most dramatically practical, vital and urgent ends. Their extraordinary ambiguity stems from the fact that, in the pursuit of the tragically real and totally unrealistic ends that emerge in situations of distress (especially when it is collective), such as the desire to triumph over death or misfortune, they apply a practical logic, produced without any conscious intention by a structured, structuring body and language which function as automatic generators of symbolic acts. It is as if ritual practices were wishes or supplications of collective distress, expressed in a language that is (by definition) collective (in which respect they are very closely related to music) – forlorn attempts to act on the natural world as one acts on the social world, to apply strategies to the natural world that work on other men, in certain conditions, that is, strategies of authority and reciprocity, to signify intentions, wishes, desires or orders to it, through performative words or deeds which make sense without any signifying intention.[12] The least inappropriate way of 'understanding' this practice might be to compare it to the private rites that situations of extreme distress, like the death of a loved one or the anxious waiting for a deeply desired event, lead one to invent, which, though they have no other purpose than to say or do something rather than nothing, inevitably borrow the logic of a language and a body which, even (and especially) when they change nothing, make common sense, generating words or actions that are both senseless and sense-full.

So one sees both the ordinary errors and their basis in an object which, like rite or myth, lends itself, by its very ambiguity, to the most contradictory readings. On the one hand, there is the lofty distance which objectivist hermeneutics seeks to keep between itself and elementary forms of thought, treated as pretexts for exercises in interpretative virtuosity, and of which the disenchantment and even aesthetic horror of Leiris's *L'Afrique fantôme* in fact represents the limiting case. On the other hand, there is the exalted participation and de-realizing enchantment of the great initiates of the gnostic tradition, who make common sense function as *lived meaning* and make themselves the inspired subjects of an objective meaning.[13] Objectivist reduction can bring to light what it calls the objective function which myths or rites fulfil (for Durkheim, functions of moral integration; for Lévi-Strauss, functions of logical integration); but, by separating the objective meaning that it brings to light from the agents who make it work, and therefore from the objective conditions and practical purposes by reference to which their practice is defined, it makes it impossible to understand how these functions are fulfilled.[14] 'Participant' anthropology, for its part – when not merely inspired by nostalgia for agrarian paradises, the principle of all conservative ideologies – regards the anthropological invariants and the universality of the most basic experiences as sufficient justification for seeking eternal answers to the eternal questions of cosmologies and cosmogonies in the practical answers which the peasants of Kabylia or elsewhere have given to the practical, historically situated problems that were forced on them in a given state of their instruments for material and symbolic appropriation of the world.[15] By cutting practices off from their real conditions of existence, in order to credit them with alien intentions, out of a false generosity conducive to stylistic effects, the exaltation of lost wisdom dispossesses them of everything that constitutes their reason and their *raison d'être*, and locks them in the eternal essence of a 'mentality'.[16] The Kabyle woman setting up her loom is not performing an act of cosmogony; she is simply setting up her loom to weave cloth intended to serve a technical function. It so happens that, given the symbolic equipment available to her for practically thinking her own practice – in particular her language, which constantly refers her back to the logic of ploughing – she can only think what she is doing in the enchanted, that is to say, mystified, form that spiritualism, thirsty for eternal mysteries, finds so enchanting.

Rites take place because, and only because, they find their *raison d'être* in the conditions of existence and the dispositions of agents who cannot afford the luxury of logical speculation, mystical effusions or metaphysical *Angst*. It is not sufficient to deride the most naive forms of functionalism to be rid of the questions of the practical functions of practices. It is clear that Kabyle marriage can in no way be understood on the basis of a universal definition of the functions of marriage as an operation intended to ensure the biological reproduction of the group in accordance with forms approved by the group. But, appearances notwithstanding, it would scarcely be better understood on the basis of a structural analysis which ignored the specific functions of the ritual practices and which failed to consider the economic and social conditions of production of the dispositions generating both these practices and the collective definition of the practical functions that they serve. The Kabyle peasant does not react to 'objective conditions' but to these conditions as apprehended through the socially constituted schemes that organize his perception. To understand ritual practice, to give it back both its reason and its *raison d'être*, without converting it into a logical construction or a spiritual exercise, means more than simply reconstituting its internal logic. It also means restoring its practical necessity by relating it to the real conditions of its genesis, that is, the conditions in which both the functions it fulfils and the means it uses to achieve them are defined.[17] It means describing the most brutally material bases of the investment in magic, such as the weakness of the productive and reproductive forces, which causes a life dominated by anxiety about matters of life and death to be lived as an uncertain struggle against uncertainty. It means trying to name, even if one cannot really hope to make it felt, this collective experience of powerlessness which is at the basis of a whole view of the world and the future (it is expressed as much in the relation to work, conceived as an unconditional tribute, as in ritual practice) and which is the practical mediation through which the relationship is established between the economic bases and ritual actions or representations. The relationship between economic conditions and symbolic practices is indeed practically realized, not in some 'articulation' between systems, but through the function that is assigned to indissolubly ritual and technical practice in the complex relationship between a mode of production and a relatively autonomous mode of perception, and through the operative schemes employed to fulfil that function.[18] To give an idea of the complexity of this network of circuits of circular causality, which mean, for example, that technical or ritual practices are determined by the material conditions apprehended by agents endowed with schemes of perception that are themselves determined, negatively at least, by these conditions (translated into a particular form of the relations of production), it is sufficient to point out that one of the functions of rites – especially those accompanying marriage, ploughing or harvesting – is to overcome in practice the specifically ritual contradiction which the ritual taxonomy sets up by dividing the world into contrary principles and by causing the acts most indispensable to the survival of the group to appear as acts of sacrilegious violence.

6

The Work of Time

So long as one only considers practices which, like rituals, derive some of their most important properties from the fact that they are 'detotalized' by their unfolding in succession, one is liable to neglect those properties of practice that detemporalizing science has least chance of reconstituting, namely the properties it owes to the fact that it is constructed in time, that time gives it its form, as the order of a succession, and therefore its direction and meaning. This is true of all practices which, like gift exchange or the joust of honour, are defined, at least in the eyes of the agents, as irreversible oriented sequences of relatively unpredictable acts. It will be recalled that, in opposition to the ordinary representation and to the famous analysis by Marcel Mauss, whom he accuses of placing himself at the level of a 'phenomenology' of gift exchange, Lévi-Strauss holds that science must break with native experience and the native theory of that experience and postulate that 'the primary, fundamental phenomenon is exchange itself, which gets split up into discrete operations in social life' (Lévi-Strauss 1987: 47), in other words, that the 'automatic laws' of the cycle of reciprocity are the unconscious principle of the obligation to give, the obligation to return a gift and the obligation to receive (1987: 43). In postulating that the objective model, obtained by reducing the polythetic to the nomothetic, the detotalized, irreversible succession to the perfectly reversible totality, is the immanent law of practices, the invisible principle of the movements observed, the analyst reduces the agents to the status of automata or inert bodies moved by obscure mechanisms towards ends of which they are unaware. 'Cycles of reciprocity', mechanical interlockings of obligatory practices, exist only for the absolute gaze of the omniscient, omnipresent spectator, who, thanks to his knowledge of the social mechanics, is able to be present at the different stages of the 'cycle'. In reality, the gift may remain unreciprocated, when one obliges an ungrateful person; it may be rejected as an insult, inasmuch as it asserts or demands the possibility of reciprocity, and therefore of recognition.[1] Quite apart from the trouble-makers who call into question the game itself and its apparently flawless mechanism (like the man the Kabyles call *amahbul*), even when the agents' dispositions are as perfectly harmonized as possible and when the sequence of actions and reactions seems entirely predictable from outside, uncertainty remains as to the outcome of the interaction until the whole sequence is completed. The most ordinary and even the seemingly most routine exchanges of ordinary life, like the 'little gifts' that 'bind friendship', presuppose an improvisation, and therefore a constant uncertainty, which, as we say, make all their *charm*, and hence all their social efficacy.

Little presents, which are halfway between 'gratuitous' gifts (*elmaâtar*, the unrequited gift, 'like a mother's milk', or *thikchi*, a thing given without recompense) and the most rigorously forced gifts (*elahdya* or *lehna*), must be of modest value and hence easy to give and easy to match ('it's nothing', as we say); but they must be frequent and in a sense continuous, which implies that they must function within the logic of the 'surprise' or the 'spontaneous gesture' rather than according to the mechanism of ritual. These presents intended to maintain the everyday order of social intercourse almost always consist of a dish of cooked food, couscous (with a piece of cheese, when they mark a cow's first milk), and follow the course of minor family celebrations – the third or seventh day after a birth, a baby's first tooth or first steps, a boy's first haircut, first visit to the market or first fast. Linked to events in the life-cycle of mankind or the earth, they involve those wishing to share their joy, and those who share in it, in what is nothing less than a fertility rite: when the dish that contained the gift is taken back, it always contains, 'for good luck' (*el fal*), what is sometimes called *thiririth* (from *er*, give back), that is to say, a little wheat, a little semolina (never barley, a female plant and a symbol of frailty) or, preferably, some dried vegetables, chick peas, lentils, etc., called *ajedjig* (flower), given 'so that the boy [the pretext for the exchange] will flower' into manhood. These ordinary gifts (which include some of those called *tharzefth*, which are visiting presents) are clearly opposed to the extra-ordinary gifts, *elkhir*, *elahdya* or *lehna*, given for the major festivals called *thimeghriwin* (sing. *thameghra*) – weddings, births, circumcisions – and *a fortiori* to *lwâada*, the obligatory gift to a holy man. Indeed, little gifts between relatives and friends are opposed to the present of money and eggs which is given by affines remote in both space and genealogy, and also in time – since they are seen only rarely, on the 'great occasions' – and the magnitude and solemnity of which makes it a kind of controlled challenge, in the same way that marriages within the lineage or neighbourhood, so frequent that they pass unnoticed, are opposed to the more prestigious but infinitely more hazardous extra-ordinary marriages between different villages or tribes, sometimes intended to set the seal on alliances or reconciliations and always marked by solemn ceremonies.

The simple possibility that things might proceed otherwise than as laid down by the 'mechanical laws' of the 'cycle of reciprocity' is sufficient to change the whole experience of practice and, by the same token, its logic. The shift from the highest probability to absolute certainty is a qualitative leap out of proportion to the numerical difference. The uncertainty which has an objective basis in the probabilistic logic of social laws is sufficient to modify not only the experience of practice, but practice itself, for example by encouraging strategies aimed at avoiding the most probable outcome. To reintroduce uncertainty is to reintroduce time, with its rhythm, its orientation and its irreversibility, substituting the dialectic of strategies for the mechanics of the model, but without falling over into the imaginary anthropology of 'rational actor' theories.

The *ars inveniendi* is an *ars combinatoria*. And one can construct a relatively simple generative model which makes it possible to give an account of the logic of practice, that is, to generate – on paper – the universe of practices (conducts of honour, acts of exchange) really observed, which impress both by their inexhaustible diversity and their apparent necessity, without resorting to the imaginary 'file of prefabricated representations', as Jakobson (1956) puts it, that would enable one to 'choose' the conduct appropriate to each situation. Thus, to account for all the observed conducts of honour, and only those, one simply needs a fundamental principle, that of equality in honour, which, although it is never explicitly posited as an axiom of all ethical operations, seems to orient practices, because the sense of honour gives practical mastery of it. The exchange of honour, like every exchange (of gifts, words, etc.) is defined as such – in opposition to the unilateral violence of aggression – that is, as implying the possibility of a continuation, a reply, a riposte, a return gift, inasmuch as it contains recognition of the partner (to whom, in the particular case, it accords equality in honour).[2] The challenge, as such, calls for a riposte, and is therefore addressed to a man deemed capable of playing the game of honour, and of playing it well: the challenge confers honour. The converse of this principle of reciprocity is that only a challenge issued by a man equal in honour deserves to be taken up. The act of honour is completely constituted as such only by the riposte, which implies recognition of the challenge as an act of honour and of its author as a man of honour. The fundamental principle and its converse imply in turn that a man who enters into an exchange of honour (by issuing or taking up a challenge) with someone who is not his equal in honour dishonours himself. By challenging a superior, he risks a snub, which would cast the dishonour back on himself; by challenging an inferior or taking up his challenge, he dishonours himself. Thus *elbahadla*, total humiliation, rebounds on to the man who misuses his advantages and humiliates his adversary to excess rather than letting him 'cover himself in shame'. Conversely, *elbahadla* would recoil on a man who imprudently stooped to take up a senseless challenge, whereas, by declining to riposte, he leaves his presumptuous challenger to bear the full weight of his arbitrary act.[3]

We thus have a very simple diagram:

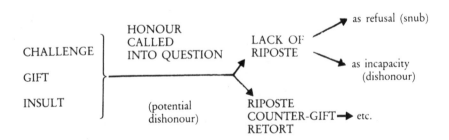

This generative model which reduces exchange to a series of successive choices performed on the basis of a small number of principles with the aid of a simple combinatory formula, and which makes it possible to give a very economical account of an infinity of particular cases of exchanges phenomenally as different as exchanges of gifts, words or challenges, reproduces, in its own order, the functioning of *habitus* and the logic of practice that proceeds through series of irreversible choices, made under pressure and often involving heavy stakes (sometimes life itself, as in the exchanges of honour or in magic) in response to other choices obeying the same logic.[4]

Similarly, it is sufficient to use a few principles of very general application obtained by combining the fundamental schemes of the mythico-ritual world-view (day/night, male/female, inside/outside, etc.) that constitute the sacred as such, with the logic of social exchanges (the principle of isotimy and its corollaries), in order to account for all the clauses of all the customary laws collected by the ethnographic tradition and even to have the means of producing the corpus of all possible acts of jurisprudence conforming to the 'sense of equity' in its Kabyle form.[5] It is these schemes, hardly ever stated as such in practice,[6] that make it possible to assess the seriousness of a theft by taking into account all the circumstances (place and time) of its commission, within the logic of *h'aram*, opposing the house (or mosque), as sacred places, to all other places, night to day, feastdays to ordinary days, etc. Other things being equal, a more severe sanction will be attached to the first term in each opposition (with, at one extreme, theft committed by night from a house, a sacrilegious violation of *h'aram* which makes it an offence against honour, and at the other extreme theft by day in a distant field). These practical principles are only stated in exceptional cases, in which the very nature of the object stolen requires that they be suspended. For example, the *qanun* of Ighil Imoula provides that 'he who steals a mule, ox or cow, by force or trickery shall pay 50 reals to the *djemâa* and pay the owner the value of the stolen animal, whether the theft be by night or by day, from inside or outside a house, and whether the animals belong to the householder or someone else' (Hanoteau and Letourneux 1873: vol. III, 338). The same basic schemes, always functioning in the practical state, apply in cases of assault. There are the same oppositions between the house and other places (the murder of an intruder caught in one's house entails no sanction, being a legitimate response to a violation of *h'urma*), between night and day, feast-days and ordinary days, together with variations according to the socially recognized status of aggressor and victim (man/woman, adult/child) and the weapons or methods used (treachery – in sleep for example – or man-to-man combat) and the degree of commission of the act (mere threats or actual violence).

But the specificity of the practical logic that generates an infinity of practices adapted to situations that are always different, on the basis of schemes so generally and automatically applied that they are only exceptionally converted into explicit principles, is revealed by the fact that the customary laws of different groups (villages or tribes) exhibit variations in the seriousness of the punishments assigned to the same offence. This vagueness and uncertainty, which are understandable when the same implicit schemes are being implemented, would be eliminated from a series of acts of jurisprudence produced by applying a single explicit code, expressly produced in a law-making operation designed to provide for all possible cases of transgression and capable of serving as a basis for homogeneous and constant, that is, predictable and calculable, acts of jurisprudence. Practical logic, based on a system of objectively coherent generative and organizing schemes, functioning in the practical state as an often imprecise but systematic principle of selection, has neither the rigour nor the constancy that characterize logical logic, which can deduce rational action from the explicit, explicitly controlled and systematized principles of an axiomatics (qualities which would also be those of practical logic if it were deduced from the model constructed to account for it). This is why practical logic manifests itself in a kind of stylistic unity which, though immediately perceptible, has none of the strict, regular coherence of the concerted products of a plan.

By producing externally, in objectivity, in the form of explicit principles, that which guides practices from inside, theoretical analysis makes possible a conscious awareness, a transmutation (materialized in the diagram) of the scheme into a representation which gives symbolic mastery of the practical principles that practical sense enacts either without representing them or while giving itself only partial or inadequate representations of them. Just as the teaching of tennis, the violin, chess, dancing or boxing extracts a series of discrete positions, steps or moves, from practices that integrate all these artificially isolated elementary units of behaviour into the unity of an organized, oriented practice, so informants tend to present either general norms (always accompanied by exceptions) or remarkable 'moves',[7] because they cannot appropriate theoretically the practical matrix from which these moves can be generated and which they possess only in practice, 'in so far as they are what they are', as Plato puts it. Perhaps the subtlest pitfall lies in the fact that agents readily resort to the ambiguous vocabulary of the rule, the language of grammar, morality and law, to explain a social practice which obeys quite different principles. They thus conceal, even from themselves, the true nature of their practical mastery as learned ignorance (*docta ignorantia*), that is, a mode of practical knowledge that does not contain knowledge of its own principles. Native theories are in fact dangerous not so much because they lead research towards illusory explanations, but rather because they bring quite superfluous reinforcement to the theory of practice that is inherent in the objectivist approach to practices, which, having extracted from the *opus operatum* the supposed principles of its production, sets them up as norms governing practices (with phrases like 'honour requires . . . ', 'propriety demands . . . ', 'custom insists . . . ', etc.).

The pedagogic work of inculcation – together with institutionalization, which is always accompanied by a degree of objectification in discourse (especially in law, designed to prevent or punish the misfirings of socialization) or in some other symbolic medium (ritual symbols or instruments, etc.) – is one of the major occasions for formulating and converting practical schemes into explicit norms. It is probably no accident that the question of the relationship between the *habitus* and the 'rule' is brought to light with the historical appearance of a specialized, explicit action of inculcation. As is suggested by a reading of Plato's *Meno*, the emergence of institutionalized education is accompanied by a crisis of diffuse education which moves directly from practice to practice without passing through discourse. Excellence (that is, practical mastery in its accomplished form) has ceased to exist once people start asking whether it can be taught, as soon as they seek to base 'correct' practice on rules extracted, for the purposes of transmission, as in all academicisms, from the practices of earlier periods or their products. The new masters can safely challenge the *kaloi kagathoi*, who are unable to bring to the level of discourse what they have learned *apo tou automatou*, no one knows how, and possess 'in so far as they are what they are'; but the upholders of old-style education have no difficulty in devaluing a knowledge which, like that of the *mathonthes*, the men of knowledge, bears the marks of having been taught. This is no doubt because the 'deviation' that is denounced in the term *academicism* is inherent in every attempt to make explicit and codify a practice that is not based on knowledge of the real principles of that practice. For example, research by some educationalists (such as René Deleplace) who have endeavoured to rationalize the teaching of sporting or artistic activities by trying to favour conscious awareness of the mechanisms really at work in these practices, shows that, if it fails to be based on a formal model making explicit the principles which practical sense (or more precisely, the 'feel for the game' or tactical intelligence) masters in the practical state and which are acquired practically through mimeticism, the teaching of sport has to fall back on rules and even formulae, and focus its attention on typical phases ('moves'). It thus runs the risk of often producing dysfunctional dispositions because it cannot provide an adequate view of the practice as a whole (for example, in rugby, training draws attention to the links between team-mates instead of giving priority to the relationship with the opposing side, from which successful teamwork derives).

It becomes clearer why that 'semi-learned' production, the rule, is the obstacle *par excellence* to the construction of an adequate theory of practice. By spuriously occupying the place of two fundamental notions, the theoretical matrix and the practical matrix, it makes it impossible to raise the question of their relationship. The abstract model that has to be constructed (for example, to account for the practices of honour) is completely valid only if it is presented for what it is, a theoretical artefact totally alien to practice – although a rational pedagogy can make it serve practical functions by enabling someone who possesses its practical equivalent to really appropriate the principles of his practice, either in order to bring them to their full realization or in order to try to free himself from them. The motor of the whole dialectic of challenge and riposte, gift and counter-gift, is not an abstract axiomatics but the sense of honour, a disposition inculcated by all early education and constantly demanded and reinforced by the group, and inscribed in the postures and gestures of the body (in a way of using the body or the gaze, a way of talking, eating or walking) as in the automatisms of language and thought, through which a man asserts himself as a real, manly man.[8] This practical sense, which does not burden itself with rules or principles (except in cases of misfiring or failure), still less with calculations or deductions, which are in any case excluded by the urgency of action 'which brooks no delay', is what makes it possible to appreciate the meaning of the situation instantly, at a glance, in the heat of the action, and to produce at once the opportune response.[9] Only this kind of acquired mastery, functioning with the automatic reliability of an instinct, can make it possible to respond instantaneously to all the uncertain and ambiguous situations of practice. For example, one can imagine the mastery of the taxonomies and the art of playing on them that are presupposed by imposing the absence of riposte as a mark of disdain when the difference between the antagonists is not very marked and when contempt can be suspected of concealing evasion. In this case, as is shown by the transgressions of the 'wise men' (*imusnawen*) who violate the official rule in the name of a higher law (cf. Mammeri and Bourdieu 1978), it is not simply a question of acting, but of commanding belief, immediately, by imposing simultaneously a response and a definition of the situation capable of getting it recognized as the only legitimate one. This requires a very exact knowledge of one's own symbolic value, the value socially accorded to one's opponent, and the probable meaning of conduct which depends first of all on the judgement that others make of it and its author.

Everything combines to show that correct use of the model, which presupposes separation, requires one to move beyond the ritual alternatives of separation and participation and to develop the theory of the logic of practice as practical participation in a game, *illusio*, and, correlatively, the theory of theoretical separation and the distance it presupposes and produces. This theory, which has nothing in common with participation in practical experience, is what makes it possible to avoid the theoretical errors that are usually encouraged by descriptions of practice. To be persuaded of the need to use this theory of practice (and of theory) as the basis for a methodical control of all scientific practice, one has to return to the canonical example of gift exchange, in which the objectivist view, which substitutes the objective model of the cycle of reciprocity for the experiential succession of gifts, is particularly clearly opposed to the subjectivist view. The former privileges practice as seen from outside, timelessly, rather than as it is lived and enacted in an experience which is summarily relegated to the state of pure appearance.

To stop short at the objectivist truth of the gift, that is, the model, is to set aside the question of the relationship between the so-called objective truth, that of the observer, and the truth that can hardly be called subjective, since it represents the collective and even official definition of the subjective experience of the exchange; it is to ignore the fact that the agents practise as irreversible a sequence of actions that the observer constitutes as reversible. Knowing the detemporalizing effect of the 'objective' gaze and the relationship that links practice to time, one is forced to ask if it is appropriate to choose between the objectively reversible and quasi-mechanical cycle that the observer's external, totalizing apprehension produces and the no less objectively irreversible and relatively unpredictable succession that the agents produce by their practice, that is, by the series of irreversible choices in and through which they temporalize themselves. To be truly objective, an analysis of exchange of gifts, words or challenges must allow for the fact that, far from unfolding mechanically, the series of acts which, apprehended from outside and after the event, appears as a cycle of reciprocity, presupposes a continuous creation and may be interrupted at any stage; and that each of the inaugural acts that sets it up is always liable to fall flat and so, for lack of a response, to be stripped retrospectively of its intentional meaning (the subjective truth of the gift can, as has been seen, only be realized in the counter-gift which consecrates it as such). Thus, even if reciprocity is the 'objective' truth of the discrete acts that ordinary experience knows in discrete form and associates with the idea of a gift, it is perhaps not the whole truth of a practice that could not exist if its subjective truth coincided perfectly with its 'objective' truth.

In every society it may be observed that, if it is not to constitute an insult, the counter-gift must be deferred and different, because the immediate return of an exactly identical object clearly amounts to a refusal. Thus gift exchange is opposed to swapping, which, like the theoretical model of the cycle of reciprocity, telescopes gift and counter-gift into the same instant. It is also opposed to lending, in which the return of the loan, explicitly guaranteed by a legal act, is in a sense already performed at the very moment when a contract is drawn up ensuring the predictability and calculability of the acts it prescribes. The difference, and particularly the delay which the 'monothetic' model obliterates, must be brought into the model not, as Lévi-Strauss suggests, out of a 'phenomenological' concern to restore the lived experience of the practice of exchange, but because the functioning of gift exchange presupposes individual and collective misrecognition of the truth of the objective 'mechanism' of the exchange, a truth which an immediate response brutally exposes. The interval between gift and counter-gift is what allows a relation of exchange that is always liable to appear as irreversible, that is, both forced and self-interested, to be seen as reversible. 'Overmuch eagerness to discharge one's obligations', said La Rochefoucauld, 'is a form of ingratitude.' To betray one's haste to be free of an obligation one has incurred, and thus to reveal too overtly one's desire to pay off services rendered or gifts received, to be quits, is to denounce the initial gift retrospectively as motivated by the intention of obliging one.

It is all a matter of style, which means in this case timing and choice of occasions; the same act – giving, giving in return, offering one's services, paying a visit, etc. – can have completely different meanings at different times, coming as it may at the right or wrong moment, opportunely or inopportunely. The reason is that the lapse of time that separates the gift from the counter-gift is what allows the deliberate oversight, the collectively maintained and approved self-deception, without which the exchange could not function. Gift exchange is one of the social games that cannot be played unless the players refuse to acknowledge the objective truth of the game, the very truth that objective analysis brings to light, and unless they are predisposed to contribute, with their efforts, their marks of care and attention, and their time, to the production of collective misrecognition. Everything takes place as if the agents' strategies, and especially those that play on the tempo of action, or, in interaction, with the interval between actions, were organized with a view to disguising from themselves and from others the truth of their practice, which the anthropologist brutally reveals simply by substituting the interchangeable moments of a reversible sequence for practices performed in time and in their own time.

To abolish the interval is also to abolish strategy. The period interposed, which must be neither too short (as is clearly seen in gift exchange) nor too long (especially in the exchange of revenge-murders), is quite the opposite of the inert gap of time, the time-lag, which the objectivist model makes of it. Unitl he has given back, the receiver is 'obliged', expected to show his gratitude towards his benefactor or at least to show regard for him, go easy on him, pull his punches, lest he be accused of ingratitude and stand condemned by 'what people say', which decides the meaning of his actions. The man who has not avenged a murder, not bought back his land acquired by a rival family, not married off his daughters in time, sees his capital diminished from day to day by passing time – unless he is capable of transforming forced delay into strategic deferment. To put off revenge or the return of a gift can be a way of keeping one's partner-opponent in the dark about one's intentions; the moment for the counter-strike becomes impossible to determine, like the really evil moment in the ill-omened periods of the ritual calendar, when the curve turns up and when lack of response ceases to be negligence and turns into disdainful refusal. Delay is also a way of exacting the deferential conduct that is required so long as relations are not broken off. It makes sense within this logic that a man whose daughter is asked for in marriage must reply as quickly as possible if he intends to refuse, lest he seem to be taking advantage of the situation and offend the suitor, whereas if he intends to agree he is free to delay his answer as long as he can, so as to maintain his situational advantage, which he will lose as soon as he gives his consent. Everything takes place as if the ritualization of interactions had the paradoxical effect of giving time its full social efficacy, which is never more active than when nothing is going on, except time. 'Time', we say, 'is working for him'; the opposite can also be true.

Thus time derives its efficacy from the state of the structure of relations within which it comes into play; which does not mean that the model of this structure can leave it out of account. When the unfolding of the action is heavily ritualized, as in the dialectic of offence (assault on *h'aram*) and vengeance, where failure to respond, even when presented as disdain, is ruled out, there is still room for strategies that consist in playing with the time, or rather the tempo, of the action, by delaying revenge so as to use a capital of provocations received or conflicts suspended, with its charge of potential revenge and conflict, as an instrument of power based on the capacity to take the initiative in reopening or suspending hostilities. This is true, *a fortiori*, of all the less strictly regulated occasions which offer unlimited scope for strategies exploiting the opportunities for manipulating the pace of the action – holding back or putting off, maintaining suspense or expectancy, or on the other hand, hurrying, hustling, surprising, stealing a march, not to mention the art of ostentatiously giving time ('devoting one's time to someone') or witholding it ('no time to spare'). We know, for example, how much advantage the holder of a transmissible power can derive from the art of delaying transmission and keeping others in the dark as to his ultimate intentions. Nor should one forget all the strategies intended simply to neutralize the action of time and ensure the continuity of interpersonal relations, making continuity out of discontinuity, as mathematicians do, through infinite addition of the infinitely small, in the form, for example, of tiny gestures and acts of 'thoughtfulness' or the 'little gifts' that are said to 'bind in friendship' ('O gift – *thunticht* – you won't make me rich but you are the bond of friendship').

This takes us a long way from the objectivist model and the mechanical interlocking of pre-set actions that is commonly associated with the notion of ritual. Only a virtuoso with a perfect mastery of his 'art of living' can play on all the resources inherent in the ambiguities and indeterminacies of behaviours and situations so as to produce the actions appropriate in each case, to do at the right moment that of which people will say 'There was nothing else to be done', and to do it the right way. We are a long way, too, from norms and rules. Doubtless there are slips, mistakes and moments of clumsiness to be observed here as elsewhere – and also grammarians of decorum able to say (and elegantly, too) what it is elegant to do and say; but they never presume to encompass in a catalogue of recurrent situations and appropriate conduct the 'art' of the necessary improvisation that defines excellence. The temporal structure of practice functions here as a screen preventing totalization. The interval inserted between the gift and the counter-gift is an instrument of denial which allows a subjective truth and a quite opposite objective truth to coexist, in both individual experience and the common judgement.[10] It is the curse of objectivism that, here as in all cases where it confronts collective belief, it can only establish, with great difficulty, truths that are not so much unknown as repressed;[11] and that it cannot include, in the model it produces to account for practice, the individual or collective, private or official, subjective illusion against which it has had to win its truth, in other words the *illusio*, belief, and the conditions of production and functioning of this collective denial.

The relationship between the objectivist model and the *habitus*, between the theoretical schema and the scheme of practical sense (which is shadowed by practical rules, partial and imperfect statements of the principles), is thus complicated by a third term, the official norm and the native theory which redouble at the level of discourse, and so reinforce, the repression of the 'objective' (that is, objectivist) truth that is inscribed in the very structure of practice and, as such, is part of the full truth of practice. Inculcation is never so perfect that a society can entirely dispense with all explicit statement, even in cases where, as in Kabylia, the objectification of the generative schemes in a grammar of practices, a written code of conduct, is limited to the absolute minimum. Official representations, which, as well as customary rules, include gnomic poems, sayings, proverbs, every kind of objectification of the schemes of perception and action in words, things or practices (that is, as much in the vocabulary of honour or kinship, with the model of marriage that it implies, as in ritual acts or objects), have a dialectical relationship with the dispositions that are expressed through them and which they help to produce and reinforce. *Habitus* are spontaneously inclined to recognize all the expressions in which they recognize themselves, because they are spontaneously inclined to produce them – in particular all the exemplary products of the most conforming *habitus* which have been selected and preserved by the *habitus* of successive generations and which are invested with the intrinsic force of objectification and with the authority attached to every publicly authorized realization of the *habitus*.

The specific force of official representations is that they institute the principles of a practical relation to the natural and social world in words, objects, practices and especially in collective, public events, such as the major rituals, deputations and solemn processions (the Greeks called them *theories* . . .), of which our processions, rallies and demonstrations, in which the group presents itself as such, in its volume and structure, are the secularized form. These ritual manifestations are also representations, theatrical performances, shows, that stage and present the whole group, which is thus constituted as the spectator of a visible representation of what is not so much a representation of the natural and social world, a 'world-view', as a practical, tacit relationship to the things of the world. Officialization is the process whereby the group (or those who dominate it) teaches itself and masks from itself its own truth, binds itself by a public profession which sanctions and imposes what it utters, tacitly defining the limits of the thinkable and the unthinkable and so contributing to the maintenance of the social order from which it derives its power.[12] It follows that the intrinsic difficulty of any explicit statement of the logic of practice is intensified by the obstacle of the whole set of authorized representations in which the group is willing to recognize itself.[13]

Objectivist critique is justified in questioning the official definition of practices and uncovering the real determinants hidden under the proclaimed motivations. The brutally materialist reduction which describes values as collectively misrecognized, and so recognized, interests, and which points out, with Max Weber, that the official rule determines practice only when there is more to be gained by obeying than by disobeying it, always has a salutary effect of demystification. But it must not lead one to forget that the official definition of reality is part of a full definition of social reality and that this imaginary anthropology has very real effects. One is right to refuse to credit the rule with the efficacy that legalism ascribes to it, but it must not be forgotten that there is an interest in 'toeing the line' which can be the basis of strategies aimed at regularizing the agent's situation, putting him in the right, in a sense beating the group at its own game by presenting his interests in the misrecognizable guise of the values recognized by the group. Strategies directly oriented towards primary profit (for example, the social capital accruing from an advantageous marriage) are often accompanied by second-degree strategies aimed at giving apparent satisfaction to the demands of the official rule, so combining the satisfactions of interest with the prestige or respect which almost universally reward actions apparently motivated by respect for the rule. There is nothing that groups demand more insistently and reward more generously than this conspicuous reverence for what they claim to revere.[14]

Strategies aimed at producing practices 'according to the rules' are one among other types of officialization strategy, aimed at transmuting 'egoistic', private, particular interests (notions which can only be defined in the relationship between a social unit and the unit which encompasses it at a higher level) into 'disinterested', collective, publicly avowable, legitimate interests. In the absence of constituted political institutions endowed with the *de facto* monopoly of legitimate violence, specifically political action can only be exerted through the officialization effect. It therefore presupposes competence (in the sense of the capacity socially granted to an authority) which is essential, especially in moments of crisis when the collective judgement hesitates, in order to manipulate the collective definition of the situation so as to bring it closer to the official definition and to mobilize the largest possible group by solemnizing and universalizing a private incident (for example, by presenting an insult to a particular woman as an assault on the *h'urma* of the whole group); or to demobilize it by disowning the person directly concerned and reducing him to the status of a private individual so devoid of reason that he seeks to impose his private reason (*idiôtès* in Greek, *amahbul* in Kabyle).

When, as in ancient Kabylia, there is no judicial apparatus endowed with the monopoly of physical or even symbolic violence, the precepts of custom can carry some weight only to the extent that they are skilfully manipulated by the holders of authority within the clan (the 'guarantors' or 'wise men') in such a way as to 'reactivate' dispositions capable of reproducing them. The assembly does not function like a tribunal pronouncing verdicts by reference to a pre-existing code but as an arbitration or family council that seeks to reconcile the adversaries' points of view and bring them to accept a settlement. Thus the functioning of the system presupposes the orchestration of *habitus*, since the arbitrator's decision can only be implemented with the consent of the 'offending' party (failing which, the plaintiff can only resort to force) and will not be accepted unless it conforms to the 'sense of equity' and is imposed in forms recognized by the 'sense of honour'. And it is clear that means of symbolic coercion such as the curse ('A man who carries off dung spread out on the market-stalls shall be fined 50 douros and a curse shall be pronounced on him that will make him an *amengur* [he will die without an heir]', Article XC of the *qanun* of Adni, reported by Boulifa 1913: 15–27) or banishment owe their efficacy to the objective complicity, the belief, of those whom they constrain.

Politics is the arena *par excellence* of officialization strategies. In their endeavours to draw the group's delegation to themselves and to withdraw it from their competitors, the agents competing for political power can only implement ritual strategies and strategic rituals, aimed at the symbolic universalization of private interests or the symbolic appropriation of official interests.[15] This is why all kinds of official representations, especially those that are objectified in language in the form of sayings, proverbs and gnomic poems, are among the most hotly contested stakes in their struggles. To appropriate the 'sayings of the tribe' is to appropriate the power to act on the group by appropriating the power the group exerts over itself through its official language. The principle of the magical efficacy of this performative language which makes what it states, magically instituting what it says in constituent statements, does not lie, as some people think, in the language itself, but in the group that authorizes and recognizes it and, with it, authorizes and recognizes itself.

Thus objectivism falls short of objectivity by failing to integrate into its account of reality the representation of reality against which it has had to construct its 'objective' representation, but which, when it is backed by the unanimity of the group, realizes the most indisputable form of objectivity. Gift exchange is the paradigm of all the operations through which symbolic alchemy produces the reality-denying reality that the collective consciousness aims at as a collectively produced, sustained and maintained misrecognition of the 'objective' truth. The official truth produced by the collective work of euphemization, an elementary form of the work of objectification which eventually leads to the legal definition of acceptable behaviour, is not only the group's means of saving its 'spiritualistic point of honour'. It also has a practical efficacy, for, even if it were belied by the practice of everyone, like a grammatical rule to which every case proved an exception, it would still remain a true description of such practices as are intended to be acceptable. The ethic of honour bears down on each agent with the weight of all the other agents; and the disenchantment that leads to the progressive unveiling of repressed meanings and functions can only result from a collapse of the social conditions of the cross-censorship that each agent may suffer reluctantly but without ceasing to impose it on others, and from the ensuing crisis of collective denial.

Urbanization, which brings together groups with different traditions and weakens the reciprocal controls (and even before urbanization, the generalization of monetary exchanges and the introduction of wage labour), results in the collapse of the collectively maintained and therefore entirely real fiction of the religion of honour. For example, trust is replaced by credit – *talq* – which was previously cursed or despised (as is shown by the insult 'credit face!', the face of a man who is so constantly humiliated that he has ceased to feel dishonour, or the fact that repudiation with restitution, the greatest offence imaginable, is called *berru natalq*). The doxic relation to the world is the most visible manifestion of the effect that occurs whenever the practices of the group show very little dispersion (a J-curve) and when each member helps to impose on all the others, willy-nilly, the same constraint that they impose on him. The idea of breaking this kind of circular control, which could only be cast off by a collective raising of consciousness and a collective contract, is excluded by the very logic of the unanimity effect, which is quite irreducible to an effect of imitation or fashion. (Contrary to what was supposed by theories of the original contract, only a contract can free a group from the contract-less constraint of social mechanisms that is sanctioned by *laissez-faire*). The fact that the primary belief of strongly integrated communities is the product of the serial constraint that the group applies to itself (which may be suffered with great impatience, as was the case with religious control in village communities, but without ever being able to spark off a revolt that could call them into question) perhaps explains why breaks (for example, in religious practice) often take a sudden, collective form. with circular control losing its efficacy as soon as there is a glimpse of the real possibility of breaking it.

7

Symbolic Capital

The theoretical construction which retrospectively projects the counter-gift into the project of the gift does not only have the effect of making mechanical sequences of obligatory acts out of the risky and but necessary improvisation of everyday strategies, which owe their infinite complexity to the fact that the giver's undeclared calculation has to reckon with the receiver's undeclared calculation, and hence satisfy his expectations without appearing to know what they are. In the same operation, it removes the conditions of possibility of the institutionally organized and guaranteed misrecognition that is the basis of gift exchange and, perhaps, of all the symbolic labour aimed at transmuting the inevitable and inevitably interested relations imposed by kinship, neighbourhood or work, into elective relations of reciprocity, through the sincere fiction of a disinterested exchange, and, more profoundly, at transforming arbitrary relations of exploitation (of woman by man, younger brother by elder brother, the young by the elders) into durable relations, grounded in nature. In the work of reproducing established relations – feasts, ceremonies, exchange of gifts, visits or courtesies and, above all, marriages – which is no less vital to the existence of the group than the reproduction of the economic bases of its existence, the labour required to conceal the function of the exchanges is as important as the labour needed to perform this function.[1] If it is true that the lapse of time interposed is what enables the gift or counter-gift to be seen as inaugural acts of generosity, without a past or a future, that is, without calculation, then it is clear that by reducing the polythetic to the monothetic, objectivism destroys the reality of all practices which, like gift exchange, tend or pretend to put the law of self-interest into abeyance. Because it protracts and so disguises the transaction that a rational contract would telescope into an instant, gift exchange is, if not the only mode of circulation of goods that is practised, at least the only one that can be fully recognized in societies that deny 'the true ground of their life', as Lukács puts it; and also the only way of setting up durable relations of reciprocity – and domination – with the interposed time representing the beginnings of institutionalized obligation.

Economism is a form of ethnocentrism. Treating pre-capitalist economies, in Marx's phrase, 'as the Fathers of the Church treated the religions which preceded Christianity', it applies to them categories, methods (economic accountancy, for example) or concepts (such as the notions of interest, investment or capital) which are the historical product of capitalism and which induce a radical transformation of their object, similar to the historical transformation from which they arose. Economism recognizes no other form of interest than that which capitalism has produced, through a kind of real operation of abstraction, by setting up a universe of relations between man and man based, as Marx says, on 'callous cash payment' and more generally by favouring the creation of relatively autonomous fields, capable of establishing their own axiomatics (through the fundamental tautology 'business is business', on which 'the economy' is based). It can therefore find no place in its analyses, still less in its calculations, for any form of 'non-economic' interest. It is as if economic calculation had been able to appropriate the territory objectively assigned to the remorseless logic of what Marx calls 'naked self-interest', only by relinquishing an island of the 'sacred', miraculously spared by the 'icy waters of egoistic calculation', the refuge of what has no price because it has too much or too little. But, above all, it can make nothing of universes that have not performed such a dissociation and so have, as it were, an economy in itself and not for itself. Thus, any partial or total objectification of the archaic economy that does not include a theory of the subjective relation of misrecognition which agents adapted to this economy maintain with its 'objective' (that is, objectivist) truth, succumbs to the most subtle and most irreproachable form of ethnocentrism. It is the same error as that incurred when one forgets that the constitution of art as art is inseparable from the constitution of a relatively autonomous artistic field, and treats as aesthetic certain 'primitive' or 'folk' practices which cannot see themselves in this way.

Everything takes place as if the specificity of the 'archaic' economy lay in the fact that economic activity cannot explicitly recognize the economic ends in relation to which it is objectively oriented. The 'idolatry of nature' which makes it impossible to think of nature as raw material and, consequently, to see human activity as labour, that is, as man's struggle against nature, combines with the systematic emphasis on the symbolic aspect of the acts and relations of production to prevent the economy from being grasped as an economy, that is, as a system governed by the laws of interested calculation, competition or exploitation.

By reducing this economy to its 'objective' reality, economism annihilates the specificity located precisely in the socially maintained discrepancy between the 'objective' reality and the social representation of production and exchange. It is no accident that the vocabulary of the archaic economy is entirely made up of double-sided notions that are condemned to disintegrate in the very history of the economy, because, owing to their duality, the social relations that they designate represent unstable structures which inevitably split in two as soon as the social mechanisms sustaining them are weakened (see Benveniste 1973). Thus, to take an extreme example, *rahnia*, a contract by which the borrower grants the lender the

usufruct of some of his land for the duration of the loan, and which is
regarded as the worst form of usury when it leads to dispossession, differs
only in the nature of the social relation between the two parties, and thus
in the detailed terms of the agreement, from the aid granted to a distressed
relative so as to save him from selling land which, even when the owner
is still allowed to use it, constitutes a kind of security on the loan.[2] As
Mauss (1966: 52) says:

'It was precisely the Greeks and Romans who, possibly following the
Northern and Western Semites, drew the distinction between personal
rights and real rights, separated purchases from gifts and exchanges,
dissociated moral obligations from contracts, and, above all, conceived of
the difference between ritual, rights and interests. By a genuine, great and
venerable revolution, they passed beyond the excessively hazardous, costly
and elaborate gift economy, which was encumbered with personal
considerations, incompatible with the development of the market, trade
and production, and, in a word, uneconomic.'

The historical situations in which the artificially maintained structures
of the good-faith economy break up and make way for the clear, economical
(as opposed to expensive) concepts of the economy of undisguised self-
interest, reveal the cost of operating an economy which, by its refusal to
recognize and declare itself as such, is forced to devote almost as much
ingenuity and energy to disguising the truth of economic acts as it expends
in performing them. For example, a much esteemed Kabyle mason, who
had learned his trade in France, caused a scandal, around 1955, by going
home when his work was finished without eating the meal traditionally
given in the mason's honour when a house is built, and then demanding,
in addition to the price of his day's work (1,000 francs), a bonus of 200
francs in lieu of the meal. His demand for the cash equivalent of the meal
was a sacrilegious reversal of the formula used in symbolic alchemy to
transmute labour and its price into unsolicited gifts, and it thus exposed
the device most commonly used to keep up appearances through a
collectively produced make-believe. As an act of exchange setting the seal
on alliances ('I set the wheatcake and the salt between us'), the final meal
at the time of the *thiwizi* of harvest or house-building naturally became a
rite of alliance intended to transfigure an interested transaction retrospectively into a generous exchange (like the vendor's gifts to the purchaser
which often rounded off the most tenacious haggling). The subterfuges
sometimes used to minimize the cost of the meals at the end of the *thiwizi*
(for example, only inviting the leading representatives of each group, or
one man per family), a departure from the principles which still paid lip-
service to their legitimacy, were viewed with the greatest indulgence, but
the reaction could only be scandal and shock when a man took it upon
himself to declare that the meal had a cash equivalent, thus betraying the
best-kept and worst-kept of secrets (since everyone kept it), and breaking
the law of silence that guaranteed the complicity of collective bad faith in
the economy of 'good faith'.

The good-faith economy, based on a set of mechanisms tending to limit and disguise the play of (narrowly) 'economic' interest and calculation, calls forth the strange incarnation of *homo economicus* known as *buniya* (or *bab niya*), the man of good faith (*niya* or *thiâuggants*, from *aâggun*, the child still unable to speak, as opposed to *thah'raymith*, calculating intelligence). The man of good faith would not think of selling certain fresh food products – milk, butter, cheese, vegetables, fruit – but always distributes them among his friends or neighbours. He practises no exchanges involving money and all his relations are based on complete trust. Unlike the shady dealer, he has recourse to none of the guarantees (witnesses, security, written documents) with which commercial transactions are surrounded. The closer the individuals and groups are in genealogy, the easier it is to reach agreements (and therefore the more frequent they are) and the more they are entrusted to good faith. Conversely, as the relationship becomes more impersonal, that is, as one moves out from the relation between brothers to that between virtual strangers (people from different villages), so a transaction is less and less likely to be established at all but it can, and increasingly does, become more purely 'economic', i.e. closer to its economic truth, and the interested calculation which is never absent from the most generous exchange (in which both parties count themselves satisfied, and therefore count) can be more and more openly revealed.[3]

Friendly transactions between kinsmen and affines are to market transactions as ritual war is to total war. The 'goods or beasts of the fellah' are traditionally opposed to the 'goods or beasts of the market', and informants will talk endlessly of the tricks and frauds that are commonplace in the 'big markets', that is to say, in exchanges with strangers. There are endless tales of mules that run off as soon as the purchaser has got them home, oxen made to look fatter by rubbing them with a plant that makes them swell (*adhris*), purchasers who band together to force prices down. The incarnation of economic war is the shady dealer, who fears neither God nor man. Men avoid buying animals from him, and from any total stranger. As one informant said, for straightforward goods, like land, it is the thing to be bought that determines the buyer's decision; for problematic goods, such as beasts of burden and especially mules, it is the choice of seller that decides, and at least an effort is made to substitute a personalized relationship for a totally impersonal, anonymous relationship. Every intermediate stage can be found, from transactions based on complete distrust, such as that between the peasant and the shady dealer, who cannot demand or obtain guarantees because he cannot guarantee the quality of his wares or find guarantors, to the exchange of honour which can dispense with conditions and rely entirely on the good faith of the 'contracting parties'. But in the great majority of transactions the notions of buyer and seller tend to be dissolved in the network of middlemen and guarantors who aim to turn the purely economic relationship into a genealogically based and guaranteed relationship. Marriage itself is no exception: it is almost always set up between families already linked by a whole network of previous exchanges, underwriting the specific new agreement. It is significant that in the first phase of the very complex negotiations that lead to the marriage agreement, the two families bring in prestigious kinsmen or affines as 'guarantors'. The symbolic capital thus displayed serves both to strengthen their hand in the bargaining and to underwrite the agreement once it is concluded.

The true nature of production is no less repressed than the true nature of circulation. The indignant comments provoked by the heretical behaviour of peasants who have departed from traditional ways draw attention to the mechanisms which inclined the peasant to maintain an enchanted relationship with the land and made it impossible for him to see his toil as labour. 'It's sacrilege, they have profaned the earth. They have done away with fear (*elhiba*). Nothing intimidates them or stops them. They turn everything upside down, I'm sure they will end up ploughing in *lakhrif* (the fig season) if they are in a hurry and if they feel like spending *lah'lal* (the licit period for ploughing) doing something else, or in *rbiâ* (spring) if they've been too lazy in *lah'lal*. It's all the same to them.' Everything in the peasant's practice actualizes, in a different mode, the objective intention revealed in ritual. The land is never treated as raw material to be exploited, but always as the object of respect mingled with fear (*elhiba*). It will 'settle its scores', they say, and take revenge for bad treatment it receives from a hasty or clumsy farmer. The accomplished peasant 'presents' himself to the land with the stance befitting one man meeting another, face to face, with the attitude of trusting familiarity he would show a respected kinsman. During ploughing, he would not think of delegating the task of leading the team, and the only task he leaves for his 'clients' (*ichikran*) is that of breaking up the soil behind the plough. 'The elders used to say that to plough properly, you had to be the master of the land. The young men were left out of it. It would have been an insult to the land to "present" it (*qabel*) with men one would not dare present to other men.' 'It is the man who faces other men', says a proverb, 'who must face the earth.'

To take up Hesiod's opposition between *ponos* and *ergon*, the peasant does not, strictly, work, he 'takes pains'. 'Give to the earth and the earth will give to you', says a proverb. This can be taken to mean that, in accordance with the logic of gift exchange, nature gives her fruits only to those who bring her their toil as a tribute. The heretical behaviour of those who leave to the young the task of 'opening the earth and ploughing into it the wealth of the new year' provokes the older peasants to express the principle of the relationship between men and the land, which could remain unformulated so long as it was taken for granted: 'The earth no longer gives because we give it nothing. We openly mock the earth and it is only right that it should pay us back with lies.' A self-respecting man should always be busy doing something: if he cannot find anything to do, 'at least he can carve his spoon'. Activity is as much a duty of communal life as an economic imperative. What is valued is activity for its own sake, regardless of its strictly economic function, inasmuch as it is seen as appropriate to the specific function of the person who performs it.

There is strong disapproval of individuals who are no use to their family or their group, 'dead men whom God has drawn from living men', in the words of a verse of the Koran often applied to them, and who 'cannot pull their weight'. To remain idle, especially when one belongs to a great family, is to shirk the duties and tasks that are an inseparable part of belonging to the group. So a man who has been out of farming for some time, because he has emigrated or been ill, is quickly found a place in the cycle of work and the circuit of the exchange of services. The group has the right to demand of each of its members that he should have an occupation, however unproductive or even purely symbolic. A peasant who provides idlers with an opportunity to work on his land is universally approved because he gives these marginal individuals a chance to integrate themselves into the group by doing their duty as men.

The distinction between productive and non-productive, or profitable and non-profitable work, is unknown. It would destroy the *raison d'être* of the countless minor tasks intended to assist nature in its labour. No one would think of assessing the technical efficiency or economic usefulness of these inseparably technical and ritual acts, the peasant's version, so to speak, of art for art's sake, such as fencing the fields, pruning the trees, protecting the new shoots from animals, or 'visiting' (*asafqadh*) and watching over the fields, not to mention practices generally regarded as rites, such as actions intended to expel evil (*as'ifedh*) or to mark the coming of spring; or of all the social acts which the application of alien categories would define as unproductive, such as the tasks that fall to the head of the family as the representative and leader of the group – co-ordinating the work, speaking in the men's assembly, bargaining in the market, reading in the mosque.[4] 'If the peasant were to count', runs a proverb, 'he would not sow.' Perhaps this implies that the relationship between work and its product is not really unknown, but socially repressed, because the productivity of labour is so low that the peasant must refrain from counting his time and measuring (as Marx does, reasoning here as an objectivist agronomist) the disparity between the working period and the production period, which is also the consumption period, in order to preserve the meaningfulness of his work; or – and this is only an apparent contradiction – that in a world in which scarcity of time is so rare and scarcity of goods so great, his best and only course is to spend his time without counting it, to squander the one thing that exists in abundance.[5]

In short, 'pains' are to labour as the gift is to trade (an activity for which, as Benveniste points out, the Indo-European languages had no name). The discovery of labour presupposes the constitution of the common ground of production, that is, the disenchanting of a natural world reduced to its economic dimension alone. Ceasing to be the tribute paid to a necessary order, activity can be directed towards an exclusively economic goal, the one that money, henceforward the measure of all things, starkly designates. This means the end of the primal undifferentiatedness which made possible the play of individual and collective misrecognition. Measured by the yardstick of monetary profit, the most sacred activities find themselves constituted negatively as symbolic, that is, in a sense the word sometimes receives, as lacking concrete, material effect, in a word, gratuitous, that is, disinterested but also useless.

In an economy which is defined by the refusal to recognize the 'objective' truth of 'economic' practices, that is, the law of 'naked self-interest' and egoistic calculation, even 'economic' capital cannot act unless it succeeds in being recognized through a conversion that can render unrecognizable the true principle of its efficacy. Symbolic capital is this denied capital, recognized as legitimate, that is, misrecognized as capital (recognition, acknowledgement, in the sense of gratitude aroused by benefits can be one of the foundations of this recognition) which, along with religious capital (see Bourdieu 1971), is perhaps the only possible form of accumulation when economic capital is not recognized.

Whatever conscious or unconscious efforts are made to regulate the routine of the ordinary course of events through ritual stereotyping and to reduce crises by producing them symbolically or ritualizing them as soon as they arise, the archaic economy cannot escape the opposition between ordinary and extra-ordinary occasions, between regular needs, which can be satisfied by the domestic community, and the exceptional needs, both material and symbolic, for goods and services, which arise in special circumstances – economic crisis, political conflict or simply the urgency of agricultural work – and which require the voluntary assistance of a more extended group. The strategy of accumulating the capital of honour and prestige which produces a clientele as much as it is produced by it, therefore provides the optimum solution to the problem that would arise from continuously maintaining the whole of the labour force that is needed during the working period (which is necessarily very short, because of the rigours of the climate and the weakness of the technical resources: 'The harvest is like lightning' – *lerzaq am lebraq*; 'When it's a bad year, there are always too many mouths to feed; when it's a good year, there are never enough hands to do the work'). It enables the great families to marshal the maximum workforce during the working period while minimizing consumption. This vital assistance provided in brief moments of great urgency is obtained at low cost since it will be rewarded either in the form of labour, but outside the period of intense activity, or in other forms, protection, the loan of animals, etc.

One is entitled to see this as a disguised form of purchase of labour power or a covert exaction of corvées, but only on condition that the analysis holds together what holds together in the object, namely the double reality of intrinsically equivocal, ambiguous practices. This is the pitfall awaiting all those whom a naively dualistic representation of the relationship between the 'native' economy and the 'native' representation of the economy leads into the self-mystifying demystifications of a reduced and reductive materialism. The complete truth of this appropriation of services lies in the fact that it can *only* take place in the disguise of *thiwizi*, voluntary assistance which is also a corvée and is thus a voluntary corvée and forced assistance, and that, to use a geometrical metaphor, it presupposes a double half-rotation returning to the starting-point, that is, a conversion of material capital into symbolic capital itself reconvertible into material capital.

In reality, *thiwizi* mainly benefits the richest farmers and also the *t'aleb* (whose land is ploughed and sown collectively). The poor need no help with their harvest. But *thiwizi* can also help a poor man in the case of the building of a house (for the transporting of beams and stones). Ostracism is a terrible sanction and is more than symbolic: owing to the limited technical resources, many activities would be impossible without the help of the group (for example, house-building, with stones to be carried, or the transporting of mill-wheels, which used to mobilize forty men in shifts for several days). Moreover, in this economy of insecurity, a capital of services rendered and gifts bestowed is the best and indeed only safeguard against the 'thousand contingencies', on which, as Marx observes, depends the maintenance or loss of working conditions, from the accident that causes the loss of an animal to the bad weather that destroys the crops.

As well as the additional labour-power which it provides at the times of greatest need, symbolic capital procures all that is referred to under the term *nesba*, that is, the network of affines and relationships that is held through the set of commitments and debts of honour, rights and duties accumulated over the successive generations, and which can be mobilized in extra-ordinary circumstances. Economic and symbolic capital are so inextricably intertwined that the display of material and symbolic strength represented by prestigious affines is in itself likely to bring in material profits, in a good-faith economy in which good repute constitues the best, if not the only, economic guarantee.[6] It is clear why the great families never miss an opportunity to organize exhibitions of symbolic capital – processions of kinsmen and allies which solemnize the pilgrim's departure or return, the bride's escort, measured by the number of 'rifles' and the intensity of the salutes fired in the couple's honour, prestigious gifts, like the sheep given for a wedding, the witnesses and guarantors who can be mobilized at any time and any place, to attest the good faith of a transaction or to strengthen the hand of the lineage in negotiating a marriage and solemnize the contract.

Symbolic capital is valid even in the market. A man may enhance his prestige by making a purchase at an exorbitant price, for the sake of his point of honour, just to 'show he could do it'; but he may also take pride in having managed to conclude a deal without laying out a penny in cash, either by mobilizing a number of guarantors, or, even better, by virtue of the credit and the capital of trust that stems from a reputation for honour as well as wealth. Because of the trust they enjoy and the capital of social relations they have accumulated, those who are said to 'be able to come back with the whole market, even if they went out empty-handed', can afford to 'go to market with only their faces, their names and their honour for money' and even 'to bid whether they have money on them or not'. The collective judgement which makes the 'market man' (*argaz nasuq*) is a total judgement on the total man which, like such judgements in all societies, involves the ultimate values and takes into account – at least as much as wealth and solvency

– the qualities strictly attached to the person, those which 'can neither be borrowed nor lent'.[7]

When one knows that symbolic capital is credit, but in the broadest sense, a kind of advance, a credence, that only the group's belief can grant those who give it the best symbolic and material guarantees, it can be seen that the exhibition of symbolic capital (which is always very expensive in material terms) is one of the mechanisms which (no doubt universally) make capital go to capital.

So it is by drawing up a comprehensive balance-sheet of symbolic profits, without forgetting the undifferentiatedness of the symbolic and the material components of a family's wealth, that it becomes possible to grasp the economic rationality of conduct which economism dismisses as absurd. For example, the decision to buy a second yoke of oxen after the harvest, on the grounds that they are needed for treading out the grain – which is a way of making it known that the crop has been plentiful – only to have to sell them again for lack of fodder, before the autumn ploughing, when they would technically be necessary, seems economically aberrant only if one forgets all the material and symbolic profit accruing from this (albeit fictitious) enhancement of the family's symbolic capital in the late-summer period when marriages are negotiated. The perfect rationality of this strategy of bluff lies in the fact that marriage is the occasion for an (in the widest sense) economic circulation which cannot be seen purely in terms of material goods. The circulation of immediately perceptible material goods, such as the bridewealth, disguises the total circulation, actual or potential, of indissolubly material and symbolic goods of which they are only the aspect that is visible to the eye of *homo economicus*. The amount of the bridewealth would not justify the hard bargaining that takes place over it if it did not take on a symbolic value of the greatest importance, by manifesting unequivocally the value of a family's products on the matrimonial market, as well as the capacity of its spokesmen to get the best price for their products through their bargaining skills.[8] Thus the profits that a group is likely to derive from this total transaction increase with its material and especially its symbolic patrimony, or, in the language of banking, with the 'credit of renown' that it can command. This 'credit-worthiness', which depends on the capacity of the group's point of honour to ensure the invulnerability of its honour, is an undivided whole, indissolubly uniting the quantity and quality of its goods and the quantity and quality of the men capable of turning them to good account. It is what enables the group, especially through marriage, to acquire prestigious affines (wealth in the form of 'rifles', measured not only by the number of men but also their quality, their point of honour) and defines the group's capacity to preserve its land and its honour, pratically the honour of its women, in short, the capital of material and symbolic strength which can actually be mobilized, for market transactions, contests of honour or work on the land.

The interest at stake in the conducts of honour is one for which economism has no name and which has to be called symbolic, although it is such as to inspire actions that are very directly material. Just as there are professions, like law and medicine, whose practitioners must be 'above all suspicion', so a family has a vital interest in keeping its capital of honour, its credit of honourability, safe from suspicion. The hypersensitivity to the slightest slur or innuendo (*thasalqubth*), and the multiplicity of strategies designed to belie or avert them, can be explained by the fact that symbolic capital is less easily measured and counted than land or livestock, and that the group, ultimately the only source of credit, will readily withdraw it and direct its suspicions at even the strongest, as if, in matters of honour, as in land, one man's wealth made others that much poorer.

The defence of 'symbolic' capital can thus lead to 'economically' ruinous conduct. This is the case when, on the basis of a socially accepted definition of the symbolic patrimony, a piece of land takes on a symbolic value disproportionate to its technical, 'economic' qualities, those that render the closest, best kept, most 'productive' fields, those most accessible to the women (by private paths, *thikhuradjiyin*), more valuable in the eyes of an ordinary purchaser. When land that has been in the family for a long time and is therefore strongly associated with the name of the family falls into the hands of strangers, buying it back becomes a matter of honour, akin to avenging an offence, and it may reach an exorbitant price. This price is purely theoretical in most cases, since, within this logic, the symbolic profits of the challenge are greater than the material profits that would accrue from cynical (hence reprehensible) exploitation of the situation. The new owners are as determined to hold on to the land, especially if its acquisition is sufficiently recent to remain a challenge, as the others are to buy it back and take revenge for the affront to the *h'urma* of their land. It may happen that a third group will step in with a higher bid, thus challenging not the seller, who only profits from the competition, but the 'legitimate' owners.

Only a partial and reductive, and therefore inconsistent, materialism can fail to see that strategies whose object is to conserve or enhance the symbolic capital of the group (like blood vengeance or marriage) are dictated by interests no less vital than inheritance or marriage strategies. The interest leading an agent to defend his symbolic capital is inseparable from tacit adherence, inculcated in the earliest years of life and reinforced by all subsequent experience, to the axiomatics objectively inscribed in the regularities of the (in the broad sense) economic order, an original investment which constitutes a given type of goods as worthy of being pursued and conserved. The objective harmony between the agents' dispositions (here, their propensity and capacity to play the game of honour) and the objective regularities of which they are the product, means that membership of this economic cosmos implies unconditional recognition of the stakes which, by its very existence, it presents as self-evident, that is, misrecognition of the arbitrariness of the value it confers on them. This primary belief is the basis of the investments and over-investments (in both the economic and psychoanalytic senses) which, through the ensuing competition and scarcity, cannot fail to reinforce the well-grounded illusion that the value of the goods it designates as desirable is in the nature of things, just as interest in these goods is in the nature of men.

8

Modes of Domination

The theory of strictly economic practices is a particular case of a general theory of the economy of practices. Even when they give every appearance of disinterestedness because they escape the logic of 'economic' interest (in the narrow sense) and are oriented towards non-material stakes that are not easily quanitifed, as in 'pre-capitalist' societies or in the cultural sphere of capitalist societies, practices never cease to comply with an economic logic. The correspondences which are established between the circulation of land sold and bought back, revenge killings 'lent' and 'redeemed', or women given and received in marriage, in other words between the different kinds of capital and the corresponding modes of circulation, require us to abandon the economic/non-economic dichotomy which makes it impossible to see the science of 'economic' practices as a particular case of a science capable of treating all practices, including those that are experienced as disinterested or gratuitous, and therefore freed from the 'economy', as economic practices aimed at maximizing material or symbolic profit. The capital accumulated by groups, which can be regarded as the energy of social physics,[1] can exist in different kinds (in the Kabyle case, these are the capital of fighting strength, linked to the capacity for mobilization and therefore to the number of men and their readiness to fight; 'economic' capital, in the form of land, livestock and labour force, this too being linked to the capacity for mobilization; and the symbolic capital accruing from successful use of the other kinds of capital). Although they are subject to strict laws of equivalence and are therefore mutually convertible, each of these kinds of capital produces its specific effects only in specific conditions. But the existence of symbolic capital, that is, of 'material' capital misrecognized and thus recognized, though it does not invalidate the analogy between capital and enery, does remind us that social science is not a social physics; that the acts of cognition that are implied in misrecognition and recognition are part of social reality and that the socially constituted subjectivity that produces them belongs to objective reality.

An unbroken progression leads from the symmetry of gift exchange to the asymmetry of the conspicuous redistribution that is the basis of the constitution of political authority. As one moves away from perfect reciprocity, which assumes a relative equality of economic situation, the proportion of counter-services that are provided in the typically symbolic form of gratitude, homage, respect, obligations or moral debts necessarily increases. If they had been aware of this continuity, those who, like Karl Polanyi and Marshall D. Sahlins, have realized the decisive role of redistribution in establishing political authority and in the functioning of the tribal economy (in which the accumulation–redistribution circuit fulfils a similar function to that of the State and public finances) would no doubt also have observed the central operation of this process, namely the conversion of economic capital into symbolic capital, which produces relations of dependence that have an economic basis but are disguised under a veil of moral relations. In focusing solely on the particular case of exchanges designed to consecrate symmetrical relations, or solely on the economic effect of asymmetrical exchanges, one is liable to forget the effect produced by the circular circulation in which symbolic added-value is generated, namely the legitimation of the arbitrary, when the circulation covers an asymmetrical power relationship.

It is important to observe, as Sahlins (1960, 962–3, 1965) does, pursuing a point made by Marx,[2] that the pre-capitalist economy does not provide the conditions necessary for an indirect, impersonal domination secured quasi-automatically by the logic of the labour market. In fact wealth can function as capital only in relationship with a specifically economic field, presupposing a set of economic institutions and a body of specialized agents with specific interests and modes of thought. Thus, Moses Finley shows that the ancient economy lacked not resources but the means 'to overcome the limits of individual resources': 'There were no proper credit instruments – no negotiable paper, no book clearance, no credit payments . . . There was moneylending in plenty but it was concentrated on usurious loans to peasants or consumers, and in large borrowings to enable men to meet political or other expenditures of the upper classes . . . Similarly in the field of business organization: there were no long-term partnerships or corporations, no brokers or agents, no guilds . . . In short, both the organizational and the operational devices were lacking for the mobilization of private capital resources' (Finley 1965a: 37; see also 1953). This analysis is valid, *a fortiori*, for ancient Kabylia, which lacked even the most elementary instruments of an economic institution. Land was almost totally excluded from circulation – though, occasionally serving as security, it was then liable to pass from one group to another. Village or tribal markets remained isolated and there was no way in which they could be linked up in a single mechanism. The opposition between the 'sacrilegious cunning' to be expected in market transactions and the good faith appropriate to transactions among kinsmen and friends – marked by the spatial distinction between the place of residence, the village, and the place of transactions, the market – mainly served to keep the calculating dispositions favoured by the market out of the universe of relations of reciprocity, and it in no way prevented the small local market from remaining 'embedded in social relationships', as Polanyi (1968, 1944) puts it.

It is paradoxical that in his contribution to a collection of essays edited by Karl Polanyi, Francisco Benet (1957) is so concerned with the opposition between the market and the village that he virtually ignores all the factors that keep the local *suq* under the sway of the values of the good-faith economy. In fact, whether one considers the small tribal markets or the great regional markets, the *suq* represented a mode of transaction that was intermediate between two extremes, neither of them completely realized. On the one hand, there are exchanges of the familiar universe, based on the trust and good faith that are possible when the buyer has virtually complete information about the products exchanged and the seller's strategies and when the relationship between the parties pre-exists and must survive the exchange; on the other hand, there are the rational strategies of the self-regulating market, made possible by product standardization and the quasi-mechanical necessity of processes. The *suq* no longer supplies all the traditional information, but neither does it yet offer the conditions for rational information. This is why all the strategies of the peasants were aimed at limiting the insecurity that accompanies unpredictability, by transforming the impersonal, instantaneous relations of the commercial transaction into durable relations of reciprocity through recourse to guarantors, witnesses and mediators.

In a general way, goods were never treated as capital. This can be seen in the case of a contract such as the *charka* of an ox, which has all the appearances of a loan with interest. In this transaction, which is only conceivable between individuals relatively distant from each other (for example, people from different villages), and which the partners tend to collude in disguising (the borrower prefers to conceal his poverty and pretend that the ox is his own, with the complicity of the lender, who has the same interest in hiding a transaction suspected of not strictly corresponding to the sense of equity), an ox is lent by its owner to a peasant too poor to buy one, in exchange for a certain number of measures of barley or wheat; alternatively, a poor peasant arranges with a richer peasant that the latter will buy a pair of oxen and lend them to him for one, two or three years, and if the oxen are sold, the profit is shared equally (the implicit principles governing transactions between acquaintances can generate an infinite variety of informal agreements, all placed under the same 'concept' by the native terminologies; thus each informant offers his own variant of *charka*). What we would be inclined to see as a simple loan, with the lender making an ox available in exchange for interest paid in wheat, the agents see as an equitable transaction with no extraction of surplus value: the lender gives the labour force of the ox, but equity is satisfied because the borrower feeds and looks after the animal in place of the lender, and the wheat handed over simply compensates for depreciation through aging.

The various kinds of arrangements concerning goats similarly divide the costs of depreciation through age between the two parties. The owner, a woman investing her nest-egg, entrusts her goats for three years to a distant, relatively poor, cousin who she knows will feed and care for them well. The goats are valued and it is agreed that the yield (milk, butter, fleece) will be shared. Each week, the borrower sends a gourd of milk, which is delivered by a child. The child cannot return empty-handed (*elfal*, the good luck charm or the warding-off of evil, has a magical significance because to return an empty vessesl, to send back emptiness, would threaten the prosperity and fecundity of the house); he is given fruit, oil, olives or eggs, according to the season. At the end of the agreed period, the borrower returns the goats and the products are divided. In one variant, the flock having been valued at 30,000 old francs, the borrower handed over 15,000 francs and half the original flock, that is, three old goats; in another case, the borrower returned the whole flock but kept all the fleeces.

Just as economic wealth cannot function as capital except in relation to an economic field, so cultural competence in all its forms is not constituted as cultural capital until it is inserted into the objective relations set up between the system of economic production and the system producing the producers (which is itself constituted by the relationship between the educational system and the family).

When a society lacks both the literacy that would enable it to preserve and accumulate in objectified form the cultural resources inherited from the past, and also the educational system that would give its agents the aptitudes and dispositions required for the symbolic reappropriation of those resources, it can only preserve them in their incorporated state.[3] Consequently, to ensure the perpetuation of cultural resources which would otherwise disappear with the agents who bear them, it has to resort to inculcation, a process which, as the example of the bards shows, may last as long as the actual period of use. The transformations that an instrument such as writing makes possible have been clearly established (see esp. Goody and Watt 1962–3: 304ff.; Goody [ed.] 1968). By detaching cultural resources from persons, literacy enables a society to move beyond anthropological limits – particularly those of individual memory – and liberates it from the constraints implied by mnemotechnic devices such as poetry, the conservation technique *par excellence* of non-literate societies;[4] it makes it possible to accumulate the culture previously conserved in the incorporated state and, by the same token, to perform the primitive accumulation of cultural capital, the total or partial monopolizing of the society's symbolic resources in religion, philosophy, art and science, through the monopolization of the instruments for appropriation of these resources (writing, reading and other decoding techniques), henceforward preserved not in memories but in texts. But capital is given the conditions of its full realization only with the appearance of an educational system, which awards qualifications durably consecrating the position occupied in the structure of the distribution of cultural.

While there are ample grounds for re-emphasizing these negative conditions of the privileged or exclusive recourse to the symbolic forms of power, it must not be forgotten that they no more account for the logic of symbolic violence than the absence of the lightning rod or the electric telegraph, which Marx refers to in a famous passage in the introduction to the *Grundrisse*, can be used to explain Jupiter or Hermes, in other words the internal logic of Greek mythology. To go further, one has to take seriously the representation that the agents offer of the economy of their own practice when this is most opposed to its 'economic' truth. The chief is indeed, in Malinowski's phrase, 'a tribal banker' who accumulates food only to lavish it on others and so build up a capital of obligations and debts that will be repaid in the form of homage, respect, loyalty and, when the occasion arises, work and services, which may be the basis of a new accumulation of material goods. But the analogy must not mislead us: processes of circular circulation such as the levying of a tribute followed by a redistribution apparently leading back to the point of departure would be perfectly absurd if they did not have the effect of transmuting the nature of the social relationship among the agents or groups involved. Everywhere they are observed, these consecration cycles perform the fundamental operation of social alchemy, the transformation of arbitrary relations into legitimate relations, *de facto* differences into officially recognized distinctions.

A rich man is 'rich in order to give to the poor'.[5] This saying is an exemplary expression of the practical denial of interest which, like Freud's *Verneinung*, makes it possible to satisfy interest but only in a (disinterested) form tending to show that it is not being satisfied (the 'lifting of repression' implying no 'acceptance of the repressed'). A man possesses in order to give. But he also possesses by giving. A gift that is not returned can become a debt, a lasting obligation; and the only recognized power – recognition, personal loyalty or prestige – is the one that is obtained by giving. In such a universe, there are only two ways of getting and keeping a lasting hold over someone: debts and gifts, the overtly economic obligations imposed by the usurer,[6] or the moral obligations and emotional attachments created and maintained by the generous gift, in short, overt violence or symbolic violence, censored, euphemized, that is, misrecognizable, recognized violence. The 'way of giving', the manner, the forms, are what separate a gift from straight exchange, moral obligation from economic obligation. To 'observe the formalities' is to make the way of behaving and the external forms of the action a practical denial of the content of the action and of the potential violence it can conceal.[7] There is a clear connection between these two forms of violence, which exist in the same social formation and sometimes in the same relationship: when domination can only be exerted in its elementary form, from person to person, it takes place overtly and has to be disguised under the veil of enchanted relations, the official model of which is presented by relations between kinsmen; in short, to be socially recognized, it must be misrecognized. If the pre-capitalist economy is the site *par excellence* of symbolic violence, this is because the only way that relations of domination can be set up within it, maintained or restored, is through strategies which, if they are not to destroy themselves by revealing their true nature, must be disguised, transfigured, in a word, euphemized. The censorship that this economy imposes on the overt manifestation of violence, especially in its crudely economic form, means that interests can only be satisfied on condition that they be disguised in and by the very strategies aimed at satisfying them.

So it would be wrong to see a contradiction in the fact that violence is here both more present and more masked.[8] Because the pre-capitalist economy cannot count on the implacable, hidden violence of objective mechanisms which enable the dominant to limit themselves to reproduction strategies (often purely negative ones), it resorts simultaneously to forms of domination which may strike the modern observer as more brutal, more primitive, more barbarous, and at the same time as gentler, more humane, more respectful of persons.[9] This coexistence of overt physical or economic violence and the most refined symbolic violence is found in all the institutions characteristic of this economy and at the very heart of each social relation. It is present in both the debt and the gift, which, despite their apparent opposition, can each provide the basis of dependence and even servitude, as well as solidarity, depending on the strategies they serve (Moses Finley [1965b] shows that a debt that was sometimes set up to create a situation of slavery could also serve to create relations of solidarity between equals). This essential ambiguity of all the institutions that modern taxonomies would incline one to treat as 'economic' is evidence that the opposing strategies that may coexist, as in the master–*khammes* relationship, are alternative, interchangeable ways of fulfilling the same function: the 'choice' between overt violence and gentle violence depends on the state of the power relations between the two parties and the integration and ethical integrity of the group that arbitrates. So long as overt violence, that of the usurer or the ruthless master, is collectively disapproved of and is liable to provoke either a violent riposte or the flight of the victim – that is, in both cases, for lack of any legal recourse, the destruction of the very relationship that was to be exploited – symbolic violence, gentle, invisible violence, unrecognized as such, chosen as much as undergone, that of trust, obligation, personal loyalty, hospitality, gifts, debts, piety, in a word, of all the virtues honoured by the ethic of honour, presents itself as the most economical mode of domination because it best corresponds to the economy of the system.

Thus, a social relationship such as that between the master and his *khammes* (a kind of sharecropper who received only a very small share of the crop, usually a fifth, with local variants), which might at first sight seem very close to a simple capital–labour relation, could not in fact be kept up without a combination or alternation of material and symbolic violence directly applied to the very person who had to be tied. The master could bind his *khammes* by a debt which forced him to renew his contract until he could find a new master willing to pay off the debt to the former employer, in other words, indefinitely. He could also resort to brutal measures such as seizing the entire crop in order to recover the value of his loan. But each particular relationship was the product of complex strategies whose efficacy depended not only on the material and symbolic strength of either party but also on their skill in arousing sympathy or indignation so as to mobilize the group. If he was not to lose what often constituted the whole profit secured by the relationship – that is to say, for many masters who were scarcely richer than their *khammes* and would have gained by cultivating their land themselves, the sheer status of master (or non-*khammes*) – the master had an interest in manifesting the virtues of his rank by excluding from the 'economic' relationship any guarantee other than the loyalty required by honour, and by making his *khammes* an associate. The *khammes*, for his part, asked nothing better than to play his part, with the complicity of the whole group, in a self-interested fiction which supplied him with an honourable representation of his position. Given that there was no real labour market and that money was rare (and therefore dear), the best way in which the master could serve his own interests was by working away, day in, day out, with constant care and attention, weaving the ethical and affective, as well as 'economic', bonds that tied his *khammes* to him. To reinforce the bonds of obligation, the master might arrange the marriage of his *khammes* (or his son) and install him, with his family, in the master's own house; the children, brought up in common, with the goods (the flock, fields, etc.) being held in common, often took a long time to discover what their real position was. It was not unusual for one of the sons of a *khammes* to go and work for wages in the town, together with one of the master's sons, and like him bring his savings to the master. In short, if the master wanted to persuade the *khammes* to devote himself over a long period to the pursuit of the master's interests, he had to associate him completely with those interests, masking the asymmetry of the relationship by symbolically denying it in all his behaviour. The *khammes* was the man to whom one entrusted one's goods, one's house and one's honour (as shown by the formula used by a master leaving to go and work in a town or in France:

'Associate, I'm counting on you; I'm going off to be an associate myself'). The *khammes* 'treated the land as if he owned it', because there was nothing in his master's conduct to belie his claim to have rights over the land on which he worked, and it was not unusual to hear a *khammes* saying, long after leaving his 'master', that the sweat of his brow entitled him to pick fruit or enter the estate. And just as he never felt entirely freed from his obligations towards his former master, so, after what he called a 'change of heart', he might accuse his master of 'treachery' in abandoning someone he had 'adopted'.

The harder it is to exercise direct domination, and the more it is disapproved of, the more likely it is that gentle, disguised forms of domination will be seen as the only possible way of exercising domination and exploitation. It would be as fallacious to identify this essentially two-sided economy with its official truth as it would be to reduce it to its 'objective' truth, seeing mutual aid as a corvée, the *khammes* as a kind of slave, and so on. 'Economic' capital can here only work in the euphemized form of symbolic capital. This conversion of capital which is the condition of its efficacy is no way automatic. As well as a perfect knowledge of the logic of the economy of denial, it requires constant labour in the form of the care and attention devoted to making and maintaining relations; and also major investments, both material and symbolic – political aid against attack, theft, offences and insults, and economic aid, which can be costly, especially in times of scarcity. It also requires the (sincere) disposition to give things that are more personal, and therefore more precious than goods or money, because, as the saying goes, they can 'neither be lent nor borrowed', such as time[10] – the time that has to be taken to do things 'that are not forgotten', because they are done properly, at the proper time, marks of 'attention', friendly 'gestures', acts of 'kindness'. If authority is always seen as a property of the person – *fides*, as Benveniste (1973: 84ff.) points out, is not 'trust' but 'the inherent quality of a person who inspires trust and is exercised in the form of protective authority over those who entrust themselves to him' – it is because gentle violence requires those who exercise it to pay a *personal* price.

'Soft' domination is thus very costly for the person who exerts it, and first in economic terms. On the one hand, the social mechanisms that imposed the repression of economic interest and so tended to make the accumulation of symbolic capital the only recognized form of accumulation, and on the other hand, the objective obstacles linked to the weakness of the means of production and the lack of 'economic' institutions, were probably sufficient to hinder or even forbid the concentration of material capital. It was no doubt exceptional for the assembly to have to intervene directly, as in a case reported by Maunier (1930: 68), and to order a man to 'stop getting any richer'. The wealthy had to reckon with the collective judgement, because they derived their authority from it, and in particular their power to mobilize the group for or against individuals or groups. They also had to reckon with the official morality, which required them to make the greatest contributions to ceremonial exchanges, the maintenance of the poor, hospitality to strangers and the organization of feast. Responsibilities such as those of the *t'amen*, the 'spokesman' or 'guarantor' who represented his group in meetings of the men's assembly or on solemn occasions (receiving his group's share from the collective sacrifice, etc.), were not much coveted or competed for. It was not uncommon for the most influential personalities of a group to refuse this role or to ask to be quickly replaced, since the *t'amen's* tasks of representation and mediation demanded much time and effort. Those whom the group honoured with the name of 'wise men' or 'the great' and who, even without any official mandate, were invested with a kind of tacit delegation of its authority, 'owed it to themselves' (as we say when a sense of obligation is dictated by self-esteem) constantly to remind the group of the values it officially recognized, both by their exemplary conduct and by their interventions in disputes. If two women in their group quarrelled, the 'wise men' would separate them, even beat them (if they were widows or if the men on whom they depended lacked authority) or fine them; if there was serious conflict between members of their clan, they would invite both sides to behave reasonably, never an easy role and sometimes a dangerous one; in any situation likely to lead to conflict among the clans (serious crime, for example), they would meet together, with the marabout, to reconcile the contending parties; and it was their responsibility to look after the interests of the poor and the clients, to make them gifts after the traditional collections, to send them food at feast times, to assist widows, see that orphans were married, and so on.

In short, in the absence of an officially declared and institutionally guaranteed delegation, personal authority can only be lastingly maintained through actions that reassert it practically through their compliance with the values recognized by the group.[11] The 'great' can least afford to take liberties with the official norms and they have to pay for their outstanding value with exemplary conformity to the values of the group. Until a system of mechanisms automatically ensuring the reproduction of the established order is constituted, the dominant agents cannot be content with letting the system that they dominate follow its own course in order to exercise durable domination; they have to work directly, daily, personally, to produce and reproduce conditions of domination which even then are never entirely certain. Because they cannot be satisfied with appropriating the profits of a social machine which has not yet developed the power of self-perpetuation, they are obliged to resort to the elementary forms of domination, in other words the direct domination of one person over another, the limiting case of which is appropriation of persons, that is, slavery. They cannot appropriate the labour, services, goods, homage and respect of others without 'winning' them personally, 'tying' them, in short, creating a bond between persons. The transformation of any given kind of capital into symbolic capital, a legitimate possession grounded in the nature of its possessor, is the fundamental operation of social alchemy (the paradigm of which is gift exchange). It always presupposes a form of labour, a visible (if not necessarily conspicuous) expenditure of time, money and energy, a redistribution that is necessary in order to secure recognition of the prevailing distribution, in the form of the recognition granted by the person who receives to the person who, being better placed in the distribution, is in a position to give, a recognition of a debt which is also a recognition of value.

Thus, contrary to simplistic uses of the distinction between infrastructure and superstructure,[12] the social mechanisms that ensure the production of compliant *habitus* are, here as elsewhere, an integral part of the conditions of reproduction of the social order and of the productive apparatus itself, which could not function without the dispositions that the group inculcates and continuously reinforces and which exclude, as *unthinkable*, practices which the disenchanted economy of 'naked self-interest' presents as legitimate and even self-evident. But the particularly important role played by the *habitus* and its strategies in setting up and perpetuating durable relations of domination is once again an effect of the structure of the field. Because it does not offer the institutional conditions for the accumulation of economic or cultural capital (which it even expressly discourages through a censorship forcing agents to resort to euphemized forms of power and violence), this economic order is such that strategies oriented towards the accumulation of symbolic capital, which are found in all social formations, are here the most rational ones, since they are the most effective strategies within the constraints of this universe. The principle of the pertinent differences between the modes of domination lies in the degree of objectification of capital. Social formations in which relations of domination are made, unmade and remade in and through personal interactions contrast with those in which such relations are mediated by objective, institutionalized mechanisms such as the 'self-regulating market', the educational system or the legal apparatus, where they have the permanence and opacity of things and lie beyond the reach of individual consciousness and power.

The opposition between, on the one hand, universes of social relations that do not contain within themselves the principle of their own reproduction and have to be kept up by nothing less than a process of continuous creation, and on the other hand, a social world carried along by its *vis insita* which frees agents from this endless work of creating or restoring social relations, is directly expressed in the history or prehistory of social thought. 'In Hobbes' view', writes Durkheim (1960: 136), 'the social order is generated by an act of will and sustained by an act of will that must be constantly renewed.'[13] And there is every reason to think that the break with this artificialist vision, which is the precondition for scientific apprehension, could not be made before the constitution, in reality, of objective mechanisms like the self-regulating market which, as Polanyi points out, was intrinsically conducive to belief in determinism.[14]

Objectification in institutions guarantees the permanence and cumulativity of material and symbolic acquisitions which can then subsist without the agents having to recreate them continuously and in their entirety by deliberate action. But, because the profits provided by these institutions are subject to differential appropriation, objectification also and inseparably tends to ensure the reproduction of the structure of the distribution of capital which, in its various kinds, is the precondition for such appropriation, and, in so doing, it tends to reproduce the structure of relations of domination and dependence.

Paradoxically, it is precisely because there exist relatively autonomous fields, functioning in accordance with rigorous mechanisms capable of imposing their necessity on the agents, that those who are in a position to command these mechanisms and appropriate the material or symbolic profits accruing from their functioning are able to dispense with strategies aimed expressly and directly at the domination of individuals. The saving is a real one, because strategies designed to establish or maintain lasting relations of personal dependence are, as we have seen, extremely costly, with the result that the means eat up the end and the actions necessary to ensure the continuation of power themselves help to weaken it. Might has to be expended to produce rights, and a great deal of it may be used up in this way.[15]

The point of honour is politics in the pure state. It inclines agents to accumulate material riches that do not have their justification 'in themselves', that is, in their 'economic' or 'technical' function, and which, in extreme cases, may be totally useless, like the objects exchanged in a number of archaic economies, but which are valued as means of manifesting power, as symbolic capital tending to contribute to its own reproduction, that is, to the reproduction and legitimation of the prevailing hierarchies. In such a context, the accumulation of material wealth is simply one means among others of accumulating symbolic power – the power to secure recognition of power. What might be called demonstrative expenditure (as opposed to 'productive' expenditure, which is why it is called 'gratuitous' or 'symbolic') represents, like any other visible expenditure of the signs of wealth that are recognized in a given social formation, a kind of legitimizing self-affirmation through which power makes itself known and recognized. By asserting itself visibly and publicly, securing acceptance of its right to visibility, as opposed to all the occult, hidden, secret, shameful and therefore censored powers (such as those of malign magic), this power awards itself a rudimentary form of institutionalization by officializing itself. But only full institutionalization makes it possible, if not to dispense completely with 'demonstration', at least to cease depending on it completely in order to secure the belief and obedience of others and to mobilize their labour power or fighting strength. And there is every reason to think that, as in the case of feudalism according to Georges Duby, the accumulation of 'economic' capital becomes possible once symbolic capital can be reproduced durably and cheaply so that the political war for rank, distinction and pre-eminence can be pursued by other, more 'economical' means. In place of the relationships between persons indissociable from the functions they fulfil, which they can perpetuate only at direct personal cost, institutionalization sets up strictly established, legally guaranteed relations between recognized positions, defined by their rank in a relatively autonomous space, distinct from and independent of their actual and potential occupants, themselves defined by *entitlements* which, like titles of nobility, property titles or educational qualifications (*titres*), authorize them to occupy these positions.[16] As opposed to personal authority, which can neither be delegated nor bequeathed, the title, as a measure of rank or order, that is, as a formal instrument of evaluation of agents' positions in a distribution, makes it possible to set up quasi-perfect relations of commensurability (or equivalence) among agents defined as aspiring to the appropriation of a particular class of goods – real estate, precedence, offices, privileges – and these goods, which are themselves classified. Thus the relations among agents can be durably settled as regards their legitimate order of access to these goods and to the groups defined by exclusive ownership of these goods.

Thus, for example, by giving the same value to all holders of the same certificate, thereby making them interchangeable, the educational system minimizes the obstacles to the free circulation of cultural capital which result from its being incorporated in particular individuals (without, however, destroying the profits associated with the charismatic ideology of the irreplaceable individual).[17] It makes it possible to relate all qualification-holders (and also, negatively, all unqualified individuals) to a single standard, thereby setting up a unified market for all cultural capacities and guaranteeing the convertibility into money of the cultural capital acquired at a given cost in time and labour. Educational qualifications, like money, have a conventional, fixed value which, being guaranteed by law, is freed from local limitations (in contrast to academically uncertified cultural capital) and temporal fluctuations: the cultural capital which they in a sense guarantee once and for all does not constantly need to be proved. The objectification performed by certificates, diplomas and, more generally, all forms of 'credentials' ('a written proof of qualification that confers credit or authority') is inseparable from the objectification that law produces by defining permanent positions which are independent of the biological individuals they call for and which may be occupied by agents who are biologically different but interchangeable in respect of the qualifications they hold. From then on, relations of power and dependence are no longer established directly between individuals; they are set up, in objectivity, among institutions, that is, among socially guaranteed qualifications and socially defined positions, and through them, among the social mechanisms that produce and guarantee both the social value of the qualifications and the distribution of these social attributes among biological individuals.

Law does no more than symbolically consecrate – by recording it in a form that renders it both eternal and universal – the structure of power relations among the groups and the classes that is produced and guaranteed practically by the functioning of these mechanisms. For example, it records and legitimates the distinction between the function and the person, between power and its holder, together with the relationship that obtains at a particular moment between qualifications and posts (depending on the bargaining power of the sellers and buyers of qualified, that is, scholastically guaranteed, labour power), a relationship that is materialized in a particular distribution of the material and symbolic profits assigned to holders (or non-holders) of qualifications. Law thus adds its specific symbolic force to the action of the whole set of mechanisms which render it superfluous constantly to reassert power relations through the overt use of force.

The effect of legitimation of the established order is thus not solely the work of the mechanisms traditionally regarded as belonging to the order of ideology, such as law. The system of cultural goods production and the system producing the producers also fulfil ideological functions, as a by-product, through the very logic of their functioning, owing to the fact that the mechanisms through which they contribute to the reproduction of the social order and the permanence of the relations of domination remain hidden. As I have shown elsewhere, the educational system helps to provide the dominant class with a 'theodicy of its own privilege' not so much through the ideologies it produces or inculcates, but rather through the practical justification of the established order that it supplies by masking – under the overt connection that it guarantees, between qualifications and jobs – the relationship, which it surreptitiously records, under cover of formal equality, between the qualifications obtained and inherited cultural capital. The most successful ideological effects are the ones that have no need of words, but only of *laissez-faire* and complicitous silence.

It follows, incidentally, that any analysis of ideologies in the narrow sense of 'legitimizing discourses' which fails to include an analysis of the corresponding institutional mechanisms is liable to be no more than a contribution to the efficacy of those ideologies. This is true of all internal (semiological) analyses of political, educational, religious or aesthetic ideologies which forget that the political function of these ideologies may in some cases be reduced to the effect of displacement and diversion, dissimulation and legitimation, which they produce by reproducing the effects of the objective mechanisms, through their oversights and omissions, in their deliberately or involuntarily complicitous silences. This is true, for example, of the charismatic (or meritocratic) ideology, a particular form of the giving of 'gifts', which explains differential access to qualifications by reference to the inequality of innate 'gifts', thereby reinforcing the effect of the mechanisms that mask the relationship between qualifications obtained and inherited cultural capital.

If it is true that symbolic violence is the gentle, disguised form which violence takes when overt violence is impossible, it is understandable that symbolic forms of domination should have progressively withered away as objective mechanisms came to be constituted which, in rendering the work of euphemization superfluous, tended to produce the 'disenchanted' dispositions that their development demanded.[18] It is equally clear why the development of the capacity for subversion and critique that the most brutal forms of 'economic' exploitation have aroused, and the uncovering of the ideological and practical effects of the mechanisms ensuring the reproduction of the relations of domination, should bring about a return to modes of accumulation based on the conversion of economic capital into symbolic capital, with all the forms of legitimizing redistribution, public ('social' policies) and private (financing of 'disinterested' foundations, donations to hospitals, academic and cultural institutions, etc.), through which the dominant groups secure a capital of 'credit' which seems to owe nothing to the logic of exploitation;[19] or the thesaurization of luxury goods attesting the taste and distinction of their possessor. The denial of the economy and of economic interest which, in pre-capitalist societies, was exerted first in the very area of 'economic' transactions, from which it had to be expelled in order for 'the economy' to be constituted as such, thus finds its favoured refuge in the domain of art and 'culture', the site of pure consumption – of money, of course, but also of time. This island of the sacred, ostentatiously opposed to the profane, everyday world of production, a sanctuary for gratuitous, disinterested activity, offers, like theology in other periods, an imaginary anthropology obtained by denial of all the negations really performed by the 'economy'.

9

The Objectivity of the Subjective

The established order, and the distribution of capital which is its basis, contribute to their own perpetuation through their very existence, through the symbolic effect that they exert as soon as they are publicly and officially declared and are thereby misrecognized and recognized. It follows from this that social science cannot 'treat social realities as things', in accordance with Durkheim's famous precept, without neglecting all that these realities owe to the fact that they are objects of cognition (albeit a misrecognition) within the very objectivity of social existence. Social science has to reintroduce into the full definition of the object the primary representations of the object, which it first had to destroy in order to achieve the 'objective' definition. Individuals or groups are objectively defined not only by what they are but by what they are reputed to be, a 'being-perceived' which, even if it closely depends on their being, is never totally reducible to this. Social science therefore has to take account of the two kinds of properties that are objectively attached to them: on the one hand, material properties, starting with the body, that can be counted and measured like any other thing of the physical world; and on the other hand, symbolic properties which are nothing other than material properties when perceived and appreciated in their mutual relationships, that is, as distinctive properties.[1]

An intrinsically twofold reality of this kind requires one to move beyond the false choice in which social science generally allows itself to be trapped, that between social physics and social phenomenology. Social physics, which often appears in the form of an objectivist economism, seeks to grasp an 'objective reality' quite inaccessible to ordinary experience by analysing the statistical relationships among distributions of material properties, quantitative expressions of the distribution of capital (in its different kinds) among the individuals competing to appropriate it. Social phenomenology, which records and deciphers the meanings that agents produce as such by a differential perception of these same properties, which are thus constituted as distinctive signs, tends towards a kind of social marginalism. The 'social order' is thus reduced to a collective classification obtained by addition of the classifying and classified judgements through which agents classify and are classified, or, to put it another way, through aggregation of the (mental) representations that one group has of the (theatrical) representations that other groups give them and of the (mental) representations that the latter have of them.

The opposition between a mechanics of power relations and a phenomenology or cybernetics of sense relations is most visible, and most sterile, in the theory of social classes. On the one hand, there are strictly objectivist definitions which, like the economistic strand of Marxism, seek the principle of class determination in properties that owe nothing to the agents' perception or action (not to mention those that identify classes as countable populations separated by frontiers traced in reality).[2] On the other hand, there are subjectivist or nominalist definitions, including Weber's theory of 'status groups' which privileges the symbolic properties constituting a life-style; empirical analyses seeking to establish whether and how classes exist in the agents' representations; and all the forms of social marginalism, which make acts of authority and submission the principle of the structures of domination and dependence and, like idealist philosophies, conceive the social world 'as will and representation', in which respect they are close to political spontaneism, which identifies a social class (and especially the proletariat) with a kind of pure surge of consciousness.[3]

The objectivist vision is able to extract the 'objective' truth of class relations as power relations, only by destroying everything that helps to give domination the appearances of legitimacy. But it falls short of objectivity by failing to write into its theory of social classes the primary truth *against* which it was constructed, in particular the veil of symbolic relations without which, in many cases, class relations would not be able to function in their 'objective' truth as relations of exploitation. In other words, objectivism forgets that misrecognition of the reality of class relations is an integral part of the reality of those relations. When the arbitrary differences recorded by statistical distributions of properties are apprehended in terms of a system of schemes of perception and appreciation objectively adjusted to the objective structures, they are recognized as legitimate; they then become signs of (natural) distinction and they function as a symbolic capital bringing in dividends of distinction directly related to their rarity (or, to put it another way, inversely related to their accessibility, their 'commonness' and 'vulgarity'). All appearances notwithstanding, the value of the properties capable of functioning as symbolic capital lies not in any intrinsic characteristic of the practices or goods in question, but in their marginal value, which, since it depends on their number, necessarily tends to decline as they are multiplied and popularized (on the struggles around titles and qualifications, see Bourdieu 1984: 160–5). Symbolic capital is the product of a struggle in which each agent is both a ruthless competitor and supreme judge (and therefore, in terms of an old opposition, both *lupus* and *deus*). This capital, or the titles that guarantee it, can only be defended, especially in times of inflation, by means of a permanent struggle to keep up with and identify with the group immediately above (either directly, for example, through marriage and all forms of public alliance and official co-option, or symbolically) and to distinguish oneself from the group immediately below.

The world of salons and snobbery as described by Proust offers a fine illustration of the struggles through which individuals or groups strive to modify, to their own advantage, the overall order of preferences arising from the whole set of judgements which constantly compete and combine in the market of symbolic values. The prestige of a salon (or a club) depends on the rigour of its exclusions (one cannot admit a person of low standing without losing in standing) and on the 'quality' of the persons received, which is itself measured by the 'quality' of the salons that receive them. Rises and falls on the stock exchange of society values, recorded in the 'court and social' columns of the 'quality' press, are measured by these two criteria, in other words a whole set of infinitesimal nuances which only an experienced eye can perceive. In a universe in which everything is classified, and therefore classifies – the places to be seen, smart restaurants, horse shows, inaugural lectures, exhibitions, conferences, the sights and shows one has to have seen, Venice, Florence, Bayreuth, the Russian Ballets, the enclaves to which not everyone is admitted, select salons and clubs – a perfect and perfectly up-to-date mastery of the classifications (which the taste-makers are quick to declare out of fashion as soon as they become too common) is required in order to get the best return from 'social' investments and avoid being identified with unfashionable groups.[4]

The struggles that take place even within spaces that are so homogeneous, at least to an outside observer, that they seem to create difference *ex nihilo*, completely belie the conservative philosophy of history, which identifies order with difference, a source of energy (creative energy, enterprise, etc., in the liberal credo), and denounces and deplores every threat to distinction as entropy, a relapse into the homogeneous, the undifferentiated, the indifferent. This 'thermodynamic' world-view, which inspires the fear of 'levelling-down', random distribution, submergence in the 'average', the 'mass', coexists with the dream of a bourgeoisie without a proletariat, nowadays expressed in the theory of the 'embourgeoisement of the working class' or the expansion of the middle classes to the limits of the social universe. It feeds on the idea that when difference declines, social energy – meaning, here, the class struggle – declines. In fact, contrary to the physicalist self-evidence which assumes that, in the case of continuous distribution, difference diminishes as proximity in the distribution grows, perceived differences are not objective differences, and social neighbourhood, the site of the *last* difference, has every chance of also being the point of greatest tension.

Minimum objective distance in social space can coincide with maximum subjective distance. This is partly because what is 'closest' presents the greatest threat to social identity, that is, differences (and also because the adjustment of expectations to real chances tends to limit subjective pretensions to the immediate neighbourhood). The logic of the symbolic makes absolute 'all or nothing' differences out of infinitesimal differences. This is, for example, the effect of the legal frontier or the *numerus clausus* (especially visible in competitive examinations) which establishes an absolute, durable distinction (between the legitimate heir and the bastard, the eldest and the younger sons, the last successful and the first unsuccessful candidate, etc.) in place of a continuity associated with different breaks in different respects. The struggle for the specific difference, the last difference, masks the generic properties, the common genus, the 'objective' solidarities, the class, which exist only for the outside observer and which the work of 'politicization' seeks to bring into the consciousness of the agents by overcoming the effects of their competititve struggles. These struggles aim not to abolish the classification or transform its principles but to modify individual positions in the classification, and they therefore imply a tacit recognition of the classification. Dividing those who are closest and most alike, they are the perfect antithesis and the most effective negation of the struggle against another class, in which the class itself is constituted.

If the symbolic struggle tends to be limited to the immediate neighbour-hood, and can only ever perform partial revolutions, this is also because it encounters its limit, as we have seen, in the institutionalization of indices of consecration and certificates of charisma such as titles of nobility or educational qualifications. objectified marks of respect calling for marks of respect, a spectrum of honours which have the effect of manifesting not only social position but also the collective recognition that it is granted by the mere fact of authorizing such a display of its importance. This official recognition implies the right and the duty ('noblesse oblige') to exhibit distinction officially and publicly in distinctive signs, officially codified and guaranteed (such as decorations), to hold the rank assigned by adopting the practices and symbolic attributes associated with it. 'Status groups' simply give an institutional, and even codified, form to the strategies of distinction, by strictly controlling the two fundamental operations of social logic, union and separation, which increase or reduce the rarity, and therefore the symbolic value, of the group. They do this as much on the symbolic terrain – by regulating the use of the symbolic attributes which manifest differences and underline ranks, that is, the distinctive signs of symbolic wealth, such as clothing or housing, or the emblems of social recognition, such as all the attributes of legitimate authority – as in real exchanges, which can imply a form of identification or, at least, mutual recognition, as in marriage, exchange of gifts or meals, or simple trade. The institutionalized strategies of distinction through which 'status groups' seek to make *de facto* differences permanent and quasi-natural, and therefore legitimate, by symbolically enhancing the effect of distinction associated with occupying a rare position in the social structure, are the self-consciousness of the dominant class.

In every social universe, each agent has to reckon, at all times, with the fiduciary value set on him, which defines what he is entitled to – among other things, the (hierarchized) goods he may appropriate or the strategies he can adopt, which, to have a chance of being recognized, that is, symbolically effective, have to be pitched at the right level, neither too high nor too low. But the extent to which differences are objectified in status barriers and sanctioned by legal frontiers setting a real limit to aspirations, rather than being marked by simple statistical limits, is the source of very important differences in symbolic practices. Everything suggests that recourse to symbolic strategies, and also their objective chances of success, increase as one moves from societies in which the limits between groups take the form of legal frontiers and where manifestations of difference are governed by sumptuary laws, to social worlds in which – as in the American middle classes, described by the interactionists – the objective indeterminacy of fiduciary value allows and encourages pretension (that is, the discrepancy between the value the subject sets on himself and the value he is officially or tacitly granted) and the bluffing strategies through which it operates.[5]

In fact, the institutionalization of distinction, inscribing it in the hard, durable reality of things or institutions, goes hand in hand with its incorporation, the surest path towards naturalization. When distinctive dispositions are accepted and acquired as self-evident from early childhood, they have all the appearances of naturally distinguished nature, a difference which contains its own legitimation. The profit of distinction is thus enhanced by the fact that the idea of supreme distinction (and therefore maximum profit) is associated with ease and naturalness in producing distinguished conduct, that is, with minimum cost of production. Thus, with the distinction that is called natural, although (as the word indicates) it only exists in the distinctive relationship with more 'common', that is, statistically more frequent, dispositions, the legitimizing theatricalization which always accompanies the exercise of power extends to all practices and in particular to consumption, which does not need to be inspired by the pursuit of distinction in order to be distinctive. The very life-style of the holders of power contributes to the power that makes it possible, because its true conditions of possibility remain unrecognized, so that it can be perceived not only as the legitimate manifestation of power but as the foundation of its legitimacy. 'Status groups' based on a 'life-style' and a 'stylization of life' are not, as Weber thought, a different kind of group from classes, but dominant classes that have denied or, so to speak, sublimated themselves and so legitimated themselves.

While, on the one hand, it has to be shown, contrary to mechanistic objectivism, that symbolic forms have a logic and an efficacy of their own which make them relatively autonomous with respect to the objective conditions apprehended in distributions, on the other hand it also has to be pointed out, contrary to marginalist subjectivism, that the social order is not formed, like an election result or a market price, by simple mechanical addition of individual orders. In the determination of the collective classification and the hierarchy of the fiduciary values set on individuals and groups, not all judgements have the same weight, and the dominant groups are able to impose the scale of preferences most favourable to their own products (in particular because they have a *de facto* virtual monopoly over the institutions which, like the educational system, establish and guarantee ranks). Moreover, the representations that agents have of their own and other agents' positions in social space (and also the representations they give of them, consciously or unconsciously, through their practices or their properties) are the product of a system of schemes of perception and appreciation which is itself the incorporated product of a class condition (that is, a particular position in the distributions of material properties and symbolic capital). It is based not only on the indices of the collective judgement but also on the objective indicators of the position really occupied in the distributions, which the collective judgement already takes into account. Even in the limiting case of 'high society', the site *par excellence* of symbolic speculation, the value of individuals and groups does not depend as exclusively as Proust suggests when he writes (1976: 22): 'Our social personality is created by the thoughts of other people' (or as Erving Goffman puts it, 'The individual must rely on others to realize his self-image'). The symbolic capital of those who dominate Proustian 'society', Charlus, Bergotte or the Duchesse de Guermantes, presupposes something more than the marks of disdain or respect, interest or indifference, which make up the play of reciprocal judgements; it is the exalted form assumed by realities as baldly objective as those that social physics records, mansions and estates, titles of property and nobility, academic distinctions, when they are transfigured by the enchanted perception, mystified and colluding, which defines snobbery (or, at another level, petit-bourgeois pretension).

The spurious alternatives of social physics and social phenomenology can only be superseded by grasping the principle of the dialectical relationship that is established between the regularities of the material universe of properties and the classificatory schemes of the *habitus*, that product of the regularities of the social world for which and through which there *is* a social world. It is in the dialectic between class conditions and 'class sense', between the 'objective' conditions recorded in distributions and the structuring dispositions, themselves structured by these conditions, that is, in accordance with the distributions, that the continuous structure of the distributions reappears, now transfigured and misrecognizable, in the discontinuous structure of hierarchized life-styles and in the representations and recognitions that arise from misrecognition of their objective truth.[6] Property and properties – expressions of the *habitus* perceived through the categories of the *habitus* – symbolize the differential capacity to appropriate, that is, capital and social power, and they function as symbolic capital, securing a positive or negative profit of distinction. The opposition between the material logic of rarity and the symbolic logic of distinction (which Saussure's use of the word 'value' reunites) provides both the principle of the opposition between a social dynamics, seeing only power relations, and a social cybernetics, attentive only to sense relations, and also the principle of its supersession.

Symbolic struggles are always much more effective (and therefore realistic) than objectivist economists think, and much less so than pure social marginalists think. The relationship between distributions and representations is both the product and the stake of a permanent struggle between those who, because of the position they occupy within the distributions, have an interest in subverting them by modifying the classifications in which they are expressed and legitimated, and those who have an interest in perpetuating misrecognition, an alienated cognition that looks at the world through categories the world imposes, and apprehends the social world as a natural world. This mis-cognition, unaware that it produces what it recognizes, does not want to know that what makes the most intrinsic charm of its object, its charisma, is merely the product of the countless crediting operations through which agents attribute to the object the powers to which they submit. The specific efficacy of subversive action consists in the power to bring to consciousness, and so modify, the categories of thought which help to orient individual and collective practices and in particular the categories through which distributions are perceived and appreciated.

Symbolic capital would be no more than another way of referring to what Max Weber called charisma, if Weber, who understood perhaps better than anyone that the sociology of religion is part of the sociology of power, had not been trapped in the logic of realist typologies. This leads him to see charisma as a particular form of power rather than as a dimension of all power, that is, another name for legitimacy, a product of recognition, misrecognition, the belief 'by virtue of which, persons exercising authority are endowed with prestige'. Snobbery or pretension are the dispositions of believers, constantly haunted by the fear of slipping, through a failure of tone or a sin against taste, and inevitably dominated by the transcendent powers to which they surrender by the mere fact of recognizing them, whether art, culture, literature, *haute couture* or other fetishes, and by the guardians of these powers, tyrannical taste-makers, couturiers, painters, writers or critics, pure creations of social belief who exercise a real power over the believers, whether it be the power to consecrate material objects by transferring on to them the collective sense of the sacred, or the power to transform the representation of those who give them their power.

Each state of the social world is thus no more than a temporary equilibrium, a moment in the dynamics through which the adjustment between distributions and incorporated or institutionalized classifications is constantly broken and restored. The struggle which is the very principle of the distributions is inextricably a struggle to appropriate rare goods and a struggle to impose the legitimate way of perceiving the power relations manifested by the distributions, a representation which, through its own efficacy, can help to perpetuate or subvert these power relations. Classifications, and the very notion of social class, would not be such a decisive stake in struggle (among the classes) if they did not contribute to the existence of the social classes, enhancing the efficacy of the objective mechanisms that determine the distributions and ensure their reproduction, by adding to them the consent of the minds which they structure. The object of social science is a reality that encompasses all the individual and collective struggles aimed at conserving or transforming reality, in particular those that seek to impose the legitimate definition of reality, whose specifically symbolic efficacy can help to conserve or subvert the established order, that is to say, reality.

BOOK II

Practical Logics

Introduction

The most obvious transformation of scientific practice that results from transforming – or more precisely, objectifying – the relationship to the object is the one that leads to abandonment of overt or implicit legalism and the language of rules and rituals, which expresses little more than the limits attached to the position of an outside observer and ignorance of these limits. In fact, the more the conditions of production of dispositions resemble the conditions in which they function to produce ordinary practices, the more socially successful, and therefore unconscious, these practices will be. The objective adjustment between dispositions and structures ensures a conformity to objective demands and urgencies which has nothing to do with rules and conscious compliance with rules, and gives an appearance of finality which in no way implies conscious positing of the ends objectively attained. Thus, paradoxically, social science makes greatest use of the language of rules precisely in the cases where it is most totally inadequate, that is, in analysing social formations in which, because of the constancy of the objective conditions over time, rules have a particularly small part to play in the determination of practices, which is largely entrusted to the automatisms of the *habitus*. This tends to prove that, in this case at least, discourse about the object says less about the object than about the author's relation to the object.   The movement that leads from rule to strategy is the same that leads from 'prelogical' thought or the 'savage mind' to the body as geometer, a 'conductive body' run through, from head to foot, by the necessity of the social world. It is the movement that leads one to situate oneself at the point of generation of practice in order to grasp it, as Marx says, 'as concrete human activity, as practice, in a subjective way'. This may be taken to mean that, to the extent that it overcomes the distant distance which constitutes practice as an object, set before the observer like a foreign body, this mode of thought enables one to become the 'theoretical subject' of other people's practice or one's own – but not at all as the eulogists of 'lived experience' suppose. This appropriation presupposes all the work needed first to objectify the objective or incorporated structures, and then to overcome the distance inherent in objectification, in order to make oneself the subject of what is other, in oneself and in others. So scientific work provides, in this case, a strange experience, bringing the stranger closer without taking away any of his strangeness, because it authorizes the most familiar closeness with the strangest aspects of the stranger while at the same time imposing a distance – the precondition for real appropriation – from the strangest aspects of what is most personal.

Anthropology then ceases to be a kind of pure art that is totally freed, by the distancing power of exoticism, from all the suspicions of vulgarity attached to politics, and becomes instead a particularly powerful form of socio-analysis. By pushing as far as possible the objectification of subjectivity and the subjectification of the objective, it forces one, for example, to discover, in the hyperbolic realization of all male fantasies that is offered by the Kabyle world, the truth of the collective unconscious that also haunts the minds of anthropologists and their readers, male ones at least. The colluding or horrified fascination that this description may arouse should not disguise the fact that the same discriminations which assign women to continuous, humble, invisible tasks are instituted, before our very eyes (increasingly so as one moves down the social hierarchy), both in things and in minds, and that it would not be difficult to find in the status accorded to homosexuals (and perhaps more generally to intellectuals) the equivalent of the image the Kabyles have of the 'widow's son' or the 'girls' boy', relegated to the most female of male tasks.

The division of sexual labour, transfigured in a particular form of the sexual division of labour, is the basis of the *di-vision* of the world, the most solidly established of all collective – that is, objective – illusions. Grounded first in biological differences, in particular those that concern the division of the work of procreation and reproduction, it is also grounded in economic differences, in particular those which derive from the opposition between labour time and production time and which are the basis of the division of labour between the sexes. More generally, every social order tends to perform a symbolic action oriented towards its own perpetuation by really endowing agents with the dispositions, and consequently the practices and properties, that the principles of di-vision assign to them. These principles, arising from social reality, contribute to the very reality of the social order by realizing themselves in bodies, in the form of dispositions which, produced by the classifications, give the appearance of a collective foundation to classificatory judgements, such as women's inclination towards 'humble and easy' tasks or flexible, submissive thinking. These dispositions are also at work in all the practices, like magic and so many other apparently more liberated forms of revolt, aimed at realizing the intention of subverting the established order in practices or discourses ordered in accordance with principles arising from that order.

1

Land and Matrimonial Strategies

The lord of an entailed estate, the first-born son, belongs to the land. It inherits him.

K. Marx, *1844 Manuscripts*

If most analysts have characterized the Béarn inheritance system as one of 'complete primogeniture' which could favour an eldest daughter as well as an eldest son, this is because their legalistic bias inclined them to see the fact of conferring on women not only part of the heritage but also the status of heir, as the distinctive feature of the system.[1] In fact, however, this transgression of the principle of male predominance, the main means of defending the interests of the lineage or (which amounts to the same thing) the patrimony, only represented a last resort in the defence of lineage and patrimony.[2] Only in the case of *force majeure* arising from the absence of any male descendant could the need to keep the patrimony in the lineage at all costs lead to the desperate solution of entrusting to a woman the task of transmitting the patrimony, the basis of the continuity of the lineage (for the status of heir did not fall to the first-born child, but to the first-born son, even if he was last in order of birth). The marriage of each of its children – older or younger, son or daughter – presented every family with a specific problem it could only solve by exploiting all the possibilities for perpetuating the patrimony offered by the tradition of succession and marriage. All means were legitimate in order to secure this overriding objective, and the family might well resort to strategies that the taxonomies of anthropological legalism would regard as incompatible. It might, for example, disregard the 'principle of predominance of the lineage', so dear to Meyer Fortes, and entrust women with the perpetuation of the patrimony; it might seek to minimize or even cancel out – if need be, through legal artifices – the consequences of inevitable concessions to a bilateral succession that would normally be disastrous for the patrimony. In a more general way, it might manipulate the relationships objectively present in the genealogical tree in such a way that they would, *ex post* or *ex ante*, justify the connections or alliances that best served the interests of the lineage, that is, the maintenance or expansion of its material and symbolic capital.

If the marrying of each of a family's children is seen as the equivalent of playing a card, then it is clear that the value of this move (measured by the criteria of the system) depends both on the quality of its 'hand' – the strength of the cards it has been dealt, as defined by the rules of the game – and on the skill with which it plays its hand. In other words, given that matrimonial strategies, at least in the best-placed families, always aimed to pull off a 'fine marriage' rather than just a marriage, that is, to maximize the economic and symbolic profits associated with setting up a new relationship, they were governed in each case by the value of the material and symbolic patrimony that could be committed to the transaction and by the mode of transmission of the patrimony, which defined the system of interests of each of the candidates for ownership of the patrimony by assigning to them different rights according to sex and order of birth. In short, for each individual, the matrimonial opportunities that are generically available to descendants of the same family by virtue of its social position, as defined, mainly though not exclusively, by the economic value of its patrimony, are specified by the mode of succession, on the basis of sex and birth rank.

While the main and most direct function of marriage strategy was to ensure the reproduction of the lineage and therefore of its labour force, it also had to ensure the continued integrity of the patrimony, in an economic environment dominated by scarcity of money. Since the share of the patrimony traditionally inherited and the compensation paid at the time of marriage were one and the same, the value of the property determined the value of the *adot* (from *adoutà*, to make a donation, dower), and this in turn determined the matrimonial ambitions of its holder. At the same time, the amount of the *adot* demanded by the family of the future spouse depended on the size of its own property. It follows that, through the mediation of the *adot*, the economy governed matrimonial exchanges, with marriages tending to take place between families of similar rank in economic terms.

The mass of the peasants was sharply differentiated from an 'aristocracy' set apart not only by its material capital but also by its social capital, measured by the value of a family's whole set of kin, in both lineages and over several generations,[3] by its style of life, which had to manifest its respect for the values of honour, and by the social consideration that surrounded it. Certain marriages were thereby defined as misalliances and were (as a principle) quite impossible. The status of the 'great' families was neither totally dependent on, nor totally independent of, their economic bases, and while considerations of economic interest were never absent when a family refused a misalliance, a 'modest house' might bleed itself white to marry one of its daughters to the eldest son of a 'great house', whereas the latter might reject an economically more advantageous match in order to marry according to his social rank. But the margin of acceptable disparity was always narrow, and beyond a certain threshold, economic differences effectively prevented alliances. In short, inequalities in wealth tended to determine the cut-off points within the field of possible partners that his or her family's position in the social hierarchy objectively assigned to each individual.

The legalistic vocabulary which informants readily use to describe the ideal norm or to account for a particular case handled and reinterpreted by notaries, reduces the complex and subtle strategies used by families – who alone are competent (in both senses) in these matters – to formal rules. Each of the younger sons or daughters was entitled to a specified share of the patrimony, the *adot*. Because this share was usually given at the time of marriage, almost always in cash to avoid fragmentation of the property and only exceptionally in the form of a piece of land (which, however, constituted no more than a security redeemable at any time through the payment of the sum agreed upon in advance), it is often mistakenly seen as a dowry. In fact, however, it was only a compensation given to the younger children in exchange for their renouncing any claim to the land. When a family had only two children, the younger child's share was assessed at one-third of the value of the property. In other cases, a quarter of the value of the property was excluded from the division and set aside for the eldest child; the younger children received a share equal to the value of the rest divided by the number of children (the first-born thus receiving a quarter plus one share).

The property would be valued as precisely as possible, with local experts, chosen by the various parties, being consulted in cases of dispute. Agreement was reached on the price of the *journade* (literally, 'day's work') of fields, woods and heaths, based on the sale price of property in the same or a neighbouring village. These calculations were fairly exact and were therefore accepted by all parties. 'For example, the T. property was valued at 30,000 francs (in about 1900). The family consisted of the father and mother and six children – a boy and five girls. The eldest son was given a quarter, 7,500 francs. That left 22,500 francs to be divided into six parts. The share of the daughters was 3,750 francs each, of which 3,000 francs was paid in cash and 750 francs in the form of clothes and linen – sheets, towels, napkins, shirts, eiderdowns – the 'wardrobe' (*lou cabinet*) that the bride always brought to the marriage' (J.-P. A., aged 85 in 1960).

In fact, division was never more than a solution of despair. The extreme rarity of liquid capital (related, at least in part, to the fact that wealth and social status was measured first and foremost by the size of landed property) sometimes made it impossible to pay the compensation, even though custom allowed payments to be spread over several years or even deferred until the death of the parents. In such cases, division had to take place when one of the younger children married or when the parents died, in order to pay the *adots* in cash or transfer their equivalent in land, with the hope of one day restoring the unity of the patrimony by somehow raising the money needed to repurchase the land that had been sold.

On the principle that property belongs less to the individual than to the lineage, the 'right of repurchase' (*retrait linager*) gave any member of the lineage the possibility of recovering possession of goods which might have been alienated. 'The "mother house" (*la maysou mayrane*) retained "rights of return" (*lous drets de retour*) on land given as a dowry or sold. In other words, when that land was sold, it was known that this or that house had rights over it and they would be given first option' (J.-P. A.).

Although my fieldwork did not include systematic questioning designed to establish the frequency of division over a given period of time, this appears to have been a rare, even exceptional occurrence which was therefore faithfully recorded in the collective memory. For example, it was said that, about 1830, the B. estate and house (a large, two-storey house, *a dus soulès*) were divided among the heirs who had not been able to settle matters amicably. As a result the estate is now 'criss-crossed with ditches and hedges'. 'After these divisions, there were sometimes two or three families living in the house, each in its own section and each with its own share of the land. The room with a fireplace always went to the eldest son. That happened with the H., Q. and D. properties. At the A.'s, there are some pieces of land that never came back. Some were bought back later, but not all. The division created terrible difficulties. In the case of the Q. property, which was divided among three children, one of the younger sons had to take his horses right round the neighbourhood to reach a far-away field that had been assigned to him' (P. L.).

But the family property would have been very poorly protected if the formula defining the *adot*, and consequently marriage itself, had been applied with the rigour of a legal rule and if there had not been other ways to avoid the threat of division, which was always regarded as a disaster. In fact, it was the parents who 'made the eldest', as the saying went, and various informants state that in earlier times the father was completely free to decide the amount of compensation to be paid to younger children, since the proportions were not fixed by any rule. In any case, since we know that in many families the children, and especially the young couple, had no information about, still less any control over the family finances, until the death of the 'old folks' (any income from important transactions, such as sale of livestock, was entrusted to the 'old lady' and locked away in the cupboard), it is unlikely that the legal rules were ever very strictly applied, except in the pathological cases brought to the attention of the law and its notaries, or those conceived in advance by legalist pessimism, which were invariably provided for in contracts but were statistically exceptional.[4]

The head of the family was in fact always at liberty to manipulate the 'rules' (starting with those of the *Code civil*) if he wished to favour one of his children, more or less secretly, by means of cash gifts or fictitious sales. It would be extremely naive to be taken in by the word 'distribution' (*partage*) which was sometimes used to describe the family 'arrangements' in fact designed to avoid the division of the property. One of these was the 'institution of the heir', which usually took place by mutual consent when one of the children married, or else was stipulated in a will (many men did this when they were called up in 1914). Following an evaluation of the property, the head of the family proceeded to define the claims of all his children: those of the 'heir', who might not be the eldest, and of the other children, who often readily endorsed provisions that were more generous to the heir than those of the *Code civil* or even of customary law. If the arrangement was made at the time of the marriage of one of the younger children, he or she would receive a portion, the equivalent of which would be given to the others either when they married or when the parents died.

The head of the family was in a position to put the interest of the patrimony before the tradition that the title of heir normally went to the first-born son. He might decide on such a course if, for example, the eldest son was unworthy of his rank or if there was a real advantage in having another child inherit (for example, in the case where a younger son, by his marriage, could easily bring about the unification of two neighbouring properties). The father's moral authority was so great and so strongly approved by the whole group that the customary heir had no choice but to submit to a decision that was dictated by the concern to ensure the continuity of the house and to give it the best possible management. The eldest son automatically lost his title if he left the household, since the heir is always the one who stays on the land, as is still seen clearly nowadays.

But we would continue to be taken in by the fallacies of legalistic thinking if we continued to cite examples of anomic or regulated transgressions against the supposed rules of succession. If it is not certain that 'the exception proves the rule', it does at least tend to confirm the existence of the rule. All means were justified when it came to protecting the integrity of the patrimony and preventing the potential division of the estate and the family which every marriage could threaten to bring about.

The principles which, through the mediation of the *adot*, tended to exclude marriages between families too unequally matched, as a result of a kind of implicit optimizing calculation aimed at maximizing the material and symbolic profit that could be gained through the matrimonial transaction while preserving the family's economic independence, were combined, in determining matrimonial strategies, with the principles that gave supremacy to men and primacy to the eldest son. The supremacy of men over women implied that, even though claims to the property could sometimes be transmitted through the female line, and even though the family (or 'house'), a monopolistic group defined by ownership of a specific set of assets, could abstractly be identified with all those who had claims to these assets, regardless of their sex, the status of heiress could, as we have seen, only fall to a woman in the last resort, namely in the absence of any male descendants. Daughters were relegated to the status of younger children, whatever their birth rank, by the existence of a single boy. This is only logical when one knows that the status of 'master of the house' (*capmaysouè*), the trustee and guarantor of the name, reputation and interest of the group, implied not only property rights but also the political right to exercise authority within the group and, especially, to speak and act on behalf of the family in its relations with other groups.[5] Within the logic of the system, this right could only fall to a man, either the eldest of the agnates or, failing this, the husband of the heiress, an heir through the female line who, if he became the spokesman of his adoptive lineage, in some cases even had to sacrifice his family name to the 'house' that had appropriated him by entrusting him with its property.[6]

The second principle, the primacy of the eldest over younger siblings, tends to make the patrimony the true subject of the economic and political decisions of the family. Identifying the interests of the designated head of the family with those of the patrimony is a more reliable way of establishing his identification with the patrimony than any expressly stated, explicit norm. To assert that power over the land, placed in the hands of the eldest son, is indivisible amounts to asserting the indivisibility of the land and to making the eldest son its guarantor and defender. (A proof that the 'right of the first-born' is only the transfigured assertion of the rights of the patrimony over the first-born can be seen in the fact that the opposition between older and younger children was only pertinent in land-owning families; it had no significance for the poor – smallholders, farm hands or domestic servants: 'There's no such thing as older or younger', said an informant, 'when there's nothing to chew on.') The arbitrariness of the act of *instituting* the eldest son as the heir, hanging a social distinction on a biological difference, often marked by visible differences in appearance, such as height, is not perceived as such: it is apparently nature which, through birth-rank, designates from the outset the person who belongs to the land and to whom the land belongs. Instituted difference will subsequently, on the whole, tend to be transmuted into natural distinction, because the group has the power to impose an objective – and therefore subjective – difference on those whom it treats differently: here, elder and younger sons, elsewhere men and women, nobles and commoners. The institution of the heir, which, like every act of institution, belongs to the logic of magic, is brought to completion through incorporation. If, as Marx says, the property appropriates its owner, if the land inherits its inheritor, this is because the inheritor, the eldest son is the land (or the firm) made flesh, incarnated in the form of a structure generating practices consistent with the fundamental imperative of perpetuating the integrity of the heritage.

The priority given to the eldest son, a simple genealogical translation of the absolute primacy of maintaining the integrity of the patrimony, combined with the pre-eminence of the male members of the lineage to favour strict homogamy, ruling out the 'upward marriages' that would be encouraged by pursuit of maximum material and symbolic profit. The eldest son must not marry too high, not only because of the fear of one day having to return the *adot*, but also and more especially because this would threaten his position in the domestic power relations. Nor must he marry too low, for fear of dishonouring himself by misalliance and being unable to dower the younger brothers. A younger brother, even more than the eldest, must avoid the material and symbolic risks and costs of misalliance and can even less indulge the temptation to marry too manifestly above his station, for fear of putting himself in a dominated and humiliating position.[7]

Despite the work of inculcation carried out by the family and constantly reinforced by the whole group, which, especially if he belonged to a 'great house', repeatedly reminded an eldest son of the duties and privileges of his rank, the identification of the inheritor with the heritage did not always proceed without conflicts and dramas. It was not free from contradictions between structures and dispositions, which might be experienced as conflicts between sentiment and duty; nor did it exclude subterfuges designed to satisfy personal interests within the limits of social acceptability. Thus parents who, in other cases, might themselves bend the custom to suit their own inclinations (for example, by allowing a favourite child to accumulate a little nest-egg),[8] felt duty-bound to forbid misalliances and to force their children, regardless of feelings, into the unions most likely to safeguard the social structure by safeguarding the position of the family within the structure. In short, they would make their eldest son pay the price of his privilege by subordinating his own interests to those of his lineage:

'I have seen people give up a marriage for the sake of 100 francs. The son wanted to marry. "How are you going to pay the younger children? If you want to marry [that girl], you can leave home!" The T.'s had five younger daughters. The parents always gave the eldest son special treatment. He always got the best bit of salt meat, and all the rest. Mothers often spoil their eldest son until he talks of marriage. . . . The daughters got no meat or anything else. When the time came for the eldest son to marry, three of the girls were already married. The boy was in love with a girl who didn't have a penny. His father said, "So you want to marry? I've already paid for three of your sisters, you must bring in the money to pay for the two others. A wife isn't made to go in the china cabinet [i.e. to be shown off]. That girl's got nothing. What can she bring?" The boy married one of the E. daughters instead and received a dowry of 5,000 francs. The marriage didn't work. He took to drink and went to pieces. He died childless' (J.-P. A.).[9]

Those who wanted to marry against their parents' will had no choice but to leave home, at the risk of being disinherited in favour of a brother or sister. This extreme solution was particularly hard for the eldest son of a 'great house', who was expected to live up to his rank: 'The eldest son of the B.'s couldn't leave. He had been the first one in the hamlet to wear a jacket. He was an important man, a municipal councillor. He couldn't run off. Besides, he wouldn't have been able to earn his living. He had become too much of a gentleman (*enmoussurit*)' (J.-P. A.).

Moreover, so long as the parents were alive, the heir had only potential rights over the property, so that he did not always have the means to uphold his rank, and had less freedom than younger sons, or eldest sons of lesser rank. '"You'll get everything", the parents would say, but in the meantime they wouldn't let go of anything.' This formula, often used ironically, because it seems to sum up the arbitrariness and tyranny of the 'old folks', goes to the heart of the tensions generated by every mode of reproduction which, like this one, carries people without transition from the class of resourceless heirs to that of legitimate owners. It depended on forcing the heirs to accept the restrictions and sacrifices of a prolonged minority in the name of the distant gratifications attendant upon their coming of age; and parental authority, which was the main means of perpetuating the lineage, could misfire and bring about the opposite result when an eldest son who could neither revolt against his parents' power nor renounce his feelings resigned himself to celibacy.

If the heir, who was privileged by the system, could not always be brought into line, how could younger sons, who were sacrificed to the imperatives of the land, be brought to co-operate? It should, of course, not be forgotten (as can happen if marriage strategies are considered in isolation) that fertility strategies could also help to solve the problem, which would disappear completely if, by chance, the first-born child was a boy. Hence the crucial importance of the sex of the first child. If it was a boy, the succession could be entrusted to an only child if procreation were suspended at that point. If the birth of a girl was never greeted with enthusiasm ('When a girl is born in a house', a proverb says, 'one of the main beams comes falling down'), it was because in all cases she was a bad card to have in one's hand, even though she could, in fact and in principle, be upwardly mobile, marrying above her station, unhindered by the social barriers imposed on a boy. For if she were the heiress, that is, an only child (though this was rare since families kept hoping for a male heir) or the eldest of several daughters, she could not ensure the preservation and continuity of the patrimony without putting the lineage at risk, since if she married an eldest son, her 'house' would be in a sense annexed to another, and if she married a younger son, domestic power (at least after her parents died) would pass to a stranger. And if she were a younger daughter, she would have to be married off, and therefore dowered, since, unlike a son, she could neither be sent away nor usefully be kept at home unmarried, because the labour she could provide would not meet the cost of her upkeep.[10]

Let us now consider the case in which the progeny included at least one son, whatever his birth-rank. Their heir might or might not be an only child. In the latter case, he might have one or several brothers, one or several sisters, or one or more of each. These various 'hands', which in themselves offered very unequal chances of success to a player with a given level of skill, required different strategies, varying in their difficulty and in the profits they could win.

When the heir was an only son,[11] one would assume that the marriage strategy would stake everything on obtaining as high an *adot* as possible through marriage with a rich younger daughter, thereby bringing in money without surrendering any. However, the endeavour to maximize the material or symbolic profit to be gained from a marriage, if need be through strategies of bluff (always difficult and risky in a world in which almost everyone knew everyone), was limited by the economic and political risks inherent in an unequal or, as it was called, an 'upward' marriage. The economic risk was the *tournadot*, return of the dowry, which could be demanded should the husband or the wife die before the birth of a child. This eventually aroused fears out of proportion to its likelihood: 'Suppose a man marries a girl from a great family. She brings him a dowry of 20,000 francs. His parents say to him: "You take the 20,000 francs and you think you have done well. In fact, you're taking a chance. You've received a dowry by contract. You're going to spend some of it. What if something goes wrong? How are you going to give it back, if you have to? You can't!"' (P. L.). Most people took care to leave the *adot* intact in case it had to be returned.[12]

What might be called the political risk was probably taken more directly into account in these strategies, since it involved one of the fundamental principles of all practices. Due to the bias in favour of the male in the cultural tradition, which judged every marriage from the male point of view (a 'downward' marriage thus always implicitly meant one between a man of higher status and a woman of lower status), there was no reason, aside from economic considerations, why the eldest daughter of a modest family should not marry a younger son from a great family, whereas the eldest son of a modest family could not marry the younger daughter of a great family. In other words, among all the marriages made for reasons of economic necessity, only one type was fully recognized, namely an alliance in which the arbitrary cultural bias in favour of the man was confirmed by a corresponding discrepancy in the social and economic status of the spouses. The greater the amount of the *adot*, the more it reinforced the position of the spouse who brought it into the marriage. Although, as we have seen, domestic power was relatively independent of economic power, the size of the *adot* was one of the foundations of the balance of authority within the family, particularly in the structural conflict between the mother-in-law and her daughter-in-law.

It used to be said of an authoritarian mother-in-law, 'She won't let go of the ladle', the symbol of authority over the household. Wielding the ladle was the prerogative of the mistress of the house. When the meal was ready and the pot boiling, she would put the 'sops' of bread in the tureen, pouring the soup and vegetables over them. When everyone was seated, she would bring the tureen to the table, stir the soup with the ladle to soak the bread, then turn the handle towards the head of the family (grandfather, father or uncle), who would serve himself first. Meanwhile the daughter-in-law was occupied elsewhere. To remind her daughter-in-law of her rank, the mother would say, 'I'm not giving you the ladle yet.'

Thus, as mistress of the household, a mother who might, in other circumstances, use all the means at her disposal to prevent a 'downward' marriage, would be the first to oppose her son's marriage with a woman of (relatively) too high status. She was well aware that it would be much easier to exert authority over a girl from a modest background than over one of those girls from a great family who, as the saying went, 'came in [as] mistresses of the household (*qu'ey entrade daune*)'. (Mention of the marriage settlement would be the clinching argument in the crises of domestic power when the usually censored 'economic' truth was revealed: 'When I think what you brought!' The imbalance was sometimes such that only when the mother-in-law died could it be said of the young wife 'Now she's the *daune*'.) The risk of asymmetry was greatest when the heir married a younger daughter of a large family. Given the approximate equivalence (shown by the ambiguity of the word *adot*) between the *adot* paid at the time of marriage and the share of the patrimony – that is, other things being equal, between patrimonies likely to be allied by marriage – the *adot* of a girl from a rich but very large family might well not be greater than that of a girl from a modest family who had only one brother. The apparent balance between the value of the *adot* and the value of the family patrimony might then conceal a discrepancy that could lead to conflict, since authority and the claim to authority depended as much on the material and symbolic capital of the family of origin as on the amount of the dowry.

Thus, by defending her authority, that is, her interest as the mistress of the house, with an authority which itself depended on her initial contribution (and here it can be seen that the whole matrimonial history of the lineage is involved in each marriage), the mother was simply defending the interests of the lineage against usurpers from outside. In other words, 'upward marriage' threatened the pre-eminence that the group assigned to its men, as much in social life as in work and domestic matters (the larger the dowry that she had brought in, the better placed the mother was to pursue the path opened up by her marriage, that is, to marry off her son in her native village or neighbourhood).

The question of political authority within the family became most acute, however, when an eldest son married an eldest daughter, especially if the heiress was the wealthier of the spouses. Except in cases where it united two neighbours and therefore two neighbouring properties, this type of marriage tended to create a permanent back-and-forth between the two homes or even led the spouses to maintain separate residences. (Hence the unanimous disapproval: 'That happened to T. when he married the D. girl. He keeps going back and forth between the two places. He's always on the road, he's everywhere, he's never at home. The master should be there' [P. L.].) What was at stake, in this open or hidden conflict over the place of residence, was, again, the predominance of one or the other lineage and the extinction of a 'house' and its name. It is significant that in all the attested cases, properties united in this way were eventually separated, often in the very next generation, when each of the children received one of them as their inheritance.

Perhaps because it approached the question of the economic bases of domestic power more realistically than other societies (it was said that, in order to assert his authority over the marriage, the groom should step on the bride's dress, if possible during the blessing, and that the bride should crook her ring finger so that the groom could not push the ring right down), perhaps because, as a consequence, its representations and strategies are closer to the objective truth, Béarnais society suggests that the sociology of the family, which is so often abandoned to the realm of pure sentiment, might be simply a particular case of political sociology. The position of the spouses in the domestic power relations and their chances of success in the competition for authority over the family, that is, for the monopoly of the legitimate exercise of power in domestic affairs, are never independent of the material and symbolic capital that they possess or have brought into the marriage (although the nature of that capital may vary according to the time and the society).

However, a male heir without siblings was a relatively rare phenomenon. In all other cases, the marriage of the heir largely determined the size of the *adot* that could be given to his younger siblings, hence the kind of marriage they could make and even their chances of marrying at all. The best strategy therefore consisted of obtaining from the parents of the heir's bride an *adot* sufficiently large to pay the *adots* of younger sons and daughters without having to divide or mortgage the property, yet not so large as to burden the patrimony with the threat of having to repay an impossibly large dowry. This means, incidentally – contrary to the anthropological tradition of treating each marriage as an autonomous unit – that every matrimonial transaction can only be understood as a stage in a series of material and symbolic exchanges, since the economic and symbolic capital that a family is able to commit to the marriage of one of its children is largely dependent on the position this exchange occupies in the entire matrimonial history of the family and the balance-sheet of these exchanges. This is obvious when the first son to be married uses up all the resources of the family, or when a younger daughter marries before her older sister, who is then more difficult to 'place' on the marriage market because she is suspected of having some hidden flaw (it was said of a father in this situation: 'He has put the one-year heifer – *l'anouille* – to the yoke before the two-year-old – *la bime*'). Appearances notwithstanding, the case of an eldest son who had a sister (or sisters) was quite different from that of one who had a brother (or brothers). As all informants spontaneously indicated, the *adot* of girls was almost always greater than that of boys, which tended to increase their chances of marriage. The reason, as has been seen, was that families had no alternative but to marry off these useless mouths, and as quickly as possible.

In the case of younger sons, there was more room for manoeuvre, the first reason being that an abundant, even superabundant, supply of labour created a hunger for land which could only benefit the patrimony. Families were therefore in less of a hurry to marry off a younger son (except, perhaps, the second son in a great family) than a younger daughter or even an eldest son. One way would be to marry him to an heiress; this was the commonest course, and the one best suited to his interests, if not necessarily to those of the lineage. If he married into a family of the same rank (as was usually the case), in short, if he brought a good *adot*, and made his mark in terms of work and fertility (a proverb puts it very realistically: 'If he's a capon, we'll eat him; if he's a cock, we'll keep him'), then he was honoured and treated as the new master. If, on the other hand, he married 'upwards', he was made to sacrifice everything to his new house: his *adot*, his labour, and sometimes his name (Jean Casenave, for example, might become Yan dou Tinou, 'Jean of the Tinou house'). Such a transgression of the principle of male pre-eminence – of which the limiting case was the marriage of a man-servant to his female employer –

incurred great disapproval. There were very few younger sons attracted by the uncertain prospects entailed by marriage with a younger daughter, sometimes called 'the marriage of hunger and thirst' and also 'sterile', *esterlou* (a destitution which the poorest of them could only avoid by hiring themselves out, with their wives, as 'kept servants'). On the other hand, the possibility of founding a family while remaining in the parental home was a privilege reserved for eldest sons. For these reasons, younger sons who failed to marry an heiress with the aid of their *adot*, sometimes supplemented with a small, laboriously accumulated nest-egg (*lou cabau*), had only two options: they could emigrate to the city or to America in the hope of setting themselves up in some craft; or they could forgo marriage and become servants either to their own family or (in the case of the very poorest) to others.

It is not sufficient to say that families were in no hurry to marry off their younger sons: quite simply, they did not press the matter. And, in a world of matrimonial *dirigisme*, this *laissez-faire* attitude was enough to lessen their chances of marriage considerably. Some families even went so far as to make payment of the *adot* conditional upon the younger son agreeing to work for the eldest for a number of years; some entered into what were nothing less than work contracts with him; and some even deferred payment by making him hope for a larger share. But there were many other ways for a younger son to become a confirmed bachelor, from the marriage that failed to materialize to the imperceptible acceptance of delay until he was 'past the marrying age', with the complicity of families who were consciously or unconsciously not disinclined to keep their 'unpaid servant' in their service, for a time at least. In opposite ways, both the son who left home to make his living in the city or to seek his fortune in America, and the son who stayed at home supplying his labour without increasing the costs of the household and without detracting from the property, contributed to the preservation of the patrimony. (In principle, the younger son had the use of his share for his lifetime; if he died unmarried, it reverted to the heir.)

Thus the younger son was, so to speak, the structural victim – the socially designated and therefore resigned victim – of a system that placed a whole armoury of protective devices around the 'house', a collective entity and an economic unit, or rather, a collective entity defined by its economic unity. The adherence, inculcated from early childhood, to the traditional values and the customary division of tasks and powers between brothers, attachment to the family estate, the house, the land, the family and, perhaps especially, to the children of the elder brother, were enough to incline many younger brothers to accept this life which, in Frédéric Le Play's superbly functionalist phrase, 'gives the serenity of bachelorhood along with the joys of the family'. Because everything led them to invest and even over-invest in a family and a patrimony that they had every reason to see as their own, the stay-at-home younger brothers represented (from the standpoint of the 'house', that is, the system) the perfect domestic servant, whose private life was invaded and annexed by his employer's family life, who was consciously or unconsciously encouraged to invest much of his time and private emotions in his borrowed family, especially in the children, and who usually had to renounce marriage as the price for the economic and emotional security of sharing in the life of the family.

It is said that occasionally, if the eldest son had no children, or left none when he died, his younger brother, now an old bachelor, would be asked to marry to ensure the continuity of the lineage. Marriage between a younger brother and the widow of the eldest, from whom he inherited (the levirate), though not really an institution, was relatively frequent. After the 1914–18 war, marriages of this type were fairly numerous: 'These things were worked out. Generally the parents pushed for it, in the interest of the family, because of the children. And the young people went along with it. Feelings had nothing to do with it' (A. B.).

Hidden, or rather denied, forms of exploitation, especially those that draw part of their strength from the specific logic of kinship relations, in other words from the experience and language of duty and feeling, have to be seen in their essential ambiguity. The disenchanted vision that brutally reduces these relationships to their 'objective' truth is, strictly speaking, no less false than the view of observers who, like Le Play, catch only the subjective, that is, mystified, representation of the relationship. Misrecognition of the 'objective' truth of the relation of exploitation is part of the full truth of the relation, which can exist in this form only to the extent that it is misrecognized. The economy of exchanges between spouses or between ascendants and descendants, which is experienced and expressed in denial and sublimation, and which is therefore predisposed to serve as a model for all gentle (paternalistic) forms of exploitation, cannot be reduced to the theoretical model of the 'objective' relation between the owners of the means of production and the sellers of labour power. On the contrary, it forces us to see that the 'objective' truth of this latter relationship would itself not have been so difficult to extract and present, if it were in all cases the truth of the subjective relation to work, with all the forms of investment in the activity itself, the material and symbolic gratifications it gives, the specific interests attached to the job and the relations it entails, and even, in many cases, attachment to the firm or its owner.

One sees how artificial or quite simply beside the point it is to ask questions concerning the relationship between structures and sentiments. Individuals and even families were capable of recognizing only the most openly respectable criteria, such as the virtue, the good health and beauty of a girl, or the dignity and zest for work of a young man, while at the same time they never ceased to identify the really pertinent criteria beneath these appearances, namely the value of the patrimony and the size of the *adot*. There are several reasons why, in the great majority of cases, the system was able to work on the basis of the criteria least pertinent in terms of the real principles of its functioning. First, family upbringing tended to ensure a very close correlation between the basic criteria demanded by the system and the characteristics most important in the eyes of the agents: thus, just as the eldest son of a 'great house' was particularly inclined to the virtues of the 'man of honour' and the 'good peasant', so the 'great heiress', or the 'good younger sister' could not settle for the average virtue that might be good enough for a girl from an ordinary family. Furthermore, the earliest learning experiences, reinforced by all subsequent social experience, tended to shape schemes of perception and appreciation, in a word, *tastes*, which were applied to potential partners as to other things: and even without any directly economic or social calculation, these tastes tended to rule out misalliances. Socially approved love, love predisposed to succeed, is nothing other than that love of one's own social destiny that brings socially predestined partners together along the apparently random paths of free choice. The exceptional, pathological cases, in which parental authority had to be openly asserted to repress individual feelings, were vastly outnumbered by cases in which the norm could remain tacit because the agents' dispositions were objectively attuned to the objective structures, in a spontaneous compliance which removes all need to point out the proprieties.

One should not be misled by the language of analysis or by the very words of the informants, who were chosen for their lucidity and provoked into lucidity by questioning. Here, as elsewhere, the agents obey the impulses of feeling or the injunctions of duty more than the calculations of interest, even when, in doing so, they conform to the economy of the system of constraints and demands of which their ethical and affective dispositions are the product. The denied truth of the economy of exchanges among kinsmen is openly expressed only in the crises which have precisely the effect of bringing back the calculation continuously repressed or sublimated into the blind generosity of feeling. This objective (or objectivist) truth remains a partial truth, neither more nor less true than the enchanted experience of ordinary exchanges. Faced with the dangers that every marriage presents for the patrimony and therefore the lineage, owing to the fact that the compensation due to the younger brothers could force the break-up of the patrimony – which the privilege of the eldest son was precisely intended to avoid – families respond with a range of actions designed to overcome this specific contradiction of the system. Their responses are not like the procedures the legal imagination invents in its efforts to bend the law (as the language inevitably used to describe it might suggest), nor even consciously calculated strategies akin to the consecrated 'winning moves' in chess or fencing. The superficially very different solutions – birth control, emigration or celibacy of younger sons, etc. – which, depending on their position in the social hierarchy, their rank in the family or their sex, the different agents produce for the practical antimonies arising from systems of demands that are not automatically compatible, have their common origin in the *habitus*, which is the product of the structures that it tends to reproduce and which implies a 'spontaneous' submission to the established order and to the orders of the guardians of that order. Marriage strategies are inseparable from inheritance strategies, fertility strategies, and even educational strategies, in other words from the whole set of strategies for biological, cultural and social reproduction that every group implements in order to transmit the inherited powers and privileges, maintained or enhanced, to the next generation. Their principle is neither calculating reason nor the mechanical determinations of economic necessity, but the dispositions inculcated by the conditions of existence, a kind of socially constituted instinct which causes the objectively calculable demands of a particular form of economy to be experienced as an unavoidable call of duty or an irresistible impulse of feeling.

2

The Social Uses of Kinship

There are the ordinary responses of codified routine, the breviary of usages and customs, the accepted values, which constitute a kind of inert knowledge. Above this, there is the level of invention, which is the domain of the *amusnaw* (the sage), who can not only implement the accepted code, but adapt it, modify it, and even revolutionize it.

Mouloud Mammeri, 'Dialogue sur la poésie orale en Kabylie'

Marriage with a parallel patrilateral cousin (*bent âamm*, father's brother's daughter), a legitimate quasi-incest, appears 'as a sort of scandal', as Claude Lévi-Strauss (1959: 13–14) puts it, only in terms of the taxonomies of the anthropological tradition. It calls into question the notion of exogamy, which is the precondition for the reproduction of separate lineages and the permanence and easy identification of the consequent groups, and so radically challenges theories of unilineal descent as well as the theory of marriage alliance, which sees marriage as the exchange of one woman for another and assumes an incest taboo, that is, the imperative of exchange. The exogamy rule clearly distinguishes alliance groups and descent groups, which, by definition, cannot coincide, genealogical lineages being by the same token clearly defined, since powers, privileges and duties are transmitted either matrilineally or patrilineally. Endogamy, by contrast, results in a blurring of the distinction between lineages. Thus, in the limiting case of a system actually based on marriage with the patrilateral cousin, a given individual would be related to his paternal grandfather equally through his father or his mother. But, on the other hand, by choosing to keep the parallel cousin, a quasi-sister, within the lineage, the group would deny itself the possibility of receiving women from outside and so forming alliances. One then has to consider whether it is sufficient to regard this type of marriage as the exception (or 'aberration') that confirms the rule, or to adjust the categories of thought that gave rise to it in order to make a place (that is, a name) for it; or whether one must radically question the categories of thought that produce this 'unthinkable' thing. Thus, it is not sufficient to observe that, while valid in the case of a society with exogamous groups that distinguishes strictly between parallel and cross kin, the use of the notion of 'preferential marriage' is no longer justified in the case of a society that has no exogamous groups. We have to go further and find in this exception a reason for questioning not only the very idea of prescription or preference and, more generally, the notion of the rule and of rule-governed behaviour (in the twofold sense of behaviour objectively conforming to the rules and determined by obedience to the rules), but also the notion of a genealogically defined group, an entity whose social identity is as invariant and univocal as the criteria that delimit it and which gives each of its members an equally distinct, permanently fixed, social identity.

The language of prescription and rules is so clearly inadequate in the case of patrilateral marriage that one is bound to endorse the questions of Rodney Needham (1958) as to the conditions of validity, perhaps never fulfilled, of such a language, which is nothing other than the language of law. But this inquiry into the epistemological status of such commonly used concepts as rule, prescription or preference inevitably challenges the theory of practice that they presuppose: one can, even implicitly, treat the 'algebra of kinship', as Malinowski called it, as a theory of kinship practices and 'practical' kinship, without tacitly postulating a deductive relationship between kinship terms and 'kinship attitudes'? And one can give an anthropological significance to this relationship without postulating that the regulated, regular relations between kinsmen are the product of obedience to rules which, though a residual Durkheimian scruple leads Radcliffe-Brown to call them 'jural' rather than legal, are assumed to control behaviour in the same way as the rules of law?[1] Finally, one can make the genealogical definition of groups the only principle for defining social units and assigning agents to these groups, thereby implicitly postulating that agents are defined in all respects, once and for all, by their membership of the group and that, in short, *the* group defines the agents and their interests more than the agents and their interests define different *groups* in terms of their interests?

RECENT THEORIES

The most recent theories of marriage with the parallel cousin, those of Frederik Barth (1953) and of Robert Murphy and Leonard Kasdan (1959), though diametrically opposed, do have in common the fact that they appeal to functions that structuralist theory either ignores or brackets off, whether economic functions, such as retentions of the patrimony within the lineage, or political functions, such as the reinforcement of lineage integration. It is difficult to see how they could do otherwise without making absurd a marriage which obviously does not fulfil the function of exchange and alliance commonly attributed to cross-cousin marriage.[2] Barth emphasizes that endogamous marriage 'plays a prominent role in solidifying the minimal lineage as a corporate group in factional struggle'. By contrast, Murphy and Kasdan criticize Barth for explaining the institution 'through reference to the consciously felt goals of the individual role players', or more precisely by reference to the lineage head's interest in keeping close control over his nephews, who represent points of potential segmentation. Thus Murphy and Kasdan relate this type of marriage to its 'structural function', that is, to the fact that it 'contributes to the extreme fission of agnatic lines . . . and, through in-marriage, encysts the patrilineal segments'. Lévi-Strauss is perfectly justified in stating that the two opposing positions amount to exactly the same thing: in fact, Barth's theory makes of this type of marriage a means of reinforcing lineage unity and limiting the tendency to fission, while Murphy and Kasdan's theory sees in it the principle of a quest for integration into larger units, founded on the appeal to a common origin and ultimately encompassing all Arabs. So both admit that parallel-cousin marriage cannot be explained within the pure logic of the matrimonial exchange system and that any explanation must necessarily refer to external economic or political functions.

Above all, both these theories accept an undifferentiated definition of the function of marriage, which reduces it to the function for the group as a whole. For example, Murphy and Kasdan (1959: 27) write: 'Most explanations of patrilateral parallel cousin marriage are of a causal-motivational kind, in which the institution is explained through reference to the consciously felt goals of the individual role players. We have not attempted to explain the origin of the custom in this paper but have taken it as a given factor and then proceeded to analyze its function, i.e. its operation within Bedouin social structure. It was found that parallel cousin marriage contributes to the extreme fission of agnatic lines in Arab society, and, through in-marriage, encysts the patrilineal segments.' Those who explain marriage strategies in terms of their effects – for example, Murphy and Kasdan's fission and fusion are effects that one gains nothing by calling 'functions' – are as far from the reality of practices as those who invoke the efficacy of the rule. To say that parallel-cousin marriage has a function of fission and/or fusion without asking for whom and for what, and to what extent (which would need to be measured), and on what conditions, is to resort, discreetly of course, to explanation by final causes instead of considering how the economic and social conditions characteristic of a social formation induce the search for satisfaction of a particular type of collective interests which itself leads to the production of a particular type of collective effects.

Jean Cuisenier simply draws out the consequences of this observation, in a construction that attempts to account for the inconsistencies noted by all observers between the 'model' and actual practice, together with at least the economic external functions of matrimonial exchanges:

'It is native thinking itself which gives us a clue to an explanatory model. This model in fact represents the alliances knit together in one group on the basis of the fundamental opposition between two brothers, of whom one must marry endogamously in order to maintain the coherence of the group, while the other must marry exogamously in order to gain alliances for the group. This opposition between the two brothers is found at all levels of the agnatic group; it expresses in the usual genealogical terminology of Arab thought a choice between alternatives which may be represented as a "partial order" diagram in which the numerical values of a and b are 1/3 and 2/3 respectively. If a represents the choice of endogamy and b the choice of exogamy, and if one follows the branchings of the two-part family tree from the root, the choice of *a* at the most superficial of the genealogical circles is the choice of the parallel cousin (1/3 of the cases)' (Cuisenier 1962).

One might be tempted to see it as a virtue of this model that it seeks to account for the statistical data, in contrast to traditional theories of preferential marriage which went no further than to state the divergence, which is attributed to secondary factors, such as demography, between the 'norm' (or the 'rule') and actual practice.[3] But one only has to adopt a more or less restrictive definition of the marriages assimilable to parallel-cousin marriage, in order to move away, to a greater or lesser extent, from the magical percentage (36% = 1/3?) which, when combined with a native maxim, generates a 'theoretical model'; and it is then clear that the model fits the facts so perfectly only because it has been made to measure to fit the facts, that is, invented *ad hoc* to account for a statistical artefact, and not built up from a theory of the principles of production of the practices. There is an equation for the curve of each face, said Leibniz; and nowadays there will always be a mathematician to prove that two cousins each parallel to a third are parallel to each other . . .

But the intention of subjecting genealogies to statistical analysis at least has the virtue of revealing the most fundamental properties of genealogies, an analytical tool which is itself never analysed. One immediately sees what is odd about the idea of calculating rates of endogamy when, as here, it is the very notion of en endogamous group, and therefore the basis of calculation, that is in question.

Cuisinier – here echoing Lévi-Strauss, who points out that 'from the structural viewpoint, one can treat marriage with the father's brother's daughter and marriage with the father's son's daughter as equivalent' (Lévi-Strauss 1959: 55) – writes: 'On the other hand, Ego may marry his paternal uncle's granddaughter or his paternal great-uncle's daughter. From the structural viewpoint, the first of these unions can be assimilated to marriage with the paternal uncle's daughter, and the second to marriage to the paternal great-uncle's granddaughter' (Cuisenier 1962: 84). When the anthropologist combines the nominalism that treats the coherence of the system of terms as the practical logic of dispositions and practices, with the formalism of statistics based on abstract divisions, he is led to perform genealogical manipulations which have a practical equivalent in the devices that the agents use to mask the discrepancies between their matrimonial practices and the ideal representation they have of them or the official image they want to give of them. (For example, when the need arises, they may subsume under the term parallel cousin not only the paternal uncle's daughter but also patrilateral cousins of the second or even third degree, such as the father's brother's son's daughter, or the father's father's brother's daughter, or the father's father's brother's son's daughter, and so on; not to mention the manipulations of kinship vocabulary involved in, for example, using the term *âamm* as a polite form of address for any older patrilateral relative.) Calculation of 'rates of endogamy' by genealogical level, an unreal intersection of abstract 'categories', leads one to treat as identical, by a second-order abstraction, individuals who, although at the same level on the genealogical tree, may be of widely differing ages and whose marriages may for this reason have been arranged in different circumstances corresponding to different states of the matrimonial market. Or, conversely, it may lead one to treat genealogically different but chronologically simultaneous marriages as different – when, for example, a man marries at the same time as one of his uncles.

Is one to be satisfied with classifications abstractly performed on paper, that is, on the basis of genealogies that have the same extent as the memory of the group, the structure and extent of which themselves vary with the functions assigned by the group to those whom it remembers and forgets? Recognizing in a lineage diagram an ideological representation resorted to by the Bedouins in order to achieve a 'primary understanding' of their present relationships,[4] E. L. Peters (1967) points out that the diagram ignores the real power relations between genealogical segments, that it forgets the women, and that it treats the most basic ecological, demographic and political factors as 'contingent accidents'.[5] Or should one adopt the divisions that the agents themselves perform on the basis of criteria that are not necessarily genealogical? It is then found that an individual's chances of making a marriage that can be socially regarded as equivalent to marriage with his *bent âamm* increase with the size of the 'practical', that is, practically mobilizable, lineage (and therefore the number of potential partners) and with the strength of the pressures and demands that incline or force him to marry within the lineage. Once the family property is divided up, and there is nothing left to underline and maintain the genealogical connection, the father's brother's daughter may be no closer, in the practically perceived social space, than any other patrilateral (or even matrilateral cousin). By contrast, a genealogically more remote cousin may be the practical equivalent of a *bent âamm* when the two cousins belong to the same strongly united 'house' living under the authority of one elder and holding all its property in common. When informants repeatedly insist that people marry less within their own lineage than they used to, they are perhaps simply victims of an illusion created by the decline of the great undivided families.

FUNCTIONS OF KINSHIP AND THE BASIS OF GROUPS

It is not sufficient to follow the example of the more circumspect observers, who prudently slip from the notion of preferential marriage with the parallel cousin to the notion of 'lineage endogamy', trusting that this vague and impressive language will resolve the problems raised by the notion of endogamy and obscured by the too-familiar concept of the *group*. It is first necessary to ask what is implied in defining a group exclusively by the genealogical relationship linking its members and in thereby implicitly treating kinship as the necessary and sufficient condition of group unity. As soon as we ask explicitly about the functions of kin relationships, or, more bluntly, about the usefulness of kinsmen, it is immediately clear that those uses of kinship that might be called genealogical are reserved for official occasions, in which they serve the function of ordering the social world and legitimating that order. They are opposed in this respect to other kinds of practical uses of kinship relations, which are a particular case of the use of relationships. The genealogical diagram of kinship relations that the anthropologist constructs merely reproduces the official representation of the social structures, which is produced by the application of a structuring principle that is dominant in a certain respect, that is, in certain situations and with a view to certain functions.

To point out that kin relationships are something that people make, and with which they do something, is not simply to substitute a 'functionalist' interpretation for a 'structuralist' one, as the prevailing taxonomies might suggest. It is radically to question the implicit theory of practice which leads the anthropological tradition to see kin relationships 'in the form of an object or an intuition', as Marx puts it, rather than in the form of the practices that produce, reproduce or use them by reference to practical functions. If everything that concerns the family were not hedged with denials, there would be no need to point out that the relations between ascendants and descendants themselves only exist and persist by virtue of constant maintenance work, and that there is an economy of material and symbolic exchanges between the generations. The same is true of affinal relationships: it is only when one records them as a *fait accompli*, as the anthropologist does when he establishes a genealogy, that one can forget that they are the product of strategies oriented towards the satisfaction of material and symbolic interests and organized by reference to a particular type of economic and social conditions.

By the mere fact of talking of endogamy and of trying, out of a laudable concern for rigour, to measure its degrees, one assumes the existence of a purely genealogical definition of the lineage. In fact, every adult male, at whatever level on the genealogical tree, represents a point of potential segmentation, which may be actualized for a particular social purpose. The further back in time and genealogical space we locate the time of origin – and nothing prevents a regression to infinity in this abstract space – the more we push back the boundaries of the lineage and the more the assimilative power of genealogical ideology grows, but only at the expense of its distinctive power, which increases as we move closer to the point of common origin. Thus the use that can be made of the expression *ath* (the descendants of, the people of . . .) obeys a positional logic altogether similar to that which, according to Evans-Pritchard, characterizes the uses of the word *cieng*: the same person may, depending on the circumstances, the situation and the interlocutor – that is, depending on the assimilative or distinctive function of the term – call himself a member of the Ath Abba, that is, a 'house' (*akham*), the most restricted unit, or, at the other extreme, a member of the Ath Yahia, that is, a tribe (*âarch*), the broadest group. The absolute relativism that would give agents unlimited power to manipulate their own social identity, or that of the adversaries or partners they seek to assimilate or exclude, by manipulating the limits of the class they each belong to, would at least have the virtue or repudiating the naive realism of those who cannot characterize a group other than as a population defined by directly visible boundaries. In fact, the structure of a group (and hence the social identity of the individuals who make it up) depends on the function which is the basis of its constitution and organization.

This is what is forgotten by precisely those who try to escape from genealogical abstraction by contrasting the 'descent line' with the 'local line' or 'local descent group', that portion of a unilineal descent group which, by virtue of common residence, is able to act collectively as a group (cf. Dumont 1971: 122–3). The effects of social distance also depend on the function that the social relationship aims to achieve. For example, while it may be assumed that the potential usefulness of a partner tends to decrease with distance, this is not the case with prestige marriages, where the more distant the people between whom the relationship is set up, the greater the symbolic profit. Likewise, if unity of residence contributes to the integration of the group, the unity that its mobilization for a common function gives to the group tends to overcome the effect of distance.

In short, although it can in theory be maintained that there are as many possible groups as there are functions, the fact remains that one cannot call on absolutely *anyone* for *any* occasion, nor can one offer one's services to *anyone* for *any* purpose. Thus, to escape from relativism without falling into realism, we may posit that the constants of the field of partners who are both usable, because they are spatially close, and really useful, because they are socially influential, cause each group of agents to tend to devote constant work to maintaining a privileged network of practical relationships. This network includes not only the set of those genealogical relationships that are kept in working order (which I shall call practical kinship) but also all the non-genealogical relationships that can be mobilized for the ordinary needs of existence (that is, practical relationships).

The negotiation and celebration of marriage provides a good opportunity to observe everything that, in practice, separates official kinship, which is unambiguous and immutable, defined once and for all by the norms of genealogical protocol, from practical kinship, whose boundaries and definitions are as numerous and varied as the users and the occasions on which it is used. Practical kin make marriages; official kin celebrate them. In ordinary marriages, the contacts preceding the official proposal (*akh'tab*) and the least avowable negotiations relating to areas which the official ideology tends to ignore, such as the economic conditions of the marriage, the status offered to the wife in her husband's home, or relations with the future mother-in-law, are left to the persons least qualified to represent the group and to speak on its behalf (who can therefore be disowned if necessary), such as an old woman, usually a sort of professional in these secret meetings, a midwife or some other woman used to moving from village to village. In the difficult negotiations between distant groups, a well-known, prestigious man from a group sufficiently distant from the 'wife-takers' to appear neutral and to be in a position to act in collusion with another man occupying roughly the same position in relation to the wife-givers (a friend or affine rather than a kinsman) will be entrusted with delivering the declaration of intent (*assiwat' wawal*). He will avoid coming straight to the point, but will try to find a seemingly chance opportunity (his apparent lack of intention implying a lack of calculation) to meet someone from the 'girl's side' and disclose to him the intentions of the interested family.

The official marriage proposal (*akht'ab*) is presented by the least responsible of those responsible, that is, the elder brother and not the father, the paternal uncle and not the grandfather, etc., accompanied, especially if he is young, by a kinsman from another line. Successively, men who are increasingly close to the prospective bridegroom and increasingly prestigious (for example, on the first occasion, the elder brother and the maternal uncle, next the paternal uncle and one of the prominent members of the group, then, the third time, the same people accompanied by several group and village notables such as the *t'aleb*, later joined by the village marabouts, then the father accompanied by notables from the adjacent villages and even the neighbouring tribe, etc.) come to present their 'solicitation' (*ah'allal*) to men in the bride's family who genealogically and spatially are increasingly distant. Eventually, the most important and most distant of the girl's kin come and intercede with the girl's mother and father on behalf of the closest and most prestigious of the young man's kin, after having been asked to do so by the latter group. Finally, acceptance (*aqbal*) is proclaimed before the largest possible number of men and conveyed to the most eminent kinsmen of the young man by the most eminent of the girl's kinsmen, who has been asked to support the proposal.

As negotiations proceed and begin to look successful, official kin begin to take the place of practical kin, the hierarchy with respect to utility being almost exactly the opposite of the hierarchy with respect to genealogical legitimacy. There are several reasons for this. First, it is not advisable in the early stages to involve kinsmen who, because of their genealogical and social position, might commit the principals too deeply – especially since the immediate inferiority of having to ask is often combined with structural superiority, when the man is marrying beneath him. Secondly, not everybody can be asked to put himself in the position of a supplicant who might encounter a refusal, and *a fortiori* to undertake negotiations which will bring no glory, are often painful, and sometimes bring dishonour on the two parties (like the practice of *thajâalts*, which consists of paying money to secure the intervention of some of the bride's kin to put pressure on the kin responsible for the decision). Finally, the search for maximum efficiency in the practical phase of negotiations directs the choice towards persons known to command great skill, to enjoy particular authority over the family in question, or to be on good terms with someone in a position to influence the decision. And it is natural that, in the official phase, those who have actually 'made' the marriage should have to make do with the place assigned to them not by their usefulness but by their position in the genealogy; having played their parts as 'utility men', they must make way for the 'leading actors'.

Thus, to schematize, the kinship that is put on display is opposed to practical kinship as the official is opposed to the unofficial (which includes the secret and the scandalous); as the collective to the particular; as the public, explicitly codified in a magical or quasi-legal formalism, to what is private, kept implicit and even hidden; as collective ritual – practice without a subject, which can be performed by collectively mandated and interchangeable agents – to private strategy, which is directed towards satisfying the practical interests of a particular individual or group. Abstract units produced by simple theoretical division, such as, here, the unilineal descent group (elsewhere, age groups), are available for all functions, in other words for none in particular, and have practical existence only for the most official uses of kinship. Thus 'representational' kinship is nothing other than the group's self-representation and the almost theatrical presentation it gives of itself when acting in accordance with that self-image. By contrast, practical groups exist only through and for the particular functions in pursuance of which they have been effectively mobilized; and they continue to exist only because they have been kept in working order by their very use and by maintenance work (including the matrimonial exchanges that they make possible) and because they rest on a community of dispositions (the *habitus*) and interests such as that which is also the basis of the undivided ownership of the material and symbolic patrimony.

If the official set of individuals amenable to definition by the same relationship to the same ancestor at the same level on the genealogical tree can sometimes constitute a practical group, this is because in this case the genealogical divisions correspond to units based on other principles, whether ecological (neighbourhood), economic (undivided patrimony) or political. The fact that the descriptive values of the genealogical criterion is that much greater when the common origin is nearer and the social unit is more limited does not mean that its unifying efficacy necessarily rises in the same way. In fact, as we shall see, the closest genealogical relationship, that between brothers, is also the site of the greatest tension, and incessant work is required to maintain solidarity. In short, the genealogical relationship never completely predetermines the relationship between the individuals it unites. The extent of practical kinship depends on the capacity of the members of the official group to overcome the tensions engendered by the conflict of interests within the common production and consumption group, and to keep up the kind of practical relationships that correspond to the official view of itself which is held by every group that sees itself as a corporate unit. On this condition, they may enjoy both the advantages accruing from every practical relationship and the symbolic profits secured by the approval socially conferred on practices conforming to the official representation of practices, that is, the social idea of kinship.

All the strategies with which agents aim to 'fall in line' with the rule and so to get the rule on their side remind us that representations, and especially kinship taxonomies, have an efficacy which, although purely symbolic, is none the less quite real. The structures of kinship fulfil a political function (like religion or any other official representation) in so far as they are used as means of knowledge and construction of the social world. Terms of address and reference are first and foremost kinship *categories*, in the etymological sense of collective, public imputations (*katègoreisthai* originally meant to accuse someone publicly), collectively approved and attested as self-evident and necessary. As such, they contain the magical power to institute frontiers and constitute groups, by performative declarations (one only has to think of all that is implied in a phrase like 'She's your sister', the only practical statement of the incest taboo) that are invested with all the strength of the group that they help to make.

The symbolic power of categoremes is most clearly seen in the case of proper names, which, as emblems concentrating all the symbolic capital of a prestigious group, are subject to intense competition. To appropriate these indices of genealogical position (so-and-so, son of so-and-so, son of so-and-so, etc.) is in a sense to take possession of a title giving special rights over the patrimony of the group. To give a new-born child the name of a great ancestor is not only to perform an act of filial piety but, as it were, to predestine the child to 'resurrect' the eponymous ancestor, to succeed him in his duties and powers. (Here as elsewhere, the present state of the relations of power and authority governs the collective representation of the past. This symbolic projection of the power relations between competing groups and individuals further helps to reinforce those power relations by giving the dominant agents the right to profess the memory of the past most likely to legitimate their present interests).

A new-born child is not normally given the name of a living relative. This is avoided because it would mean 'bringing him back to life' before he was dead, thereby throwing down an insulting challenge, and worse, casting a curse on him. This is true even when the break-up of the undivided patrimony is consecrated by a formal sharing out or when the family splits up on moving to the city or emigrating to France. A father cannot give his son his own first name, and when a son does bear his father's name it is because the father has died leaving him 'in his mother's womb'. But, here as elsewhere, there is no lack of subterfuges and loopholes. Sometimes the name the child was first given is changed so as to give him a name made available by the death of his father or grandfather (the original name is then reserved for private use, by his mother and the women of the family). Sometimes the same first name is given in slightly different forms to several children, with an element added or and removed (for example, Mohand Ourabah instead of Rabah, or vice versa), or with a slight alteration (Beza instead of Mohand Ameziane, Hamimi or Dahmane instead of Ahmed). Similarly, although giving a child the same name as his elder brother is avoided, certain associations of names that are very close to one another or derived from the same name are much appreciated (Ahcene and Elhocine, Ahmed and Mohamed, Meziane and Moqrane, etc.), especially if one of them is the name of an ancestor.

The most prestigious first names, like the noblest pieces of land, are the object of regulated competition, and, because it continuously proclaims the genealogical relationship with the ancestor whose memory is preserved within and beyond the group, the 'right' to appropriate the most coveted first name is distributed according to a hierarchy analogous to the one that governs the obligations of honour in the case of vengeance or the rights to land belonging to the patrimony in the case of sale. Thus, since first names are transmitted in direct patrilineal line, a father may not give his child the name of his own *âamm* or his own brother (the child's *âamm*) if the latter have left sons who are already married and thus in a position to give their father's name to one of their own sons or grandsons. Here as elsewhere, one should not be misled by the convenient language of norms and obligations ('must', 'may not', etc.). Thus, a younger brother has been known to take advantage of a favourable balance of power to give his son the first name of a prestigious brother who had died leaving only young children; the children subsequently set their point of honour on retaking possession of the first name which they saw as legitimately theirs, whatever confusion might ensue. The competition is particularly evident when several brothers wish to give their children their father's first name. Whereas the need to rescue it from neglect and fill up the gap that has appeared requires that the name should be given to the first boy born after the death of its bearer, the eldest son may delay using it and save it for one of his grandsons, instead of leaving it for the son of one of his younger brothers, thus jumping a genealogical level. But it can also happen that, for lack of male descendants, a name threatens to escheat; the responsibility for 'resurrecting' it falls first to the collaterals and then on the group as a whole, which thereby demonstrates that its integration and its wealth in men enable it to re-use the names of all its direct ascendants and also to make good any gaps arising elsewhere (one of the functions of marriage with the daughter of *âamm*, when the latter dies without male descendants, is to enable his daughter to ensure that her father's name does not disappear).

Kinship categories institute a reality. What is commonly called conformism is a form of the sense of reality (or, to put it another way, an effect of what Durkheim called 'logical conformism'). The existence of an official truth – which, with the whole group behind it, as is the case in a relatively undifferentiated society, has the objectivity of what is collectively recognized – defines a form of specific interest, attached to the correctness of the official. Marriage with the parallel cousin is backed by the reality of the ideal. If native discourse is taken too seriously, one is liable to present the official truth as the norm of practice; but if one distrusts it too much, one is liable to underestimate the specific efficacy of the official and to fail to understand the second-order strategies through which agents seek to secure the profits associated with conformity by disguising their strategies and interests under the veil of obedience to the rule.[6]

The true status of kinship taxonomies, principles of structuration of the social world, which, as such, always fulfil a political function, is most clearly seen in the different uses that men and women may make of the same field of genealogical relations, especially in the different 'readings' and 'uses' they make of genealogically ambiguous kinship ties (which arise fairly often because of the narrow area of matrimonial choice). In all cases of genealogically ambiguous relationship, one can always bring a remote relative closer, or move closer to him, by emphasizing what unites, and one can equally well distance the closest relative by emphasizing what separates. What is at stake in these manipulations, which it would be naive to regard as fictitious on the grounds that they deceive no one, is nothing other than the definition of the practical limits of the group, which can be made to run, as required, beyond or short of a person one wants to exclude or annex. The uses made of the term *khal* (literally, 'mother's brother') give an idea of these subtleties: used by a marabout to a common, lay peasant, it expresses his desire to set himself apart, by indicating, within the limits of courtesy, the absence of any legitimate kin relationship; used by one peasant to another, it indicates the willingness to set up a minimal relationship of familiarity by invoking a distant, hypothetical affinal relationship.

The anthropologist is accepting the official reading when, for example, with his informants' blessing, he assimilates to parallel-cousin marriage the relationship between second-degree patrilateral parallel cousins, one of whom is himself the child of a parallel-cousin marriage, and *a fortiori* when both are children of such a marriage (as in the case of the exchange of women between the sons of two brothers). The male, that is to say, the dominant, reading, which is imposed with particular force in all public, official situations – in short, in all the relationships of honour, where one man of honour is speaking to another – privileges the noblest aspect, the one most worthy of public proclamation, in a multi-faceted relationship that links each of the individuals to be situated to his or her patrilineal forebears and, through the latter, to the patrilineal forebears they have in common. It represses the other possible pathway, albeit more direct and often more convenient practically, which would reckon through the women. Thus (see figure 1, case 1), genealogical propriety requires Zoubir to be regarded as having married in Aldja his father's father's brother's son's daughter, or his father's brother's daughter's daughter, rather than his mother's brother's daughter, even if, as was actually the case, this latter relationship was the origin of the marriage; or again, to cite another case from the same genealogy, that Khedoudja should be seen as her husband Ahmed's father's father's brother's son's daughter, instead of being treated as a cross cousin (father's sister's daughter), which she equally well is (case 2). The heretical reading, which privileges the relations through women that are excluded from the official account, is reserved for private situations, or even for magic, which, like insults, designates its victim as 'his mother's son'. Apart from the cases in which women are speaking to women about a woman's kin relationships, when the language of kinship through women is taken for granted, this language may also be current in the most intimate sphere of family life, that is, in a woman's conversations with her father and his brothers or her husband, her sons or even perhaps her husband's brother, when it takes on the value of an assertion of the intimacy of the group of interlocutors.

But the multiplicity of readings has an objective basis in the fact that marriages that are identical purely in terms of genealogy may have different and even opposite meanings, depending on the strategies to which they belong. These strategies can only be understood by reconstructing the whole system of relations between the groups thereby associated and the state of these relations at a given moment in time. As soon as one ceases to consider only the genealogical properties of marriages and looks at the strategies and the conditions that made them possible and necessary, that is, the individual and collective functions they have fulfilled, it becomes clear that two marriages between parallel cousins may have nothing in common, depending on whether they were concluded in the lifetime of the common paternal grandfather, and possibly by him (either with the consent of the two fathers or 'over their heads'), or by direct agreement between the two brothers; in the latter case, depending on whether they were concluded when the future spouses were still children or already of marriageable age (not to mention cases where the bride is already 'past' the age), depending on whether the two brothers work and live separately or have maintained completely undivided ownership of the whole estate (land, livestock and other goods) and the domestic economy (a 'common

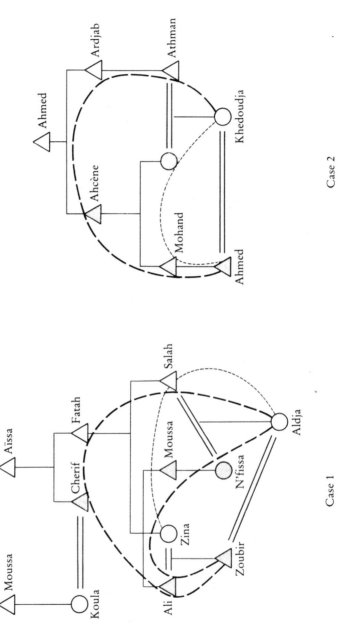

Case 1

Case 2

Figure 1

cooking-pot'), not to mention cases where they only keep the appearances of non-division; depending on whether it is the elder brother (*dadda*) who gives his daughter to his younger brother or who takes the latter's daughter, since difference in age and especially birth rank may be associated with differences in social rank and prestige; depending on whether the brother who gives his daughter has a male heir or is without male descendants (*amengur*); depending on whether both or only one of the brothers is alive at the moment when the marriage is arranged, and, more precisely, whether the surviving brother is the groom's father, the natural protector of the girl he takes for his son (especially if she has no adult brother), or whether the girl's father can take advantage of his dominant position to exert power over his son-in-law. And, as if to compound the ambiguity of this marriage, it is not uncommon for the obligation to sacrifice oneself, to be the 'veil cast over shames' and protect a suspect or disgraced girl, to fall to a man from the poorest branch of the lineage; it is then easy, convenient and praiseworthy to praise his eagerness to perform a duty of honour towards the daughter of his *âamm* or even to exercise his 'right' as a male member of the lineage.[7]

In practice, marriage with the parallel cousin only becomes unavoidable in extreme circumstances, such as the case of the daughter of the *amengur*, the man who has 'failed' by not producing a male heir. In this case, interest and duty coincide to require the marriage of the parallel cousins, since the *amengur*'s brother and his children will in any case inherit not only the land and the house of the 'failed' man but also his obligations towards his daughters (particularly in the case of widowhood or repudiation), and since this marriage is, moreover, the only way of avoiding the threat that marriage to a stranger (*awrith*) would present to the honour of the group and perhaps to its patrimony.

The obligation to marry the parallel cousin also applies when a daughter has not found a husband, or at least not found one worthy of her family. 'He who has a daughter and does not marry her off must bear the shame of it.' The relationship between brothers is such that a man cannot withhold his daughter when his brother, especially an elder brother, asks for her for his son. In this limiting case, when the taker is also the giver, inasmuch as he is the equivalent of and substitute for the father, to shirk the obligation is scarcely conceivable, as when an uncle asks for his niece on behalf of someone to whom he has given a commitment. It would, moreover, be a serious slight to a man's brothers for him to marry off his daughter without informing and consulting them, and a brother's disapproval, often invoked to justify a refusal, is not always a ritual pretext. The demands of solidarity are even more binding, and refusal is unthinkable, when, going against all propriety (it is always the man who 'asks' for the woman in marriage), the girl's father offers her for his nephew, hinting at it as discreetly as possible – although, to go against custom in this way, one has to be able to count on a very strong bond between closely united brothers. The fact remains that, since honour and dishonour are held in common, the two brothers have the same interest in 'covering up the shame before it is unveiled', or, in the language of symbolic interest, before the family finds that its symbolic capital has been devalued by the lack of takers for its daughters on the matrimonial market.

Here too, however, every sort of compromise and, of course, strategy is to be found. Although, in the case of land, the best-placed relative may be aware that more distant kin would willingly steal a march on him and win the symbolic and material advantages accruing from such a meritorious purchase, or, in the case of the vengeance of honour, that a rival avenger is ready to step in and take over the revenge and the ensuing honour, nothing similar occurs in the case of marriage, and many ploys are used to evade the obligation. Sometimes the son takes flight, with his parents' connivance, thereby providing them with the only acceptable excuse that a brother can be given. Short of this extreme solution, it is not uncommon for the obligation to marry left-over daughters to devolve upon the 'poor relations', who are 'obliged' in all sorts of ways to the richer members of the group. There is no better proof of the ideological function of marriage to the parallel cousin (or to any female cousin in the paternal lineage, however distant) than the use that may be made, in such cases, of the exalted representation of this ideal marriage.

In short, even in extreme cases where the choice of the parallel cousin becomes a compelling obligation, there is no need to appeal to ethical or juridical rules in order to account for practices which are the result of strategies consciously or unconsciously oriented towards the satisfaction of a particular type of material or symbolic interests.

Informants constantly remind us by their very incoherences and contradictions that a marriage can never be fully defined in genealogical terms, and that it may take on different, even opposite, meanings and functions, according to the conditions that determine it. They also remind us that parallel-cousin marriage may be the worst or the best of marriages depending on whether it is seen as voluntary or forced, that is, depending primarily on the relative positions of the families in the social structure. It can be the best of marriages ('marriage with your *âamm*'s daughter is honey in your mouth'), not simply from the mythic point of view but also in terms of practical advantages, since it is the least onerous economically and socially – the negotiation and material and symbolic costs being reduced to a minimum – and at the same time the safest: the same terms are used to contrast a close marriage with a distant one as are used to contrast direct exchanges between peasants with market transactions.[8] It can also be the worst kind of union ('The marriage of "paternal uncles" – *azwaj el laâmum* – is bitter in my heart; I pray you, O my God, preserve me from that misfortune' [Hanoteau 1867: 475]), and also the least prestigious ('Friends have come who are greater than you; you remain, you who are black'), whenever it is forced on the group as a last resort. In short, the apparent incoherence of the informants' discourse in fact draws our attention to the practical ambiguity of a genealogically unequivocal marriage, and thereby to the manipulations of the objective meaning of practice and its product which this combination of ambiguity and clarity allows and encourages.

One example will suffice to give an idea of the economic and symbolic inequalities which may be hidden behind the mask of the genealogical relationship between classificatory parallel cousins and also to bring to light the political strategies cloaked in the legitimacy of this relationship (see figure 2). The spouses both belong to the 'house of Belaïd', a great family both in terms of numbers (ten or so men of working age and some fifty people in all) and economic capital. Because

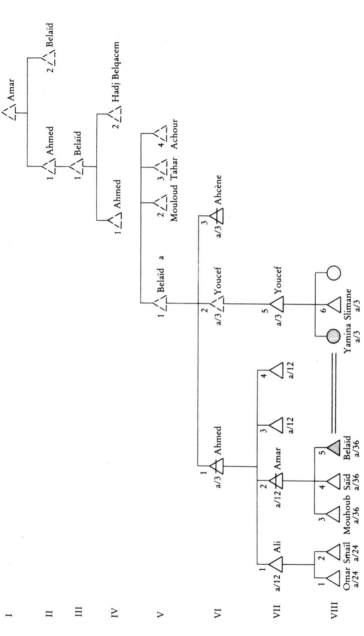

Figure 2 This simplified genealogy (which omits marriages other than those between VIII5 and the daughter of VII5, and omits all daughters except those of VII5) shows the structure of kinship at the time of the marriage in question, and therefore does not include the sons born subsequently

undivided ownership is never anything other than a refusal to divide, the inequalities which separate the potential 'shares' and the respective contributions of the different lines are strongly felt. Thus the line of the descendants of Ahmed, from which the bridegroom comes, is much richer in men than the line of Youcef, to which the bride belongs, and which is correspondingly richer in land. Wealth in men, considered as reproductive strength and therefore as the promise of still greater wealth in men, is related, provided one knows how to make the capital work, to a number of advantages, the most important of which is authority in the conduct of the internal and external affairs of the house: 'The house of men is greater than the house of cattle *(akham irgazen if akham izgaren)*'. The pre-eminent position of the line of Ahmed is shown by the fact that it has been able to take over the first names of the remote ancestors of the family and that it includes Ahcène, who represents the group in all major external encounters, whether conflicts or ceremonies, and Ahmed, the 'wise man' who by his mediation and counsel ensures the unity of the group. The bride's father (Youcef) is totally excluded from power, not so much on account of the difference in age between him and his uncles (Ahcène and Ahmed), since Ahmed's sons, although much younger than him, are associated with the decisions, but above all because he has cut himself off from competition among the men, from all exceptional contributions and even to a certain extent from work on the land. An only son, and, moreover, 'son of the widow', coddled by a whole set of women (mother, aunts, etc.) as the one hope of the lineage, kept away from the games and work of the other children in order to go to school, he has remained in a marginal position all his life. After a period of army service and then agricultural labour abroad, now that he is back in the village he takes advantage of his favourable position as the possessor of a large part of the patrimony with only a few mouths to feed, restricting himself to the work of overseeing, gardening and tending – those tasks that require the least initiative and entail the least responsibility, in short, the least male of male jobs.

These are some of the elements that have to be borne in mind in order to understand the internal and external political function of the marriage between Belaïd, the last son of Asmar, himself the son of Ahmed, the uncle of Youcef – and Youcef's daughter Yamina, his classificatory parallel cousin (father's father's brother's son's daughter). This marriage, arranged by Ahmed the 'wise man' and Ahcène the diplomat, the holders of power – as usual, without consulting Youcef, and leaving his wife to protest in vain against a union bringing little profit – reinforces the position of the dominant line, strengthening its links with the line rich in land, without in any way compromising its external prestige, since the domestic power structure is never declared outwardly.

Thus the complete truth of this marriage resides in its twofold truth. The official image, that of a marriage between parallel cousins in a large family anxious to demonstrate its unity by a marriage that reinforces it at the same time as displaying its adherence to the most sacred of the ancestral traditions, coexists without contradiction, even for outsiders, who are always well enough informed never to be taken in by the representations they are given, with knowledge of the objective truth of a union which sanctions the forced alliance between two social units sufficiently attached to each other negatively, for better or worse, that is, genealogically, to be forced to unite their complementary riches. Endless examples could be given of this sort of collective bad faith.

There is no case in which the objective meaning of a marriage is so strongly marked as to leave no room for symbolic transfiguration. Thus it is only in folk tales and the writings of ethnographers that the marriage of the so-called *mechrut* ('the man on condition'), by which a man who has no male offspring gives his daughter to an 'heir' (*awrith*) on condition that he comes and lives in his father-in-law's house, takes the form of the kind of purchase of a son-in-law, recruited for his productive and reproductive powers, that a mechanical application of the principles of the official world-view would lead one to see in it.[9] Those informants who mention it are right in saying that it is unknown in their region and only found in other areas. The most attentive reading of genealogies and family histories will not reveal a single case that perfectly matches the definition ('I give you my daughter, but you will come to my home'). None the less, one is equally entitled to claim that there is no family that does not include at least one *awrith*, but an *awrith* disguised under the official image of the 'associate' or the 'adopted son'. The word *awrith*, the 'heir', is an official euphemism allowing people to name the unnameable, that is, a man who could only be defined, in the house that receives him, as the husband of his wife. It is clear that the man of honour who plays the game fairly can count on the benevolent complicity of his own group when he attempts to disguise as an adoption a union which, in the cynical form of a contract, represents the inversion of all the honourable forms of marriage and which, as such, is no less dishonourable for the *awrith* ('he plays the bride', it is said) than for kinsmen sufficiently self-interested to give their daughter to this kind of unpaid domestic servant. And the group is quick to join in the circle of self-serving lies tending to conceal its failure to find an honourable way of saving the *amengur* from resorting to such an extreme measure in order to prevent the 'bankruptcy' (*lakhla*) of his family.

The second-order strategies that aim to transform useful relationships into official relationships all tend to make practices that really obey other principles *look* as if they are deduced from the genealogical definition. They thus achieve an additional, unexpected outcome, in that they give a representation of practice which might also be made to confirm the representation that the 'ritualistic' anthropologist spontaneously has of practice. Appeal to the 'rule', that last resort of ignorance, makes it possible to avoid drawing up the complete balance-sheet of material and symbolic costs and benefits that contains the reason and the *raison d'être* of practices.

THE ORDINARY AND THE EXTRA-ORDINARY

Far from obeying a norm which would designate an obligatory spouse from among the whole set of official kin, the arrangement of marriages depends directly on the state of the practical kinship relations – relationships through men usable by the men, relationships through women usable by the women – and on the state of the power relations within the 'house', that is, between the lineages united by marriage in the previous generation, which allow and favour the cultivation of one or the other field of relationships.

If it is accepted that one of the main functions of marriage is to reproduce the social relations of which it is the product, then it is immediately clear why the different types of marriage that can be distinguished by the dual criterion of the objective characteristics of the groups brought together (their position in the social hierarchy, their geographical distance, etc.) and those of the ceremony itself, particularly its solemnity, correspond very closely to the characteristics of the social relations which have made them possible and which they tend to reproduce. The set of official kin, publicly named and socially recognized, is what makes possible and necessary the official marriages which provide its only opportunity to mobilize practically as a group and thereby to reaffirm its unity, a unity as solemn and artificial as the occasions on which it is celebrated. Practical kinship, the field of relationships that are constantly re-used and thus reactivated for further use, is where ordinary marriages are set up, with a frequency that itself condemns them to the insignificance of the unmarked and the banality of the everyday. In accordance with the general law of exchanges, the higher a group is placed in the social hierarchy, and hence the richer it is in official relationships, the greater the proportion of its work of reproduction that is devoted to reproducing such relationships. It follows that the poor, who have little to spend on solemnities, tend to settle for the ordinary marriages that practical kinship provides for them, whereas the rich, that is, those richest in kinsmen, expect more from – and sacrifice more to – all the more or less institutionalized strategies aimed at maintaining social capital, the most important of which is undoubtedly the extra-ordinary marriage with prestigious 'strangers'.

Perhaps the most insidious of the distortions inherent in informants' spontaneous ethnology is the exaggerated emphasis they place on extra-ordinary marriages, which are distinguished from ordinary marriages by a positive or negative mark. As well as the various *curiosa* with which the anthropologist is often presented by well-meaning informants, such as marriage by exchange (*abdal*, two men 'exchange' their sisters), or by 'addition' (*thirni*, two brothers marry two sisters, the second sister being 'added' to the first; the son marries the sister or even the daughter of his father's second wife), or the levirate, a particular case of marriage as 'reparation' (*thiririth*, from *err*, to give or take back), native discourse privileges the extreme cases: parallel-cousin marriage, the most perfect mythically, and marriage uniting the headmen of two tribes or two different clans, the most perfect politically.

Thus the tale, a semi-ritualized parable paraphrasing the proverb or saying which provides its moral, only ever relates marked, remarkable marriages. First, there are the various types of parallel-cousin marriage, whether intended to preserve a political heritage or to prevent the extinction of a lineage (in the case of an only daughter). Then there are the most flagrant misalliances, like the marriage of the tawny owl and the eagle's daughter – a pure model of upward marriage (socially, but also mythically, since up is opposed to down as day, light, happiness, purity, honour, to night, darkness, misfortune, impurity and dishonour), between a man at the bottom of the social scale, an *awrith*, and a woman of a family of higher rank, in which the traditional relationship of assistance is inverted because of the discrepancy between the partners' positions in the social and sexual hierarchies. It is the giver, in this case the higher placed, who must go to the aid of the taker, in this case the lower: the eagle has to take his son-in-law, the tawny owl, on his back, to spare him a humiliating defeat in the contest with the young eagles – a scandalous situation, denounced in the proverb: 'giving him your daughter and adding wheat'.

Contrary to these official representations, observation and statistics indicate that, in all the groups observed, most marriages, by far, are ordinary marriages, generally arranged by the women, within the area of the practical kinship or practical relationships which make them possible and which they help to strengthen.

For example, in an important family in the village of Aghbala in Lesser Kabylia, of the first marriages of 218 men, 34 per cent were with families outside the limits of the tribe. Only 8 per cent, those with the spatially and socially most distant groups, present all the features of prestige marriages. These are all the work of one lineage, which has sought to distinguish itself from other branches by original matrimonial practices. The other distant marriages (26 per cent) merely renew established relationships (relationships 'through the women' or 'through the maternal uncles', constantly maintained on the occasion of weddings, departures and returns, funerals and sometimes even large work projects). Two-thirds (66 per cent) of the marriages were arranged within the tribe (made up of nine villages). Apart from marriages with the opposing clan, which are very rare (4 per cent) and always have a political significance (especially in the older generations), because of the traditional antagonism between the two groups, all the other unions fall within the class of ordinary marriages. Only 6 per cent of the marriages were set up within the lineage (as against 17 per cent with the other lineages and 39 per cent in the field of practical relationships); of these, 4 per cent are with the parallel cousin and 2 per cent with another cousin (and two-thirds of the families in question had, moreover, abandoned undivided ownership). In a recent study, Bassagana and Sayad (1974) found, among the Ath Yenni, a minute proportion of marriages with the parallel cousin (2 out of 610) or a close agnate (6 out of 610) and a significantly higher proportion of marriages with the maternal uncle's daughter (14 out of 610) or a close ally (58 out of 160).

Ordinary marriages, arranged between families united by frequent, long-standing exchanges, are marriages of which there is nothing to be said, as with everything that can be taken for granted because it has always been as it is. They have no other function, apart from biological reproduction, than the reproduction of the social relationships that make them possible.[10] Generally celebrated without great ceremony, they stand in the same relationship to extra-ordinary marriages – which are arranged by the men, between different villages or tribes, or, more simply, outside practical kinship, and for this reason are always sealed by solemn ceremonies – as the exchanges of everyday life to the extra-ordinary exchanges of extra-ordinary occasions which involve the official kin.

The common feature of extra-ordinary marriages is that they exclude the women. Parallel-cousin marriage, which is arranged between brothers, or at any rate the men of the lineage, with the blessing of the patriarch, differs in this way alone from ordinary marriages, which are unthinkable without the intervention of the women.[11] By contrast, a distant marriage is officially presented as political. Contracted outside the zone of practical relationships, celebrated with ceremonies which mobilize extensive groups, its sole justification is political, as in the limiting case of the marriages intended to set the seal on peace or an alliance between the 'heads' of two tribes.[12] More often, it is the marriage of the market-place, a neutral ground from which women are excluded and where lineages, clans and tribes meet warily. It is 'published' in the market by the crier, unlike other marriages which, since they only bring together kinsmen, do not entail solemn invitations. It treats the woman as a political instrument, as a sort of pledge or liquid asset that can be used to win symbolic profits. Being an opportunity to exhibit the family's symbolic capital publicly and officially, and hence perfectly legitimately, to make a *show* of kinship ties, and so to increase this capital, at the cost of considerable economic expenditure, it conforms at each stage to the logic of the accumulation of symbolic capital. (Thus, whereas marriage to a stranger who has been cut off from his group and taken refuge in the village is despised, marriage to a stranger living at a distance is prestigious because it bears witness to the extent of the group's influence; similarly, unlike ordinary marriages which follow well-worn tracks, political marriages cannot be repeated, since the alliance would be devalued by becoming common.) Here too, this kind of marriage is fundamentally masculine, and often causes friction between the bride's father and her mother, who is less sensitive to the symbolic profit it can bring and more concerned about the drawbacks it may entail for her daughter, who is condemned to a life of exile (*thaghribth*, the exile, she who has 'gone west').[13] Because it brings large groups into contact through the lineages and families directly involved, it is totally official and every aspect of the celebration is strictly ritualized and magically stereotyped. The stakes are so high and the chances of a rift so great that the agents dare not rely entirely on the regulated improvisation of orchestrated *habitus*.

The ritual acts grow in intensity and solemnity as one moves from marriages arranged within the undivided family or within practical kinship towards extra-ordinary marriages. The latter present in its most elaborate form a ceremonial which is reduced to its simplest expression when the marriage takes place in the everyday world. Marriages concluded within the privileged sub-market (that of the *akham*) which the authority of the elder and agnate solidarity set up as a kind of protected zone from which rival bids are excluded, are far less costly than extra-ordinary marriages. The union is generally regarded as self-evidently necessary, and when it is not, discreet intervention by the women of the family is sufficient to bring it about. The celebration of the wedding is reduced to the strict minimum. First, the expenses (*thaqufats*) incurred by the reception of the wedding procession by the girl's family are very modest. The *imensi* ceremony, at which the bridewealth is presented, brings together only the most important representatives of the two families (perhaps twenty men). The bride's trousseau (*ladjaz*) is limited to three dresses, two scarves and a few other items (a pair of shoes, a *haik*). The sum agreed upon as the bridewealth, negotiated in advance in relation to what the bride's parents have to buy in the market to equip their daughter (a mattress, a pillow, a trunk, as well as the blankets which are the family's own work and are handed down from mother to daughter), is handed over without great ceremony and without bluff or disguise. The wedding-feast expenses are minimized by arranging for the feast to coincide with Aïd. The sheep traditionally sacrificed on that occasion is sufficient for the requirements of the wedding, and the invited guests are more likely to be kept at home then and to send their regrets.

Compared with these ordinary marriages which the old peasant morality eulogizes (in contrast to marriages which, like 'widows' daughters' marriages', go beyond the bounds socially defined for each family), extra-ordinary marriages differ in every respect. To conceive the ambition of seeking a wife at a distance, one has to be predisposed to do so by the habit of keeping up relationships that are out of the ordinary, which implies possession of the skills, especially the linguistic ones, indispensable in such circumstances. One also needs a large capital of very costly distant relationships, the only source of reliable information and mediators without whom the project cannot succeed. In short, to be able to mobilize this capital at the right moment, it is necessary to have invested a lot and for a long time. For example, to take just one case, the heads of marabout families who have been asked to act as mediators are paid back in countless ways: the taleb of the village and *a fortiori* the religious figure of higher rank who takes part in the procession (*iqafafen*) is given new clothes and shoes by the 'master of the wedding', and the gifts he traditionally receives, in cash at the time of religious festivals, in kind at harvest time, are roughly proportionate to the services rendered. The Aïd sheep he is given that year is simply compensation for the 'shame' he has incurred by going to solicit a layman (who, however powerful, does not 'hold in his heart' Koranic knowledge) and consecrating the marriage with his faith and his wisdom.

Once the agreement is reached, the ceremony of 'pledging' (*asuras*, the handing-over of the pledge, *thimristh*), which functions as an appropriation rite (*aâayam*, naming, or *aâallam*, marking, comparable to that of the first plot of land ploughed; or more exactly *amlak*, appropriation on the same terms as land), is in itself almost a wedding. Presents are brought not only for the bride (who receives her 'pledge', a jewel of value, and money from all the men who see her on that day – *thizri*), but also for all the other women of the house. The visitors also bring provisions (semolina, honey, butter), and some cattle, to be slaughtered and eaten by the guests or to constitute a capital for the bride. The men of the family demonstrate how numerous they are with the noise of their rifle volleys, as on the wedding day. All the feasts that take place between this ceremony and the wedding are opportunities to bring the fiancée (*thislith*) her share. Great families at a great distance from each other cannot be content with exchanging a few dishes of couscous; presents appropriate to the persons they unite are added. Though betrothed, that is to say, 'given', 'appropriated' and 'recalled to mind' by the many 'shares' she has received, the girl is not yet acquired: a point of honour is set on allowing her family the time it wishes to wait and keep the groom's family waiting.

The celebration of the wedding is naturally the high point in the symbolic confrontation of the two groups, and also the moment of greatest expense. The girl's family is sent *thaqufats*, at least 200 kilos of semolina, 50 kilos of flour, abundant meat (on the hoof) – which the sender knows will not all be eaten – honey (20 litres) and butter (10 litres). A case was mentioned of a wedding in which the girl's family was taken a calf, five live sheep and a carcass (*ameslukh*). The *iqafafen* delegation consisted, it is true, of forty rifle-bearing men, together with all the kinsmen and notables too old to shoot, fifty men in all. The bride's trousseau, which may in such cases consist of up to thirty items, is matched by a similar number of items given to the various other women of the family. And if one often hears it said that between great families there are no *chrut* (conditions laid down by the father for his daughter before he grants her hand), this is because the status of the family is in itself a guarantee that the 'conditions' that are spelled out elsewhere will here be surpassed. To demand a large payment for one's daughter, or to pay a large sum to marry off one's son, is in either case to assert one's prestige and thereby to acquire prestige. Each side seeks to prove its own 'worth', either by showing what price men of honour, who know how to appreciate it, set on an alliance with them, or by making a brilliant demonstration of their assessment of their own value through the price they are prepared to pay to have partners worthy of them. Through a sort of inverted haggling, disguised under the appearance of ordinary bargaining, the two groups tacitly agree to step up the amount of the payment by successive bids, because they have a common interest in raising this indisputable index of the symbolic value of their products on the matrimonial exchange market. And no feat is more highly praised than the prowess of the bride's father who, after vigorous bargaining has been concluded, solemnly returns a part of the sum received. The greater the proportion returned, the greater the ensuing honour, as if, in crowning the transaction with an act of generosity, the intention was to make an exchange of honour out of haggling which could be so overtly keen only because the pursuit of maximum material was masked under the contest of honour and the pursuit of maximum symbolic profit.

Distant marriages, the fruit of elaborate strategies which are expected to yield alliances, are a kind of long- and short-term investment designed to maintain or increase social capital, particularly through the quality of the 'maternal uncles' they procure. They are not discarded lightly, and the oldest and most prestigious relationships are of course those best protected against casual breakdown. If repudiation becomes inevitable, all sorts of subterfuges are used to avoid loss of the capital of alliances. The parents of the repudiated wife may be visited and 'begged' to send her back; excuses are made for the immaturity, the thoughtlessness, the verbal brutality of a husband too young to appreciate the value of alliances; or it is claimed that the formula of repudiation was not pronounced three times, but once, impetuously, without witnesses. The divorce becomes a mere tiff (*thutchh'a*). A whole new wedding (with *imensi* and a trousseau) may even be offered. If the repudiation proves to be final, there are several ways of 'separating'. The more important and solemn the marriage was, and the more that was 'invested' in it, the greater the interest there is in safeguarding relations with those from whom one is separating, and the more discreet the break. Return of the bridewealth is not demanded immediately, and it is not refused ('free' repudiation is a grave insult); and it may not be expected until the bride remarries. The accounts are not examined too closely, and witnesses, especially outsiders, are kept away from the divorce settlement.

As for marriage with the parallel cousin, the pre-eminent position it enjoys in native discourse, and therefore in anthropological discourse, is due to the fact that it is the marriage most perfectly consistent with the mythico-ritual representation of the sexual division of labour, and more particularly of the functions assigned to the men and the women in inter-group relations. First, it constitutes the most absolute affirmation of the refusal to recognize the relationship of affinity for what it is, that is, when it does not simply appear as a doubling-up of the relationship of filiation:

'woman', it is said, 'neither unites nor separates' (it has to be remembered that a husband is – theoretically – free to repudiate his wife; that a wife coming from outside remains a quasi-outsider until she has produced her first son, and sometimes even beyond that time; and the relationship between nephew and maternal uncle is an ambivalent one). There is much praise for the specific effect of a marriage between parallel cousins, namely that the resulting children ('those whose extraction is unmixed, whose blood is pure') can be attached to the same lineage through their father or their mother ('He took his maternal uncles from where he had his own roots – *ichathel, ixhawel*'; or, in Arabic, 'His maternal uncle is his paternal uncle – *khalu âammu*'). Since we also know that woman is seen as the source from which impurity and dishonour threaten to enter the lineage ('Shame is the maiden', the proverb says, and the son-in-law is sometimes called 'the veil cast over shames'),[14] it is also clear that the best, or least bad, of women is the woman sprung from agnates, the patrilateral parallel cousin, the most 'male' of women – the extreme instance of which, the figment of a patriarchal imagination, is Athena, sprung from Zeus' *head*. 'Marry the daughter of your *âamm*; even if she chews you, she won't swallow you.' The patrilateral parallel cousin, a cultivated, straightened woman, is opposed to the matrilateral parallel cousin, a natural, twisted, maleficent, impure woman, as the male-female to the female-female, that is, in accordance with the structure (of the type $a : b : b_1 : b_2$) which also organizes the mythic space of the house or the agrarian calendar.[15] Marriage to the father's brother's daughter is the most blessed of all marriages, and likely to bring blessings to the group. It was used as the opening rite of the marriage season, intended, like the homologous rite in the case of ploughing, to exorcize the threat contained in the coming together of male and female, fire and water, sky and earth, ploughshare and furrow, in acts of unavoidable sacrilege.[16]

Every informant – and almost every anthropologist – will assert that in Arab and Berber countries a boy has a 'right' to his parallel cousin. 'If the boy wants his father's brother's daughter, he has a *right* to her,. But if he doesn't, he isn't consulted. It's the same as with land.' This remark by an informant, although infinitely closer to the reality of practice than anthropological legalism, which does not even suspect the homology between a man's relation to the women of his lineage and his relation to land, masks the real, much more complex relationship linking an individual to his parallel cousin. A man's supposed right to his *bent âamm* may in fact be a duty which obeys the same principles as the obligation to avenge a kinsman or to buy up a tract of land coveted by strangers, and is therefore strictly binding only in rather exceptional circumstances. The fact that, in the case of land, the right of pre-emption (*achfaâ*) is formulated and codified by the learned legal tradition (furnished with institutionalized authority and guaranteed by the courts) as well as by 'custom' (*qanun*) in no way implies that the juridical or customary rule can be made the principle of the practices actually observed when land changes hands. Because the sale of a piece of land belonging to the patrimony is first and foremost an internal matter for the lineage, it is entirely exceptional for the group to have recourse to the authorities (the clan or village assembly) which transmute the obligation of honour into a right; and if they do invoke the right or custom of *chafaâ* (or *achfaâ*), they are almost always motivated by principles that have nothing to do with those of law (such as the intention to challenge the purchaser by requesting the annulment of an allegedly illegal sale) and which govern most practices of land sale or purchase.

The obligation to marry a woman who is in a similar state to that of fallow land, neglected by its masters (*athbur*, maiden; *el bur*, fallow land), is simply less pressing than the obligation to buy land put up for sale by a group member, or to buy back land fallen into the hands of outsiders, land ill defended and ill possessed; and infinitely less pressing than the obligation not to leave the murder of a member of the group unavenged. In all these cases, the force of the duty depends on the agents' positions in the genealogy, and also, of course, on their dispositions. Thus, in the case of revenge, the obligation of honour may become a right to honour in the eyes of some (the same murder is sometimes avenged twice), while others will back out or bring themselves to do it only under pressure. In the case of land, the material advantage of purchase is clear, and the hierarchy of rights to honour and obligations to buy is both more visible and more often transgressed, with conflicts and very complex dealings between those members of the family who feel obliged to purchase but cannot afford to, and those who have lesser duty-rights to purchase but could afford to.

In fact, *pace* the whole anthropological tradition, which simply takes over the official theory (that is, the one corresponding to male interests) that every man has a kind of right of preemption over his parallel cousin (in accordance with the official representation giving men the upper hand, and therefore the initiative, in all relations between the sexes), it has to be pointed out that marriage with the parallel cousin may in some cases be forced on the group with a necessity which is not, however, that of a genealogical rule.

In practice, this ideal marriage is often a forced choice which the group seeks to present as a choice of the ideal, thus making a virtue of necessity. As has been seen, it is often found in the poorest lineages or the poorest lines of the dominant groups. It tends in any case to be the choice of groups characterized by a strong desire to assert their distinction, because it always has the objective effect of reinforcing the integration of the minimal unit and, consequently, its distinctiveness vis-à-vis other units. It is predisposed by its ambiguity to play the role of poor man's prestige marriage, and it offers an elegant solution for all those who, like a ruined nobleman unable to manifest his refusal to derogate other than symbolically, seek in the affectation of rigour the means of affirming their distinction. This can be the case with a lineage cut off from its original group and anxious to maintain its originality; a family seeking to assert the distinctive features of its lineage by going one better in purism (almost always the case with one family in the marabout communities); a clan seeking to mark its distinction from the opposing clan by strict observance of the traditions (like the Aït Madhi at Aït Hichem), etc. Because it can appear as the most sacred and, in certain conditions, the most 'distinguished' marriage, it is the cheapest form of extra-ordinary marriage, obviating expenditure on the ceremony, hazardous negotiations and a costly bridewealth. Thus there is no more accomplished way of making a virtue of necessity and putting oneself in line with the 'rule'.

However, any given marriage is meaningful only in relation to the totality of simultaneously possible marriages (or, more concretely, in relation to the set of possible partners). In other words, it is situated somewhere on a continuum running from parallel-cousin marriage to marriage between members of different tribes. These two marriages represent the points of maximum intensity of the two values which all marriages try to maximize: on the one hand, the integration of the minimal unit and security, on the other hand, alliances and prestige, that is, opening up to the outside world, towards strangers. The choice between fission and fusion, the inside and the outside, safety and adventure, arises anew with each marriage. If it ensures the maximum of integration for the minimal group, parallel-cousin marriage merely duplicates the relationship of filiation with a relationship of alliance, a kind of redundancy which squanders the opportunity of making new alliances which marriage represents. Distant marriage, on the other hand, secures prestigious alliances at the cost of lineage integration and the bond between brothers, the foundation of the agnatic unit.

Native discourse repeats this obsessively. The centripetal drive – exaltation of the internal, of security, autarky, purity of blood, agnate solidarity – always calls forth, if only to oppose it, the centrifugal drive, exaltation of the prestigious alliance. Concealed behind the apparent categorical imperative there is always calculation of the maximum and the minimum, the search for the maximum of alliance compatible with maintained or enhanced integration between brothers. This can be seen in the informants' syntax, which is always that of preference: 'It is better to protect your point of honour (*nif*) than to reveal it to others'; 'I don't sacrifice *adhrum* (the lineage) to *aghrum* (wheatcake); 'The inside is better than the outside'; 'First madness (act of daring, risky step): to give the daughter of *âamm* to other men. Second madness: to go penniless to the market. Third madness: to vie with the lions on the mountain tops.' This last saying is the most significant, because under the guise of an absolute condemnation of distant marriage, it explicitly recognizes the logic to which this marriage belongs, that of the exploit, prowess, prestige. It takes great prestige and wild audacity to go to market without money intending to buy things, just as it takes enormous courage to challenge lions, the courageous strangers from whom the founders of the villages snatch their wives, according to many legends of origin.

MATRIMONIAL STRATEGIES AND SOCIAL REPRODUCTION

The characteristics of a marriage, and in particular the position it occupies at a particular point on the continuum running from political marriage to parallel-cousin marriage, depend on the ends and means of the collective strategies of the groups involved. The outcome of each 'round' of the matrimonial game depends partly on the 'deal' and partly on the player's skill: that is to say, first on the material and symbolic capital of the families concerned, their wealth in instruments of production and in men, considered both as productive and reproductive power, and also, in an earlier state of the game, as fighting strength and therefore symbolic strength; and secondly on the competence that enables the strategists to make the best use of this capital, since practical mastery of (in the widest sense) economic logic is the precondition for the production of practices regarded as 'reasonable' within the group and positively sanctioned by the objective laws of the market in material and symbolic goods.

The collective strategy that leads to any given 'move' (whether in marriage or any other area of practice) is nothing other than the product of a combination of the strategies of the agents involved which tends to give their respective interests the weight corresponding to their position in the structure of domestic power relations at the moment in question. It is, in fact, remarkable that matrimonial negotiations are really the business of the whole group, with everyone eventually playing his or her part and therefore contributing to the success or failure of the project. First, the women make unofficial, deniable approaches, making it possible to start semi-official contacts without risking a humiliating rebuff; then the notables most representative of the representational kinship, acting as expressly mandated guarantors of the will of their group and as its explicitly authorized spokesmen, provide their mediation and intercession as well as an imposing display of the symbolic capital of a family that can mobilize such prestigious figures; finally the two groups in their entirety intervene in the decision, with intense discussion of the marriage projects, the accounts of the reception given to the delegates' proposals, and the course to be followed in the subsequent negotiations. In other words – for the benefit of anthropologists who think they have done their job when they have characterized a marriage purely in terms of its genealogical determination – through the quasi-theatrical representation that each group gives of itself during this process, the two groups carry out a systematic inquiry aimed at establishing the complete set of variables characterizing not only the two spouses (age and especially difference in age, previous matrimonial history, birth rank, theoretical and practical kin relationship with the holder of authority within the family, etc.) but also their lineages. The various bargaining and negotiating sessions required by major, distant marriages are an opportunity to exhibit and assess the capital of honour and men commanded by each lineage, the quality of the network of alliances it can rely on and of the groups to which it is traditionally opposed, the family's position in its group – particularly important information, since the display of prestigious kinsmen may conceal a dominated position within an eminent group – and the state of its relations with the other members of its group, that is, the degree of family integration (non-division, etc.), the structure of the power and authority relations within the domestic unit (and more especially, when a daughter is to be married, among the women of the household), and so on.

In a social formation oriented towards simple reproduction – that is, the biological reproduction of the group and the production of the quantity of goods required for its subsistence, and, inseparably from this, the reproduction of the structure of the social and ideological relations within which and through which the activity of production is carried on and legitimated, the strategies of the different categories of agents whose interests may clash within the domestic unit (over the marriage, among other things) derive from the systems of interests objectively assigned to them by the system of dispositions characterizing a given mode of reproduction. These dispositions, which orient fertility, filiation, residence, inheritance and marriage by reference to the same function, namely the biological and social reproduction of the group, are objectively concerted.[17] In an economy characterized by relatively equal distribution of the means of production (usually owned jointly by the lineage) and by weak and stable productive forces which do not allow the production and accumulation of large surpluses and the consequent development of clear-cut economic differentiation, the family's labour is directed towards the maintenance and reproduction of the family rather than the production of values.

In these conditions, an abundance of men would no doubt constitute a burden if, adopting a strictly economic standpoint, one saw them only as 'hands' and, by the same token, 'mouths to feed' (the more so since Kabylia always had a fluctuating labour force of paupers who would form itinerant teams, moving from village to village in the season for major projects). In fact, however, the political insecurity which perpetuated itself by generating the dispositions needed to respond to war, brawling, thefts or revenge was probably the basis of the valorization of men as 'rifles', that is, not only as labour power but also as fighting strength: land has value only through the men who cultivate it – and also defend it. The patrimony of the lineage, symbolized by its name, is defined not only by possession of its land and its house, precious and therefore vulnerable assets, but also by possession of the means of protecting them, that is, its men, because land and women are never regarded as simple instruments of production or reproduction, still less as chattels or 'property'. An attack on these material and symbolic assets is an attack on their master, on his *nif*, his 'potency', his very *being* as defined by the group. Alienated land, unavenged rape or murder, are different forms of the same offence, which always elicits the same riposte from the group's point of honour. Just as a murder is 'paid back', but at a higher rate, by striking if possible at the person closest to the murderer or at the most prominent member of his group, so a piece of ancestral land, even a not very fertile one, is 'bought back' at any price in order to wipe out the standing challenge to the group's point of honour. This is because, in the logic of challenge and riposte, the best land, technically and symbolically, is the land most closely bound up with the patrimony, just as the man through whom one can most solemnly, and therefore most cruelly, strike at the group is its most representative member. The ethos of honour is the transfigured expression of this economic logic. More generally, it is the ethos corresponding to the interest of social formations, groups or classes whose patrimony, as here, contains a large element of symbolic capital.

A clear-cut distinction was drawn between *nif*, the point of honour, and *h'urma*, honour, which is everything that is *h'aram*, that is, forbidden, everything that makes the group vulnerable, its most sacred possession (from which there follows the distinction between the challenge, which touches only the point of honour, and sacrilegious outrage). The simple challenge to the point of honour (*thirzi nennif*, the act of challenging; *sennif*, 'by *nif*, I challenge you! I dare you!') is distinguished from the offence which calls *h'urma* into question. There is derision for the *nouveau riche* who tried to redress a slur upon his *h'urma* by challenging his offender to beat him in a race or lay out more thousand-franc notes on the ground, for he was confusing the realm of the challenge with the realm of the offence. An attck on *h'urma* tends to rule out evasions and settlements such as *diya*, compensation paid by the murderer's family to the victim's family. Of the man who accepts this, people say, 'He's the man who's agreed to eat his brother's blood; for him, only the belly counts. In the case of an offence, albeit committed indirectly or thoughtlessly, the pressure of opinion is such that the only alternative to revenge is dishonour and exile.

Only the vigilance and susceptibility of the point of honour (*nif*) can guarantee the integrity of honour (*h'urma*) – which, being sacred, is inherently exposed to sacrilegious outrage – and win the consideration and respectability granted to the man who has sufficient point of honour to keep his honour safe from offence. *H'urma* in the sense of the sacred (*h'aram*), *nif*, and *h'urma* in the sense of respectability, are inseparable. The more vulnerable a family is, the more *nif* it must possess to defend its sacred values, and the greater are the consideration and esteem it enjoys. Thus poverty, far from contradicting or prohibiting respectability, only enhances the merit of a man who manages to win respect although he is particularly exposed to outrage. Conversely, the point of honour has a meaning and a function only in a man for whom there are things worthy of being defended. A being devoid of the sacred (for example, a confirmed bachelor) could dispense with the point of honour, because he would be in a sense invulnerable. What is *h'aram* (that is, literally, taboo), is essentially the sacred of the left hand, that is, the inside and more precisely the female universe, the world of what is secret, the enclosed space of the house, as opposed to the outside, the open world of public space, reserved for men. The sacred of the right hand is essentially the 'rifles', that is, the group of agnates, the 'sons of the paternal uncle', all those whose death must be avenged by blood and all those who are bound to carry out blood vengeance. The rifle is the symbolic embodiment of the *nif* of the agnatic group, *nif* defined as that which can be challenged and which enables one to take up the challenge. Thus, opposed to the passivity of *h'urma*, female in nature, there is the active susceptibility of *nif*, the male virtue *par excellence*. It is ultimately on *nif*, its (physical or symbolic) fighting capacity, that the defence of the group's material and patrimony – the source both of its power and its vulnerability – depends.

Men constitute a political and symbolic strength without which the group cannot protect and expand its patrimony, defend itself and its goods against violent encroachments, still less impose its domination and satisfy its interests. Consequently, the only threat to the power of the group, apart from the sterility of its women, is the fragmentation of the material and symbolic patrimony which results from quarrels among the men. Hence the fertility strategies which aim to produce as many men as quickly as possible (through early marriage), and the educational strategies which inculcate an exalted attachment to the lineage and to the values of honour (a transfigured expression of the objective relationship between the agents and their ever-threatened material and symbolic patrimony) and so help to strengthen lineage integration and to channel aggressive tendencies outwards. 'The land is copper (*neh'as*), men's arms are silver.' The very ambiguity of this saying – *neh'as* also means jealousy – points to the principle of the contradiction generated by the mode of inheritance. For, on the one hand, by handing down equal shares it binds all the available men to the patrimony, but at the same time it threatens the ancestral lands with disintegration in the event of equal division among many heirs; and above all it sets at the very heart of the system the principle of competition for power over the domestic economy and politics – competition and conflict between the father and the sons, whom this mode of transmission of power keeps in a subordinate position so long as the patriarch is alive (many parallel-cousin marriages are arranged by the 'old man' without the fathers being consulted); competition and conflict among the brothers or the cousins who, at least when they in their turn become fathers, inevitably find that they have antagonistic interests.[18] The agnates' strategies are dominated by the antagonism between the symbolic profits of political unity and the economic non-division that guarantees it, and the material profits of a break-up, which are constantly recalled to mind by the spirit of economic calculation. The urge to calculate, repressed in men, finds more overt expression in women, who are structurally inclined to be less sensitive to the symbolic profits accruing from political unity, and freer to attend to strictly economic profits.

Lending among women is regarded as the antithesis of the exchange of honour. It is indeed closer to the economic truth of exchange than men's dealings. Of a man who, unlike the man of honour anxious not to squander his capital of 'credit', too readily seeks loans, especially of money, a man who has so often blanched with shame on asking for a loan that he has a 'yellow face', it is said that 'his borrowing is like that of women'. The opposition between the two 'economies' is so marked that the phrase *err arrt'al*, also applied to the taking of revenge, means the return of a gift, an exchange, in the men's speech, whereas it means 'repaying a loan' when used by the women. Loan conduct is certainly more frequent and more natural among the women, who will lend and borrow anything for any purpose. It follows that the economic truth, contained in the exchange of exact equivalents, is closer to the surface in female exchanges in which there can be specific deadlines ('until my daughter gives birth') and precise calculation of the quantities lent.

In short, the symbolic and political interests attached to the unity of land ownership, to the extent of alliances, to the material and symbolic strength of the agnatic group and to the values of honour and prestige which make a great house (*akham amograne*) militate in favour of the strengthening of corporate bonds. Conversely, as is shown by the fact that the breaking up of joint ownership has become increasingly frequent with the generalization of monetary exchanges and the corresponding spread of the spirit of calculation, economic interests (in the narrow sense), especially those relating to consumption, are conducive to the break-up of undivided ownership.[19]

Even in cases in which the holder of domestic power has long prepared for his succession by manipulating individual aspirations, channelling each of the brothers towards the 'speciality' that suited him in the division of domestic labour, competition for internal power is almost inevitable, and it can be sublimated into a competition of honour only at the cost of continuous self-control by the men and control by the group over each of them. But the cohesive forces represented by the non-division of the land and the integration of the family – mutually reinforcing institutions – clash constantly with fissive forces such as the 'jealousy' aroused by unequal distribution of powers or responsibilities, or the imbalance between individual contributions to production and consumption ('the hard-working man's labour has been eaten up by the man who leans against the wall').[20] In general, authority over the delegation of work, the control of expenditure and the management of the patrimony, or over the family's external relations (alliances, etc.) resides in fact in a single person, who thus appropriates the symbolic profits that accrue from going to the market, attending clan assemblies or the more exceptional gatherings of tribal notables, etc. – not to mention the fact that these duties have the effect of dispensing the person who assumes them from the continuous, and therefore less noble, tasks of the everyday routine.

Objectively united, for worse if not for better, the brothers are subjectively divided, even in their solidarity. 'My brother', said an informant, 'is the man who would defend my honour if my point of honour failed, who would save me from dishonour but put me to shame.' Another informant reported an acquaintance as saying: 'My brother is he who, if I died, could marry my wife and would be praised for it.' The homogeneity of the mode of production of *habitus* (that is, the material conditions of existence and pedagogic action) produces a homogenization of dispositions and interests which, far from excluding competition, may in some cases engender it by inclining those who are the products of the same conditions of production to recognize and pursue the same goods, whose rarity may arise entirely from this competition. The domestic unit, a monopolistic grouping defined, as Weber said, by the exclusive appropriation of a determinate type of goods (land, names, etc.), is the site of competition for capital, or rather, for control over this capital, a competition which continuously threatens to destroy the capital by destroying the fundamental condition of its perpetuation, that is, the cohesion of the domestic group.

The relationship between brothers, the keystone of the family structure, is also its weakest point, and a whole set of mechanisms are designed to support and strengthen it.[21] The foremost of these is parallel-cousin marriage, the resolution in ideology, sometimes achieved in practice, of the specific contradiction of this mode of reproduction. If parallel-cousin marriage is a matter for men,[22] consistent with the men's interests, that is, the higher interests of the lineage, often arranged without the women being consulted, and against their will (when the two brothers' wives are on bad terms, one not wanting to let the other's daughter into her house and the other not wishing to place her daughter under her sister-in-law's authority), this is because it is designed to counteract, practically, the principles of division between the men. This is so much taken for granted that the father's ritual advice to his sons, 'Don't listen to your wives, stay united amongst yourselves!' is naturally taken to mean: 'Marry your children to one another.' Everything takes place in fact as if this social formation had had to allow itself officially a possibility rejected as incestuous by most societies, in order to resolve ideologically the tension which is at its very heart. Perhaps the exaltation of marriage with *bent âamm* would have been better understood if it had been realized that *bent âamm* has come to designate the enemy, or at least, the intimate enemy, and that enmity is called *thabenâammts*, 'that of the children of the paternal uncle'. It would be a mistake to underestimate how much the system of values and the schemes of mythico-ritual thought contribute to the symbolic reduction of tensions, especially those that run through the agnatic group, whether tensions between brothers or tensions between generations.

There is no need to insist on the function of legitimating the division of labour and power between the sexes that is fulfilled by a mythico-ritual system entirely dominated by male values. But it is perhaps less obvious that the social structuring of time, which organizes representations and practices and which is most solemnly reaffirmed in the rites of passage, fulfils a political function by symbolically manipulating age limits, that is, the boundaries that define age groups but also the limitations imposed at different ages. The mythico-ritual categories cut up the age continuum into discontinuous segments, constituted not biologically (like the bodily signs of ageing) but socially, and marked by the symbolism of cosmetics and dress, decorations, ornaments and emblems, the tokens that express and underline the representations of the uses of the body that are appropriate to each social age, or inappropriate, because they would tend to dislocate the system of oppositions between the generations (like rejuvenation rites, the exact inversion of rites of passage). The social representations of the different ages of life, and of the properties attached by definition to them, express, in their own logic, the power relations between the age-classes. They help to reproduce both the union and the division of those age-classes by means of temporal divisions tending to produce both continuity and rupture. They thereby rank among the institutionalized mechanisms maintaining the symbolic order, and hence among the mechanisms reproducing the social order whose very functioning serves the interests of those occupying a dominant position in the social structure, the men of mature age.[23]

In fact, the technical and symbolic forces of cohesion are embodied in the person of the 'patriarch', *djedd*, whose authority is based on the power to disinherit, the threat of malediction, and above all on adherence to the values symbolized by *thadjadith* (from *djedd*, father's father, the set of ascendants common to those who claim the same real or mythic ancestor), the original and historical community which is the basis of the official units. The patriarch ensures equilibrium among the brothers by his very existence, since all power and prestige are concentrated in him, and also, of course, by maintaining strict equality among them (and their wives) both in work (the women, for example, take turns to do the housework, prepare the meals, fetch water, etc.) and in consumption. It is no accident that crisis so often arises when the father dies leaving adult sons none of whom wields a clearly established authority (because of the age gap or any other principle). But, at the level of the domestic unit as in larger units like the clan or the tribe, the extremely variable strength of the tendencies to fusion or fission depends fundamentally on the relationship between the group and the external units. Insecurity provides a negative principle of cohesion capable of making up for the lack of positive principles:[24] 'I hate my brother, but I hate the man who hates him.'

If it is true that marriage is one of the major opportunities to preserve, enhance or (by misalliance) diminish the capital of authority conferred by strong integration and the capital of prestige stemming from an extensive network of affines (*nesba*), the fact remains that the members of the domestic unit who take part in arranging the marriage do not all identify their particular interest to the same degree with the collective interest of the lineage. The successional tradition which prevents woman from inheriting, the mythic world-view which allows her only a limited existence and never grants her full participation in the symbolic capital of her adoptive lineage, the division of labour between the sexes which restricts her to domestic tasks while leaving representational functions to men – everything combines to identify the interests of the men with the material and more especially the symbolic interests of the lineage, the more so the greater their authority within the agnatic group. And indeed, the typically 'male' marriages – parallel-cousin marriage and political marriage – demonstrate unequivocally that the interests of the men are more directly identified with the official interests of the lineage and that their strategies are more directly designed to strength the integration of the domestic unit or the family's network of alliance.

As for the women, it is no accident that the marriages for which they are responsible belong to the class of ordinary marriages or, more precisely, that they are left responsibility only for such marriages.[25] Being excluded from representational kinship, they are thrown back on to practical kinship and the practical uses of kinship, and they invest more economic (in the narrow sense) realism than men in seeking a spouse for their son or daughter.[26] Male and female interests are most likely to diverge when it is a question of marrying a daughter. Not only is the mother less sensitive to the 'family interest' which tends to see the daughter as an instrument for strengthening the integration of the agnatic group or as a sort of symbolic money enabling prestigious alliances to be set up with other groups; but also, by marrying her daughter into her own lineage and so strengthening the exchanges between the groups, she tends to strengthen her own position in the domestic unit. The marriage of a son raises for the old mistress of the house first and foremost the question of her dominance over the domestic economy. Her interest is only negatively adjusted to that of the lineage: in taking a daughter from the family she herself came from, she is following the path traced by the lineage, and a conflict among the women resulting from a bad choice would ultimately threaten the unity of the agnate group.

The marriage of the son often gives rise to conflict between the parents – albeit undeclared, since the mother can have no official strategy – with the father tending to favour marriage within the lineage, that is, the one that the mythical representation, the ideological legitimation of male domination, presents as the best, while the mother directs her secret approaches towards her own lineage, and at the opportune moment will invite her husband to give his official sanction to the outcome. The women would not devote so much ingenuity and effort to the matrimonial prospecting that is generally left to them by the sexual division of labour, at least up to the moment when official dialogue can be established between men, if their son's marriage did not potentially imply the subversion of their own power. The in-marrying women (*thislith*), depending on whether she is linked to her husband's father (and if so, whether by her father, or more generally by a man, or by her mother) or to his mother will have very different weight in the power relationship with her husband's mother (*thamgharth*); this relationship clearly also varies according to *thamgharth*'s relationship to the men of her lineage (that is, to her husband's father). Thus, the patrilateral parallel cousin finds herself in a position of strength from the outset when she has to deal with an 'old woman' from outside the lineage, whereas the 'old woman's' position may be strengthened, in her dealings with *thislith*, but also, indirectly, in her dealings with her own husband, when *thislith* is her own sister's daughter, and *a fortiori* her brother's daughter.

In fact, the interests of the 'old man' (*amghar*) and the 'old woman' are not necessarily antagonistic. Realizing the advantage for himself of choosing a young woman fully devoted to a *thamgharth* herself devoted to the lineage, he may well authorize *thamgharth* to seek out a docile girl from her lineage. Moreover, since the whole structure of the practical relationships between kinsmen is present in each particular relationship, he may deliberately choose to take as his son's wife the daughter of his own sister (patrilateral cross cousin), or even, without seeming to do so, encourage his wife to marry him to her brother's daughter (matrilateral cross cousin), rather than strengthen the hold of a brother already dominant (by age or prestige), by agreeing to take his daughter (patrilateral cross cousin).

The interest of the men is most forcefully asserted when the agnatic group is well integrated (as is indicated indirectly when one of the arguments used in favour of non-division is that it enables the women to be kept under closer control) and when the father's lineage is at least equal in the social hierarchy to the mother's lineage. It is hardly an exaggeration to claim that the group's whole matrimonial history is present in the internal discussions over each intended marriage. The interest of the lineage, that is, the men's interest, requires that a man should not be placed in a subordinate position within the family by being married to a girl of markedly higher status: a man, it is said, can raise a woman, but not the opposite; one gives (a daughter) to a superior or an equal, one takes (a daughter) from an inferior. This male interest is therefore more likely to predominate when the man who is (at least officially) responsible for the marriage has not himself married above his status. In fact, a whole set of mechanisms, including the amount of the bridewealth and the wedding expenses, which rise with the prestige of the marriage, tend to exclude alliances between groups that are too unequal in economic or symbolic capital. The frequent cases in which the family of one of spouses is rich in one kind of capital – for example, in men – while the other possesses more of another kind of wealth – for example, land – are far from being exceptions: 'You ally with your equals', it is said.

In short, the structure of the objective relations between the kinsmen responsible for the matrimonial decision, as a man or a woman and as a member of a particular lineage, helps to define the structure of the relationship between the lineages to be united by the planned marriage.[27] In fact, it would be more accurate to say that the decisive relationship, that between the lineage of the person to be married and the lineage offering a possible partner, is always mediated by the domestic power structure. In order to describe completely the multi-dimensional and multi-functional relationship between the two groups, it is not sufficient to take into account the spatial, social and economic distance between them at the time of the marriage, in terms of economic and also symbolic capital (measured by the number of men and men of honour, the degree of family integration, etc.). One also has to consider the state, at that particular moment, of the balance-sheet of their material and symbolic exchanges, that is, the whole history of the official, extra-ordinary exchanges, brought about or at least consecrated by the men, such as marriages, and also the unofficial, ordinary exchanges continuously conducted by the women with the complicity of the men but sometimes without their knowledge, a mediation through which the objective relations predisposing two groups to come together in marriage are prepared and realized.

Whereas economic capital is relatively stable, symbolic capital is more precarious. The death of a prestigious head of the family, not to mention the breakup of undivided ownership, is sometimes sufficient to diminish it severely. Fluctuations in the group's symbolic fortunes are followed by corresponding changes in the whole representation the family seeks to give of itself and in the objectives it assigns to its marriages. Thus, in the space of two generations, a great family, whose economic situation was in fact improving, has declined from 'male' marriages – marriages within the close kin or extra-ordinary marriages – to ordinary marriages, generally set up by the women within their own networks of relationships. This change in matrimonial policy coincided with the deaths of the two eldest brothers, the long absence of the oldest men (who had gone to France), and the weakening of the authority of *thamgharth*, who had become blind. Because it was not clear who was to succeed the 'old woman' who imposes order and silence ('obedience to the old woman is silence'), the power relations among the wives reflect the power relations among the husbands, leaving the role of mistress of the house vacant. In such circumstances, marriages tend to go towards the women's respective lineages.

The structural characteristics generically defining the value of a lineage's products on the matrimonial market are obviously specified by secondary characteristics such as the matrimonial status of the person to be married, his/her age, sex, etc. Thus, the group's matrimonial strategies and the resulting marriage are quite different depending on whether the man to be married is a bachelor 'of marriageable age' or already 'past his prime', or an already married man looking for a co-wife, or a widower or divorcee seeking to remarry (and, in this case, on whether there are children from the first marriage). For a woman, the variations are similar, except that the depreciation resulting from previous marriages is infinitely greater (because of the value set on virginity and despite the fact that a reputation as 'a man who repudiates' is at least as damaging as that of 'a woman to repudiate').

This is only one aspect of the asymmetry between the situation of the man and the woman before marriage. 'The man', runs the saying, 'is always a man, whatever his state; it is up to him to choose.' Having the strategic initiative, he can afford to wait. He is sure to find a bride, even if he has to pay for his delay by making do with a woman who has already been married, or is of lower social status, or has some disability. The girl being the one traditionally 'asked for' and 'given' in marriage, it would be the height of absurdity for a father to solicit a husband for his daughter. Another difference is that 'the man can wait for the woman [to be of age], but the woman cannot wait for the man'. A father with daughters to marry can play with time in order to prolong the conjunctural advantage he derives from his position as the receivers of offers, but only up to a certain point, or he will see his products devalued because they are thought to be unsaleable, or are simply past their prime.

One of the most important constraints is the urgency of marriage, which naturally tends to weaken the player's position. Among the reasons for hurrying a marriage may be the great age of the parents, who hope to attend their son's wedding and to have a daughter-in-law to look after them, or the fear of seeing a girl they had counted on being given to someone else (to avoid this, the parents 'present a slipper', thus 'marking' the girl at a very early age, and sometimes even have the *fatih'a* recited). An only son is also married young, so that he can continue the lineage as soon as possible. The symbolic profit accruing from remarrying after a divorce before the ex-spouse does leads both spouses to arrange hasty marriages (such marriages are unlikely to last, which explains why some men or women seem 'destined' to marry many times). But there is great asymmetry on this point too. A man, divorced or widowed, is expected to remarry, whereas a divorced woman is devalued by the failure of her marriage, and a widow, even a very young one, is excluded from the matrimonial market by her status as a mother expected to bring up her husband's child, especially if it is a boy. 'A woman cannot remain [a widow] for another woman': a widow who only has daughters will be encouraged to remarry, whereas a mother of sons is praised for her sacrifice, which is all the greater if she is young and will have to live as an outsider among her husband's sisters and his brothers' wives. But her situation also varies depending on whether she has left her children with her husband's family or taken them back with her to her own family (in which case she is less free and hence harder to marry). An interesting option arises: she may either be taken to wife by a member of her husband's family (the official custom, particularly recommended if she has sons) or she may be found a husband by her father's family (which is more common when she is childless) or by her husband's family. It is difficult to establish the set of variables (no doubt including local traditions) determining the 'choice' of one or the other of these strategies.

But it also has to be borne in mind, contrary to the tradition that treats each marriage as an isolated unit, that the marrying of each of the children of the same family unit (that is, depending on the case, the children of the same father or the grandchildren of the same grandfather) depends on the marrying of all the others. It therefore varies as a function of each individual's position (defined mainly by birth, rank, sex and relationship to the head of the family) within the particular configuration of the set of children to be married, which is itself characterized by their number and sex. Thus, for a man the situation is more favourable the closer his kin relationship to the statutory holder of authority over the marriage (which may range from son–father to younger brother–elder brother or even the relationship between distant cousins). Moreover, although there is no official privilege favouring the eldest (son, of course), everything in fact conspires to advantage him at the expense of his younger brothers, to marry him first and as well as possible, that is, outside rather than inside the lineage, the younger sons being destined for production rather than the exchanges of the market or the assembly, for work on the land rather than the external relations of the house.[28] But there is great difference in situation between the eldest of several sons and one who bears all his family's hopes as an only child or as a son followed by several daughters.

'Spontaneous psychology' perfectly describes the 'girls' boy' (*aqchich bu thaqchichin*), coddled and cosseted by the women of the family who are always inclined to keep him with them longer than other boys. He eventually identifies with the social role destiny created for him and becomes a sickly, puny child, 'eaten up by his many long-haired sisters'. The same reasons that lead the family to lavish care on a product too rare and precious to be allowed to run the slightest risk – to spare him farm work and to prolong his education, thus setting him apart from his friends by his more refined speech, cleaner clothes and more elaborate food – will also lead them to arrange an early marriage for him. By contrast, a girl's value rises with the number of her brothers, the guardians of her honour (in particular, her virginity) and potential allies for her future husband. Tales express the jealousy inspired by the girl with seven brothers, protected sevenfold like 'a fig among the leaves': 'A girl who had the good fortune to have seven brothers could be proud, and there was no lack of suitors. She was sure of being sought after and appreciated. When she was married her husband, her husband's parents, the whole family, and even the neighbours and their wives respected her: had she not seven men on her side, was she not the sister of seven brothers, seven protectors? If there was the slightest argument, they would come and set things right, and if their sister committed a fault, or ever came to be repudiated, they would have taken her back home with them, lavishing attention on her. No dishonour could touch them. No one would dare to enter the lions' den.'

A family with many daughters, especially if they are 'ill protected' (by brothers), and therefore less valued because they offer few allies and are vulnerable, is in an unfavourable position and is forced to incur debts towards the families that receive its women. By contrast, a family rich in men has great freedom of manoeuvre. It can choose to 'invest' each of its sons in a different way according to the circumstances: to increase its alliances with one of them, strengthen its integration with another, and even put a cousin who only has daughters under an obligation by taking one of his girls for a third son. In this case, the strategist's skill can have free rein and can effortlessly reconcile the irreconcilable, reinforcing integration *and* expanding alliances. The man who only has daughters, or who has too many of them, is restricted to negative strategies, and his skill has to be limited to manipulating the relationship between the field of potential partners and the field of possible competitors, by playing off the near against the distant, the request of a close kinsman against that of a stranger (in order to refuse without offence or make him wait), so that he reserves the right to choose the most prestigious offer.

This takes us a long way from the pure – infinitely impoverished – realm of the 'rules of marriage' and the 'elementary structures of kinship'. Having defined the system of principles from which the agents are able to produce (and understand) regulated, regular matrimonial practices, we could use statistical analysis of the relevant information to establish the weight of the corresponding structural or individual variables. In fact, the important thing is that the agents' practice becomes intelligible as soon as one is able to construct the system of principles that they put into practice when they immediately identify the socio-logically matchable individuals in a given state of the matrimonial market; or, more precisely, when, for a particular man, they designate for example the few women within practical kinship who are in a sense promised to him, and those whom he might at a stretch be permitted to marry – and when they do so in such a clear and final way that any deviation from the most probable trajectory, marriage into another tribe for example, is felt as a challenge to the family concerned, and also to the whole group.

3

Irresistible Analogy

The purpose and shape of the spoon make it an instrument ideally suited to the gesture indicating the desire to see rain fall. The opposite gesture, that of inverting a spoon, should automatically, as it were, provoke a contrary action. This is what the wife of a *fqih* does, among the Mtouggas, to ward off imminent rainfall.

> E. Laoust, *Mots et choses berbères*

'I think I've made a new theological discovery . . .'
'What is it?'
'If you hold your hands upside down, you get the opposite of what you pray for!'

> Charles M. Schulz, *There's No One Like You, Snoopy*

The extent to which the schemes of the *habitus* are objectified in codified knowledge, transmitted as such, varies greatly between one area of practice and another. The relative frequency of sayings, prohibitions, proverbs and strongly regulated rites declines as one moves from practices linked to or directly associated with agricultural activity, such as weaving, pottery and cuisine, towards the divisions of the day or the moments of human life, not to mention areas apparently abandoned to arbitrariness, such as the internal organization of the house, the parts of the body, colours or animals. Although they are among the most codified aspects of the cultural tradition, the precepts of custom which govern the temporal distribution of activities vary greatly from place to place and, in the same place, from one informant to another.[1] We find here again the opposition between official knowledge, which is also the knowledge most marked by interferences with the Islamic tradition (and – confirming the connivance between anthropology and all forms of legalism – the knowledge most strongly represented in ethnographic collections), and all kinds of unofficial or secret, even clandestine, knowledge and practices which, though they are the product of the same generative schemes, obey a different logic. What is called the 'calculation of moments' (*lawqat lah'sab*) is more especially imparted to the 'dignitaries', that is, the oldest men of the most respected families, to whom it falls to recall the dates of the great collective ceremonies, official and imperative rites which, like the agrarian rites, involve the whole group because they fulfil one and the same function for all members of the group, or to establish and impose the ban on harvesting ('When the ears of corn are ripe', said an informant in Aïn Aghbel, 'the senior men get together and fix the date of the harvest. It will be a feast-day. They come to an agreement. Everyone begins on the same day.') By contrast, it is among blacksmiths and old women that one most often finds the greatest competence in private magic, minor rites intended to satisfy private ends, such as rites of malign or curative magic or love magic, which generally employ a fairly transparent symbolism, and ritual strategies such as the transfer of evil on to a person or a thing.

As soon as one sets out to draw up a synoptic 'calendar' combining the most frequently attested features and indicating the most important variants (instead of presenting the record of what was really derived from a particular informant), one finds that identical 'periods' are given different names and, even more frequently, that identical names cover periods of very different duration, situated at different dates depending on the region, the tribe, the village and even the informant.[2] So care must be taken not to see anything more than a theoretical artefact in the diagram that brings together in condensed, synoptic form the information accumulated by a process of collection that was initially oriented by the semi-conscious intention of combining all the productions recorded so as to construct a kind of unwritten 'score' of which all the 'calendars' actually collected would be imperfect, impoverished 'performances'. However, although they are perfectly inadequate theoretically, the synoptic diagram and the linear text which makes its contents explicit by successively unfolding 'moments' and 'periods' (treating the rival 'readings' as 'variants') are useful in two distinct ways.[3] First, they offer an economical way of giving the reader information reduced to its pertinent features and organized in accordance with a principle that is both familiar and immediately visible. Secondly, they make it possible to show some of the difficulties that arise from the endeavour to combine and linearize the available information and to give a sense of the artificiality of the 'objectified calendar', the idea of which has been taken for granted and has oriented all collections of rites, proverbs or practices, including my own.[4]

A question as innocuous in appearance as 'What next?', inviting an informant to situate two periods in relation to each other in a continuous time, which does no more than state what the chronological diagram does implicitly, has the effect of inducing an attitude to time which is the exact opposite of the attitude involved practically in the ordinary use of temporal terms and of notions which, like that of a 'period', are not at all self-evident. Proof that *eliali*, which every informant mentions, is not 'a period of forty days' (all that is said is 'We enter *eliali*') but a simple scansion of passing time, is found in the fact that different informants assign different durations and different dates to it. One of them even located the first day of *ennayer* both in the middle of winter and in the middle of *eliali*, although he did not set *eliali* in the (geometric) middle of winter, thereby demonstrating that the practical grasp of the structure that led him to think of *eliali* as the winter of winter overrides calculating reason.

This logic is also found in the belief that certain 'periods', benign in themselves, contain a malign moment, which cannot be precisely situated, and during which certain actions are avoided, the 'period' then being nothing other than the field of uncertainty between two reference-points. This is true of a 'period' of intense cold, *laâdidal*, which no one can situate exactly (it was referred to by an informant in the Djurdjura region, and is also mentioned in a song sung by women working at the flour mill: 'If for me *laâdidal* are like the nights of *h'ayan*, tell the shepherds to take refuge in the village'). It is also, according to various informants in Djurdjura, during a night in the month of *jember* – no one knows which one – that water turns to blood: a person who drinks it may die and will be thirsty all day. Similarly, *nisan*, a benign month, contains a sinister moment (*eddbagh*), unknown to anyone (except perhaps a few peasants who keep it a close secret), during which any tree that is touched or any animal stung by an insect (or shedding blood) will die instantly. This is a perfect example of the dialectic of poverty and insecurity engendering the magic ritual which is intended to combat them but in fact intensifies them.

As well as the form that the questioning has to take in order to elicit an ordered sequence of answers, everything in the relationship of inquiry itself betrays the 'theoretical' disposition of the questioner, inviting the respondent to adopt a quasi-theoretical stance. Because it excludes any reference to the use and conditions of use of the temporal reference-points, such questioning tacitly rejects discontinuous reference-points, used for practical purposes, in favour of the calendar as an object predisposed to be unfolded as a totality existing outside of its 'applications' and regardless of the needs and interests of its users. This explains why, apart from the primordial oppositions such as *eliali* and *es'maïm*, informants who are invited to rehearse the calendar often start by setting out what they recall of scholarly series such as *mwalah'*, *swalah'* and *fwatah'*, or *izegzawen*, *iwraghen*, *imellalen* and *iquranen*. In short, by tacitly excluding all reference to the practical interest that a particular person – man or woman, adult or shepherd-boy, farmer or blacksmith – may have in each case in dividing up the year in this or that way and using this or that temporal marker, one unwittingly constructs an object which only exists by virtue of this unconscious construction of both it and its operations.[5]

This inevitable effect produced by graphic construction has to be borne constantly in mind when 'reading' the diagram opposite and its commentary on pp. 204–9. They are no more than shorthand descriptions designed to give the reader a convenient overview of the practices which the generative model will have to re-produce.

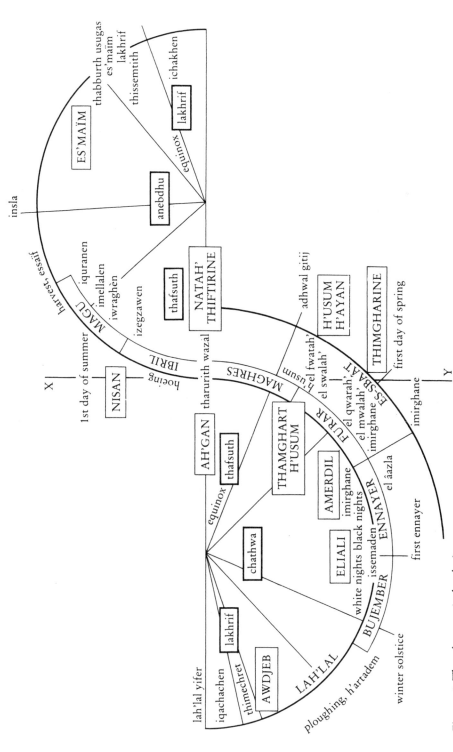

Figure 1 The abstract 'calendar'

The calendar and the synoptic illusion

Most informants spontaneously start their account of the year with autumn (*lakhrif*). Some of them locate the beginning of this season around the 1st of September in the Julian calendar; for others, it starts about the 15th of August, on the day called 'the door of the year' (*thabburth usugas*), which marks the entry into the wet period, after the dogdays of *es'maïm*. On that day, each family sacrifices a cock, and associations and contracts are renewed. But for other informants, the 'door of the year' is the first day of ploughing (*lah'lal natsh'arats* or *lah'lal n thagersa*), which marks the most decisive turning-point in the transitional period.

The 'period' devoted to ploughing (usually called *lah'lal*, but sometimes *h'artadem*) begins with the inauguration of ploughing (*awdjeb*), after an ox bought collectively (*thimechreth*) has been sacrificed and the meat shared out amongst all the members of the clan (*adhrum*) or village. Ploughing and sowing, which begin immediately after the opening ceremony (which is also a rain-making rite), as soon as the land is sufficiently moist, may go on until mid-December, or even longer, depending on the region and year.

In fact, it is probably incorrect to refer to *lah'lal* as a 'period'. The term *lah'lal*, and the corresponding temporal unit, are defined practically, within the universe of the wet season, in opposition to *lakhrif* (ploughing and sowing are then opposed to the picking and drying of figs, gardening work in *thabh'irth*, the summer garden, and *laâlaf*, the special attention given to oxen weakened by treading-out, so as to prepare them for ploughing). But within the same universe it can also be defined in opposition to *eliali*, the slack moment in winter. Within a quite different logic, it can also be contrasted with all the other periods held to be licit for a particular type of work which would be *h'aram*, illicit, if done outside these periods. For example, *lah'lal lafth*, the licit period for sowing turnips (from the 17th day of autumn, our 3rd of September), *lah'lal yifer*, the licit period for stripping fig trees (late September), etc.

Winter (*chathwa*) begins, for some informants, on the 15th of November, for others on the 1st of December, without any special rite (which tends to show that the opposition between autumn and winter is not strongly marked). Still other informants even say it is impossible to know which is the first day of winter. The heart of winter is called *eliali*, 'the nights', a period of forty days which all informants divide into two equal parts, *eliali thimellaline*, the white nights, and *eliali thiberkanine*, the black nights, a distinction which, as is suggested by its range of applications, is the product of a quite abstract, formal principle of division, although informants find justifications for it in climatic changes. Once the autumn work is over, the slack period begins. This period is opposed, as such, to *es'maïm*, the slack period of the dry season, or, as has been seen, to *lah'lal*, a time of intense activity; but it is contrasted in another respect with the transition from winter to spring (*es-sbaât* or *essubuâ*, the 'sevens'); and from yet another standpoint, these are the 'great nights' (*eliali kbira*) as opposed to the 'lesser nights' (*eliali esghira*) of February and March, to the 'shepherd's nights' and to the 'nights of H'ayan'. At the heart of winter, the first day of *ennayer* (January) is marked by a whole set of renewal rites and taboos (in particular on sweeping and weaving), which some informants extend to the whole period of *issemaden* (the cold days) running from late December to early January.

The end of *eliali* is marked by the ritual celebration of *el âazla gennayer*, 'the separation from *ennayer*'. Life has emerged on the face of the earth, the first shoots are appearing on the trees, it is 'the opening' (*el ftuth'*). The farmer goes out into the fields and sets up oleander branches, which have the power to drive away *maras*, the cockchafer grub; as he does so, he says: 'Come out, Maras! The *khammès* is going to crush you!' (according to other informants, in Collo, this rite is performed on the first day of spring). On the same day, it is said, the peasants go to their stables and shout in the ears of the oxen: 'Good news! *Ennayer* is over!' Some informants say *âazri*, bachelor, for *âazla*, separation, 'because from that day on, spring is coming and marriages start to be celebrated', with a kind of play on words which is probably also a play on mythic roots. This is the beginning of a long transitional period, a time of waiting, covered by a terminology as rich as it is confused. Whereas autumn, as one informant put it, 'is a whole', the passage from winter to spring is a patchwork of moments which are ill-defined, almost all malign, and variously named.

Thus the term *thimgharine*, the old women, or *thamghart*, the old woman (names evoking the legend of the borrowed days that tells how, by borrowing a few days from the following period, Winter – or January, or February, etc. – was able to punish an old woman – or a goat, or a Negro – who had defied her), or the term *amerdil*, loan, designate either the moment of transition from one month to another (December to January, or January to February, or February to March, or even, at Aïn Aghbel, March to April) or the moment of transition from winter to spring. *H'usum*, a learned term of Arabic origin which refers to a sura of the Koran, is used alongside *h'ayan* (or *ah'gan*) to designate the transition from *furar* to *maghres*. (Although it must not be forgotten that to bring together a set of features present in a region in the form of a series is in itself a quite artificial syncretic operation, the three main series are indicated on the diagram, viz. (1) *imirghane, amerdil, thamghart, ah'gan* or *thiftirine, nisan*; (2) *thimgharine, ha'yan, nisan*; (3) *el mwalah', el qwarah', el swalah', el fwatah', h'usum, natah', nisan*. These series could roughly be said to correspond to the Djurdjura region, to Lesser Kabylia, and, in the last case, to the most Islamized regions or to literate informants.)

But the logic of magic insists that it is never possible to know exactly which is the most unpropitious moment in a period which is uncertain as a whole, so that the terms *thimgharine* or *h'usum*, indicating highly unpropitious periods, are sometimes used to designate the whole transition from late January to mid-March. In this case, they are made to include the four 'weeks' that divide up the month of February, known collectively as *es-baât* (the sevens): *el mwalah'* (sometimes called *imirghane*), the salty days; *el qwarah'*, the pungent days; *el swalah'*, the benign days; *el fwatah'*, the open days. This semi-scholarly series is sometimes called *ma, qa, sa, fin,* applying a mnemonic device used by the marabouts, in which each name is represented by its initial. Similarly, it is thanks to its mnemonic properties that informants almost always cite the series of the divisions of the beginning of summer – *izegzawen, iwraghen, imellalen, iquranen*; the series is also sometimes designated by the first consonants of the roots of the Berber words for the divisions: *za, ra, ma, qin*. We find here one of the semi-learned dichotomies, similar to that within the nights of January, which always involve an attempt at rationalization: the first two periods are malign and come at the end of winter; the last two are benign and come at the beginning of spring. In the same way, informants who locate *h'usum* in the fortnight straddling the end of January and the beginning of February, concentrating within it all the features characteristic of the period as a whole, distinguish a first, dangerous week and a second, more favourable week. And similarly, numerous informants (especially in Djurdjura) distinguish two *ah'gans* (or *h'ayans*) – *ah'gan bu akli*, the *h'ayan* of the Negro, seven intensely cold days during which work is suspended, and *ah'gan u hari*, the *h'ayan* of the freeman, seven days in which 'everything on earth comes back to life'.

During '*h'ayan* week' (the first week of March), life completes its work. Man must not disturb it by going into the fields or orchards. Other taboos of *h'ayan'* and *h'usum* concern ploughing, weddings, sex, working at night, making and firing pottery, preparing wool and weaving. At Aïn Aghbel, during the period of *el h'usum*, all work on the land is forbidden; this is *el faragh*, emptiness. It is inauspicious to 'start any building work, celebrate a marriage, hold a feast, or buy an animal'. In a general way, people refrain from any activity involving the future. The animals too seem to have completed their growth: weaning (*el h'iyaz*) is carried out at the end of *h'ayan* week, on the day of the spring equinox (*adhwal gitij*, the lengthening of the sun). A tin can is struck to make a noise that will prevent the oxen – who can understand human speech on that day – from hearing what is said about 'the lengthening of the days', lest they 'take fright at having to work harder'. By virtue of its position, *h'usum* (or *h'ayan*) is endowed with an inaugural and augural character very similar to that conferred on morning in the cycle of the day. For example, if it rains, this is a sign of plenty; if it starts with snow, there will be many partridge eggs. It is therefore a time for acts of propitiation (almsgiving) and divination.

Once the days of the old woman and *h'usum* are over, the flock is reckoned to be safe. It is now *el fwatah'*, the time for coming out, the time for births, both on the cultivated land and among the flock, and the younglings are no longer threatened by the rigours of winter. The first day of spring (*thafsuth*), the feast of greenness and infancy, has already been celebrated. All the ritual of this inaugural day of an augural period is placed under the sign of joy and of objects that bring good fortune and prosperity. The children go out into the fields to meet spring. In the open air they eat a semolina of grilled cereals and butter. The couscous served on that day (*seksu wadhris*) is cooked in the steam of a broth containing *adhris*, thapsia, a plant that causes swelling. The women cast off the taboos of the ploughing period and dye their hands with henna. They go off in groups and gather shrubs to make brooms, the euphemistic name for which is *thafarah'th*, from *farah'*; made in joy, they will bring joy.

The days grow longer. There is not much work to be done (apart from tillage in the fig orchards); man has to wait for life to do its work. 'In March', they say in Great Kabylia, 'go and look at your crops, and take a good look'; and elsewhere: 'the sun of the flowering [that of the leguminous plants, and especially the long-awaited broad beans] empties the *douar*'. The food stocks are exhausted and the lengthening of the days is made more burdensome by the ban on going out into the fields (*natah'* is not yet past) and on eating beans or other green vegetables. Hence the proverbs: 'March (*maghres*) climbs like a hillside'; 'The days of March are seven-snack days.'

With *natah'* or *thiftirine*, the transitional period comes to an end. These terms, which denote the same period to within a few days, are both of Arabic origin and are rarely known to the peasants of the Djurdjura region (where *h'ayan*, or rather *ah'gan*, as it is called locally, has shifted to this time of the year). During *natah'*, 'the trees are shaken and knock together'; heavy rain is likely, and the weather is so cold that 'the boar shivers'. As in *h'usum*, it is forbidden to enter the cultivated fields or the orchards (for fear of causing the death of a person or a beast). *Natah'* is also the season of nature's awakening, the blossoming of crops, life and marriages. It is (along with autumn) the time for weddings (according to a scholarly tradition, 'all living beings on earth marry'; sterile women are recommended to boil and eat herbs gathered in *natah'*); and it is the time for village feasts. Applying a familiar device, some informants divide *thiftirine or natah'* into an unfavourable period, in March ('the difficult days') and a favourable period, in April ('the easy days').

The passage from the wet season to the dry season is situated during *natah'*, on the day called 'the return of *azal*', the date of which varies from region to region because of climatic differences, coming either in March, after weaning, or a little later, in April, at sheep-shearing time or shortly after, or, at the very latest, at the beginning of May. It is marked by a change in the rhythm of daily activity. From that day on, the flock, which previously went out late in the morning and returned relatively early, now leaves early in the morning and comes back to spend the moment called *azal* in the village (*azal* designates broad daylight, as opposed to night and morning, and more precisely the hottest moment of the day, devoted to rest); it then goes out again in early afternoon and returns at sunset.

The time of bad weather is over for good. The green fields and the gardens are now ready to receive the rays of the sun. This is the start of the cycle of dryness and ripening. With *ibril*, a particularly benign month ('April is a downward slope'), a trouble-free period of relative plenty begins. Work of all sorts starts up again. In the fields, where the critical growth period is over, the men can start hoeing, the only important activity; in the gardens, the first beans are picked. During the period of *nisan*, whose benign rain, bringing fertility and prosperity to every living thing, is invoked with all sorts of rites, the sheep are shorn and the new lambs branded. The fact that *nisan*, like all transitional periods (*natah'* for example), is an ambiguous period, ill-defined in terms of the opposition between the wet and the dry, is here expressed not in a division between two periods, one auspicious and the other inauspicious, but by the existence of inauspicious moments (*eddbagh*), which no one can situate exactly, when one should avoid pruning or grafting trees, celebrating weddings, whitewashing houses, setting up the loom, setting eggs to be hatched, etc.

As the period known as *izegzawen*, 'the green days', comes to an end, the last traces of greenery fade from the landscape; the cereal crops, previously as 'tender' (*thaleqaqth*) as a new-born baby, begin to turn yellow. The changing appearance of the cornfields is indicated by the names of the ten- or seven-day periods into which the month of *magu* (or *mayu*) is divided. After *izegzawen* come *iwraghen*, the yellow days, *imellalen*, the white days, and *iquranen*, the dry days. Summer (*anebdhu*) has begun. The characteristic tasks of the wet season, tillage (in the fig-orchards) and sowing, which are still permitted in the 'green' days, are absolutely banned from the period known as the 'yellow' days. The only concern is to protect the ripening crops against the dangers that threaten them (hail, birds, locusts, etc.), with the aid of showers of stones, shouts (*ah'ah'i*) or scarecrows. The collective expulsion rites (*as'ifedh*) that are also used to drive malignant forces out of the territory to be protected, into a cave, bush or heap of stones, after 'fixing' them on objects (dolls) or animals (for example, a pair of birds), which are then sacrificed, are simply applications of the scheme of the 'transfer of evil' which is set to work in treating a large number of diseases – fever, madness (possession by a *djinn*), sterility – and also in rites performed on fixed dates in certain villages.

According to most informants, summer begins on the 17th day of the month of *magu*. Just as acts of fecundation are excluded from the month of May, so sleep is excluded from the first day of summer. Men take care not to sleep during that day, for fear of falling ill, or losing their courage or their sense of honour (the seat of which is the liver). Probably for the same reason, earth gathered on that day is used in the magical rites intended to weaken or destroy the point of honour (*nif*) in a man, or the stubbornness in an animal which makes it resistant to training. By the last day of *iquranen*, known as 'a fiery ember has fallen in the water', an expression that alludes to the quenching of iron by the blacksmith, everyone should have started harvesting (*essaïf*), which is completed around *insla*, the day of the summer solstice (24 June), when fires are lit everywhere. Smoke, the mingling of the dry and the wet that is obtained by burning the wet (green plants, branches and vegetation gathered from damp spots, such as poplars or oleander) is believed to have the power to 'fecundate' the fig trees; fumigation is identified with caprification. When treading-out and winnowing are completed, the forty dog-days of *es'maïm* begin and work is suspended, as it is during *eliali*, a period to which *es'maïm* is always opposed (for example, it is often said that if there is a severe sirocco in *es'maïm*, there will be cold weather and snow in *eliali*).

In opposition to harvesting and treading-out, *lakhrif* appears as a slack period in the agrarian year, or rather in the grain cycle. It is also a period devoted to rest and to the celebrations of a plentiful harvest. As well as the newly harvested grain there are figs, grapes and various fresh vegetables – tomatoes, sweet peppers, gourds, melons, etc. *Lakhrif* is sometimes said to begin in mid-August, at *thissemtith* (from *semti*, to start ripening), the moment when the first figs appear and when the ban (*el haq*) on fig picking is imposed, with fines for disobedience. When *ichakhen* comes round (*ichakh lakhrif*, 'it is *lakhrif* everywhere'), the fig-harvest is in full swing, and the men, women and children all join in. The 1st of October is *lah'lal yifer*, when the leaves may be stripped from the fig trees (*achraw*, from *chrew*, to strip) to feed the oxen. This date is the signal for the 'withdrawal of life', the work of *iqachachen* ('the last days'), which are devoted to a thorough cleaning of the kitchen gardens, orchards and fields, with *thaqachachth lakhrif* (the last fruit is shaken from the trees and the remaining leaves are stripped off) and 'the rooting-up of the garden'. When all traces of life persisting in the fields after the harvest have thus been removed, the land is ready for ploughing.

THE GENERATIVE FORMULA

Figure 1 and its commentary are useful not only for the sake of more economical exposition. They would differ from the richest of previous collections only in the quantity and density of the pertinent information they assemble, if their synthetic and synoptic capacity did not make it possible to apply greater logical control and therefore to go further in bringing to light both the coherence and the incoherences. Indeed, the specifically 'structuralist' intention of constructing the network of relationships constituting the system of ritual practices and objects as a 'system of differences', has the paradoxical effect, when one tries to carry it through to its conclusion, of thwarting the very ambition it contains, namely that of finding confirmation of the validity of this kind of self-interpretation of the real in the coherence and systematicity of the interpretation and of the interpreted reality. The most rigorous analysis cannot manifest all the possible coherence of the products of practical sense without at the same time bringing to light the limits of this coherence. It thereby forces one to pose the question of the functioning of the analogical sense which produces practices and works that are less logical than structuralist pan-logicism would have it and more logical then the inchoate, uncertain evocation of intuitionism would suggest.

The principle of ritual practice lies in the need to re-unite socio-logically the contraries that socio-logic has separated (for example, the rites of ploughing or marriage) or to divide the product of this re-union (as in the rites of harvesting). Both operations must be performed in a socio-logically acceptable way, that is, in the only way that is both logical and legitimate in terms of a given cultural arbitrary. A vision of the world is a division of the world, based on a fundamental principle of division which distributes all the things of the world into two complementary classes. To bring order is to bring division, to divide the universe into opposing entities, those that the primitive speculation of the Pythagoreans presented in the form of 'columns of contraries' (*sustoichiai*). The limit produces difference and the different things 'by an arbitrary institution', as Leibniz put it, translating the '*ex instituto*' of the Scholastics. This magical act presupposes and produces collective belief, that is, ignorance of its own arbitrariness. It constitutes the separated things as separated, and by an absolute distinction, which can only be crossed by another magical act, a ritual transgression. *Natura non facit saltus*: it is the magic of institution which, in the natural continuum, the network of biological kinship or the natural world, introduces the break, the division, *nomos*, the frontier which makes the group and its specific customs ('vérité en deçà des Pyrénées, erreur au-delà'), the arbitrary necessity (*nomô*) through which the group constitutes itself as such by instituting what unites it and what separates it. The cultural act *par excellence* is the one that traces the line that produces a separate, delimited space, like the *nemus*, a sacred wood apportioned to the gods, the *templum*, a precinct delimited for the gods, or simply the house which, with the threshold, *limen*, a dangerous line where the world is reversed and all signs are inverted, provides the practical model of all rites of passage. As Arnold van Gennep (1960: 12) correctly observed, all rites of passage have something in common: they aim to regulate magically the crossing of a magical limit where, as at the threshold of the house, the world 'pivots'.

Particularly in the presence of vulnerable people, whose life is threatened because they are at a threshold between two states – the new-born, the newly married, recently circumcised boys – euphemisms are used instead of all the words that contain an idea of cutting, closing and finishing: 'finish', replaced by 'be happy' or 'become rich'; 'be finished' (applied to the harvest, provisions, milk, etc.), replaced by 'there is plenty'; die, extinguish, leave, break, spread, close (cf. the ritual formula that a woman addresses to her husband when he goes off to the market: 'Cut and it grows again, may God make things easy and open' [Genevois 1968: vol. I, 81]). Similarly, all the terms suggesting violence against life are avoided: 'water' is used for 'blood' during the forty days that follow calving or childbirth. Because it implies the imposition of a limit, a cut (bread is not cut with a knife), the operation of measuring is surrounded by all sorts of euphemisms and magical precautions. The master avoids measuring his own crop and has this done by a *khammès* or a neighbour. Euphemistic expressions are used to avoid certain numbers; ritual formulae are used, such as 'May God not measure out his bounty to us!'

The sense of the limit which separates, and of the sacred, which is separated, is indissoluble from the sense of regulated and therefore legitimate transgression of the limit which is the form *par excellence* of ritual. The principle of the ordering of the world is again the basis of the ritual actions intended to sanction, by denying them, the necessary or inevitable transgressions of the limits. All the acts that defy the original *diacrisis* are critical acts, which present danger for the whole group, and first and foremost for the person who performs them for the group, that is, in its place and name, on its behalf. Transgressions of the limit (*thalasth*) threaten the order of the natural world and the social world: 'everyone for himself', the Kabyles say, 'the hen crows [like the cockerel] on its head', that is, at its own risk [its throat will be cut]. The rainbow or the mixture of hail, rain and sun that is called the 'jackal's wedding' is another case of unnatural union, that is, union contrary to the classification, like the marriage of the jackal and the camel, presented in a tale as an exemplary form of misalliance.

The limit *par excellence*, that between the sexes, will not brook transgression. A man who flees from battle is subjected to nothing less than a degradation ritual. He is bound, by women – the world upside down – who tie a scarf, a typically female attribute, around his head, blacken him with soot, and pluck hairs from his beard and his moustache, the symbol of *nif*, 'so that the next day it will be seen that a woman is better than him', and he is led before the assembly which solemnly excludes him from the world of men (Boulifa 1913: 278–9). Regarded as *lkhunta*, that is, neuter, hermaphrodite, sexless, beyond the pale of what can be thought and named, he is reduced to nothing, like the objects that are cast away, to get rid of them for ever, on the grave of a stranger or at the boundary between two fields.

At Aït Hichem, the earth contained in the dish used to catch the blood of a circumcised boy was gathered on the boundary between two fields and taken back to the same place (the same observation is made by Rahmani (1949), who reports that the dish that has received the blood is used for target practice). Rites to expel evil make much use of soil taken from between two limits, a point which, being situated outside thinkable space, outside the divisions produced by the principles of division, represents the absolute outside. The 'tomb of the stranger', or of a man without issue, another of the points outside space to which evil is expelled, represents absolute death, without return; the stranger (*aghrib*) being not only the man who is in a sense twice dead because he died in the west, towards the setting sun, the place of death, but also the man who, because he died in foreign territory, in exile (*elghorba*), has no one to come and resurrect him (*seker*).

The fearful character of every operation reuniting contraries is particularly emphasized in the quenching of iron, *asqi*, which also means broth, sauce and poisoning. *Seqi*, to sprinkle, to moisten the dry, is to unite the dry and the wet in the action of sprinkling couscous with sauce, to unite the hot and the cold, fire and water, the dry and the wet, in quenching iron (*seqi azal*), to pour the 'burned (and burning) water' (*seqi essem*), poison (and also, according to Dallet, to immunize magically against poisoning). The quenching of iron is a terrible act of violence and cunning, performed by a terrible and guileful being, the smith, whose ancestor, Sidi-Daoud, could hold red-hot iron in his bare hands and would punish tardy payers by offering them one of his products with an innocent air after first heating it white-hot. Excluded from matrimonial exchanges ('blacksmith, son of a blacksmith' is an insult), the smith, the maker of all the instruments of violence – ploughshares, but also knives, sickles, axes and choppers – does not sit in the assembly but he is consulted on questions of war and violence.

The intersection of antagonistic forces can never be approached without danger. Circumcision (*khatna* or *th'ara*, often replaced by euphemisms based on *dher*, to be clean, neat), is supposed to give the protection which, as Durkheim (1976: 314–15) suggests, is needed in order to confront the fearful forces contained in the vagina[6] and especially those unleashed by the act of uniting contraries in sexual intercourse. Similarly, the ploughman puts on a white woollen skull-cap and *arkasen*, leather sandals that must not enter the house, as if to avoid making himself the meeting-point of sky and earth and their antagonistic forces at the very moment when he brings them together (whereas, for their gleaning and hoeing, the women, who partake of earthly things, go barefoot into the fields). As for the harvester, he puts on a leather apron, which Servier (1962: 217) rightly associates with the blacksmith's apron, and whose meaning becomes clearer when one knows that, as Devaux (1859: 46–7) reports, it was also worn in battle.

The most fundamental ritual actions are in fact denied transgressions. The rite must resolve the specific contradiction that the original dichotomy makes inevitable by constituting, as separate and antagonistic, principles that have to be reunited to ensure the reproduction of the group. It must do so through a socially approved and collectively endorsed operation, that is, in accordance with the objective intention of the very taxonomy which gives rise to the contradiction. Through a practical denial, which is not individual, like that described by Freud (1961: 235–6), but collective and public, it aims to neutralize the dangerous forces that can be unleashed by transgression of the sacred limit, violation of the *h'aram* of woman or the earth that the limit has produced.

The magical protections that are set to work whenever the reproduction of the vital order requires transgression of the limits that are the foundation of that order, especially whenever it is necessary to cut or kill, in short, to interrupt the normal course of life, include a number of ambivalent figures who are all equally despised and feared. These agents of violence, like the instruments of violence that they use, the knife or the sickle, etc., can also keep away evil and protect against violence. Negroes, blacksmiths, butchers, corn-measurers, old women, partaking by nature of the maleficent forces that have to be confronted or neutralized, are predisposed to play the role of magic screens, interposing themselves between the group and the dangerous forces arising from unnatural division (cutting) or uniting (crossing). It is almost always the blacksmith who is appointed to perform the sacrilegious, sacred acts of cutting, whether it be the slaughter of the sacrificial ox, circumcision, or the castration of mules; in some villages, he is even entrusted with the inaugural ploughing. In a village in Lesser Kabylia, the person charged with starting the ploughing, the last descendant of the man who had found a piece of iron in the earth at the spot where lightning had struck, and had made his ploughshare out of it, was responsible for all the acts of violence by fire and iron (circumcision, sacrification, tattooing, etc.). More generally, the man charged with the solemn opening of ploughing, sometimes called 'the man of the wedding', acts as the delegate of the group and as a scapegoat designated to confront the dangers inherent in the transgression.[7] And the primary function of the sacrifice, performed publicly and collectively, at the time of the great transgressions of ploughing or the assembly of the loom (when the warp and the upright of the loom are smeared with the blood of a sacrificial animal – Anon. FDB 1964) is again to keep away the evil implied in the transgression.[8] However, as is seen very clearly in the case of the slaughter of the ox or the cutting of the last sheaf, it is always the ritualization itself that tends to transmute the inevitable murder into a necessary sacrifice by denying sacrilege in the very moment of its performance.

Magical transgression of the frontier installed by magical logic would not be so imperatively necessary if the contraries to be united were not life itself, and their dissociation a murder, the condition of life; if they did not represent reproduction, substance and subsistence, fecundated earth and woman, which are thus snatched from the deadly sterility which is that of the female principle when left to itself. In fact, the union of contraries does not abolish the opposition and, when united, the contraries are still as opposed as ever, but quite differently, manifesting the dual truth of the relationship that unites them, at once antagonistic and complementary, *neikos* and *philia*, and what might appear as their dual 'nature' if they were conceived outside of this relationship. Thus the house, which has all the negative characteristics of the dark, nocturnal, female world and which is, in this respect, the equivalent of the tomb or the maiden, changes its meaning when it becomes what it also is, the site *par excellence* of the cohabitation and marriage of contraries, which, like the wife, 'the lamp of the inside', contains its own lamp.[9] Each thing thus receives different properties, depending on whether it is considered in the state of union or separation, and neither of these two states can be regarded as its final truth, of which the other is simply an imperfect or adulterated form. Thus cultivated nature, the sacred of the left hand, the male-female or masculinized female, such as the wife or fecundated land, is opposed not only to the male as a whole – in the state of union or separation – but also and more especially to natural nature, which is still wild and untamed – the maiden or fallow land – or has returned to the twisted, malign naturalness into which it falls outside marriage – the harvested field or the old witch, with the cunning and treachery that relate her to the jackal.

This opposition between a female-female and a male-female is attested in countless ways. The female woman *par excellence* is the woman who does not depend on any male authority, who has no husband, no children and no honour (*h'urma*). She is sterile, akin to fallow land (a sterile woman must not plant in the garden or carry seeds) and the wilderness. She has affinities with the dark forces of uncontrolled nature. Being linked to everything that is twisted (*aâwaj*, to twist; 'she is of bad wood', 'twisted wood') and everything that is warped and warping (she is credited with *thiâiwji*, the suspect skill and guile that also characterize the blacksmith), she is predisposed to magic, especially the magic which uses the left hand, the cruel, deadly hand (a 'left-hander's blow' is lethal), which turns things from right to left (as opposed to man, who uses the right hand, the hand used in swearing oaths, and who turns things from left to right). She is also skilled in the art of slyly 'twisting her gaze' (*abran walan*) away from the person of whom she wishes to express her disapproval or annoyance –· *abran*, to turn from right to left, to fork (the tongue), in short, to turn the wrong way, is opposed to *qeleb*, to turn (the back), to reverse, as a discreet, furtive, passive movement, a female side-stepping, a 'twisted' move, a magical device, to open, honest, straightforward male aggression. The negative extreme of womanhood, the old woman, who concentrates all the negative properties of the female (that is, everything in woman that arouses terror in men, so characteristic of 'male-dominated' societies), has as her own extreme limit the old witch (*stut*), the villain of many tales (Lacoste-Dujardin 1970: 333–6), credited with extraordinary powers ('toothless, she crunches beans, blind, she spins cotton, deaf, she peddles gossip everywhere'). Whereas men, as they grow older, grow in wisdom, women grow in wickedness – despite the fact that, 'being finished for this world' (because they are no longer concerned with sexuality), they can pray daily (Anon. FDB 1964). Disputes between women are often attributed to old women from outside the family (they are called 'the ruin of the house'). A man concerned for the harmony of his household will keep them at a distance; and they steer clear of families where there is authority (*elhiba*).

The unbridled, sterile old woman, who no longer has any 'restraint', brings the potentialities inherent in every woman to their full realization. Like the young shoot which, left to itself, tends to the left, and has to be brought back to the

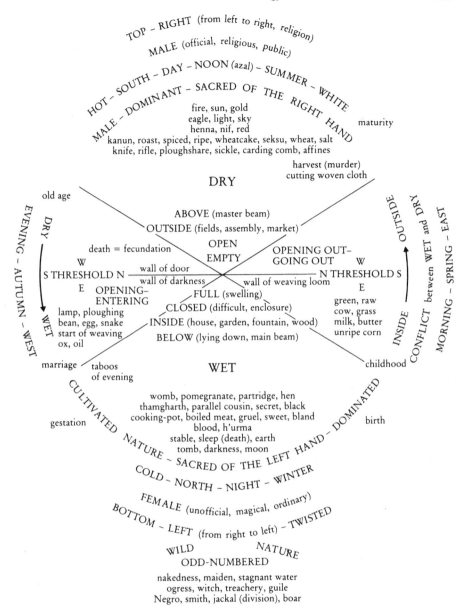

Figure 2 Synoptic diagram of pertinent oppositions

right (or made upright) at the cost of a twisting, a 'knot' ('woman is a knot in the wood'), every woman partakes of the diabolic nature of the female woman, especially during the menstrual period, when she must not prepare food, work in the garden, plant, pray or fast. 'Woman is like the sea' (where filth accumulates). *Elkalath*, the collective noun for 'womankind', also means emptiness, the void, the desert, ruin.

The pre-eminence given to the male principle, which enables it to impose its effects in every union, means that, unlike the female-female, the male-male is never overtly condemned, despite the disapproval of certain excesses of the male virtues in the pure state, such as 'the Devil's point of honour (*nif*)' (one of its incarnations is the redhead,[10] who sows discord everywhere, who has no moustache, whom no one wants as a companion and who refuses indulgence at the last judgement, when everyone forgives offences, and so on, or, in a quite different way, the *amengur*, the man without male issue).

The fundamental division runs through the social world from end to end, from the division of labour between the sexes and the associated division of the agrarian cycle into labour periods and production period, through ritual practices and into representations and values. The same practical schemes, inscribed at the deepest level of the bodily dispositions, are at the heart both of the division of labour and of the rites or representations that tend to reinforce or justify it.[11] The empirical work that establishes the 'columns of contraries' on which each cultural system is based in its arbitrary, that is, historical, singularity, makes it possible to grasp the principle of the fundamental separation, the founding *nomos* which one is tempted to see as situated at the origin, in a kind of initial act of constitution, and which is in fact instituted in each of the ordinary acts of ordinary practice, such as those regulated by the division of labour between the sexes – this unconscious, collective, continuous creation being the basis of its durability and its transcendence with respect to individual consciousnesses.

The distribution of activities between the sexes (as shown in the synoptic table, figure 3) can be accounted for by combining three cardinal oppositions: the opposition between movement inwards (and, secondarily, downwards) and movement outwards (or upwards); the opposition between the wet and the dry; and the opposition between continuous actions, aimed at maintaining and managing the united contraries, and short, discontinuous actions, aimed at uniting contraries or separating united contraries. There is no need to dwell on the opposition between the inside, the house, cooking, or inward movement (storing provisions), and the outside, the field, the market, the assembly, or outward movement, between the invisible and the visible, the private and the public, etc. The opposition between the wet and the dry, which partly overlaps with the former, assigns to woman everything that has to do with water, green things, grass, the garden, vegetables, milk, wood, stone, earth (women hoe barefoot and knead the clay for pottery or the inner walls with their bare hands). But the last opposition, the most important one in terms of ritual logic, distinguishes male acts, brief, dangerous confrontations with the liminal forces – ploughing, harvesting, slaughter of the ox – which use instruments made with fire and are accompanied by prophylactic rites, and female acts of gestation and maintenance, continuous attention aimed at ensuring continuity – cooking (analogous to gestation), rearing children and livestock (which implies cleaning, sweeping, carrying away dung, the smell of which

men's work	women's work
INDOORS	
feeding cattle at night	**bringing in** supplies and water, managing supplies, tying up cattle back from fields
	cooking (kitchen, fire, pot, couscous), feeding children and livestock (cows, hens) looking after children
(taboo on broom)	sweeping (cleaning)
	weaving (and spinning wool)
	milling
	kneading clay (pottery and plastering inner walls)
OUTDOORS	**milking** cow (and churning butter)
taking out goats and sheep, going to market	
working in fields (remote, open, yellow, cereals) ploughing (ploughshare, shoes) sowing harvesting (sickle, apron) treading out winnowing	**looking after** garden (close, closed, green, vegetables) (threshing floor taboo)
transporting and **raising** beams (men's 'corvée'), building roof transporting dung to fields (on back of animals)	**transporting** seed-corn, dung (on back), water, wood, stones and water for house building (women's 'corvée)
knocking down (climbing trees and beating down olives, felling trees – for house building) **cutting** wood and diss (carving wooden kitchen utensils with chopper or knife)	**picking up** (gathering) olives (beating-down taboo), figs, acorns, woods (twigs, brushwood) and tying up (faggots) gleaning hoeing (barefoot, trailing dress)
	treading olives (cf. kneading)
slaughtering	(taboo on slaughter)
	kneading clay (for house and threshing floor – with dung) by hand

Figure 3 The division of labour between the sexes

causes livestock and children to fade away), weaving (seen from one standpoint as bringing up a life), managing the reserves, or mere picking and gathering, all these activities being accompanied by simple propitiatory rites. Supremely vulnerable in herself, that is, in her life and her fertility ('a pregnant woman has one foot in this world and one foot in the other'; 'her grave is open from conception to the fortieth day after confinement') and in the lives for which she is responsible, those of the children, the livestock and the garden, woman, the guardian of the united contraries, that is, of life itself, must manage and protect life, both technically and magically.

Constantly threatened as guardians of life, women are responsible for all the magical practices intended to safeguard life (for example, all the *asfel* rites against the evil eye). All the rites they practise are designed to maintain the life for which they are responsible and the generative power of which they are the bearers (women are always blamed for sterility). To avoid the death of the child she bears, a pregnant woman washes next to a bitch that has been separated from its young. When a woman has lost a young child, she sprinkles water in the stable and the child's clothes are buried near its grave, along with the spade used to bury them (this is 'selling the spade'; a mother who has lost a child is told, 'May that spade by sold for ever!'). Conversely, all the acts linked to fertility (planting, putting henna on the hands of the bridegroom, *isli*, combing the bride, *thislith*, touching anything that must multiply and increase) are forbidden to a sterile woman. It is also a woman's duty to keep away the dangers that come through words: a child, like a garden, is spoken of in euphemisms, even antiphrases ('what a little nigger', is said of a child), so as to avoid defying fate (with a kind of hubris or complacency) or arousing envy, which would attract the evil eye, in other words the greedy, jealous gaze of envious desire, especially of women. Envy brings misfortune and is a particular threat to women, as the bearers and trustees of life (it is said that someone who sees a cow, likes the look of it and wishes he owned it, makes it ill; compliments are dangerous; envy is expressed in praise). 'Gardens', it is said, 'love secrecy (*esser*) and politeness.' Euphemism, which is a blessing, is opposed to cursing and blasphemy. A slanderer's talk is dangerous, 'like the woman who raises the loom' (the only time when a woman performs a crossing, running a danger analogous to that of a man when ploughing or harvesting). It is also the woman who applies the magic antidotes, which all belong to the realm of fire and the dry, to damp concupiscence (the evil eye, *thit'*, is also sometimes called *nefs*), such as scented fumigation, tattooing, henna, salt, and all the bitter substances, assa foetida, oleander, tar, etc., used to separate, dispel and drive away (Devulder 1957: 343–7)

Thus, the opposition between the male discontinuous and the female continuous appears as much in the order of reproduction – with the opposition between conception and gestation – as in the order of production, with the opposition, which structures the agrarian cycle, between labour time and production time, devoted to the gestation and tending of natural processes. 'A man's business – one sigh and it's over. For a woman, seven days pass and her business is not done' (Genevois 1969). 'The wife follows her husband; she finishes what he leaves behind him'; 'A woman's work is light (*fessus*), but there's no end to it.' Through the division between the sexes of labour that is inseparably technical and ritual, the structure of ritual practice and representations is articulated with the structure of production. The major moments of the farming year, those that Marx (1956) designates 'working periods', when men perform the uniting of contraries or the separation of united contraries, that is, specifically agricultural acts (as opposed to acts of simple gathering, left rather to women), are marked by quite different sanctioning rites contrasting, in their gravity, solemnity and imperative character, with the prophylactic and propitiatory rites which – during the rest of the 'production periods' when, like the pottery set out to dry or the child in its mother's womb, the grain undergoes a purely natural process of transformation – are performed mainly by the women and the children (shepherds) and have the function of assisting nature in its labour (see figure 4).

The agrarian calendar reproduces, in a transfigured form, the rhythm of the farming year, or more precisely, the climatic rhythms as translated into the alternation of labour periods and production periods which structures the farming year. The pattern of rainfall is characterized by the opposition between the cold, wet season, from November to April – with the greatest precipitation coming in November and December, followed by a decline in January and an increase in February and March, though this may come later or not at all – and the hot, dry season, from May to October, with rainfall at a minimum in June, July and August and a much-awaited increase in September. The farmers' dependence on the climate was obviously exacerbated by the limited traction power available (for ploughing) and the inefficiency of the techniques used (swingplough and sickle). Similarly, the symbolic equipment the rites can use naturally depends on what is in season (although in some cases reserves, of pomegranates, for example, are set aside especially for ritual use); but the generative schemes make it possible to find substitutes and to turn external necessities and constraints to good account within the logic of the rite itself (and this explains the perfect harmony between technical reason and mythic reason to be found in more than one case, for example, in the orientation of the house).

There is no need to show how, through the division of ritual and technical labour between the sexes, the table of male and female values is linked to the fundamental opposition of the agrarian year. The price set on the values of virility and fighting spirit, in the case of a boy, can be understood when it is known that, particularly in ploughing, harvesting and the sexual act, the man is the one who must perform the uniting of contraries or the separation of united contraries, in an act of violence that is likely to unleash violence, in order to produce life and the means of satisfying the most vital needs. By contrast, woman, being responsible for the continuous tasks of gestation and care, is logically called upon to cultivate the negative virtues of protection, reserve and secrecy, which define *h'urma*.

The magical frontier is thus everywhere, in things and in bodies, in other words, in the nature of things, the order of things, the routine and banality of everyday life. This is what must never be forgotten, though it disappears as much in accounts 'full of sound and fury, signifying nothing' as in the mystical evocation which makes a kind of inspired liturgy out of the almost mechanical, maniacal routine of works and days, the strings of stereotyped words expressing pre-thought thoughts (hence the recurrent 'it is said', and 'as the saying goes', or 'we say' that punctuate informants' discourse), the commonplaces in which people feel comfortable, at home with themselves and with others, and the series of pre-formed acts, more or less mechanically performed. It has to be borne in mind that mere description changes the whole status of the words and actions which make up the ordinary order, 'making sense' without any signifying intention, and which, through the simple power of discourse, become meditated utterances and premeditated acts; and that this change of status particularly affects all the gestures of ritual, which, rendered both eternal and banal

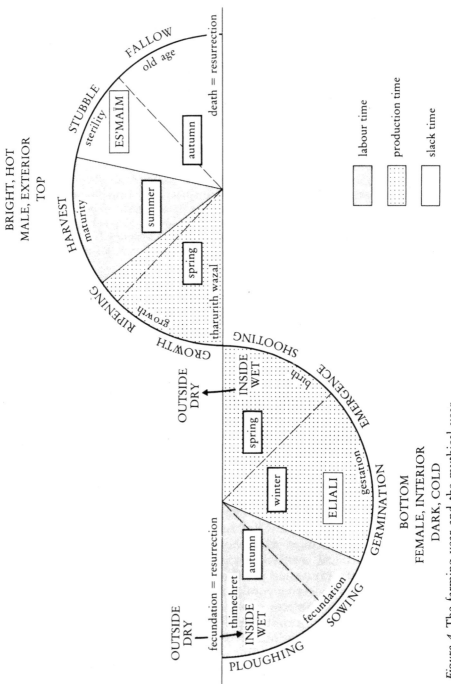

Figure 4 The farming year and the mythical year

by what Weber calls 'magical stereotyping', translate the most characteristic operations of ritual logic – uniting, separating, transferring, inverting – into unthought motions – turning right or left, turning upside down, going in or coming out, tying or cutting.

'On that day, the shepherd sets out early in the morning and comes back at *azal*. He picks a little of all the wild herbs . . . He makes them into a bouquet, also called *azal*, which will be hung over the threshold. Meanwhile, the mistress of the house has made a milk pudding . . .' (Hassler 1942). Behind each of the ordinary phrases in an ordinary description such as this, one has to be able not only to detect a meaning not consciously mastered by the agents, but also to see a banal scene of everyday life, with an old man sitting in front of the door while his daughter-in-law prepares the milk pudding, the animals returning, the woman fettering them, the boy coming back clutching a handful of flowers that he has picked with the help of his grandmother, his mother who takes them and hangs them over the door, the whole thing accompanied by everyday actions and everyday remarks: 'Let me see what you've brought', 'Well done, they're lovely', 'Anything to eat?', and so on.

And perhaps nothing would give a clearer sense of the practical function and functioning of the social principles of division than a description, at once realistic and evocative, of the sudden, total transformation of daily life that occurs on the 'return of *azal*'. Everything, without exception, in the activities of the men, women and children is suddenly changed by the switch to a new temporal rhythm: the comings and goings of the flock, of course, but also the men's work and the women's domestic activity, the place where cooking is done (the fire is brought out and the *kanun* set up in the courtyard), the times of meals, the place where they are eaten, the very nature of the food, the times and routes of the women's movements and tasks outside the house, the rhythm of meetings in the men's assembly, ceremonies, prayers, meetings outside the village, and markets.

In the wet season, in the morning, before *doh'a*, all the men are in the village. Except for the meeting sometimes held on Friday after collective prayer, this is when the clan assembly and all the conciliation committees (to deal with division of estates, repudiations, etc.) are always held. It is also the time when announcements directed to all the men (such as the call to take part in collective work) are made from the top of the minaret. About the time of *doh'a*, the shepherd boys set off with their flocks and the men go off to the fields or gardens, either to carry on with the great seasonal tasks such as ploughing or hoeing, or to occupy themselves with the minor activities that fill out the 'slack periods' of the agrarian year or day (gathering grass, digging and clearing ditches, gathering wood, extracting stumps, etc.). When rain, snow or cold winds rule out all work in the fields, or the earth is too wet to be trodden without compromising the future crop or the ploughing, when the bad state of the roads and the fear of being detained far from home interrupt traditional relations with the outside world, the imperative that drives the men to stay outside during the middle of the day brings them together in the assembly house, whatever their divisions. At this time of the year, not a man is missing from the village, to which the inhabitants of the *azib* – hamlet – retreat directly after *thaqachachth* (late October).

The evening meal (*imensi*) is served very early, as soon as the men have taken off their moccasins and work clothes and had a brief rest. By nightfall, everyone is at home, except for those who want to offer the evening prayer in the mosque, where the last prayer (*el âicha*) is generally brought forward to coincide with the *maghreb* prayer. Because the men eat all their meals indoors (except their midday snack), the women, dispossessed of their own space, endeavour to reconstitute a world apart by preparing the meal over by the wall of darkness, in the afternoon, while the men are out, and they try not to attract attention, even when fully occupied, or to be caught doing nothing. The loom, which remains assembled throughout the wet season, provides them with a kind of veil behind which they can withdraw, as well as the alibi of a constantly available activity. The same strategies are seen in the use of the village space: the presence of men prevents younger women from going to the fountain in the morning, and the slippery ground anyway creates the risk of falling. So, in the morning, the 'old woman' fetches water and, if there is no little girl available to do it, shoos chickens and animals away from the mat on which the olives or grain waiting to go to the press or the mill are spread out.

The group's withdrawal into itself, and into its own past and traditions – with the stories and tales recounted in the room reserved for men – contrasts sharply with its opening-up to the external world in the dry season.[12] The awakening of the village, which is very discreet in the wet season, is accompanied, once *azal* returns, by much noise and agitation. After the clip-clop of the mules accompanying the men going to the market, comes the noise of the flocks as they go out in unbroken succession, and then the clattering hooves of the donkeys, signalling the men's departure for the fields or the forest. Around the time of *doha*, the shepherd boys bring back their flocks and some of the men return to the village for their midday rest. The muezzin's call to the *ed-dohor* prayer is the signal for the second going-out of the day. In less than half an hour, the village empties, almost completely this time. In the morning, the women were kept in the house because it would be improper for them either to take their midday rest (*lamqil*) outdoors, under a tree, as the men do, or to hurry on their way back home; but in the afternoon, almost all of them accompany the men, at one time or another. First of all, there are the 'old women', who, after giving their instructions to the daughter-in-law whose turn it is to prepare the evening meal, go and make their contribution to the work and assert their authority in their own way, inspecting the gardens, making good the men's negligence – picking up a stray piece of wood, a handful of fodder dropped on the way, a branch abandoned under a tree – and bringing back, in the evening, on top of the jar of water freshly drawn from the garden spring, a bunch of herbs, vine leaves or maize, for the domestic animals. The young wives too, especially in the fig season, join in the work, following their husbands to pick up the figs they have knocked down, sorting them and laying them out on racks, and returning in the evening, each walking a few paces behind her husband, either alone or accompanied by the 'old woman'.

Thus, the double going-out delimits *azal*, a sort of 'dead' time in the strong sense, which everyone feels he must respect. Everything is silent, tense and austere. It is 'the desert' in the streets. Most of the men are scattered outside the village, some living in the *azib*, others kept permanently away from the house to look after the garden or the yoke of oxen being fattened, others watching over the fig-drying shelter (in this season, every family's fear is that it would not be able to muster its men in an emergency). It is not clear whether the external space of the village belongs now to men or to women; so both take care not to occupy it. There is something suspect about anyone who ventures on to the streets at this time. The few men who have not remained in the fields to sleep under a tree are taking their siesta in a convenient shade, in a porchway, behind a hedge, in front of the mosque, on the flagstones, or at the house, in the courtyard or in a side room if they have one. Furtive shadows flit across the street, from one house to another: the women, equally idle, are taking advantage of the very limited presence of the men to visit one another or meet in groups. Only the shepherd boys, who have returned to the village with their flocks, bring life to the outer crossroads and minor meeting-places with their games – *thigar*, sparring with the feet, *thighuldadth*, throwing stones at targets, *thimristh*, a kind of draughts, etc.

THE FUNDAMENTAL DIVISION

To escape from the forced choice between intuitionism and positivism, without falling into the interminable interpretation to which structuralism is condemned when, having failed to go back to the generative principles, it can only endlessly reproduce the logical operations which are merely their contingent actualizations, one needs to apply a generative model that is both very powerful and very simple. Knowing the fundamental principle of division (the paradigm of which is the opposition between the sexes), one can recreate – and therefore fully understand – all the practices and ritual symbols on the basis of two operational schemes which, being natural processes culturally constituted in and through ritual practice, are indissolubly logical and biological, like the natural processes they aim to reproduce (in both senses), when they are conceived in terms of magical logic. On the one hand, there is the reuniting of separated contraries, of which marriage, ploughing or the quenching of iron are exemplary cases, and which engenders life, as the realized reunion of contraries; and on the other hand, there is the separation of reunited contraries, with, for example, the sacrifice of the ox and harvesting, enacted as denied murders.[13] These two operations, of reuniting that which the fundamental division (*nomos*: distribution and law, law of partition, principle of division) separates – male and female, dry and wet, heaven and earth, fire (or fire-forged instruments) and water – and separating that which the ritual transgression, ploughing or marriage, the pre-condition of all life, has reunited, are both acts of inevitable sacrilege, necessary and unnatural transgressions of an arbitrary yet necessary limit. In short, once the fundamental principle of division and these two classes of operations have been identified, it is possible to re-produce the whole set of pertinent data in a *constructed description* that is quite irreducible to the endless and always incomplete enumeration of rites and their variants which renders most previous analyses so bewildering or bewitching.

The fundamental division, which counterposes male and female, dry and wet, hot or cold, is the basis of the opposition, which informants always cite, between the two high moments of the year, *eliali*, 'the nights', the time of the wet and the female, or rather, of the reunited contraries, the full house, fecundated earth and woman, and *esmaïm*, the dog-days, the time of the dry and the male in their pure state, the state of separation, two moments that condense and bring to their highest intensity the properties of the wet season and the dry season. Around these two poles, the rites are organized in two classes. On the one hand, there are the sanctioning rites, aimed at denying or euphemizing the violence inherent in all acts that unite the antagonistic principles, in ploughing, the quenching of iron or the sexual act, or, conversely, the separation of reunited contraries, in murder, harvesting or the cutting of woven cloth. On the other hand, there are the propitiatory rites, designed to ensure or facilitate the insensible and always threatened transitions between the opposing principles, to 'manage' life, that is, the reunited contraries, and to cause men and the elements to respect 'the order of time' (*chronou taxis*), that is, the order of the world: feminization of the male in autumn, with ploughing and sowing and the rain-making rites that accompany them, and masculinization of the female in spring, with the progressive separation of the grain and the earth that is completed with the harvest.

The main reason why informants always mention *eliali*, 'the nights', and always in relation to *esmaïm*, the dog-days, is that the winter of winter and summer of summer in a sense concentrate within themselves all the oppositions structuring the world and the agrarian year. The period of forty days which is believed to represent the time that the seed sown in autumn takes to emerge, is the prime example of the slack periods when nothing happens and all work is suspended, and which are marked by no major rite (except a few divining rites).

Divining practices are particularly frequent on the first day of *ennayer* (in the middle of *eliali*, at the threshold between the 'black' nights and the 'white' nights) and at the time of the renewal rites which mark the beginning of the new year and which are centred on the house and the *kanun* (replacing the three stones of the hearth, whitewashing the house). For example, at dawn, the sheep and goats are called out, and it is an unlucky sign if a goat comes out first (the goat is associated with the female-female, like the old woman [the 'days of the old woman' are also called 'the days of the goat']; the hearthstones are coated with a paste of wet clay: the year will be wet if the clay is still damp in the morning, dry if the clay is dry. This is explained not only by the inaugural role of the first day of *ennayer* but also by the fact that it comes in a period of waiting and uncertainty, when there is nothing to be done but to try to anticipate the future. This is why the divination rites concerning family life and especially the coming harvest are similar to those applied to pregnant women.

The fecundated field, duly protected – like a woman[14] – with a prickly fence (*zerb*), the sacred limit which produces the sacred, the taboo (*h'aram*), is the site of a mysterious, unpredictable labour which no external sign betrays and which resembles the cooking of wheat or beans in the pot or the work of gestation in a woman's womb. This period is indeed the winter of winter, the night of night. Homologous with night, winter is the time when the oxen sleep in the stable, the night and north the house, and the time of sexual relations. Like the boar,[15] the partridge, whose eggs are symbols of fertility, mates in *eliali*. It is the time when the natural world is given over to the female forces of fecundity, which can never be regarded as perfectly, finally masculinized, that is, cultivated and domesticated. The continuing assaults of winter, cold and night serve to remind men of this hidden violence of female nature which constantly threatens to turn to evil, the left hand, fallowness, the sterility of natural nature. In the 'quarrel between winter and man' (Lanfry 1947a), winter is presented as a woman (the name of the season, *chathwa*, being treated as a personified woman's name), and usually an old woman, the incarnation of the evil forces of disorder and division, death and destruction ('I will kill your cattle', she says. 'When I arise, the knives will set to work'); she is forced to renounce her lust for violence and show more moderation and clemency when defeated in her struggle with man. This origin myth emphasizes that winter, like woman, is dual-natured. It contains in it the purely female woman, unadulterated and untamed, who is incarnated in the old woman, empty, dry and sterile, that is, the female principle reduced by old age to its purely negative reality (the return of bad weather is sometimes explicitly blamed on the malevolence of the 'old women' of one village or another of the tribe or a neighbouring tribe, that is, witches, each of whom has her own day of the week); but it also contains tamed, domesticated woman, woman fulfilled, and fertility, the work of gestation and germination, that is performed by nature when fecundated by man. The whole of cultivated nature – the earth with its buried seed, and also the womb of woman – is the site of a struggle akin to that between the cold and darkness of winter and the springtime forces of light, of opening up and going out (out of the earth, the womb and the house) with which man is associated. This logic gives the key to the 'days of the old woman', a moment of transition and rupture between winter and spring (or between two months of winter): an old woman, who has various names, insults one of the months of winter (January, February or March) or Winter herself, defying her to harm her animals; the month (or Winter) asks the next month to lend it a few days so as to punish the old woman (Galand-Pernet 1958: 44 and bibliography). In all the legends of the borrowed days (*amerdil*, loan), which are probably more than just a way of explaining an unexpected return of bad weather, a being that is linked to nature, and even to winter, usually an old woman (like Winter herself), or a goat (Ouakli 1933a; Hassler 1942), or a Negro, is sacrificed by winter, or rather, sacrificed to winter, as a scapegoat. This is the price that has to be paid for the old witch Winter to agree to respect the limits assigned to her, as she does when she asks the period that follows to lend her a few days.

This hypothesis is confirmed by the fact that, in a legend recorded at Aït Hichem, the role of the old woman is taken by a Negro, a despised and malign figure. Distinguishing within the period known as *ah'ayan* a benign period called *ah'ayan u h'uri* (*ah'ayan* of the free man, the white man), during which one may sow and plant, and a malign period called *ah'ayan bu akli* (*ah'ayan* of the Negro), a week of cold and frost during which work stops, an informant referred to a legend which touches on the transgression of the limits constituting the social order: a Negro wanted to marry the daughter of a white man; anxious to prevent this impious union, the father asked the suitor to stand under a waterfall for seven days to wash himself white. The Negro endured this for six days, but on the seventh, God, who was against the marriage, unleashed rain accompanied by a rainbow (as for the jackal's marriage) and a frost, which killed the Negro (a variant of this legend is found in Bourrilly 1932). In a variant recorded at Aïn Aghbel, it is an old woman who, reversing the usual division of roles and transgressing the limits assigned to the different ages, asks her children to find her a husband; her children make her stay out in the cold for seven days and she dies. Another unnatural marriage is evoked in the tale of 'the jackal's marriage'. This animal which, like the impious old woman or the shameless goat, incarnates natural disorder, undomesticated nature ('he has no house'), marries outside his species, against nature, with a camel, and compounds the outrage by not celebrating the wedding. Once again the sky sends hail and a storm, as if the transgression of the temporal limits which structure the natural order could only be justified by the need to prevent or punish a transgression of the social limits.

In most variants, the old woman is characterized by verbal intemperance, which leads her into defiance and insults and that form of *hubris* that consists in presuming on the future and overstepping the limit *par excellence*, which is temporal ('Farewell uncle Ennayer, you've gone off without doing anything to me'). But, above all, being ugly, wicked, sterile and wild, exceeding the bounds of decency (in one legend, the old woman of *ennayer* urinates on children; her substitute, the nanny-goat, always has its tail lifted shamelessly, a flat, empty belly, and greedy, destructive, dessicating teeth), she is predisposed to confront the evil forces of which she partakes and which have to be driven back into the past, exorcised, in inaugural and liminal periods. In short, akin in this respect to the Negro and the blacksmith, she is cast as the figure who can fight evil with evil (as she does in the raising of the loom) and lead the fight, on behalf of the group, against winter, her *alter ego*, a battle in which she sacrifices herself or is sacrificed.

Es'maïm, the dog-days, is to the dry season exactly what *eliali* is to the wet season. This slack period, which is opposed to *essaïf*, the harvest, just as within the wet season *eliali*, another slack period, is opposed to *lah'lal*, ploughing, presents all the properties of the dry season in their most extreme form. The dry, sterile kingdom of summer (and therefore of fire, the dry and the salty) is entered in May, a month regarded as unpropitious for any act of procreation, and hence for weddings (May marriages are doomed to failure and every misfortune; the 'accursed broom of May' is the exact opposite of the blessed broom of the 'first day of spring': it brings ruin, emptiness and sterility to the house or stable where it is used). The rites that mark the 'first day of summer',[16] and even more, the rites of the summer solstice, *insla*, at the beginning of *es'maïm*, include tattooing, preventive or curative scarification with a stick of oleander, a plant not used in the *azal* bouquet (like scilla, *thiberwaq*, which is used to separate fields), preventive application of red-hot iron to the head, piercing of the little girls' ears, and bleeding performed on men and animals. These rites make use of iron, fire and tools made or associated with fire – the ploughshare, the sickle, the carding-comb and the dagger (and also the blacksmith's fire and poker) – which are used to cut and sever (especially the throats of sacrificial animals, and of men), to pierce, burn and bleed, and also to drive away the evil forces of the kingdom of the wet, such as *djnun*. The night of *insla*, when sterile, purifying fires are lit, in the house, in the midst of the flock, in the orchards, by the hives, on the threshing-floor, etc., is given over to sterility. It is said that women cannot conceive then, and that children born on that day are themselves condemned to sterility (as are marriages celebrated then).

According to Destaing, at the time of *insla*, the Beni Snous used to leave a cooking-pot (a symbol of the wetness and blackness of winter) in the kitchen garden (the site of female cultivation), upside down, with its base whitewashed (whitening of blackness). The scheme of turning round and turning over is set to work in all the rites intended to bring about a radical change, in particular an abrupt passage from the dry to the wet and more especially from the wet to the dry. Reversing operations – the verbal equivalent of which is the absurd lie, sometimes used to bring about a reversal of the course of events – such as those performed to induce a change in the weather, differ from transgressions in that they still recognize the order they reverse. They are always based on moving an object or an animal from its natural site and its normal position so as to provoke a tension the resolution of which gives the desired effect (for example, to make rain, a tortoise is put upside down in a tree [Destaing 1907: 254]). The threshold, which is itself a reversal, is one of the favourite spots for such rites; mirrors are another. The same scheme makes it possible to conceive any inversion: a shameless liar is said to have 'put the east in the west'.

The time of the dry is also the time of the salty, of roasted, spicy food which is both virile and virilizing, like the dried herbs that season it, wheatcake and oil ('the sun is burning as oil') which is to the food of summer as butter is to the food of spring.

Salt is strongly associated with the dry and with virility: the words meaning to be hot, scorching, also mean to be spicy, strong and virile ('I am the man who eats salty food and rejects insipid food', says a war-chant from the Rif [Biarnay 1915]), as opposed to bland, without bite, without intelligence (salt is sprinkled on babies so that they will not be insipid, graceless, witless). Salty, spiced food is intended for men, because it generates courage and virility (a piece of salt is put in a little boy's clothing when his father takes him to the market for the first time). Male, dry salt dessicates and sterilizes that which is wet (for example, it dries up a cow's milk). The exorcizing rites in which salt is used include sentences such as: 'Just as salt does not grow, so may misfortune not grow on me'; 'Just as salt cannot take root in the ground, so may cares and troubles not grow here.' A man who acts frivolously is said to 'think he is scattering salt' – he thinks his actions have no consequences.

Es'maïm, which presents all the features of summer in their pure state, without admixture or attenuation, is to the year what *azal* (the hottest time of the day), and more precisely 'the middle of *azal*', is to the cycle of the day. Like *azal*, *es'maïm*, the desert (*lakhla*) of the harvested fields, the time of iron and fire, violence and death (the edge of the sword, *s'emm*), is the male time *par excellence*.

The transitional periods have all the properties of the threshold, the boundary between two spaces, where the antagonistic principles confront one another and the world is reversed. Boundaries are where battles take place: boundaries between fields, which are the sites or the causes of very real struggles (a well-known refrain refers to old men who 'shift the boundaries'); boundaries between the seasons, with, for example, the fight between winter and spring; the threshold of the house, where the antagonistic forces meet and all the changes of state occur that are linked to the transition from inside to outside (all the 'first goings-out' – of the woman after giving birth, of the child, the milk, the calf, etc.) or from outside to inside (such as the bride's first entry, the conversion of fallowness into fertility); the boundary between day and night ('the hour when day and night fight it out'). The rites associated with these moments also obey the principle of the maximization of magical profit. They aim to ensure the concordance of mythical chronology and climatic chronology, with its whims and vagaries, by ensuring that rain comes at the right moment – ploughing time – by accompanying or if need be accelerating the passage from the dry to the wet in autumn, or from the wet to the dry in spring, in short, by striving to precipitate the coming of the benefits brought by the new season while seeking to conserve the profits of the declining season for as long as possible.

Autumn is the point where the course of the world turns round and everything is turned over to enter its opposite, the male into the female, the seed into the womb of the earth, men and beasts into the house, light (with the lamp) into darkness, until the next reversal, in spring, which will set back on its feet a world turned upside down, momentarily abandoned to the supremacy of the female principle – the womb, woman, the house, and the darkness of night. And consumption visibly mimes this paradoxical inversion: autumn food, generated in accordance with the scheme of soaking the dry, is made up of dry foods (cereals, dry vegetables, dried meat) which are boiled in water, unspiced, in the cooking-pot or (which amounts to the same thing) steamed or raised with yeast. The same objective intention also informs all the autumn rites intended to aid the coming of rain, that is, the descent of the dry male, the fecundating seed, into the female wetness of the earth: the sacrifice of an ox (*thimechreth*), which must not be russet, a colour associated with the dry (it is said of a lazy redhead, 'the red ox leaves its land fallow') or the start of ploughing (*awdjeb*) which, inasmuch as it ritually mimes the fearful union of contraries, is in itself an invocation of rain.

In times of severe drought and distress, when the logic of despair is particularly compelling, the practices that are intended to hasten the transition from the dry to the wet by playing on the attraction that the dry exerts on the wet (as in the collective invocation of rain when old men, carrying a ladle dressed as a doll, go through the village begging for flour – see Picard 1958: 302ff.), or by performing reversals and inversions (in the Collo region, the people pray together wearing their clothes inside out), often take the form of rites of supplication and sacrifice, in which poverty and suffering, even life itself, are offered as tributes. Thus, at Sidi Aïch, the poorer families come together to beg for rain. A virtuous widow is chosen to ride, wearing a dirty burnous, on an emaciated donkey; escorted by the children and the poor, she goes begging from house to house. She is sprinkled with water. This is followed by a collective meal, a couscous containing crushed broad beans, called *tatiyaft*). (This rite is found in various places in simplified forms – for example, three old men from a family of marabout status go and collect gifts.) The supplication designed to arouse pity (at the same time as attracting the wet on to something dry and sterile, the old woman) is most fully developed in the ceremony called 'the appeal for mercy': at Aïn Aghbel, when there was prolonged drought, the assembly would meet and a pious man would offer himself to be subjected to the funeral rites (washing, a shroud, etc.); he was laid in the mosque, facing eastwards. The imam recited the prayer, the man was carried home, and he died (Genevois [1962] similarly relates that Si Lhadj Azidan gave his life for his village, Tawrirt n-At-Mangellat).

This rite is perhaps the limiting case of all the collective practices of which ball games like *kura*, symbolic confrontations between dry and wet, east and west, which give rise to terrible violence, are particular cases. Their function seems to be to make an offering of the sufferings and humiliations that certain individuals, usually old men, designated as scapegoats, receive from the others or inflict on each other. For example, there is the collective battle called *awadjah* (public humiliation), described by the same informant at Aïn Aghbel; after a prayer led by the taleb and reserved for the men, the assembly secretly asks two or three men and two or three women (never married to each other) to lead the game. The men dress as women (inversion) and with two pieces of wood make a doll which they dress as a woman (with a headscarf); the women dress as men and make a male doll. They come out of their houses, the women first, and the inhabitants of the *zerba* hit them with sticks and stones (sometimes axes); the women scratch their faces (hence, it is said, the name given to the ceremony, *awadjah*, from *wadj*, face). If the game begins in the morning, there is no midday meal. Anyone meeting one of the male transvestites must either give him some water and a kick or a punch, or, if there is no water, put a coin in his sleeve, or at least hit him; the women wait to be given something, always in silence. The men, but not the women, can return the blows they receive, but always without speaking. There is then a general battle which lasts until nightfall.

In fact, more so than autumn, which is dominated by the sharp break that ploughing marks, and by the specific logic of fecundation, interwoven with the ritual work of moistening the dry, spring is an interminable transition, constantly suspended and threatened, between the wet and the dry, beginning immediately after *eliali*; or, more accurately, it is an uncertain struggle, with unceasing reversals and changes in fortune, between the two principles. The role of mankind in this struggle, which resembles the battle fought out each morning between darkness and light, can only be that of impotent onlookers; and this perhaps explains the profusion of calendar terms, almost all describing states of the weather or the crops. In this time of waiting, when the fate of the sown seed depends on an ambiguous, female nature, and man cannot intervene without danger, the virtual cessation of activity reflects his limited control over the processes of germination and gestation. It falls to woman to play the part of a midwife and to offer to nature, in its labour, a kind of ritual and technical assistance, with hoeing, for example, the only agricultural activity reserved solely for women. Analogous to their work in the garden, this gathering of the green (the name *waghwaz*, related to *azegzaw*, the green and the raw, is given to the raw, green plants, such as dandelions, which the women gather in the cultivated fields while hoeing, and which are eaten raw) – performed barefoot, with a hoe, with the body bent towards the earth – is opposed both to ploughing and to harvesting, acts of defloration or murder which may not be performed by a woman (or a left-handed man).[17]

The moment called 'the separation from *ennayer* (*el âazla gennayer*) is associated with the idea of a break in continuity. There is 'separation' in the fields: some farmers perform the ritual expulsion of 'Maras' by setting up oleander branches in the fields. There is 'separation' in life, with the boys' first haircut. This time of interruption has the same role in the grain cycle as that played in the human life-cycle by the rites designed to ensure the progressive masculinization of the boy (initially a female being), which begin as soon as he is born, and particularly all the ceremonies that mark the stages in the passage to the male world, such as the first visit to the market or the first haircut, and the culminating ceremony of circumcision.

Despite variations in detail, there are clear analogies between all the separation rites, because they apply the same scheme of cutting and separating, and use a set of objects capable of symbolizing these operations (knife, dagger, ploughshare, coin, etc.). Thus, when the bride leaves home, the break with her original family (and especially with her father) is symbolized by dressing her in a burnous (brought by the groom's family), slipping a piece of silver (provided by the groom's father) into her shoe, and advising her not to turn round or talk. While her father gives her water to drink from his hands, a song is sung, variants of which are sung for other passages and breaks – a boy's first visit to the market, circumcision, the veiling of the bride and the application of henna to her hands.

A new-born boy is placed to the right of his mother, who herself lies on her right side, and between the two are placed a carding comb, a large knife, a ploughshare, one of the stones from the fireplace, and a pot full of water (the informant who attributed transparent functions to some of these objects – the knife 'so that he will be a fighter', the ploughshare 'so he will work the earth' – indicated that only steel, rather than any particular object, was indispensable). According to another source, the objects include coins, a tile, some steel, a large flat plate, and a calabash full of water (Genevois 1968). Until he first goes out of the house, the little boy is under female protection, symbolized by the lesser beams, and this will cease as soon as he crosses the threshold. So a favourable period is chosen for his first emergence, either ploughing time – when he will be taken to the fields to touch the handle of the plough – or spring (preferably the inaugural days of the season).

The first haircut is so important because hair is seen as female and as one of the symbolic ties that link the child to the maternal world. It is the father's task to perform the first haircut (with a razor, a male instrument), on the day of the 'separation from *ennayer*' (*el âazla gennayer*). This rite was performed shortly before taking the boy to the market for the first time, between the ages of six and ten; until then, younger children had only their right temple shaved by their fathers.[18] When the time came for the boy to accompany his father to the market for the first time, at an age which varied according to the family and the child's position within it, he was dressed in new clothes and his father would put a silk band around his head. He was given a dagger, a padlock and a small mirror; in the hood of his burnous, his mother would put a fresh egg. He set off on the back of a mule, in front of his father. At the entrance to the market, he would break the egg (a virile act, also performed at the start of ploughing), open the padlock and look at himself in the mirror, an operator of reversal ('so', it was said, 'that afterwards he will see what is going on the market'). His father guided him through the market, introducing him to everyone and buying him all sorts of sweetmeats. On their return, they procured an ox's head, probably a phallic symbol (like the horns), associated with *nif* – 'so that he will become a "head" of the village' – and shared a festive meal with all their kinsmen.

All the characteristic features of this difficult transition are in a sense concentrated in the series of critical moments, like *h'usum* and *natah'*, times of crisis when all the evil powers of winter seem to revive and to threaten growth and life one last time, or *nisan*, which though regarded as benign is not without threats. These are ambiguous periods: even at their worst, they contain the hope of the best, and at their best they contain the threat of the worst. It is as if each of them bore within it the conflict that overshadows the whole season – and also the uncertainty about the future that causes these augural periods (especially *h'usum* or the first day of spring) to be, like morning, times for divination rites and inaugural practices.

This ambiguity is inscribed in the season itself. Spring implies growth and childhood, to be celebrated with joy, like the first day of the season: *thafsuth*, spring, is related to the root FS, *efsu*, to undo (the piles of fig racks), to untie, to stretch (wool) and, in the passive, to bud, blossom, bloom, open up (Laoust 1920; Dallet 1953 no. 714; Servier 1962: 151). But it also implies the vulnerability and fragility of all beginnings. Spring is to summer as green, raw (*azegzaw*) and tender (*thalaqaqth*) things (unripe corn or the baby) and green produce, the eating of which is seen as an untimely destruction (*aâdham*), are to full-grown, yellow (*iwraghen*), ripe, dry, hardened produce.[19] As a mother, the repository and guardian of the reunited contraries, a woman is logically designated to perform all the tasks concerned with protecting things that grow and shoot, that are green and tender. It is women's duty to watch over the growth of the young humans and young animals, the morning of life, a threatened hope. As has been seen, as well as hoeing, women's work includes gathering herbs and vegetables in the garden, looking after the cow, milking it and making butter, a female product which is opposed to oil as the inside and the wet to the outside and the dry.

Spring is the time for the garden and for *asafruri*, leguminous plants, especially broad beans, some of which are eaten green; and the time of milk, which is produced in abundance by cattle fed on [green] silage, in the stable or near the house, and is consumed in all its forms (whey, curds, butter, cheese, etc.). The wish to have everything at once, to have both the one and the other (as children try to do, according to Plato), to hold for as long as possible the balance between opposing forces which defines life, to enter the dry, as the separation rites sought to do, while retaining the wet and preventing the dry from taking away the milk and butter, is declared quite explicitly in a rite, performed on the day of *azal*, when the woman of the house buries a cloth bag, containing cumin, benzoin and indigo, in front of the stable entrance, with the words: 'O green, restore the balance, keep it [the butter] from waning!' The same intention is also clearly seen in all the rites associated with the cow and its milk, which must be kept flowing, kept from drying up (the *azal* siesta, the daytime of the day, is the best time for stealing milk). Thus, fighting the dry with the dry, the mistress of the house who wants to protect the cow, the calf and the milk against people who cast 'salty looks' – dry, dessicating glances (salt is synonymous with sterility: cf. 'sowing salt') – picks up a handful of earth from the place where the calf dropped to the ground, mixes it with salt, wheat flour and seven hawthorn or prickly pear thorns ('sharp' is equivalent to spicy, salty), and rolls it into a lump which she sticks first on the cow's horn and then on the churn. For three days following the birth of the calf, she will not take out the fire; only on the fourth day will she start to bring milk out of the cowshed, after she has sprinkled a few drops on the edge of the hearth and on the threshold, and thrown burning embers from the fire into the vessel she will use to take milk to her neighbours (Rahmani 1936). And to 'return the milk' to a cow that has been milked dry, she takes (among other things) a sickle, a ploughshare, some rue, a grain of salt, a horseshoe, a steel ring and a spindle weight, which she turns seven times over the cow, asking for the milk and butter to be restored (Genevois 1968: vol. II, 77).

Among the rites that women perform to protect their children, the most typical are those known as the rites of the association of the month (*thucherka wayur*). These are designed to defend a child against the evil-transferring rites that may be performed by the mother of a child born in the same month. According to an informant, women keep a close watch on other women with whom they share the month (*icherqen ayur*). Fearing that the other might divert every misfortune on to her own child, each one tries to be the first to say, while uncovering her brow, 'I turn the evil back on you' (*aqlab*, change). When a child has been struck in this way, his mother says 'He's been changed, turned the wrong way'. To protect themselves, two women may share bread, pledging themselves in this way not to betray each other. A woman who has suffered *qibla* and who has identified the cause of her misfortune grills wheat on *bufrah*' (the blackened dish) turned upside down, that is, turned the wrong way, and secretly goes and throws it on the roof of the other woman's house, saying 'I give you back what you gave me'. The rite called *thuksa thucherka wayur*, the breaking of the association of the month, is performed on the 3rd, 7th, 14th, 30th and 40th days after the birth (known as the days 'of the association of the month'). A powder is made of caraway, incense, alum, salt, the 'association nut' (*ldjuz ech-cherk*), zanjar and henna; an egg in a bowl of water is left by the child's head all night. In the morning, at breakfast if it is a girl, in the middle of the day if it is a boy ('A girl is the morning', she must be receptive immediately; 'a boy is the afternoon', he can be counted on in the long run), the midwife mixes the powder with the water in the bowl, using the egg as a beater, and draws a circle around each of the child's joints with the egg, dipped in the mixture. She also draws a line across the child's brow and another from the brow to the chin, while reciting a ritual formula. The same rite, with variants, is performed on the other 'days of association' (for example, on the 14th day a hundred gorse thorns are stuck into a reed as tall as the child, which is then thrown into a stream; on the 30th day, a hundred grains of wheat are stuck into an onion, which is then planted on the boundary between two plots). The midwife proceeds in the same way (with an egg sprinkled with the blood of the sacrificial sheep) on the day of Aïd. In fact, *thuckerka* designates all the obstacles and difficulties that stand in the way of good fortune, marriage or success. Thus, for a girl who cannot find a husband, the midwife 'cuts' the *thuckerka*; and she undoes *thucherka* on the eve of a wedding by washing the bride in a big dish.

The precise locus of the threshold, where the order of things turns upside down 'like a wheatcake in the pan', is explicitly marked by the 'return of *azal*' (*tharurith wazal*), the point of division between the wet season and the dry season, where the year tips over. The rhythm of the working day – defined by the departure of the flocks – changes, and with it, as has been seen, the group's whole existence. The fire is brought out of the house and the *kanun* set up in the courtyard. The flock with its shepherd boy, the housewife who awaits him, who milks the cow and treats the milk, bring new elements into the rites, partaking more of the dry than of the wet. The flock ceases to be fed on tender, green plants from the cultivated fields and grazes instead on wild, dry plants. The herbs, flowers and branches that the shepherd brings back on his first return at the hour of *azal*, which make up the bouquet, also called *azal*, that is ritually hung above the threshold – fern, cytisis, bramble, thyme, lentisk, male fig-tree branches, asparagus, elm, thapsia, myrtle, rosemary, tamarind, heather, broom, in short, 'everything the wind shakes in the countryside' (Rahmani 1936; Yamina 1952) – are the wild products of fallow land – and not the product, albeit parasitic, of cultivated land, like the plants the women gather while hoeing. The change in food is even clearer: the special dishes of the 'return of *azal*' give a prominent place to milk, as in the previous period, but it is now eaten in cooked or boiled form.

TRANSGRESSION DENIED

The times of separation, when the opposing principles exist in a sense in the pure state, as in the dog-days, or threaten, in the case of winter, to return to it, and the times of transition, when the dry returns to the wet, in autumn, or the wet returns to the dry, in spring – processes opposed to one another, in which union and separation take place without any human intervention – are in turn opposed, but in a different way, to the times when the reunion and separation of contraries take a critical form because it falls to man himself to bring them about. The opposition between the propitiatory rites of the transitional periods, almost all performed by women, and the sanctioning rites, which are obligatory for the whole group and above all for the men, during the periods of human intervention in nature, harvesting and ploughing, in fact reproduces in the specific logic of ritual the opposition, structuring the agrarian year, between the time of work and the time of gestation (that is, the remainder of the production cycle), during which the grain undergoes a purely natural process of transformation.[20]

The function of the rites that accompany ploughing or marriage is to disguise and thereby sanction the collision of two opposing principles, *coincidentia oppositorum*, that is performed by the peasant, who is obliged to force nature, to do it violence, using tools – ploughshare, knife and sickle – that are in themselves fearful because they are made by the blacksmith, the master of fire. The aim is to make carefully euphemized ritual actions out of the objectively sacrilegious actions of separating, cutting and dividing (in harvesting, cutting the thread in weaving, and slaughtering the sacrificial ox) that which nature (that is, the *nomos*, the taxonomy) has joined,[21] or, conversely, of reuniting – in quenching, marriage or ploughing – that which nature (the taxonomy) has separated. Sacrilegious transgressions may be delegated to an inferior being, both feared and despised, a sacrificer and scapegoat whose role is to 'take away ill fortune'.[22] This is the case with the quenching of iron, entrusted to the blacksmith, or the slaughter of the ox in the collective sacrifices, entrusted to the smith or a Negro. When these acts have to be committed by those who are responsible for and benefit from them, like the defloration of the bride, turning the first furrow, cutting the last thread in weaving, or harvesting the last sheaf, they are transfigured by a collective dramatization intended to give them a collectively proclaimed meaning, that of a sacrifice, which is the exact opposite of their socially recognized, and therefore no less objective reality, which is that of murder. The whole truth of magic and collective belief is contained in this game of twofold objective truth, a double game played with truth, through which the group, the source of all objectivity, in a sense lies to itself, by producing a truth whose sole function and meaning are to deny a truth known and recognized by all, a lie that would deceive no one, were not everyone determined to deceive himself.

In the case of the harvest, the social truth to be collectively denied is unambiguous: harvesting (*thamegra*) is a murder (*thamgert'* designates the throat, violent death, revenge; and *amgar*, the sickle), through which the earth, fertilized by ploughing, is stripped of the fruits it has brought to maturity. The ritual of the last sheaf, of which we have countless descriptions, no doubt because Frazer's analyses (1912: 214–69) drew attention to it, and therefore almost as many variants, almost always consists fundamentally in symbolically denying the inevitable murder of the field or 'the spirit of the corn' (or 'the field'), the principle of its fecundity, by transforming it into a sacrifice that will ensure the resurrection of the sacrificed life. The sacrifice is always accompanied by various compensatory tributes which seem to be substitutes for the life of the 'master of the field' himself. As in weaving, where the sacrifice preceding the cutting of the cloth is justified by explicitly stating the principle 'a life for a life', the logic adopted is that of blood vengeance (*thamgert'*), a 'throat' for a 'throat', and the 'master of the field' risks paying with his life for the life he takes from the field by cutting the throat of the last sheaf, an act which he must always undertake personally. (Even when what seems to be the original form of the ritual has disappeared, as in Great Kabylia, it is still the master of the field who cuts the last sheaf and carries it back to the house, where it is hung from the main beam.) This is underlined by the treatment often inflicted on the 'master of the field' as if to obtain from him the equivalent of *diya*, a compensation that was sometimes used to break the cycle of revenge killings. In one case, for example, the harvesters leap on him as he is about to cut the last sheaf, bind him, and drag him to the mosque, where he negotiates his ransom – honey, butter, and sheep, which are immediately sacrificed and eaten in a feast attended by all the harvesters (Bourrilly 1932: 126).

From the names given to the last sheaf, it seems that the 'spirit of the field' whose perpetuation is to be affirmed is practically identified, depending on the variant, either with an animal (informants speak of 'the mane of the field' or 'the tail of the field') or with a bride, *thislith*, destined to die after having borne her fruit (others speak of 'the curl of the field' and 'the plait of the field'). To these different representations correspond different rituals. In some villages, it is held to be a sin to reap the last sheaf, which is left standing in the middle of the field for the poor, the oxen or the birds; elsewhere, it is mown (or uprooted by hand to avoid contact with the sickle) but always in accordance with a special ritual. The ritual murder of the field may be enacted in the murder of an animal (the magical compensation for inevitable crime) which is both its embodiment and its substitute (the miraculous properties of the meat of the sacrificed animal are appropriated in a communal meal; in several cases, the tail of the animal receives special treatment – it is hung up in the mosque – as if, like the last sheaf, sometimes known as the 'tail of the field', it concentrated the vital potency of the whole). It may also be performed on the last sheaf itself, treated like a sacrificial animal. In one case (Servier 1962: 227–30) the master of the field turns to face the east, lays the last sheaf on the ground with its 'head' facing eastwards, as it if were an ox, and simulates cutting its throat, letting a handful of soil trickle from his left hand in the middle of the wound as if to mimic bleeding. Elsewhere, the master of the field, or his son, cuts the last sheaf while reciting the ritual prayer of the dying, *chahada* (Lévi-Provençal 1918: 97; Bourrilly 1932: 126–8), or exhorting it with a whole accompaniment of laments to accept death and expect resurrection:[23] 'Die, die, O field, our master will bring you back to life!' In some cases the 'spirit of the field' is even treated like a dead person: the last sheaf, into which it has in a sense retreated, is buried in a grave, facing eastwards (Servier 1962: 227–30). And the interference between the denial of murder and the exchange of one life for another is seen in the fact that these same chants were sung when the carpet was detached from the loom: 'Die, die, our field or barley; glory to him who does not die! But Our Lord can restore your life. Our men will plough you and our oxen will tread you out' (H. Basset 1922: 158, and many earlier authors, such as Westermarck, on the harvest chants).

The ritual denial of murder is accompanied by propitiatory acts intended to favour resurrection, which the performative language of the ritual chants both calls for and announces, applying the scheme of the uniting of contraries. Resurrection is nothing other than the reunification or, so to speak, the marriage, of life principles which the inevitable murder separates – heaven and earth, male and female. This is why the harvest rites return to the logic of the rain-making rites at a time when rain is not needed for its purely technical function (which is never autonomized) and can have no other purpose than to regenerate the grain or the field. Thus the whole apparatus of the rain-making rites reappears, with the characters (Anzar and his wife Ghonja, he representing the rain and the sky, and she the young virgin soil, the bride, etc.) and the objects (dolls, banners) that figure in it.

Another ritual aimed at sanctioning the uniting of contraries, the ploughing ceremonies, cannot be fully understood unless it is realized that the period that follows the harvest and its rites aimed at ensuring the perpetuation of the fecundating principle is a time of separation, devoted to the manly virtues, the point of honour, and fighting.[24] *Lakhrif* – from the Arabic verb *kherref* (Dallet 1953 no. 1191), to pick and eat fresh figs, and also to joke (*akherraf*, joker, buffoon), sometimes to ramble, to rave – is an extra-ordinary period of plenty and rest which cannot be defined either as a labour period, like ploughing and harvesting, or a gestation period, like winter and spring. It is the male time *par excellence*, when the group opens up to the outside world and must confront outsiders, in feasts and in war, so as to knit alliances which, like extra-ordinary marriages, are far from excluding challenge.[25] Like the grain set aside as seed-corn, which will be kept in a state of separation, the young boy is symbolically torn from the maternal, female world by circumcision. This ceremony, from which women are rigorously excluded, has the function of co-opting the boy into the world of men by means of an operation which is regarded as a second birth, a purely male affair this time, and which, as the saying goes, 'makes men'. In one variant of the ritual, the newly circumcised boys are surrounded by two or three concentric circles of men seated on ploughshares with their rifles in their hands. The men who encircle them are all the members of the clan and sub-clan, together with the male kinsmen of their mothers, the affines, to whom the boys have been presented, escorted by a delegation of men from the sub-clan, bearing their rifles, in the week preceding the ceremony (a rite also performed before marriage and called *aghrum*, wheatcake, the dry, male food *par excellence*).[26] The land itself is cleared of every trace of life as the trees are stripped of leaves, the last fruit picked and any remaining vegetation uprooted from the fields and gardens. The state of separation ends, for the natural world, with *awdjeb*, the solemn inauguration of the ploughing, which celebrates the marriage of the sky and the earth, the ploughshare and the furrow, by the collective enactment of a whole set of mimetic practices, including human marriages.

The return to the ordinary order is also marked by the reassertion of the primacy of the strengthening of kin-group unity over the pursuit of distant alliances, with *thimechret*, the sacrifice of an ox at 'the door of the year'; its throat is cut, its blood sprinkled on the ground, calling down rain, and the consecrated meat shared out among all the members of the community. The division into equal shares which treats the sacrificed ox as a kind of practical image of the social body, a schema of the division into families, delimits the group, solemnly reaffirming, by giving them each a share, the bonds of real or official consanguinity that unite all the living members (*thaymats*) of the clan (*adhrum*) in and through the original community (*thadjadith*). At the same time, it institutes the specifically political law of this participation, namely isonomy, tacitly recognized by taking part in the communal meal and taking a share equal to that of all the others. It thus takes on its full meaning as a nomothetic act, collectively and solemnly producing and reproducing the fundamental law of distribution and division that constitutes the group as a human group in opposition to the savage world, incarnated in the jackal, a kind of outlaw. This anomic being, ignorant of the law tacitly recognized by the oath implied in commensality (one swears by the sharing of *aghrum* and salt), feeds on raw flesh and even eats the corpses it is supposed to bury. It has no 'house' and shows the same savagery in the order of sexuality by making an unnatural marriage, outside its species, with the camel.

This philosophy of history, implicit in all ritual practice, is expressed in a tale in the form of an origin myth: 'The animals once met together in an assembly and swore not to prey on one another any longer. They chose the lion to be their king . . . devised laws, and laid down sanctions . . . The animals lived in peace . . . Life would have been fine if Jackal, Lion's counsellor, had not ruined everything. He was an old hand at every sort of treachery . . . and he regretted the former state of affairs. The smell of fresh meat and warm blood would send him into a frenzy . . . He decided to use cunning and secretly to incite the courtiers, one after another, to disobey – the work of a demon' (Zellal 1964).

The jackal has many properties in common with women, or, more precisely, old women. He has the task of fetching water. He is irredeemably twisted: 'They put the jackal's tail down a rifle barrel for forty days, and when they took it out it was just the same.' He is subject to immediate and insatiable desire: 'As the jackal said, I wish spring lasted two years.' As a counsellor and *éminence grise*, he always tends to bring back disorder and division (he is always referred to with euphemisms: he is 'the short one' or 'the animal in *arkasen*', because he drags corpses like the sandals made of uncured leather from the skin of the sacrificial ox). The jackal is also assimilated to the redhead, without beard or moustache, who, as has been said, sows discord and at the last judgement refuses to pardon someone who had stolen his pickaxe.

The sacrifice of the ox, an act of denied violence intended to deny the violence contained in imposing the human order on fertile but wild nature – fallow land or the maiden – is a meal of alliance, a collective pledge through which the group institutes itself by proclaiming the specifically human, that is, male, order against nostalgia for the struggle of all against all, also embodied in the jackal – or in woman, who is excluded both from the sacrifice and from the political order it establishes – and its sacrilegious cunning (*thah'raymith*). Like the natural world, whose domestic fertility contains the only half-tamed forces of a wild nature (those embodied in and mobilized by the old witch), the social order arising from the pledge that raises the assembly of men from the disorder of individual interests remains haunted by repressed nostalgia for the state of nature.

The ploughing ritual which represents the culminating point of the agrarian year derives its complexity from the fact that – in accordance with the essentially multifunctional logic of magical practice which, as practice, ignores the rigorous differentiation of functions, and, as magical practice, seeks to put all the odds on its own side – it applies different generative schemes, whose relative weight can vary according to local traditions, 'municipal laws' as Montaigne put it, historically constituted and often perpetuated by the concern for distinction. These schemes, although reducible to one another in the last analysis, have sufficient autonomy to produce actions or symbols that are partially discordant or, at least, overdetermined, polysemic and multifunctional.[27] The products of several different practical schemes can thus be seen, as if superimposed. First, there is the scheme, which has already been encountered, of denial of the violence contained in ploughing or defloration and, at the second degree, in the murder-sacrifice of the ox, which, in the logic of gift exchange (*do ut des*), represents the equivalent of the violence done to the earth. Then there is the scheme of reuniting, which is its positive counterpart, with all the symbols of the couple and coupling, from the yoke of oxen to the marriage lamp; and, brought in by the concern to make the reunion successful, the schemes of virilization of the male (with the rifle shots and target shooting) and fertilization of the female, with all the fertility rites (which are autonomized when a sterile woman renews the marriage rites – see Genevois 1968: vol. II, 26–7). Finally, and in a very secondary role, there is the scheme of separation and reversal of status (which applies mainly to the bride, separated from her original family and joined to the new family in a rite of passage in van Gennep's sense).

The ritualization which officializes the transgression, making it a regulated and public act, performed before all, collectively shouldered and approved, albeit performed by one individual, is, in itself, a denial, the most powerful one of all, because it has the backing of the whole group. Belief, which is always collective, is consolidated and legitimated by becoming public and official, asserting and flaunting itself instead of remaining hidden, as illegitimate ritual (in other words, dominated ritual, such as female magic) does, thereby recognizing legitimacy, and its own illegitimacy (like the thief, according to Weber). In the case in question, where the aim is to sanction a transgression,[28] the group authorizes itself to do what it does through the work of officialization, which consists in collectivizing the practice by making it public, delegated and synchronized.

It follows from this that the degree of legitimacy (and the social importance) of a rite can be measured by the form of collective organization that it imposes. Thus there are the major rites of public interest which bring the whole group together in the same place at the same time, such as the sacrifice of an ox (*thimechreth* 'at the door of the year', or for a funeral or to make rain); the rites performed at the same time but separately by each family, such as the sacrifice of the Aïd sheep or rites which, though of private interest, are performed publicly, such as immolation on behalf of a house, or the threshing floor, or the weaving; rites that are performed without disguise and at any time, such as the rite to cure styes; and finally the private, clandestine rites which can only be performed in secret, at ungodly hours, such as the rites of black magic. Everything seems to indicate that the symbolism applied is that much more unconscious (being the product of a forgotten history) when rites are more official and collective, and that much more conscious, because it is more instrumental, when the aims they pursue are more private and more secret.

Thus, the rites to transfer evil (*asfel*), such as birth rites, divination rites, etc., appeal to very simple and transparent associations of ideas (rather as tales do), because their logic is derived quite directly from their function, which provides the guiding scheme. For example, to cure a whitlow, the *qibla* covers the affected limb with earth (from the tomb of a stranger), performs the giration rite with an egg and buries it for a moment; she then cooks the egg until it bursts, then sacrifices a pigeon, which she buries in the hole with the egg. After ablutions and fumigations with bitter herbs, the instruments used are left on the spot when everyone leaves, at the moment when the sun touches the sea. Bursting, transfer, expulsion, accentuation of breaks (the objects and the evil are abandoned to the night) – the symbolism is transparent. The same is true in a typical rite intended to make teeth grow: the baby's head is covered with a cloth and pancakes (*thibuâjajin*) are made with semolina, which as it cooks produces bubbles that burst immediately. The divination rites are even clearer, because they borrow less from the deep symbolism: for example, a person will receive money if he feels itching in the palm of his right hand; if his left hand itches, he will give money. Often, the meaning explicitly assigned to the rite, either in the practice itself or in response to questioning by an outsider, masks its deeper significance, as when, for example, it is explained that the rite of the padlock, on a boy's first visit to the market, is intended to make life easy; or when a woman scatters the leaves stripped from gourds in a place where cattle pass, so that the gourd will spread its fruit in all directions, as the cattle drop their dung. Such rites are optional and subject to individual improvisation, because the stakes are not high; they can do no harm, and no harm will come from not doing them.

In fact, the degree of freedom varies with the degree of collectivization of the rite and the (corresponding) degree of institutionalization, that is, officialization. But it also varies with the position of the individuals in the official hierarchy, which is always a hierarchy with respect to the official. Those who are dominant identify with the official (the competence conferred by status predisposes agents to recognize and acquire competence). By contrast, those who are dominated, in this case the women, are relegated to the unofficial and the secret, means of struggle against the official power which they are denied. As is shown by analysis of female magic, symbolism is simultaneously and without contradiction a common code and a means of struggle, used both in the domestic struggles between women – especially the mother-in-law and daughter-in-law – and in the struggles between men and women. Just as there is an official, male, truth of marriage, and a practical truth, manipulated by women, so there is an official, public, solemn extra-ordinary use of symbolism, a male use, and a secret, private, guilty, everyday use by women.

The institution of licit (*lah'lal*) periods or moments, the mandating of persons who serve as 'screens' (the family charged with opening the ploughing, inaugural parallel-cousin marriage, etc.) and the organization of major collective ceremonies, in which the group authorizes itself, are three aspects of the same operation, which is essential to all legitimate ritual (one confuses everything by identifying the distinction between legitimate and illegitimate magic with the – socially contested – distinction between religion and magic). The authority which the group grants itself, on its own authority, either as a whole or in the person of one of its mandated members, is the basis of the illocutionary force at work in all social rituals. The specifically magic character of this completely social force is invisible so long as it is exercised only on the social world, separating or uniting individuals or groups with frontiers or bonds (marriage) no less magic than those instituted by the knife or the knot in magic, transmuting the social value of things (like the fashion designer's label) or persons (like the educational qualification). On the other hand, it appears quite openly when, in a kind of innocence, confidence or abandonment imposed by extreme distress and disarray, groups attempt to use the power that they give themselves, in one of the circular operations which are the basis of the entirely efficacious magic of the collective, beyond the limits of its validity, that is, on the natural world which does not depend on the group but on which the group depends – when they try to turn a pumpkin into a coach in the same way that they turn a king's son into a king or a baptized baby into a Christian, in short, when they try to set up with things the same kinds of relations that obtain between people, giving them orders or making them gifts, uttering wishes or supplications.

In ploughing as in harvesting, sacrilege is symbolically denied in the very moment of being performed. The man assigned to open the ploughing, 'the man of the wedding' as he is sometimes called, acts, at a time designated by the group, as the mandated representative of the group, to perform the sacrilegious reuniting of celestial fire and the wet earth, the ploughshare and the furrow.

The ploughshare is the equivalent of the thunderbolt. Both blessed and feared, it must not be washed or brought into the house between two days' ploughing. Laoust (1920: 189) indicates that lightning is sometimes called 'the ploughshare of the sky', that, in the Aurès, *thagersa* means both 'ploughshare' and 'thunderbolt' and that 'there is a widespread belief among the Berbers that lightning falls in the shape of a ploughshare' (so that a lightning-strike is practically identified with the quenching of iron). The words used to designate the plough, *thagersa* (*thayirza*), but also *saâqa* or *sihqa*, are used, probably as euphemisms, to refer to lightning that strikes the ground (as opposed to flashes of lightning). The frame of the plough is often designated by a word, *lmâun*, which, in view of its root (mutual help, with a connotation of blessing which recalls the phrase *Allah iâaunik*, a greeting used to someone working), is no doubt another euphemism. A man struck by lightning is regarded as the victim of a curse, and if he survives, he sacrifices an ox.

At Sidi Aïch, the inauguration of ploughing (or rather, 'the going-out to the first ploughing'), the task of ritually cutting the first furrow, falls to a family referred to as *abruâ*, 'bringer of luck'. (*Abruâ* is also used to refer to the tail of the ox chosen for the sacrifice and the long trailing dress of the woman who carries the seed-corn, and it figures in the invocations endlessly recited by women as they work in the garden: 'Give a plentiful harvest to every patch that my skirt, *abruâ*, and the soles of my feet have touched' [Genevois 1969]. 'The people, that is to say all the members of the clan, go out through the house of Yusef' (which, as is also said, 'goes out on behalf of the others'). To explain the functions assigned to this family, which also monopolizes all the technical acts involving fire or objects made with fire (ignipuncture, tattooing, bone-setting, circumcision), it is said that lightning struck the land of one of its ancestors, who 'grafted' on to his ploughshare the piece of sharpened, hardened iron that he found at the point of impact, and also that one stormy day a ewe brought in its fleece a little sickle which was 'grafted' on to the sickle used for ignipuncture.

The rites of ploughing must also favour a paradoxical state of the union of contraries in which the female principle temporarily has the upper hand. The seed, locked for a time in dryness and sterility, can return to life only by being immersed in female wetness. The earth, like the ewe, may not bring forth (*thamazgulth*). It may return to sterility or the wild fertility of fallow land, and the future of the seed is at the mercy of female powers to which the act of fecundation has had to do violence. The 'door of the year' is not the moment when the year begins (it has no beginning, but is an endless renewal); rather, it is a threshold, a period of uncertainty and hope ('at every turn, people say "God willing"'), when everything is renewed, starting with contracts and associations (Maury 1939), an inaugural moment when the year, like the house, which must remain open to the fertilizing light of the sun, opens up to the male principle which fertilizes and fills it. Ploughing and sowing mark the completion of the movement from outside to inside, from the empty to the full, the dry to the wet, sunlit sky to dark earth, the fertilizing male into the fertile female.

In this context it is relevant to cite a well-known tale, the story of Heb-Heb-er-Remman, in which all the fertility symbolism implemented in the marriage and ploughing rites is organized around the snake that is often represented on the stone jars used to store the grain kept for consumption and seed-corn. A girl who has seven brothers and is therefore seven times blessed falls foul of the jealousy of her sisters-in-law, who make her eat seven snake's eggs, concealed in dumplings. Her belly swells and people think she is pregnant; she is driven from the house. A wise man discovers the cause of her ailment. To cure her, a sheep must be slaughtered and its meat roasted, with a lot of salt. The girl must eat it and then be suspended by her feet with her mouth open over a pan of water. When this is done, the snakes come out and they are killed. The girl marries. She has a child whom she calls Heb-Heb-er-Remman, 'pomegranate seeds'. She goes back to her seven brothers, who recognize her when she tells them the story, showing them the seven snakes which she has dried and salted. It can immediately be seen that to produce this narrative, or at least decode it in general terms, it is sufficient to possess the set of schemes that are at work in the production of any fertility rite. To fertilize is to penetrate, to introduce something that swells or causes swelling. The ingestion of food, and of food that swells, is homologous with sexual intercourse and ploughing. In another tale, a snake which a woman had brought up as her son is rejected by its first wife; the snake draws itself up, swells, and breathes at her a jet of poisonous flame which reduces her to ashes. But here there is a false fertilization. The snakes, a symbol of the male life-principle, seed, which must die to be reborn, and thus of the dry, are ingested in the form of eggs, that is, in their female state, and they return to maleness inopportunely, in the girl's stomach. (In a fertility rite reported by Westermarck, it is the heart – a male part of the snake – that is eaten.) The swelling that results from this inverted procreation is sterile and pernicious. The cure is self-evident. The dry must be made to move in the opposite direction, from high to low – the girl simply has to be turned upside down – and from inside to outside – which cannot be done by a simple mechanical operation: the dry must be further dried, parched, by adding to it what is pre-eminently dry, salt, and so reinforcing its propensity towards the wet, which, in normal fecundation – procreation or sowing – carries it towards the inside, into the damp womb of woman or of the earth opened by the ploughshare. At the end of the story, the girl's fecundity is proved by the birth of Heb-Heb-er-Remman, 'pomegranate seeds' (the symbol *par excellence* of female fertility, identified with the womb), that is, the many sons born (or to be born) from the fertile womb of a woman herself sprung from a womb rich in men (her seven brothers). And the seven snakes end up dried and salted, that is, in the state to which they are structurally assigned as symbols of male seed, capable of growing and multiplying through the cycle of immersion in the wet followed by emergence towards the dry.

The reuniting of the male and the female, the dry and the wet, in ploughing or marriage, is called for by all the performative symbolism of the ritual, which is there to *signify*, that is, to state with authority, the reuniting of principles that are condemned to sterility so long as they remain separate, 'uneven' and imperfect. Hence the use, in the rituals of marriage and ploughing, of everything that can signify pairing and coupling, starting with the yoke of oxen (*thayuga* or *thazwij*, from *ezwej*, to marry, be married), the perfect example of 'evenness' because the ox is in itself a symbol and portent of prosperity. The man mandated to open the ploughing, sometimes called 'the man of the wedding', is also called the 'old man with the yoke of oxen' (*amghar natyuga*).

It is the ox that says 'Where I have lain, there will be no famine', and 'Moo! Out of there, hunger, make way for fullness' (Genevois 1968: vol. I, 29). This is why a new yoke of oxen's entry into the house is a blessing marked by rites entrusted to the mistress of the house. As when the bride enters, on the threshold she places *alemsir*, the sheepskin that receives the flour from the mill, also called 'the door of provisions' (*bab-errazq*), so that they will bring plenitude and prosperity. She greets them ('Welcome, happy one!'), gives them water, strokes them, ties them up and unties them, moves beneath them. These traditions, observed at Aït Hichem, have many features in common with those seen when the flocks return at *azal* (Rahmani 1936). In Lesser Kabylia, the sheepskin is replaced by a bean-sieve and they are not given water. Other blessed pairs include: a double ear of wheat (on the same stem), called the 'ear of blessing', which merits the slaughter of a goat and which is kept in the house; twins (according to some informants, a mother of twins has the privilege of being allowed to sacrifice animals).[29] In divining, things that come in pairs portend good (even if they are intrinsically bad omens, such as crows). Conversely, things that are 'uneven', single and solitary, like the bachelor or spinster, are bad omens, being symbols of sterility (an unmarried girl and an ox that refuses the yoke are both called *afrid*).

Another way of *signifying* the success of the coupling can be seen in the handling of the seed-corn. According to various informants, the grain that will be sown is never mingled with the grain that will be eaten or sold. It always includes some grains from the last sheaf cut, sometimes grain from the last sheaf threshed or dust taken from the last patch harvested or from the threshing floor when the last sheaf is threshed, or dust from the mausoleum of a saint (Servier 1962: 229, 253), salt, etc. It is kept in the house, in chests or jars (*thikufiyin*) beside the dividing wall and prepared in accordance with rites and taboos designed to maintain its properties. In other words, it is domesticated by its long stay in the place *par excellence* of procreation, of the reuniting of male and female which is manifested, in the architecture itself, by the union of the female fork and the male beam which it bears, as the earth holds up the sky.[30]

The clearest evidence of the signified union is, however, the lighted lamp (*mes'bah'*) which was carried before the wedding procession (Devulder 1957; Yamina 1960) and which burned all night in the bridal chamber, just as, according to some traditions, it accompanied the ploughman to the field on the first day of ploughing and was kept alight until the first plot (*thamtirth*) had been sown. The ordinary lamp is the symbol of man through whom light comes ('Man is light, woman darkness'; the motif representing the lamp, in wall paintings, when it is surmounted by a sort of M, symbolizing a woman lying with her legs open – like the fork of the house – signifies coupling [Devulder 1951]). But, like the hearth, it has the ambiguity of the female-male: it is the light of the inside, the male in the female, which is what has to be reproduced.[31]

In the marriage lamp that is carried in the procession bringing the bride from her house to the bridegroom's, the old woman who has prepared it puts salt, honey and a product, also used in the rites of the 'association of the month', called the 'nut of the association' (Devulder 1957). It is a bad omen – which the old woman tries, by her words, to prevent – if it goes out on the way, and it has to burn through the wedding night and the following days until the oil runs out, without ever being put out. The wall-painting motif called the 'wedding lamp' contains both the M, the crossroads, the *thanslith* (from the root NSL, to begin, engender), a motif consisting of two triangles joined at their apexes, which is 'at the beginning of all weaving and all life' (Chantréaux 1941–2: 219–21; Servier 1962: 132). As for the motif, also called 'the wedding lamp', in which the lamp is surmounted by two white triangles representing eggs, it stands for another wedding lamp called *mes'bah' thamurth*, the lamp of the land, which was described to me (among the Ouadhias) and which is characterized by the fact that the wick runs right through an egg (the practical equivalent of the pomegranate or a woman's belly) with two holes in it.

The lamp, a symbol of union, as well as being the light of the inside, is also a symbol of man and his virility. It is thus a principle of virilization, like the rifle shots, in even number, that accompany the bride, and especially those that the bridegroom's male relatives, the guardians and guarantors of his virility, fire at the target set up in their path (a rite which was also practised when a boy was born and to celebrate a circumcision). It is said that formerly the children would set up a kind of ambush, on the outskirts of the village, for the delegation of kinsmen of the bridegroom bringing the bride to her new home. Placing a stone (female) or a raw egg, a symbol of the womb and its fertility, in the hollows of an embankment or a tree-trunk, they would draw the attention of the escort party to this target and challenge them to shoot it down. The procession would stop until the target was hit and laid low. If this could not be done, the whole escort had to pass under a donkey's packsaddle (a symbol of submission, often invoked in domestic struggles, especially when involving magic). In fact, the adults took care to prevent such (excessive) humiliation of the visitors, and the tradition of target shooting was progressively abandoned, probably because of the risks it entailed, reappearing, though stripped of its character as a competition of honour, in the form of a game, played by the members of the delegation in their own village, that is, within their own group (any outsiders being mere guests), the day after the bride's arrival, while awaiting the meal. The specifically sexual symbolism of shooting (confirmed by many other indices)[32] is particularly seen in the fact that, to make the riflemen miss their aim, the eggs to be used as targets were passed three times (downwards) under a maiden's dress, so that they would remain 'virgin' (Rahmani 1949); and that, to break the charm, a man who was an outsider to the village and the escort had to pierce the eggs with a needle.

Rifle shots, which are frequently used in rain-making rites as symbols of male sprinkling capable of unbinding what is bound, are naturally associated with all the taboos on tying, binding or knotting, which is opposed as much to the male action of opening as to the female action of being open(ed) and swelling. Always seeking to maximize the magical profits, ritual in a sense kills two birds with one stone by playing on the coincidence between 'opening' and 'being opened' (which is reflected in the ambiguity of the stative verbs) to forbid actions that would tend to hinder the action of opening, which is female in its passive form and male in its active form (just as the so-called iron-binding rites, aimed at rendering a man or woman incapable of sexual relations, implement the scheme of cutting). The bride must wear no belt for seven days, and on the seventh day her belt is tied by a mother of many sons; similarly, the woman who carries the seed-corn must tie her belt loosely and wear a long dress which trails behind her for good luck (*abruâ*). The bride must not tie up her hair for seven days; the woman who carries the seed-corn wears her hair untied.

(Likewise, at the moment of childbirth, all forms of knotting – crossing the arms or legs, wearing knots or belts, rings, etc. – or closing – of doors, chests, locks, etc. – are forbidden and the opposite actions recommended.) As well as acts of closing, the taboos around ploughing and marriage rule out all acts of purification and expulsion: sweeping, whitewashing the house, shaving, cutting the hair or nails; and all contact with objects that are dry or associated with dryness, such as the use of kohl and henna or the eating of spices.

As acts of procreation, that is, of re-creation, marriage and ploughing are practically treated as male acts of opening and seeding intended to provoke a female action of swelling.[33] The ritual *mise-en-scène* plays on all the ambiguities of objects or practices, mobilizing on the one hand everything that opens (keys, nails) and everything that is open (untied hair and girdles, trailing garments), everything that is sweet, easy and white (sugar, honey, dates, milk), and on the other hand everything that swells and rises (pancakes, fritters, wheat, chick-peas, broad beans – *ufthyen*), everything that is multiple and tightly packed (grains of *seksu*, couscous, or *berkukes*, coarse couscous, pomegranate or fig seeds), everything that is full (eggs, walnuts, almonds, pomegranates, figs); and the most productive symbols are those that combine several of these properties. Such are the egg, the symbol *par excellence* of what is full and pregnant with life, or the pomegranate, which is at once full, swollen and multiple, of which one riddle says, 'Granary upon granary, inside the corn is red', and another: 'No bigger than a pounding-stone, and more than a hundred children' (Genevois 1963: 73). And a whole aspect of the multi-functional action performed in ploughing and marriage is summed up in the ploughman's act of breaking (*felleq*, to burst, split, deflower) a pomegranate or an egg on the ploughshare.

The rites accompanying the first entry of the yoke of oxen into the stable, the first ploughing, and the bride's arrival in her new house, give a very clear idea of the products of the practical sense which, oriented towards the performance of several functions that are not clearly distinguished, takes maximum advantage of the polysemy of actions and things so as to produce symbolically and functionally over-determined actions, each tending to attain the ends in view in several ways simultaneously. The sieve that is presented to the bride at the threshold of the door evokes the 'ploughing sieve' (Servier 1962: 141). It contains wheat, walnuts, dried figs and dates, symbols of male fertility, eggs, fritters and pomegranates. But, as has been seen in other cases (for example, the rites to welcome the yoke of oxen and the rites of *azal*), it is only in the uses made of them that the practical meaning of these always interchangeable and always ambiguous objects is fully defined and that one sees the equivalence with rites that are apparently different but produced from the same schemes and oriented towards the same functions. The bride breaks the eggs on the head of the mule that bears her, wipes her hands on its mane, and throws the contents of the sieve behind her; the children who have followed her scramble (number implies abundance) to pick up the titbits (Genevois 1955b no. 49). In another variant, the sieve contains branches of pomegranate tree and nettles, a mirror, eggs and wheat; the bride throws water behind her and breaks the egg against the lintel of the door, while the mother-in-law smears the loom wall with egg (Yamina 1960). According to another informant (Aït Hichem), the mother-in-law spreads a mat in front of the door, on *alemsir*, 'the door of provisions' (there is a clear analogy with the rite of the 'first entry of the yoke of oxen', intended to produce fullness). She puts on it wheat and broad beans (*ajedjig*) and prepares an egg and a pot of water; the bride does the same (she goes and throws *ajedjig* in the fountain a few days later). As well as wheat, broad beans and eggs, the sieve, which is also called the 'sieve of the traditions' (*laâwayed*), can also contain fritters, a food which swells, like *ajedjig*, and which is supposed to cause swelling (Boulifa 1913). In a general way, the bride is sprinkled by the *qibla*, or the bridegroom's mother, who, in at least one case (Sidi Aïch), gives her water to drink (elsewhere, whey) from her hands, as does the father when she leaves (but sometimes he too sprinkles her). She throws the contents of the sieve behind her (walnuts, dates, fritters, hard-boiled eggs), except for the wheat and broad beans – the promise of an abundance of men – which she takes three times in her hands (Aït Hichem) and replaces in the sieve after kissing them.

It can be seen incidentally that analysis of the variants confirms the freedom inherent in improvising on the basis of implicit practical schemes rather than executing an explicit model. The same objects and the same acts reappear everywhere, as does the overall meaning of the practice, but with all kinds of substitutions, of the agents (the *qibla*, the mother-in-law, the bride, for example), the objects and the actions performed (and this is what disqualifies the search for the 'correct', most complete, most significant variant, which at least initially oriented my own collecting). Everything takes place as if, through improvisation, semi-codified by local traditions, the agents generated all the practices that could be generated from one (or several) schemes, selected in relation to the dominant intention of the rite: the scheme of 'increasing and multiplying', the scheme of 'breaking' (or 'deflowering') with the breaking of the egg used as a target, the egg in the sieve or the plate which held the henna and which the bridegroom must break with a kick (Sidi Aïch), the scheme of reversal of the world, with the crossing of the threshold without contact (on the back of a 'magic screen', sometimes a Negro) and the mirror.

Similarly, the 'ploughing sieve' (*agherbal elh'erth*, hence the name of the rite, *thagerbalt*), brought to the ploughman by his wife, accompanied by the village children, a symbol of multiplication, at various times depending on the village (in the morning, when he leaves the house, or when he reaches the field and harnesses the oxen, or at the time of the midday meal), always contains pancakes, dried broad beans, wheat and a pomegranate. In one tradition, the ploughman stops work, feeds the oxen, and then, standing in front of the oxen, throws first the seeds, then the pancakes (which the children try to catch), over the oxen (taking care to touch them) and over the plough or on the ground; it is a gesture of generosity, ensuring prosperity, and also a sacrifice. Setting the children at a distance, he then throws the pomegranate, which the most skilful must catch. The children run from field to field in this way. In another recorded version of this rite (Hénine 1942), the sieve also contains a carding-comb; after chanting some religious words, the wife places the two fresh eggs in the most recent furrow and the husband ploughs a new furrow before letting the oxen rest and eat. If the eggs remain intact, the year will be good. After the woman has buried an amulet in a corner of the field, the participants eat the contents of the sieve. One more of the innumerable variants: the ploughman breaks two pomegranates, some wheatcakes and a few fritters on the ploughshare, then distributes the rest among those present; the offerings are buried in the first furrow.

Endless examples could be given of meetings between the two rituals. The bride (and her procession) are sprinkled with milk, and she herself often sprinkles water and milk as she enters her new house, just as the mistress of the house sprinkles the plough with water or milk when it leaves for the field. The bride is presented with a key with which she strikes the lintel of the door (elsewhere, a key is put under her clothes as she is being dressed); a key is put in the bag of seed-corn and is sometimes thrown into the furrow.

The denial of murder and the promise of resurrection that were contained in the ritual of harvesting are here enacted in the denial of the rape and violence which are the precondition for the resurrection of the seed.[34] The sacrifice and collective consumption of the ox can be understood as a mimetic representation of the cycle of the grain which has (to consent) to die to feed the group. This sacrifice is all the more remarkable because it concerns the animal closest to humans, most closely associated with their life, their work and their anxiety in the face of the uncertainty of the cosmic rhythms (which it depends on and takes part in as closely as does mankind).

At the winter solstice, when the earth, which rests on the horns of a bull, passes from one horn to another, there ensues a great uproar, heard only by the oxen, who would waste away, too terrified to eat, did not the whole family make a loud noise in the stable, banging on receptacles and shouting, 'Fear nothing, O oxen, it's only the sun declining.' At the spring equinox, when 'the sun turns' and the days will grow longer, more noise 'so that the oxen will not hear that their working time will grow longer' is made in the stable (according to other informants, the day of the 'loan', at the end of *ennayer*, is when people go into the stable, before daybreak, to shout in the oxen's ears, 'Rejoice, oxen, *ennayer* is over!').

This denied murder – the sacrifice of a quasi-human animal, the intermediary and mediator between the natural world and the human world, whose body is treated as an image of and substitute for the social body – is accomplished in the communal meal, which practically enacts the resurrection of the dead in the living, in an ultimate application of the axiom 'a life for a life' which led to the accepted sacrifice of the old man closest to the ancestors, in exchange for rain and the survival of the group. All the more so since the communal meal bringing together the whole group contains an evocation of the dead. As is underlined by the status of the stranger (*aghrib*), who cannot 'cite' any ancestor and who will not be 'cited' (*asker*, to cite and to resurrect) by any descendant, membership of the group, which is affirmed by meeting and eating together, implies the power to invoke and evoke ancestors and the assurance of being invoked and evoked by descendants.[35]

The resurrection of the dead in the living is called for by every aspect of symbolism, especially that of cuisine. Thus, the broad bean, the dry, male seed *par excellence*, akin to the bones, the refuge of the soul awaiting resurrection, together with chick peas and wheat, composes *ufthyen* (or *ilafthayen*), grains which increase and multiply in cooking,[36] and which are eaten at the start of ploughing (and also on the eve of *ennayer* and especially the eve of *Achura*). It is also used in *abisar*, a dish reserved for men; it is one of the things thrown into the first furrow. This almost transparent symbol of the dead (a riddle: 'I put a broad bean in the ground, it didn't come up' – a dead man [Genevois 1963: 10]), and the food of the dead ('I saw the dead nibbling broad beans' – I almost died) is predisposed to carry the symbolism of death and resurrection, being a dessicated seed which, after ritual burial in the damp womb of nature, swells and comes up again, more numerous, in spring, when it is the first sign of plant life to appear.

In the case of weaving (see figure 5) – the structure of which, as H. Basset (1922: 154) observed long ago, is, even in its ambiguity, perfectly homologous with the structure of the agrarian cycle, but even clearer, because it is reduced to its two high points, the assembly of the loom, linked to the start of ploughing, and the removal of the woven cloth, associated with the harvest – the axiom that governs the whole logic of the sacrifice is spelled out almost explicitly.

As well as the homology of structure, a very large number of indices directly confirm the correspondence between the agrarian cycle and the cycle of weaving. The loom is assembled under a crescent moon in autumn ('the figs and blackberries are ripe and we have no blankets'). The upper beam, called the east beam (at Aït Hichem) or the sky beam (Servier 1962: 65), and the lower beam, called the west beam or earth beam, delimit a space analogous to the space the ploughman defines when starting his ploughing, and within which the weaving is done upwards, that is, from west to east. The woman who is to start the weaving abstains from all dry food; the evening meal, called the 'meal of the warp', invariably consists of moist food, couscous and fritters (*thighrifin*), etc. (Chantréaux 1941–2: 88). There are various indications that the weaving cycle, like the grain cycle, is practically identified with procreation, that is, resurrection. *Thanslith*, the triangular motif with which weaving starts, and which, as has been seen, appears on the 'marriage lamp', is a symbol of fertility. It is said that the art of weaving was taught by Titem Tahittust, the wife of a blacksmith from Ihittusen, in the Aït Idjer, a place celebrated for its carpets, who copied her pattern from a piece of marvellous cloth, found on a dunghill, depicting the back of a snake (more symbols of resurrection) (Chantréaux 1941–2: 219).

The decisive moment in the dangerous operation of uniting contraries, particularly the crossing of the threads which produces *erruh'*, the soul, a euphemism designating something dangerous, is always entrusted to an old woman, who is both less precious and less vulnerable (Chantréaux 1941–2: 110). According to one informant, the bringing of the loom, that is, a new person, into the house has to be paid for with a life; to conjure this threat, a hen is slaughtered on the threshold, its blood is poured on one of the uprights of the loom, and its flesh is eaten in the evening (or a hank of wool 'that has not seen water' may be washed in the courtyard and the water then be sprinkled on the loom). Just as the last sheaf is often cut by hand, by the master of the field, so it is sometimes the mistress of the house who must detach the woven cloth, without using iron and after sprinkling it with water, as is done to the dying, while singing harvest chants (H. Basset 1922: 159). Elsewhere, this dangerous operation is entrusted to an old woman who, it is said, 'cuts the throat' of the warp with a knife, after sprinkling it, while pronouncing the *chahada* (A. Basset 1963: 70; Genevois 1967: 71). These different ways of denying murder

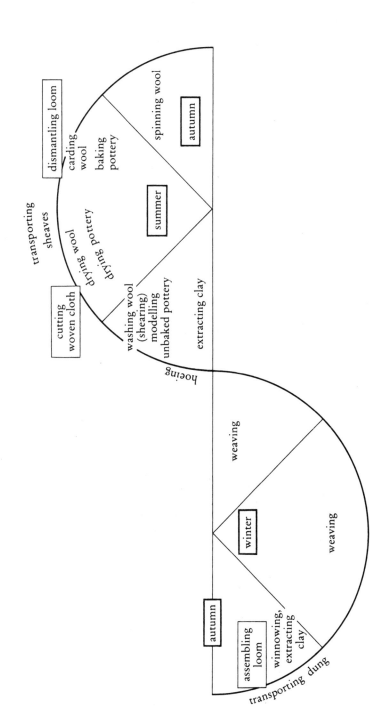

Figure 5 The cycle of the women's activities

and so escaping the law of revenge, a 'soul' for a 'soul' – which means that men are kept away from the cutting operation – are also intended to call for resurrection, like the rain-making rites of the harvest, which the sprinkling recalls, by calling down the fecundating rain of heaven on to the loom which, like the harvested field, has now returned to the state of sterile dryness.

Wool and pottery, natural products, have a very similar cycle. Pottery, being derived from the earth, partakes of the life of the field; the clay is collected in autumn, but it is never worked in that season, nor in winter, when the earth is pregnant, but in spring. The unfired, 'green' (*azegzaw*) pottery dries slowly in the sun (wet-dry) while the ears of corn are ripening (the wet-dry period) (Servier 1962: 164–6). So long as the earth bears the ears, it cannot be baked. It is only after the harvest, when the earth is bare and no longer producing, and fire is no longer liable to dry up the ears (dry-dry period) that baking can be carried out, in the open air (dry-dry). The wool, which is sheared at the end of the cold period, is washed with soap and water, at the moment when everything is opening and swelling, and boiled in a pot into which some wheat and beans (*ufthyen*) have been thrown, so that the flocks of wool will swell like the ears of corn in the fields. It dries at the same time as the pottery, in the wet-dry period. It is carded with instruments as typically 'dry' and male as the carding-comb, the symbol of separation and male roughness, a product of the work of the blacksmith which is used in virilization rites and in the prophylactic rites intended to ward off the diseases associated with evening and dampness.

SCHEME TRANSFER AND HOMOLOGY

As the case of weaving shows clearly, the basis of the homologies that analysis discovers between the different areas of practice is the application of practically interchangeable schemes. Thus, for example, the major features of the series of ordinary or extra-ordinary dishes which, on account of the mimetic-rite function conferred on eating,[37] are associated with the different periods of the agrarian year (see figure 6), can be understood in terms of the opposition between two classes of foods and two classes of operations. On one side, there are the dry foods – cereals (wheat and barley), dry vegetables (beans, peas, chick-peas, lentils, etc.) and dried meat – which are boiled in water, unspiced, in the cooking-pot, indoors, or steamed, or raised with leaven (fritters), operations which all make food swell; and on the other side, there are raw, green or fresh foods (three meanings of the word *azegzaw*, associated with spring and unripe corn), which are eaten raw (as tends to be the case in spring) and/or roasted or grilled on the griddle (*bufrah'*), outdoors, and heavily spiced. (Except very occasionally, when an animal has been sacrificed, or there are sick people to be fed, for example, meat is too precious to be cooked on the fire. In summer, sweet peppers and tomatoes are cooked on the *kanun*. However, meat is always boiled in autumn whereas it can be roasted in spring.) The variations observed can be fully accounted for when it is further noted that the first combination is characteristic of late autumn and winter, the

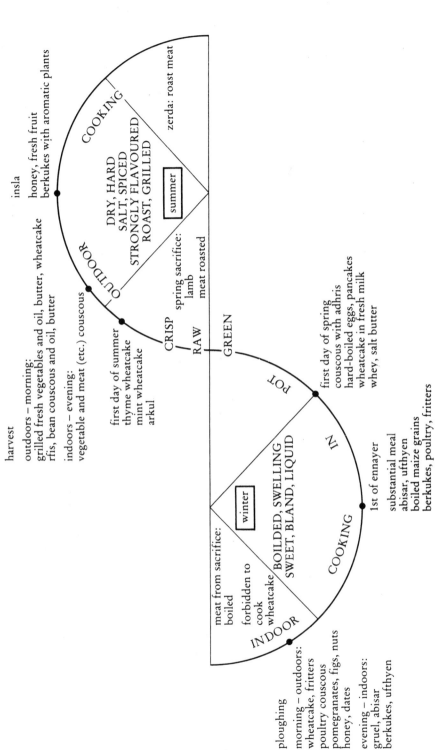

Figure 6 The cuisine cycle

period when the dry is moistened and the fecundated earth and woman are expected to swell, whereas the second is associated with spring, a transitional season, and summer, the period of dessication of the wet and separation from the female, when everything that has developed inwardly, like grains of wheat and beans, must open out and ripen in the light of day.

Winter food is, overall, more female, summer food more male. In every season, women's food is, as one might expect, a moist form of the corresponding male food. The men's food is solid and nourishing, based on wheatcake (*aghrum*) and couscous. A guest one wants to honour, the male *par excellence*, is offered at least a couscous, even if it has to be made with barley, and if possible a meat couscous; never soup, not even wheat soup, or boiled semolina. Women's food is more liquid, less nourishing, less highly spiced, based on boiled cereals, broths and sauces; their couscous is made with barley or even bran and flour (*abulbul*).[38] But in fact, things are not so simple. Semolina dumplings, which may appear as female because they are boiled in water, are also the most masculine of female foods, and are therefore sometimes eaten by men, because they can accompany meat. Conversely, *berkukes*, a male food, can be eaten by women because it is boiled, unlike couscous, which is simply sprinkled.

Without entering into a description – strictly speaking, an interminable one, owing to the innumerable variants – of the feast-day dishes which concentrate the characteristic properties of the cuisine associated with the various periods, it is none the less possible to indicate their pertinent features, while bearing in mind that the dishes differ not so much in their ingredients as in the processes applied to them, which strictly define a cuisine. Thus certain polysemous products reappear at very different moments of the year and in very different rites: wheat, for example, of course, but also broad beans, which figure in the meals of ploughing time, the first day of January, harvest time, funerals, etc., or eggs, a symbol of female fertility also used in virilization rites, on the first day of spring. On ploughing days, the meal eaten outside, in the fields, is always more male, that is, 'drier', than autumn and winter food as a whole, which is boiled or steamed, like the food eaten at the time of weddings or burials; but the meal taken in the evening of the first day's ploughing always consists of boiled cereals or unspiced coarse-grained couscous, a dish that is sometimes explicitly excluded from the meal of the first day of spring ('because the ants would multiply like the grains of semolina'), or *ufthyen*, made from grains of wheat and beans cooked in water or steam, or *abisar*, a sort of thick bean purée, the food of the dead and of resurrection (these dishes are always associated with many-seeded fruit, pomegranates, figs, grapes, nuts, or sweet foods, honey, dates, etc., symbols of 'easiness'). Wheatcake, the dry, male food *par excellence*, must not be cooked during the first three days of ploughing. It is even said that if roast meat were eaten (the meat of the *thimechret* ox is boiled), the oxen would before long be injured in the neck. The couscous (*berkukes*) eaten on the first day of *ennayer* contains poultry, typically female (among other reasons because the fowl are the women's personal property). But it is perhaps on the eve of this day (sometimes called the 'old women' of *ennayer*) that the generative scheme of winter food, that of moistening the dry, shows through most clearly. On that day, people must eat nothing but boiled, dry grains (sometimes with fritters) and they must eat their fill. They must not eat meat ('so as not to break the bones') or dates ('so as not expose the stones'). The meal eaten on the first day of *ennayer* (*Achura*) is very similar to that of the first day of ploughing: it is always substantial (being an inaugural rite) and consists of *abisar* or *berkukes* and fritters, or boiled cereal.

From the first day of spring, as well as the traditional elements of fertility-giving food (couscous cooked in the steam of *adhris*, thapsia, which causes swelling, and hard-boiled eggs, which must be eaten to satiety) – at the time when the women first dye their hands with henna – the diet includes grilled cereals (semolina), which the children eat outdoors, raw, green produce (beans and other vegetables) and milk (warmed or cooked).

With the return of *azal*, *thasabwath*, dry pancakes crumbled and dipped in boiling hot milk, *thiklilth*, a cheese made of cooked churned milk which is only eaten on that day (Hassler 1942) and semolina with butter, announce the dry, male food of summer. The combination characterizing the feast-day meals of the dry season is wheatcake and grilled meat with or without couscous (depending mainly on whether it is eaten in the fields or at the house). More ordinary meals consist of wheatcake dipped in oil (a dry, male food contrasting with moist, female butter) and dried figs and also, for meals at the house, grilled fresh vegetables.

The structure of the day (which integrates the five Moslem prayers very naturally) constitutes another, particularly legible, product of the application of the same principles. The wet-season day is nocturnal even in its diurnal part. Because the flock goes out and returns only once in the course of this day, it appears as an incomplete form of the dry-season day (see figure 7). On the day called 'the return of *azal*', the threshold of the dry season, when the mistress of the house brings the fire out into the courtyard, there is an abrupt change-over to a more complex rhythm defined by the double departure and return of the flocks. They go out for the first time at dawn and come back as soon as the heat becomes burdensome, that is, around *doh'a*; the second departure coincides with the midday prayer, *dohor*, and they return at nightfall.

Just as the year runs from autumn towards summer, moving from east to west, so the day (*as*) runs from the evening towards noon; the evening meal (*imensi*) is the first and main meal of the day. Although the whole system is organized in accordance with the perfect cycle of an eternal recurrence – evening and autumn, old age and death, being also the locus of procreation and sowing – time is none the less oriented towards the culminating point represented by noon, summer or mature age (see figure 8). Night, in its darkest part, the 'shadows' of the 'middle of the night', which brings men, women and children together in the most secret part of the house, close to the animals, in the closed, damp, cold place of sexual relations, a place associated with death and the grave, is opposed to the day, and more precisely to its summit, *azal*, the moment when the light and heat of the sun at its zenith are at their strongest. The link between night and death, which is underlined by nocturnal sounds like the howling of dogs or jackals or the grinding of the sleepers' teeth, similar to that of the dying, is marked in all the taboos of evening: the practices forbidden – bathing, or even wandering by expanses of water, especially stagnant, black, muddy water, looking in mirrors, anointing the hair,

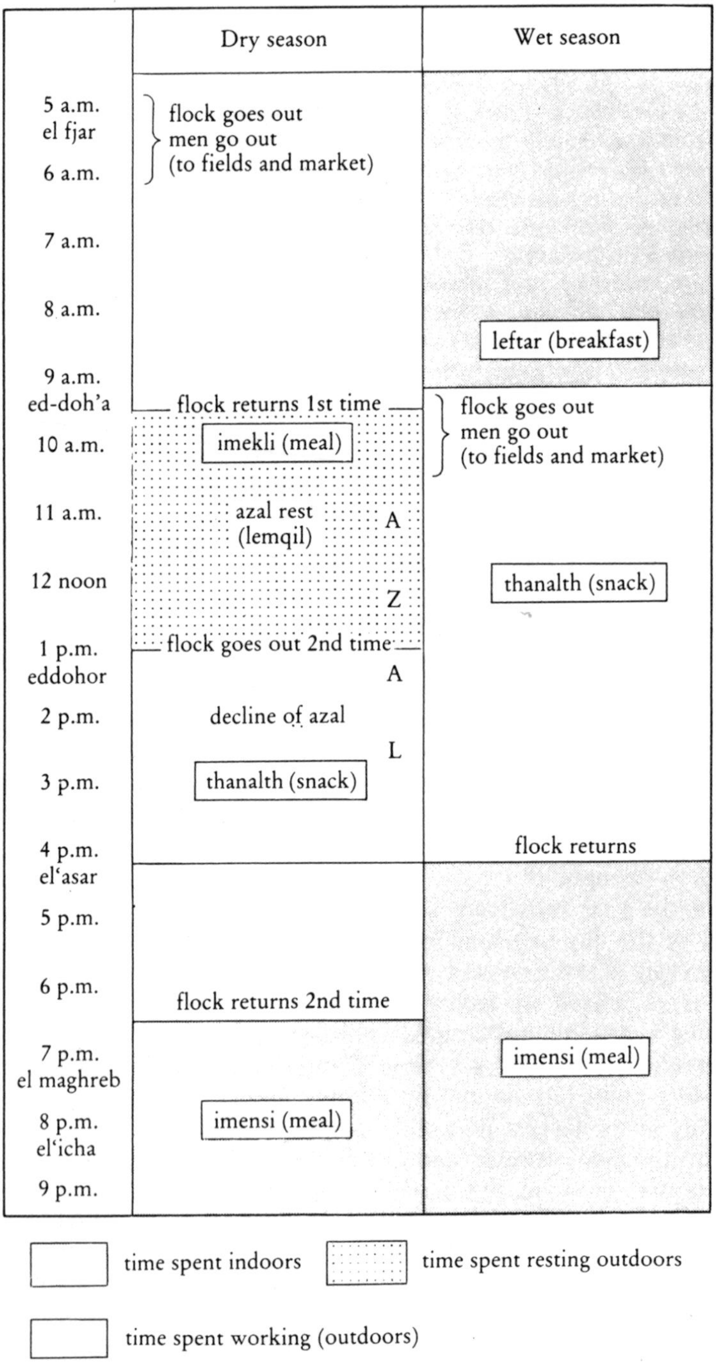

	Dry season	Wet season
5 a.m. el fjar 6 a.m.	flock goes out men go out (to fields and market)	
7 a.m.		
8 a.m.		leftar (breakfast)
9 a.m. ed-doh'a	flock returns 1st time	flock goes out
10 a.m.	imekli (meal)	men go out (to fields and market)
11 a.m.	azal rest (lemqil) A	
12 noon	Z	thanalth (snack)
1 p.m. eddohor	flock goes out 2nd time A	
2 p.m.	decline of azal	
3 p.m.	thanalth (snack) L	
4 p.m. el'asar		flock returns
5 p.m.		
6 p.m.	flock returns 2nd time	
7 p.m. el maghreb		imensi (meal)
8 p.m. el'icha	imensi (meal)	
9 p.m.		

☐ time spent indoors   ⬚ time spent resting outdoors

☐ time spent working (outdoors)

Figure 7 Daily rhythms in summer and winter

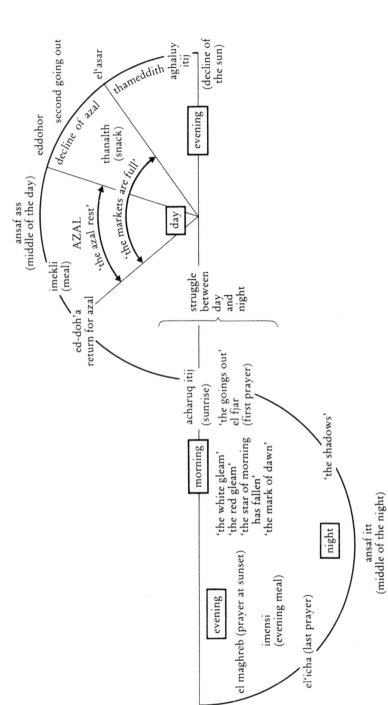

Figure 8 Structure of the dry-season day

touching ashes – would have the effect of, as it were, doubling the malignancy of the nocturnal darkness through contact with substances which are all endowed with the same properties (and are in some cases interchangeable – hair, mirrors, dark waters).

The morning is a moment of transition and rupture, a threshold. It is during the hours before daybreak, when day wins its battle against the night, that the rites of expulsion (*asfel*) and purification are performed (for example, this is the moment when, at the foot of a solitary bramble bush, semolina left overnight near the head of jealous baby, or one afflicted by transferred evil, *aqlab*, is poured over him; likewise, in some expulsion rites, a person goes to a place in the evening – a place of separation, such as the boundary between two fields – and leaves it early in the morning, so as to leave evil behind there). As in many rites performed in spring, the aim is to accelerate and accentuate the break with darkness, evil and death, so as to 'be in the morning', that is, open to the light, the goodness and the good fortune that are associated with it. The rites of inauguration and separation which mark the days of transition are all performed at daybreak: the waking of the cattle in the stable at the winter solstice, the renewal rites on the first day of the year (*ennayer*), the shepherds' departure to gather plants on the first day of spring, the flock's going-out on the 'return of *azal*', etc. Every morning is a birth. Morning is the time for going out, the opening of the day and an opening-up to light (*fatah'*, to open, blossom, is synonymous with *s'ebah'*, to be in the morning). It is the moment when the day is born (*thallalith wass*, the birth of the day), when 'the eye of the light' opens and the house and the village, which closed in upon themselves for the night, pour out their men and flocks into the fields. Morning is the best moment for decisions and new undertakings.

'Morning', it is said, 'means easiness'. 'The market is the morning' (it is when good business is done). 'The hunters' game is shared out by the morning; woe to the sleepers.' On the morning of the first day of spring, the morning of the morning of the year, children are woken with the words: 'Wake up children, the further you walk before sunrise, the longer you will live.' To get up early is to place oneself under favourable auspices (*leftah'*, opening, good augury). The early riser is safe from the encounters that bring misfortune, whereas the man who is late in setting out on the road will have no other companion than the one-eyed man (associated, like the blind man, with night) who waits for broad daylight before setting out, or the lame man who lags behind. To rise at cockcrow is to put one's day under the protection of the angels of the morning and to do them honour. It is also in the morning, an inaugural moment, that divination rites are very often performed: for example, very early the goats, the ewes and the cows are called out and, depending on whether the ewes (or cows) or the goats come first, the year will be good or bad.

The morning, like the homologous periods in the agrarian year or human life, spring or childhood, would be entirely favourable – since it marks the victory of light, life and the future over night, death and the past – if its position did not confer on it the fearful power to determine the future to which it belongs and which it governs as the inaugural term of the series. Though intrinsically benign, it is fraught with the danger of misfortune, inasmuch as it can decide, for good or ill, the fate of the day. We must take a closer look at this logic, which is not fully understood because it is too well half-understood on the basis of the quasi-magical experience of the world which, under the effect of emotion, for example, imposes itself even on those whose material conditions and institutional environment best protect them against this 'regression'. When the world is seen as a system governed by fate, whose starting-point is its cause, what happens in the world or what one does in it governs what must happen. This future is already inscribed in the present in the form of omens. Mankind must decipher these warnings, not in order to submit to the future as a destiny, but in order to be able, if necessary, to modify it. This is only an apparent contradiction, since the hypothesis of a system governed by fate is what justifies trying to remake the future announced by the present, by remaking a new present. Magic is fought with magic: the magical potency of the omen-present is fought with conduct aiming to change the starting-point, in the name of the belief, which was the whole strength of the omen, that the system's starting-point is its cause.

Men watch anxiously for the signs (*esbuh'*, the first encounter of the morning, portending good or ill) through which evil forces may announce their imminence, and then strive to exorcize their effect. A man who meets someone carrying milk takes this as a good omen; a man who, while still in bed, hears the shouts of an argument, takes it as a bad omen; a man who meets at dawn a blacksmith, a lame or one-eyed man, a woman carrying an empty goatskin bottle, or a black cat, must 'remake his morning', return to the night by crossing the threshold in the opposite direction, sleep again and remake his 'going-out'. The whole day (sometimes the whole year, or a man's whole life, when it is the morning of an inaugural day like the first day of spring) can depend on this. The magical power of words and things works with particular intensity here, and it is more than ever necessary to use euphemisms. Of all the forbidden words, the most fearful, in the morning, are all those which express terminal acts or moments – shutting, extinguishing, cutting, or, to a lesser extent, finishing, exhausting, leaving, spreading – and which might invoke an interruption, an untimely destruction, emptiness or sterility. Faith in the power of words implies that certain forms must be observed in one's relations with the world. Any transgression of the prescribed forms, in words or actions, could have cosmic effects. So one must watch one's tongue, especially in the presence of young children, recently circumcised boys or the newly married, all highly vulnerable beings whose future – their growth, virility and fertility – is in question. Similarly, a number of the taboos and prohibitions of spring are practical euphemisms intended to avoid endangering the fertility of nature by the performative power of word or deed. Ultimately the ritualizing of practices tend in itself, through stereotyping, to avoid the errors associated with improvisation, which could trigger off social conflicts or natural disasters. Just as, in the relations between groups who are strangers to each other, the ritualizing of exchanges and conflicts (target shooting, *thawsa*, or the formalisms of etiquette) tends in advance to reduce the potential for unfortunate gestures or words, so too, in the relationship with natural forces, the great collective rites, performed by the agents most capable of committing the future of the whole group, tend to regulate

strictly those exchangse between mankind and the natural world that are most vital
– in the literal sense, since, as in the exchanges of honour, one gives 'a life for
life' – and to leave no room for individual invention or idiosyncrasy. As is shown
by comparison with optional or secret rites, in which the psychological function
and private interest come to the forefront and directly govern the choice of words
and actions, the obligatory, collective rites not only have the effect of avoiding the
damaging effects of intemperate words or gestures or precipitation, which might
give rise to untimely undertakings, by regulating the form, place and time of these
practices; but they also have the effect of censoring psychological experience, even
to the extent of cancelling it out or, which amounts to the same thing, of producing
it by making the action the product of obedience to a kind of categorical imperative.
The fact of collective practice takes the place of intention and can have the effect
of producing a subjective experience and a sense of institution.

It is characteristic of the cultural imperative that it performs a kind of
culturalization or denaturalization of everything it touches, whether it be biological
or psychological necessities, which are thus transfigured and sublimated, like
laughter or tears, or climatic or morphological necessities. This is true of the ritual
divisions of time, which are to climatic divisions as institutionalized tears or
laughter are to 'spontaneous' laughter and tears. Thus the characteristic rhythm of
the winter day is maintained as much in the coldest moments as in the warmest
and already 'springlike' periods of the wet season. The autonomy of the logic of
ritual with respect to objective conditions is even clearer in the case of clothing,
which, as a symbol of social status, cannot be subordinated to climatic variations.
How can a man take off his burnous in summer, if a man without a burnous is
dishonoured? How could anyone fail to put on his winter mocassins to go scything
or to make a long mountain journey, when everyone knows that this footwear
specifically characterizes the genuine peasant or the strong walker? How could the
mistress of the house give up the traditional pair of blankets, worn pinned in front,
which symbolize her authority, her ascendancy over her daughters-in-law and her
power over the running of the household, as does the girdle on which she hangs
the key to the household stores?

Azal, and in particular the middle of azal (*thalmas'th uzal*), the moment
when the sun is at its zenith, when '*azal* is hottest', broad daylight, is
opposed both to winter and to morning, first light, the nocturnal part of
the day. Homologous with the hottest, driest, brightest time of the year,
it is the day of the daytime, the dry of the dry, in a sense bringing the
characteristic properties of the dry season to their fullest expression. It is
the male time *par excellence*, the moment when the markets, paths and
fields are full (of men), when men are outside at their men's tasks. (In a
rite performed to hasten a girl's marriage, the sorceress lights the lamp,
mes'bah', the symbol of the hoped-for man, at *azal*.) Even the sleep of
azal (*lamqil*) is the ideal limit of male rest, just as the fields are the limit
of the usual places for sleep, such as the threshing floor, the driest and
most masculine area in the space close to the house. It is clear why *azal*,
which in itself partakes of the dry and the sterile, should be strongly
associated with the desert (*lakhla*) of the harvested field.

Eddohor, the second prayer, roughly coincides with the end of the *azal*
rest. This is the start of 'the decline of *azal*', the end of the fiercest heat
(*azghal*), when for the second time the flocks set out for the fields and

the men go off back to work. With the third prayer, *elâasar, azal* ends and *thameddith* (or *thadugwath*) begins. Now 'the markets have emptied', and the taboos of evening come into effect. The 'decline of the sun', which 'slopes to the west', is in a sense the paradigm of all forms of decline, in particular old age and all kinds of political decadence ('his sun has fallen') or physical decay. To go westward, towards the setting sun (*ghereb*, as opposed to *cherraq*, to go towards the rising sun), is to go towards darkness, night, death, like a house whose west-facing door can only receive shadows.

Pursuing the analysis of the different fields of application of the system of generative schemes, one could also build up a synoptic diagram of the cycle of life as structured by the rites of passage. The whole of human existence, being the product of the same system of schemes, is organized in homology with the agrarian year and the other major temporal 'series'. Thus procreation (*akhlaq*, creation) is very clearly associated with evening, autumn and the nocturnal, damp part of the house. Likewise, gestation corresponds to the underground life of the grain, that is, the 'nights' (*eliali*). The taboos of pregnancy, those of fecundity, are the taboos of the evening and or mourning (looking in a mirror at nightfall, etc.); a pregnant woman, like the earth swollen in springtime, partakes of the world of the dead (*juf*, which designates the belly of the pregnant woman, also means north, the homologue of night and winter). Gestation, like germination, is identified with cooking in the pot. After giving birth, the mother is served the boiled food of winter, of the dead and of ploughing, particularly *abisar* (the meal of the dead and of funerals) which is otherwise never eaten by women, and, on the fortieth day, she eats coarse couscous boiled in water (*abazin*), a symbol of fertility and multiplication (also eaten on the first day of ploughing), fritters, pancakes and eggs. Birth is associated with the 'opening' of the end of winter and the same prohibitions on acts of closing are observed (crossing the legs, hands and arms, wearing bracelets and rings, etc.). The homology between spring, childhood and morning, periods of inaugural uncertainty and expectation, is manifested *inter alia* by the abundance of divination rites and rites intended to assist the break with the domestic and maternal world and emergence into the male world (such as the first haircut and the first visit to the market).

A number of rites of passage are explicitly associated with a homologous moment of the year. For example, the beginning of autumn is appropriate for circumcision, but not winter, and *elâazla gennayer*, a moment of separation, is a propitious time for the first haircut, one of the important stages in the transition towards the male world. Autumn and spring (after *elâazla*) are appropriate for marriage, which is ruled out on the last day of the year, in *h'usum* and *nisan*, and in May and June. The springtime rites (especially those of the first day of spring and the return of *azal*) set to work a symbolism which applies as much to the unripe corn, still 'bound, fettered, tied' (*iqan*), as to the limbs of the baby that cannot yet walk (*aqnan ifadnis*) and remains in a sense attached to the earth. Those rites of passage that are not linked to a particular period of the year always owe some of their properties to the ritual characteristics of the period in which they are performed, a fact that explains the essential features of the variants observed. For example,

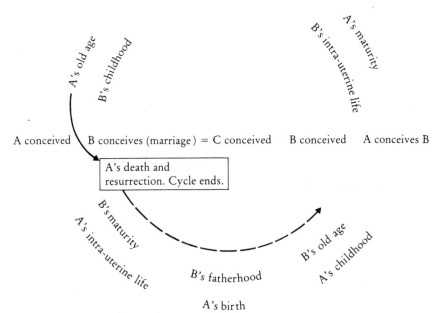

Figure 9 The cycle of reproduction

the beneficent water of *nisan*, a necessary component in the rites specific to that period (like the first milk in spring, the ears of the last sheaf in summer, etc.), also appears in the rites of passage that take place at that time.

Although described as an untimely destruction (*anâadam*), the harvest is not a death without issue (*maâdum*, the bachelor who dies childless); and magic, which enables the profits of contradictory actions to be combined without contradiction, is expected to bring about resurrection in and through a new act of fecundation. Similarly, old age, which faces the west, the setting sun, night and death, the dark direction *par excellence*, is at the same time turned towards the east of resurrection in a new birth. The cycle ends in death, that is, the west, only for the outsider (*aghrib*). In a universe in which a man's social existence requires that he be linked to his ancestors and 'cited' and 'resurrected' by his descendants, the death of the outsider, the man of the west (*el gharb*) and of exile (*el ghorba*), a man without descendants (*anger*), is the only absolute form of death.

The different generations occupy different positions in the cycle that thus emerges. They are diametrically opposed for successive generations, those of father and son (since the first conceives when the second is conceived, or enters old age when the second is in childhood), and identical for alternate generations, those of grandfather and grandson (see figure 9). Such is the logic which, by making birth a rebirth, leads the father whenever possible to give his first son the name of his own father (the verb for 'to name' is *asker*, to resurrect). And the fields go through a perfectly homologous cycle, that of two-year rotation: just as the cycle of generation is completed by the death and resurrection of A, that is, when B conceives C, so the cycle of the field is completed when field A, which has lain fallow, waiting to be resurrected, for the duration of the life of the fecundated field B, is 'raised from the dead' by ploughing and sowing, that is, at the moment when field B is laid fallow.

It can be seen how the denial of murder by cyclicalization tends to extend to 'natural' death itself. It follows that, contrary to scholarly illusion, the expectation of the 'resurrection' of the dead might be simply the product of a transfer of schemes constituted in the area of practice most directly turned towards the satisfaction of temporal needs.

Thus, practical logic owes its efficacy to the fact that, through the choice of the fundamental schemes that it applies and through its exploitation of the polysemy of the symbols that it uses, it adjusts in each case to the particular logic of each area of practice. This explains the uncertainties and even incoherences that are encountered as soon as one tries to compare methodically all the particular applications of the systems of schemes. Just as the same word receives a different sense in each of its broad areas of use while remaining within the limits of a 'family of meanings', so the fundamental structures are realized in meanings which are very different between one area of practice and another, although they always share some feature with at least one other element in another series and all have in common a kind of 'family look' which is immediately intuited. It is no accident that the difficulties of the Greek and Chinese exegetes began when they tried to construct and superimpose *series* (in the sense of asymmetrical, transitive, 'connected' relationships that Russell gives the word in his *Introduction to Mathematical Philosophy*) similar to those that have been successively examined here. When one tries to push the identification of the different series beyond a certain degree of refinement, behind the fundamental homologies all sorts of incoherences begin to appear.[39] True rigour does not lie in an analysis which tries to push the system beyond its limits, by abusing the powers of the discourse that gives voice to the silences of practice, exploiting the magic of the writing that tears practice and discourse out of the flow of time, and above all by putting the essentially mandarin questions of coherence or logical correspondence to the most typically practical of practices.[40]

It is only when the transfer of schemes that is effected on the hither side of discourse becomes *metaphor* or *analogy* that it becomes possible, for example, to wonder like Plato whether 'it was the earth that imitated woman in becoming pregnant and bringing a being into the world, or woman that imitated the world' (*Menexenus*, 238a). The slow evolution 'from religion to philosophy', as Cornford and the Cambridge school put it, that is, from analogy as a practical scheme of ritual action to analogy as an object of reflexion and a rational method of thought, is correlative with a change in function. Rite and especially myth, which were 'acted out' in the mode of belief and which fulfilled a practical function as collective instruments in a symbolic action on the natural and social world, tend to have no other function than the one they receive in the competitive relations between the scholars who question and interpret their letter by reference to the questions and readings of past and contemporary interpreters. Only then do they become explicitly what they always were, but only implicitly or practically so, that is, a system of solutions to the cosmological or anthropological problems which scholarly reflexion thinks it finds in them but which it in fact causes to exist as such by a *misreading* that is implied in any *reading* ignorant of its own objective reality.

Thus, having failed to conceptualize all that was implied in its status as a learned reading of practices and in particular its ignorance of the logic of practice, of which archaic societies have no monopoly, anthropology has become locked in the antinomy of otherness and identity, the 'primitive mentality' and the 'savage mind'. The principle of this antinomy was indicated by Kant in the *Appendix to the Transcendental Dialectic*: depending on the interests which inspire it, 'reason' obeys either the 'principle of specification' which leads it to seek and accentuate differences, or the 'principle of aggregation' or 'homogeneity', which leads it to observe similarities, and, through an illusion that characterizes it, 'reason' situates the principle of these judgements not in itself but in the nature of its objects.

THE USES OF INDETERMINACY

Practical logic has nothing in common with logical calculation as an end in itself. It functions in urgency, in response to life-or-death questions. It therefore never ceases to sacrifice the concern for coherence to the pursuit of efficiency, making maximum possible use of the *double entendres* and dual purposes that the indeterminacy of practices and symbols allows. Thus, the propitiatory *mise-en-scène* through which ritual action aims at creating the conditions favourable to the resurrection of the grain by reproducing it symbolically in a set of mimetic acts, one of which is marriage, presents a number of ambiguities, which are particularly seen in the ritual of the last sheaf. As if there were hesitation between a cycle of the death and resurrection of the grain and a cycle of death and resurrection of the field, the last sheaf is treated practically, in some places, as a female personification of the field ('the strength of the earth', 'the bride'), on whom male rain, sometimes personified as Anzar,[41] is called down; elsewhere, it is a male (phallic) symbol of 'the spirit of the corn', destined to return for a while to dryness and sterility before inaugurating a new cycle of life by pouring down in rain on to the parched earth. The same ambiguities reappear in the ploughing ritual, although at first sight the acts tending to favour the world's return to wetness, in particular the rites specifically intended to provoke rain, which are practised in identical form in spring, can be combined quite logically with the actions intended to favour the act of fecundation (ploughing or marriage), as the immersion of the dry in the wet, celestial seed in the sterile earth. In the presence of rain, dry water, which partakes of solar maleness by virtue of its celestial origin, but also of the wet, terrestrial female, the system of classification hesitates. The same is true of tears, urine and blood, much used in the homoeopathic strategies of the rain-making rites, and also of semen, which gives new life to woman as rain does to the land, and of which it may be said indifferently either that it swells or that it causes swelling, like beans or wheat in the cooking-pot. Hence the hesitations of magical practice, which, far from being troubled by these ambiguities, takes advantage of them.

After systematically cataloguing the multiple variants of the rain-making rites, Laoust, the only observer who has seen the contradiction clearly (Laoust 1920: 192–3 and 204ff.), infers the female nature of *thislith*, the betrothed, or *thlonja*, the ladle, a doll made out of a ladle dressed as a bride, which is paraded in a procession while rain is called down. The very meticulousness of his inventory provides the means of grasping the properties that make the 'doll' of the rain-making rites, hoeing rites (it is 'Mata' whose abduction is simulated) and harvest rites, a being which is unclassifiable from the point of view of the very system of classification of which it is the product. The female name, *thislith*, which may be no more than a euphemism to designate a phallic symbol, and the clothing (headscarf, necklace, dress) most often used to dress the ladle (although it has been seen that, in one case, old women carry a male doll and men a female doll), probably conflict in practice with the properties of the ladle which is generally used to make the doll (referred to in many places by the name of the ladle) and which, though not without ambiguity for the taxonomy itself, since it can be treated as a hollow liquid-filled object that sprinkles or as something hollow and empty that asks to be filled, belongs rather to the order of the male.

Here is series of scattered observations which tend to confirm this: (1) A divination rite: on her wedding day, the bride plunges the ladle into the pot; she will bear as many sons as she brings up pieces of meat. (2) A proverb: 'Whatever there is in the cooking-pot, the ladle will bring it up.' (3) A divination rite: the ladle is hung on a piece of string so that it balances horizontally, in front of a piece of wheatcake; if it dips towards the wheatcake, the hoped-for event will occur. (4) Of a man who cannot do anything with his hands: 'He's like the ladle.' (5) A taboo: you must never hit anyone with a ladle; either the implement would break (there is only one in the house) or the person struck would 'break'. (6) A taboo: a man must never eat out of the ladle (to taste the soup, as women do): the consequence would be storms and rain on his wedding day. (7) To someone using a tool clumsily: 'Would you eat with the ladle?' – someone who does is liable to be cheated. (8) If a man scrapes the bottom of the cooking-pot with the ladle, it is bound to rain on his wedding day. Obviously linked with marriage, rain and fertility, the ladle, which is also used to pour the sauce, burning water, hot and spicy, which virilizes, is to the cooking-pot, which it penetrates and fecundates, as the male to the female. (The equivalence between the ingestion of food and sexuality explains the prohibition of men's use of the ladle to eat, seen as the equivalent of passive, female sexuality, which, as in most male traditions, is associated with the idea of being dominated and deceived.)

Everything suggests that practice hesitates between two usages: the object can either be treated as something that asks to be sprinkled, like woman or earth which calls for male rain, or as something that sprinkles, like celestial rain. In fact, for practice, this distinction, which has worried the best of interpreters, is of no importance: whether sprinkling or sprinkled, the old men and old women who perform the rain-making rites, and the objects they bear, themselves both sprinkling and sprinkled, mime the intended effect, *signify* the rain which is inseparably sprinkling and sprinkled, depending on the male or female standpoint which is adopted, the two perspectives being equally valid by definition when it is a matter of reuniting contraries. The ritual practice which aims to realize a collective desire symbolically and so help to satisfy it in reality, seizes eagerly on encounters which, as here, offer everything at once, and there is no reason why it should seek to analyse a double reality that satisfies it doubly. This is particularly true in situations like drought, when the importance of what is at stake, a whole year's harvest, requires the threshold of logical requirements to be lowered even further so as to exploit all the available resources.

Because the meaning of a symbol is never completely determined in and through the actions into which it is put and because, in addition to the liberties it takes with a view to maximizing magical profit, the logic of ritual is often intrinsically ambiguous since it can use the same object to produce the property that characterizes it (for example, the dry) or to neutralize that property (for example, to destroy the dry), like the sickle which can be used to dry up a cow's milk or to restore its yield, the uncertainties of scholarly interpretation do no more than reflect the uncertainties of the uses that the agents may themselves make practically of a symbol so overdetermined that it becomes indeterminate even in terms of the schemes that determine it.[42] The error would here lie in trying to decide the undecidable.

There is another factor of indeterminacy which derives from the very basis of practical knowledge. Like all knowledge, it is based, as we have seen, on a fundamental operation of division, and the same principle of division can be applied not only to the whole set (which may be a continuous distribution) but also to each of its parts. It can thus perform, in accordance with the same principle of division, a partition within the part, producing for example a division between the big and the small even within the small, so giving rise to the sequences of interlocking partitions (of the form $a : b :: b_1 : b_2$) which are so frequent both in the organization of groups and in the organization of symbolic systems. It necessarily follows that all the products of a second-degree partition, such as the one that divides the (female) house into a female part and a male part, carry within them duality and ambiguity. This is true of all female activities which lie on the side of fire, the dry and the east, such as cooking and especially weaving, a female activity which, within the female universe, performs a uniting of contraries and a division of contraries that is very similar to ploughing, harvesting or the slaughter of the ox, typically male actions that are forbidden to women. As has been seen, the loom, which is a world in itself, with its up and down, its east and west, its heaven and earth, derives some of its properties and its uses (in the swearing of oaths, for example) to the position, defined according to the same principles as its own internal divisions, that it occupies in the space of the house, which in turns stand in the same microcosm–macrocosm relation to the world as a whole. Nothing better defines the practical logic of magic than its capacity to take advantage of these ambiguities, such as those that result from the fact that the internal space of the house has its own orientation, inverted in relation to that of external space, so that one can both enter and leave the house while always facing east.

Among the objects whose properties are a challenge to the system of classification, perhaps the most characteristic is embers, *times* (in the presence of men, the word is taboo and is replaced by euphemisms). This female fire which smoulders under the ashes, like passion (*thinefsith*, a diminutive of *nefs*), a sly, hypocritical fire like unassuaged revenge ('that which does not forgive'), *times* evokes female sexuality (as opposed to the flame, *ah'ajaju*, which purifies and sets ablaze, like the sun, red-hot iron, lightning – or the plough). According to an informant, the site of spilt blood (*enza*) is made up of three stones, arranged like those of the hearth (*ini*) and delimiting the patch of soil which drank the blood; and a riddle says of the *kanun*, the lighted hearth: 'Here an edge, there an edge, in between poison.' (Poison, *es'em*, water that burns, is associated with the idea of quenching iron, and also, through its root, with the edge of the sword and the dog-days.)

One could also cite moonlight (*tiniri*), the light of the night, a symbol of unlooked-for opportunity; or the sickle, which, as a object made with fire and used for violence and murder, is distinctly male, but which, as a curved, twisted, devious object, evoking confusion and discord ('they are like sickles' means 'they are at odds' – also indicated by crooking two fingers of each hand), partakes of the female. Even an object as clearly marked as the egg, the symbol *par excellence* of female fertility, is not without ambiguity, as can be seen from some of its uses, because it also partakes of the male through its colour (white) and its name (*thamellalts*, egg; *imellalen*, 'whites' [masc.], a man's testicles; *thimellalin*, 'whites' [fem.], eggs, a boy's testicles).

All the factors of indeterminacy seem to be combined in the case of a technical object like the loom. Even more than *thislith*, which is made specially for the specific purposes of its rite, the loom can be involved in uses that tend to confer different, even opposite, meanings on it. These will vary depending on whether attention is focused on the loom as a whole or on one or another of its parts, which can themselves receive different values, within limits, depending on the practical (syntagmatic) context in which they are placed, on which of the properties of its form or function are emphasized, and so on. Thus attention may focus on the external appearance of the object itself: its verticality, rigidity and tension then make it a symbol of uprightness (Lefébure 1978). This view of the loom is aided by the fact that, by virtue of its position in the house, in front of the (inner) eastern wall, the 'wall of light', the 'wall of the angels' that one faces on entering, where an honoured guest is invited to sit (in some cases the loom itself is treated as a guest to be welcomed), it evokes the posture of the man of honour, the 'upright' man who faces one, and is faced, full-square. Because of these properties, and probably also because it produces woven cloth, the veil and protection of nakedness and intimacy (a woman who weaves covers her husband 'unlike Shem who uncovered his father'), it is invoked as 'the barrier of the angels', that is, a shelter, a refuge, a magical protection, cited as a guarantor in oaths ('by the breath of the warp', 'by the seven-souled warp', etc. [Genevois 1967: 25]) and appealed to ('by the loom') to urge someone not to shirk his duty.

But it goes without saying that the most important meanings of the loom are given to it by its functions, particularly through the homology between ploughing and weaving, between the cycle of weaving or the loom and the cycle of the grain or the field. All the symbolic uses of the loom are marked by the ambiguity stemming from the fact that, just as the practical definition of the agrarian cycle hesitates between the cycle of the field and the cycle of the grain, so some practices treat the loom itself as a person who is born, grows up and dies, while others treat it as a field that is sown and then emptied of the crop it has borne, the cycle of the woven cloth being identified with that of the grain or the person (the wool is also said to 'ripen'). The emphasis may be placed more on the loom, and in particular on the assembly of the loom and the start of weaving, that is, on the dangerous act of crossing and knotting, uniting opposites as in ploughing, quenching and marriage; or on the product of this act, the thing that is knotted, the knot seen as a durable crossing of united opposites, a living being that has to be protected or cut (killed) like the wheat and its grain, but with a denial of this inevitable murder. The benign object is also a dangerous object which, like the crossroads or the blacksmith, can bring sterility as well as fertility (thus a repudiated woman who wants to remarry bestrides a reed and runs along shouting; but one must never straddle the loom, for fear of causing the death of someone in the family, and a slanderer's tongue is said to be as dangerous as a woman assembling the loom).

The dangerous character of the loom, which combines within itself the two forms of male violence, crossing and cutting, is reinforced by the properties attached to some of its parts, such as *ilni* (the strings separating the threads of the warp), an ambivalent object, evoking cutting and tying, which is used in rites of malign magic as well as in prophylactic magic. Without telling him, a woman measures her husband with the string, ties seven knots in it, takes a piece of one of his old garments, wraps the string in it with a bouquet of *asa foetida*, often used in expulsion rites, and buries everything in the grave of a stranger (Chantréaux 1941–2: 93) or at the boundary between two fields. To measure is to make a double, a substitute for the thing measured and so gain power over it (the reed with which a corpse is measured is always buried at the bottom of the grave to prevent women from making magic use of it). This measuring – that is, cutting – operation, performed with an object associated with cutting and dryness, is also applied to a cow to prevent theft of the milk (Rahmani 1936) or to a child in the rites to protect against the evil eye (Genevois 1968: vol. II, 56).

There we must stop, but it would not be difficult to show, in relation to this object which is particularly charged and over-charged with meaning by virtue of its plurality of uses and functions, that, without falling into incoherence, practical logic sometimes refers back the things of the world to the plurality of aspects which they present until the cultural taxonomy frees them from it by making its arbitrary selection.

In fact, practical logic can only function by taking all sorts of liberties with the most elementary principles of logical logic. Practical sense, working as a practical mastery of the sense of practices and objects, makes it possible to combine everything that goes in the same sense, everything that at least roughly fits together and can be adjusted to the ends in view. The presence of identical symbolic acts or objects in the rituals associated with such different events in the life of mankind or the field as funerals, ploughing, harvests, circumcision or marriage, has no other explanation. The partial coincidence of the meanings that the practical taxonomies confer on these events is matched by the partial coincidence of ritual acts and symbols whose polysemy perfectly suits practices that are essentially multifunctional. Without any need for symbolic mastery of the concepts of (lasting) swelling and resurrection, the dish called *ufthyen*, a mixture of wheat and broad beans that swells when it is boiled, can be associated with wedding, ploughing and funeral ceremonies, on the basis of what is there subsumed by the function of resurrection; equally, the same dish will be excluded ('because the gums would stay swollen') from moments like the cutting of teeth (in favour of *thibuâjajin*, a kind of pancake which as it cooks produces bubbles that immediately burst), or circumcision, a rite of purification and virilization, that is, separation from the female world, which belongs to the register of dryness, fire and violence (target shooting plays an essential role in it) and is accompanied by roast meat. Yet this does not prevent *ufthyen* from being associated with target shooting in one variant of a multifunctional ceremony like marriage, in which 'intentions' of virilization (opening) and fertilization (swelling) are combined.

The freedom with the constraints of ritual logic that comes from perfect mastery of that logic is what makes it possible for the same symbol to refer back to realities that are opposed in terms of the axiomatics of the system itself. Consequently, although it is not inconceivable that a rigorous algebra of practical logics might one day be written, it will never be done unless it is understood that logical logic, which only speaks of them *negatively*, if at all, in the very operations through which it constitutes itself by denying them, is not equipped to describe them without destroying them. It is a question of reconstituting the 'fuzzy', flexible, partial logic of this *partially integrated* system of generative schemes which, being *partially mobilized* in relation to each particular situation, produces, in each case, below the level of the discourse and the logical control that it makes possible, a 'practical' definition of the situation and the functions of the action (which are almost always multiple and interlocking), and which, with the aid of a simple yet inexhaustible combinatory, generates the actions best suited to fulfil these functions within the limits of the available means. More precisely, one only has to compare the diagrams corresponding to the different areas of practice – the farming year, cuisine, women's work, the structure of the day – to see that the fundamental dichotomy is specified in each case in different schemes which are its efficient form in the area in question: oppositions between dry and wet, hot and cold, full and empty, in the farming year; between dry and wet, boiled and roasted (the two variants of the cooked), bland and spiced, in cuisine; dark and light, cold and hot, inside (or closed) and outside, in the structure of the day; female and male, soft (green) and hard (dry), in the life-cycle. When other structured universes, such as the space of the house or the parts of the body, are added, further principles (up/down, east/ west, right/left, etc.) can be seen at work.

These different schemes are both partly independent and partly inter-changeable, and therefore more or less closely interconnected. For example, from in front/behind one moves quite naturally to male/female, not only because the real division of labour leaves the woman the task of picking up what the man has cut or dropped, or because the rule of deportment requires a wife to walk a few paces behind her husband, but because the front is what distinguishes a man from a woman: in the wall paintings, woman is represented by two diamonds corresponding to the anus and the uterus, man by one diamond (Devulder 1957); the man is the one who goes forward, who faces forward (and here we reconnect with all the connotations of *qabel*). Similarly, the totality of the relationships constitut-ing the system could be recreated from a relatively minor opposition such as that between right and left, right hand and left hand, straight and curved (or twisted).

The left-hander is awkward and clumsy (and akin to the club-footed man and the one-eyed man). He brings ill luck; to meet a left-handed man in the morning is of ill omen. No one will employ him as a ploughman. He may not cut the throat of the sacrificial ox – unless he uses his right hand (we return here to the opposition between male and female, dry and wet). If he ties up an animal, the tether will break and the animal will escape. Eating, alms-giving, offering or taking food or drink, and greeting are all done with the right hand, which must not be used for dirty acts such as touching one's genitals or wiping one's nose (likewise, one spits to the left). The left hand is the hand of malign magic. As opposed to licit amulets, made by the marabout, which are worn on the right, 'magical' amulets (a tooth, a phalanx from a corpse, a miniature ploughshare, etc.) are worn on the left (just as medical magic, which is benign, is performed facing east, whereas malign magic is performed facing west). To eat with the left hand is to feed the devil. The left hand is also the cruel hand; a 'left-hander's shot' (whether it be a rifle shot or the throwing of a stone) is lethal. Woman is associated with the left hand. Naturally inclining towards the left, she goes to the right only if she is straightened (she is 'a knot in the wood'). The right hand is the hand *par excellence*, the hand used in swearing oaths. *Thiâawji*, which designates the craftsman's skill, may, according to a popular etymology, be connected with the idea of twisting, and twisting leftwards, the wrong way (a wicked man is said to be like a piece of twisted wood, he puts out one or both of your eyes). Likewise, the verb *abran* (BRN) which designates the action of turning – an object, the head, the eyes, the tongue (forking) – from right to left, backwards, in short, the wrong way, is opposed to *qaleb* (QLB) – turning the back or the eyes frankly – as the female to the male, as passive refusal, devious avoidance and flight, to active, manifest, frank confrontation. Beyond this, the opposition between going leftwards, turning from right to left, ill-omened movements, and going rightwards, turning from left to right, beneficent movements, connects up with the distinction between 'going west', towards exile and misfortune, and facing east, facing up (*qabel*), the posture of the body and way of presenting oneself that befits a man of honour, and from which one can generate the most fundamental values of the culture, in particular those inscribed in the scheme of spatial orientation: *qabel* is also, as we have seen, to face the east (*lqibla*), the noble direction *par excellence*, that of halcyon days, good omens, the future (*qabel*) (and *qebbel* is to orient eastwards, as is done with the dead in the tomb and the ox that is to be slaughtered with the right hand); it is to receive and welcome someone who arrives, to honour; it is also to accept, to grant. *Cherreq*, to go eastwards, is likewise to go the right way, towards good luck. By contrast, the movement towards the west (*lgharb*), exile (*lghorba*), often identified with death or the tomb, is ill-omened: 'The west is darkness.' 'A maiden', it is said of the father with many daughters, 'is twilight (*lmaghreb*).'

In other words, all the oppositions constituting the system are linked to all the others, but through longer or shorter pathways (which may or may not be reversible), that is, at the end of a series of equivalences which progressively empty the relationship of its content. Moreover, every opposition can be linked to several others in different respects by relationships of varying intensity and meaning (for example, spiced/bland can be connected directly to male/female and hot/cold and more indirectly to strong/weak or empty/full, through – in the last case – male/female and dry/wet, which are themselves interconnected). It follows that the oppositions do not all have the same weight in the network of relationships that bind them together. It is possible to distinguish secondary oppositions which specify the main oppositions in a particular respect and which therefore have relatively low yield (yellow/green, a simple specification of dry/wet) and central oppositions (such as male/female and wet/dry), strongly connected with all the others by logically very diverse relationships, which constitute a cultural arbitrariness (female/male and inside/outside or left/right, twisted/straight, below/above). Since, in practice, only one sector of a system of schemes is mobilized at a time (though without ever entirely breaking all the connections with the other oppositions), and since the different schemes mobilized in different situations are partly autonomous and partly linked to all the others, it is quite natural that all the products of the application of these schemes – a particular rite or a whole series of ritual actions, such as the rites of passage – should be partly congruent and should strike anyone who possesses practical mastery of the system of schemes as roughly, practically, equivalent.[43]

That is why, at the risk of being sometimes understood as a regression towards intuitionism (which at best mimes the practical mastery of a system of schemes that is not theoretically mastered), the description through construction that is made possible by mastery of the generative formula of practices has to remain within the limits that are set on practical logic by the very fact that it derives not from this formula but from its practical equivalent – a system of schemes capable of orienting practice without entering consciousness except in an intermittent and partial way.[44] The theoretical model that makes it possible to recreate the whole universe of recorded practices, in so far as they are sociologically determined, is separated from what the agents master in the practical state, and of which its simplicity and power give a correct *idea*, by the infinitesimal but infinite distance that defines awareness or (it amounts to the same thing) explicit statement.

Appendix

The Kabyle House or the World Reversed[1]

The interior of the Kabyle house is rectangular in shape and divided into two parts, at a point two-thirds of the way along its length, by a small openwork wall half as high as the house. The larger of the two parts, some fifty centimetres higher and covered with a layer of black clay and cowdung which the women polish, is reserved for human use. The smaller part, paved with flagstones, is occupied by the animals. A door with two wings gives access to both rooms. On top of the dividing wall are kept, at one end, the small earthenware jars or esparto-grass baskets used to store the provisions kept for immediate consumption, such as figs, flour and leguminous plants, and at the other end, near the door, the water jars. Above the stable is a loft where, next to all kinds of tools and implements, quantities of hay and straw to be used as animal fodder are piled up. It is here that the women and children usually sleep, especially in winter. Against the gable wall, known as the wall (or more precisely the 'side') of the upper part or of the *kanun*, stands a brickwork construction, in the recesses and holes of which the kitchen utensils (the ladle, the cooking pot, the dish used to cook wheatcake – *aghrum* – and other earthenware objects blackened by the fire) are kept, and at each end of which are placed large jars filled with grain. In front of this construction is the fireplace, a circular hollow three or four centimetres deep at its centre, around which, arranged in a triangle, are three large stones to hold the cooking utensils.[2]

In front of the wall opposite the door, generally referred to by the same name as the outside wall that is seen from the rear courtyard (*tasga*),[3] or else called the weaving-loom wall or the 'facing' wall (one faces it on entering), stands the weaving loom. The opposite wall, where the door is, is called the wall of darkness, or the wall of sleep, of the maiden, or of the tomb (it is also said 'the maiden is the dusk', or 'the maiden is the wall of darkness', or 'when a boy is born, the walls of light rejoice, when a dead man leaves the walls of darkness weep' [Bassagna and Sayad 1974]). A bench wide enough for a mat to be spread out on it is set against this wall. This is the place set aside for the festal sheep or small calf, sometimes for the wood or the water pitcher. Clothes, mats and blankets are hung, in the daytime, on a peg or a wooden crossbar next to the wall of darkness, or else they are put under the dividing bench. Thus, the *kanun* wall is

back door

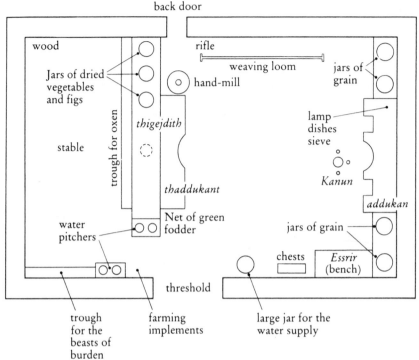

Figure 1 Plan of the house

opposed to the stable as the high to the low (*adaynin*, stable, comes from the root *ada*, the bottom), and the loom wall is opposed to the door wall as the light to the dark. One might be tempted to give a purely technical explanation of these oppositions, since the loom wall, facing the door, which itself faces east, is the most brightly lit and the stable is indeed at a lower level than the rest (the house usually being built at right angles to the contour lines, to facilitate the drainage of animal waste and dirty water). However, a number of indices suggest that these oppositions are the centre of a cluster of parallel oppositions, the necessity of which never stems directly from technical imperatives and functional requirements.

The dark, nocturnal, lower part of the house, the place for things that are damp, green or raw – jars of water placed on the benches on either side of the stable entrance or next to the wall of darkness, wood, green fodder – and also the place for natural beings – oxen and cows, donkeys and mules – natural activities – sleep, sexual intercourse, childbirth, and also death – is opposed to the light-filled, noble, upper part. This is the place for human beings and especially the guest, for fire and things made with fire, such as the lamp, kitchen utensils, the rifle – the attribute of the male point of honour (*nif*) which protects female honour (*h'urma*) – and the loom, the symbol of all protection. It is also the site of the two specifically cultural activities performed within the house: weaving and cooking. In fact, the meaning objectified in things or parts of space is fully yielded only through practices structured according to the same schemes that are organized in relation to them (and vice versa). An honoured guest is invited to sit in front of the loom (the verb *qabel*, to honour, also means to face up to someone and to face the east). When a man has been badly received, he will say: 'He made me sit beside his wall of darkness, as in a grave.' The wall of darkness is also called the invalid's wall, and the phrase 'to keep to the wall' means to be ill and, by extension, idle; a sick person's bed is in fact placed next to this wall, especially in winter. The connection between the dark part of the house and death is also shown in the fact that the washing of the dead takes place at the entrance to the stable. The homology between sleep and death is explicitly stated in the precept that on going to bed one should first lie for a moment on one's right side and then on one's left, because the first position is that of the dead in the tomb. The funeral chants represent the grave, 'the house underground', as an inverted house (white/dark, up/down, adorned with paintings/roughly dug out), sometimes exploiting a homonymy associated with analogy in shape, as in a chant sung at wakes, quoted by Genevois (1955a: 27): 'I found people digging a tomb, With their pickaxes they carved out the walls, They were making benches (*thiddukanin*), with mortar below the mud.' *Thaddukant* (plural *thiddukanin*) is the name of the bench set against the dividing wall, opposite the gable wall (*addukan*) and also of the bank of earth on which a man's head rests in the grave (the slight hollow in which a woman's head is laid is called *thakwath*, as are the small recesses in the walls of the house, in which women keep small objects). It is traditionally said that the loft, which is made entirely of wood, is supported by the stable as the corpse is carried by the bearers; *thaârichth* designates both the loft and the stretcher used to transport the dead.[4] It is clear why a guest cannot, without offence, be invited to sleep in the loft, which is opposed to the loom wall in the same way as is the wall of the tomb.

It is also in front of the loom wall, facing the door, in full daylight, that the young bride is made to sit, as if to be shown off, like the decorated plates that hang there. When one knows that a baby girl's umbilical cord is buried behind the loom and that, to protect a maiden's virginity, she is made to step through the warp, from the side facing the door to the side next to the loom wall, then the function of magical protection attributed to the loom becomes clear.[5] Indeed, from the standpoint of her male kin, the girl's whole life is in a sense summed up in the successive positions she successively occupies vis-à-vis the loom, the symbol of male protection. Before marriage she is placed behind the loom, in its shadow, under its protection, just as she is kept under the protection of her father and brothers; on her wedding day she is seated in front of the loom, with her back to it, with the light upon her, and thereafter she will sit weaving, with her back to the wall of light, behind the loom.

The low, dark part of the house is also opposed to the upper part as the female to the male. Not only does the division of labour between the sexes (based on the same principle of division as the organization of space) give the woman responsibility for most of the objects belonging to the dark part of the house, the carrying of water, wood, manure, for instance; but the opposition between the upper part and the lower part reproduces, within the internal space of the house, the opposition between the inside and the outside, between female space – the house and its garden – and male space.

The opposition between the part reserved for receiving guests and the more intimate part (an opposition also found in the nomad's tent, which is divided by a curtain into two parts, one open to guests, the other reserved for the women) is expressed in ritual forecasts such as the following. When a cat, a beneficent animal, enters the house with a feather or a thread of white wool in its fur, if it goes towards the hearth, this portends the arrival of guests, who will be given a meal with meat; if it goes towards the stable, this means that a cow will be bought, if this occurs in spring, or an ox if it is the ploughing season. The cat, an accidental intruder which is chased away, is only there as a bearer of symbols that performs practically the movement of entering. The feather is implicitly treated as equivalent to the wool, probably because these substances are seen as bearers of a beneficent quality, whiteness. The opposition between the hearth and the stable, which structures the whole sequence – that is, that between the noble part where meat, the food *par excellence* for guests, is roasted, and where guests are received, and the lower part, reserved for the livestock – only has to be combined with the opposition between two seasons – autumn, the time of collective sacrifice, the ox and ploughing, and spring, the time of milk – to yield the ox and the cow.

The lower part of the house is the place of the most intimate secret within the world of intimacy, that is, the place of all that pertains to sexuality and procreation. More or less empty during the daytime, when all the (exclusively female) activity in the house is centred on the fireplace, the dark part is full at night, full of human beings and also full of animals, since the oxen and cows, unlike the mules and donkeys, never spend the night outdoors; and it is never fuller than in the wet season, when the men sleep indoors and the oxen and cows are fed in the stable. The relationship that links the fertility of humans and the fields with the dark part of the house, a privileged instance of the relation of equivalence between fertility and the dark, the full (or the process of swelling) and the damp, is here established directly. Whereas the grain intended for consumption is kept in large earthenware jars next to the wall of the upper part, on either side of the fireplace, the grain kept for sowing is stored in the dark part of the house, either in sheepskins or in wooden chests placed at the foot of the wall of darkness, sometimes under the conjugal bed; or else in chests placed under the bench against the dividing wall (Servier 1962: 229, 253).[6] When one knows that birth is always the rebirth of an ancestor, it can be understood how the dark part of the house can simultaneously and without contradiction be the place of death and of procreation.

At the centre of the dividing wall, between 'the house of the humans' and 'the house of the animals', stands the main pillar, supporting the 'master beam' and the whole framework of the house. The master beam (*asalas alemmas*, a masculine term) which extends the protection of the male part of the house to the female part, is explicitly identified with the master of the house, whereas the main pillar, a forked tree trunk (*thigejdith*, a feminine term), on which it rests, is identified with the wife (according to Maunier the Beni Khellili call it *Masâuda*, a feminine first name meaning 'the happy one'), and their interlocking symbolizes sexual union – represented in the wall paintings, in the form of the union of the beam and the pillar, by two superimposed forked shapes (Devulder 1951).

Around the main beam, the symbol of male potency, there is coiled another symbol of the fertilizing power of man and also of resurrection: the snake, the 'guardian' of the house. The snake is sometimes represented (in the Collo region, for example) on the earthenware jars made by the women and containing the seed-corn. It is also said to descend sometimes into the house, into the lap of a sterile woman, calling her 'mother'. At Darma, a sterile woman ties her girdle to the central beam (Maunier 1930); the foreskin and the reed that has been used for circumcision are hung from the same beam; if the beam is heard to crack, those present hasten to say 'may it be for the good', because this portends the death of the head of the family. When a son is born, the wish is made that 'he may be the master beam of the house', and when he has completed the ritual fast for the first time, he takes his first meal on the roof, that is, on the central beam (in order, so it is said, that he may be able to carry beams). A number of riddles and sayings explicitly identify woman with the central pillar. A young bride is told: 'May God make you the pillar firmly planted in the middle of the house.' Another riddle says: 'She stands upright but she has no feet.' This fork open upwards is female nature, fertile, or rather, capable of being fertilized.

Thus this symbolic summary of the house, the union of *asalas* and *thigejdith*, which extends its fertilizing protection over all human marriage, is, like ploughing, a marriage of heaven and earth. 'Woman is the foundations, man the master beam', says another proverb. *Asalas*, defined in another proverb as 'born in the earth and buried in the sky' (Genevois 1963), fertilizes *thigejdith*, which is rooted in the soil and open towards the sky.

Thus, the house is organized in accordance with a set of homologous oppositions – high : low :: light : dark::day : night :: male : female :: *nif* : *h'urma* :: fertilizing : able to be fertilized. But the same oppositions also exist between the house as a whole and the rest of the universe. Considered in relation to the male world of public life and farming work, the house, the universe of women, is *h'aram*, that is to say, both sacred and illicit for any man who is not part of it (hence the expression used in swearing an oath: 'May my wife (or, my house) become illicit (*h'aram*) to me if . . .'). A distant relative (or a close one, but through women, such as the wife's brother) who is brought into the house for the first time will give the mistress of the house a sum of money that is called 'the sight' (*thizri*). As the place of the sacred of the left hand, *h'urma*, with which all the properties associated with the dark part of the house are bound up, it is placed in the safekeeping of the male point of honour (*nif*) just as the dark part of the house is placed under the protection of the master beam. Every violation of the sacred space therefore takes on the social meaning of sacrilege. Thus, theft from an inhabited house is treated in customary law as a heinous act – an outrage upon the *h'urma* of the house and an offence against the *nif* of the head of the family.

The woman can be said to be confined to the house only so long as it is also pointed out that the man is kept out of it, at least in the daytime. A man's place is outside, in the fields or in the assembly; boys are taught this at a very early age. Hence this formula, which the women repeat, meaning by it that men are unaware of much that goes in the house: 'O man, poor wretch, out in fields all day like a donkey put out to pasture!' As soon as the sun has risen, in summer a man must be out in the fields or at the assembly; in winter, if he is not in the fields, he must be at the assembly or on the benches set in the shelter of the pentroof over the door to the courtyard. Even at night, at least in the dry season, the men and the boys, as soon as they are circumcised, sleep outside the house, either near the haystacks, on the threshing floor, beside the shackled mule and donkey, or on the fig-drying floor, or in the fields, or more rarely in the assembly house, *thajmaâth*.[7] A man who spends too much time at home in the daytime is suspect or ridiculous; he is a 'house man', who 'broods at home like a hen in its nest'. A self-respecting man must offer himself to be seen, be constantly in the eyes of others, confront them, face up to them: he is the man among men (*argaz yer irgazen*). Relations among men are established outdoors: 'Friends are outdoor friends, not *kanun* friends.'

It is understandable that all biological activities, sleeping, eating, procreating, should be banished from the external universe ('The hen does not lay in the market') and confined to the house, the sanctuary of privacy and the secrets of nature, the world of woman, who is assigned to the management of nature and excluded from public life. In contrast to man's work, which is performed outdoors, woman's work is essentially obscure and hidden ('God conceals it'): 'Inside the house, woman is always on the move, she bustles like a fly in the whey; outside the house, nothing of her work is seen.' Two very similar sayings define woman's estate as that of one who can know no other abode than the tomb: 'Your house is your tomb'; 'Woman has but two dwellings, the house and the tomb.'

Thus, the opposition between the women's house and the men's assembly, private life and public life, the full light of day and the secrecy of night, corresponds exactly to the opposition between the dark, nocturnal, lower part of the house and the noble, brightly lit, upper part.[8] The opposition between the external world and the house only takes on its full significance when it is seen that one of the terms of this relation, that is, the house, is itself divided in accordance with the same principles that oppose it to the other term. So it is both true and false to say that the external world is opposed to the house as the male to the female, day to night, fire to water, etc., since the second term in each of these oppositions splits, each time, into itself and its opposite.

The house, a microcosm organized by the same oppositions and homologies that order the whole universe, stands in a relation of homology to the rest of the universe. But, from another standpoint, the world of the house, taken as a whole, stands in a relation of opposition to the rest of the world, an opposition whose principles are none other than those that organize both the internal space of the house and the rest of the world and, more generally, all areas of existence. Thus, the opposition between the world of female life and the city of men is based on the same principles as the two systems of oppositions which it opposes to one another. The application to opposing areas of the same *principium divisionis* that establishes their opposition ensures economy and a surplus of consistency, without involving confusion between those areas. The structure $a : b :: b_1 : b_2$ is doubtless one of the simplest and most powerful that a mythico-ritual system could use, since it cannot counterpose without simultaneously uniting, and is capable of integrating an infinite number of data into a single order by the endlessly repeated application of the same principle of division. Each of the two parts of the house (and, by the same token, each of the objects that are put there and each of the activities carried on there) is, in a sense, qualified at two degrees, that is, first as female (nocturnal, dark) in so far as it belongs to the universe of the house, and secondly as male or female in so far as it belongs to one or other of the divisions of that universe. Thus, for example, when the proverb says 'Man is the lamp of the outside, woman is the light of the inside', this must be taken to mean that man is the true light, the light of day, and woman the light of darkness, a dark light; and we know in other ways that woman is to the moon as man is to the sun. Similarly, by her work on wool, woman produces the beneficent protection of weaving, whose whiteness symbolizes happiness ('white' days are happy days, and a number of marriage rites, such as the sprinkling of milk, seek to make the bride 'white'). The loom, the instrument *par excellence* of female activity, *raised* facing the east like a man and like the plough, is at the same time the east of the internal space and has a male value as a symbol of protection. Again, the hearth, the navel of the house (which is itself identified with the belly of a mother), where the embers smoulder with a secret, hidden, female fire, is the domain of the woman of the house, who is invested with total authority in all matters concerning cooking and the management of the food stores.[9] She takes her meals by the fireside, whereas the man, turned towards the outside, eats in the middle of the room or in the courtyard. However, in all the rites in which they play a part, the fireplace and the stones surrounding it derive their magical power, whether to give protection from the evil eye or from illness, or to bring fine weather, from the fact that they belong to the order of fire, the dry, and the heat of the sun.[10] The house itself is endowed with twofold significance. Though opposed to the public world as nature to culture, it is also, from another standpoint, culture; it is said of the jackal, the incarnation of wild nature, that he builds no house.

The house, and by extension, the village, the 'full country' (*laâmara* or *thamurth iâamaran*), the precinct peopled by men, are opposed in one respect to the fields empty of men which are called *lahkla*: empty, sterile space. Thus the inhabitants of Taddert-el-Djeddid believed that those who build their houses outside the village boundary run the risk of their family dying out (Maunier 1930). The same belief is found elsewhere and the only exceptions made are for the garden, even when remote from the house, the orchard, or the fig-dryer, all of which are places that are in some way linked to the village and fertility. But the opposition does not exclude the homology between the fertility of humans and the fertility of the field, each of which is the product of the union of the male principle and the female principle, solar fire and the wetness of the earth. This homology in fact underlies most of the rites intended to ensure the fertility of human beings and the earth, whether the rites of cooking, which are closely dependent on the oppositions that structure the farming year and are therefore tied to the rhythms of the farming calendar; the rites of renewing the fireplace and its stones (*iniyen*), which mark the passage from the wet season to the dry season, or the beginning of the calendar year; and, more generally, all the rites performed within the microcosm of the house. Whenever the women play a part in the specifically agrarian rites, it is again the homology between agricultural fertility and human fertility, the form *par excellence* of all fertility, that underlies their ritual actions and endows them with their magical potency. A considerable number of rites that take place within the house are only apparently domestic rites, since they aim simultaneously to ensure the fertility of the fields and the fertility of the house, which are inextricably linked. For, in order for the field to be full, the house must be full, and woman contributes to the prosperity of the field by dedicating herself, *inter alia*, to accumulating, economizing and conserving the goods that man has produced and to fixing, as it were, within the house all the goodness that can enter it. 'Man is the conduit, woman the basin'; one supplies, the other holds and keeps. Man is 'the hook on which the baskets are hung'; like the beetle, the spider and the bee, he is the provider. It is women who say: 'Handle your riches like a log on the fire. There is today, there is tomorrow, there is the grave; God forgives those who have saved, not those who have eaten.' And again: 'A thrifty woman is worth more than a yoke of oxen ploughing.' Just as 'the full country' is opposed to 'empty space', so 'the fullness of the house' (*laâmmara ukham*), that is to say, usually, the 'old woman' who saves and accumulates, is opposed to 'the emptiness of the house' (*lakhla ukham*), usually the daughter-in-law. In summer, the door of the house must remain open all day long so that the fertilizing light of the sun can enter, and with it prosperity. A closed door means dearth and sterility; sitting on the threshold, and so blocking it, means closing the passage to happiness and prosperity. To wish someone prosperity, the Kabyles say 'May your door remain open' or 'May your house be like a mosque'. A rich and generous man is one of whom it is said: 'His house is a mosque, it is open to all, rich and poor alike, it is made of wheatcake and couscous, it is full' (*thaâmmar* – applied to a woman, *âammar* means to be a good, thrifty housewife). Generosity is a sign of prosperity which guarantees prosperity.

Most of the technical and ritual actions that fall to women are oriented by the objective intention of making the house, like *thigejdith* opening its fork to *asalas alemmas*, the receptacle of the prosperity that comes to it from without, the womb which, like the earth, receives the seed the male has put into it; and, conversely, the intention of thwarting all the centrifugal forces that threaten to dispossess the house of the goods entrusted to it.

For example, it is forbidden to give anyone a light from the fire on the day a child or a calf is born, and also on the first day of ploughing;[11] when the threshing has been done, nothing must leave the house and the woman retrieves all the objects that she has lent; the milk produced in the three days following calving must not leave the house; the bride must not cross the threshold before the seventh day after her wedding; a woman who has given birth must not leave the house before the fortieth day; the baby must not go out before the Aïd Seghir; the hand-mill must never be loaned and must not be left empty for fear of bringing famine upon the house; woven cloth must not be taken out before it is finished; sweeping, an act of expulsion, is, like giving embers to make a fire, forbidden during the first four days of ploughing; when someone has died, the removal of the corpse is 'facilitated' so that prosperity does not leave with it;[12] the first 'goings-out', the cow's, for example, four days after calving, or the newborn calf's, are marked by sacrifices.

'Emptiness' can result from an act of expulsion. It can also find its way in with certain objects, such as the plough, which must not enter the house between two days' ploughing, or the ploughman's shoes (*arkasen*), which are associated with *lakhla*, empty, sterile space (like the solitary spendthrift, called *ikhla*); or certain people may bring it in, such as old women, because they are bearers of sterility (*lakhla*) and have caused many houses to be sold or to be visited by thieves. Conversely, a number of ritual acts aim to ensure the 'filling' of the house, such as those that consist of casting the remains of a marriage lamp (whose shape represents sexual union and which plays a part in most fertility rites) into the foundations, after first sacrificing an animal; or of making the bride sit on a leather bag full of grain, on first entering the house. Every first entry into the house is a threat to the fullness of the world inside, a threat which the threshold rites, at once propitiatory and prophylactic, must ward off. A new yoke of oxen is met by the mistress of the house, 'the fullness of the house', who places on the threshold the sheepskins on which the hand-mill stands at other times and which receives the flour. Most of the rites intended to bring fertility to the stable and, therefore, to the house ('a house without a cow is an empty house') tend to give magical reinforcement to the structural relationship between milk, the colour blue-gren (*azegzaw*, which is also the raw, *thizegzawth*), grass, springtime – the childhood of the natural world – and human childhood. At the spring equinox, on the 'return of *azal*', the young shepherd, who has twofold affinities with the growth of the fields and the cattle on account of his age and his task, gathers a bouquet to be hung from the lintel of the door, made up of 'all that the wind shakes in the countryside' (Rahmani 1936). A little bag of herbs, containing cumin, benjamin and indigo, is buried at the threshold of the stable, with the words: 'O blue-green (*azegzaw*), keep the butter from waning!' Freshly picked plants are hung on the butter-churn, and the receptacles used for the milk are rubbed with them.

Above all, the young bride's entry is fraught with consequences for the fertility and plenitude of the house. While she is seated on the mule that has brought her from her father's house, she is presented with water, grains of wheat, figs, nuts, cooked eggs, or fritters, all of which (whatever the local variants) are things associated with the fertility of women and the land. She throws them towards the house, thus ensuring that she is preceded by the fertility and plenitude she must bring there herself. She crosses the threshold carried on the back of one of the bridegroom's kinsmen or sometimes (Maunier 1930) on the back of a Negro, who interposes himself to intercept the malignant forces, concentrated on the threshold, which might affect her fertility. A woman must never sit on the threshold holding her child; and a child or a bride, who, like all beings that are in a liminal position, are especially vulnerable, must not cross it too often. Thus woman, through whom fertility comes to the house, makes her own contribution to the fertility of the fields. Consigned to the world of the inside, she also acts on the outside by ensuring fullness for the inside and, in her role as guardian of the threshold, by supervising those unequal exchanges which only the logic of magic can conceive, through which each part of the universe expects to receive from the other nothing but fullness while giving it only emptiness.[13]

But one or the other of the two systems of oppositions that define the house, either in its internal organization or in its relationship with the external world, is brought to the forefront depending on whether the house is considered from the male or the female point of view. Whereas for the man the house is not so much a place he goes into as a place he comes out of, the woman is bound to give opposite importance and meaning to these two movements and to the different definitions of the house they imply, since, for her, movement outwards consists above all in acts of expulsion, while inward movement is her specific concern. The significance of outward movement is most clearly demonstrated by the rite performed by a mother, seven days after giving birth, 'in order that her son may be valorous': striding across the threshold, she sets her right foot upon the carding comb and simulates a fight with the first boy she meets. Going out is the essentially male movement, which leads towards other men and also towards the dangers and trials that must be confronted with the determination of a man who, in matters of honour, is as prickly as the spikes of the carding comb.[14] A self-respecting man must leave the house at daybreak. Hence the importance of the things encountered, which are a portent for the whole day, so that in the event of an undesirable encounter (a blacksmith, a woman carrying an empty leather bag, shouts or a quarrel, a deformed being), it is best to go back and 'remake one's morning' or one's 'going out'.

It is now clear why it is so important which way the house faces. The front of the main house, the one which shelters the head of the family and which contains a stable, almost always faces east, and the main door – as opposed to the low, narrow door, reserved for women, which leads to the garden – is commonly called the east door (*thabburth thacherqith*), or the street door, the upper door, or the great door.[15] The aspect of the villages and the lower position of the stable mean that the upper part of the house, with the fireplace, is in the north, the stable in the south and the loom wall in the west. It follows from this that the movement by which one enters the house is oriented east–west, in opposition to the movement effected when coming out, in accordance with the orientation *par excellence*, towards the east, that is, towards the high, the bright, the good and the prosperous. The ploughman turns his oxen to face the east when he harnesses and unharnesses them, and he starts his ploughing from west to east; the harvesters work eastwards, and the sacrificial ox is slain facing east. Countless actions are performed in accordance with this cardinal orientation; they include all portentous acts, that is, all those involving the fertility and prosperity of the group.[16]

If we now go back to the internal organization of the house, we can see that its orientation is exactly the reverse of that of external space, as if it had been obtained by a half-rotation on the axis of the front wall or the threshold. The loom wall, which a man entering the house immediately faces on crossing the threshold, and which is lit directly by the morning sun, is the daylight of the inside (just as woman is the lamp of the inside), that is, the east of the inside, symmetrical to the macrocosmic east from which it draws its borrowed light. The dark, inside face of the front wall represents the west of the house, the place of sleep, which one leaves behind as one moves towards the *kanun*; the door corresponds symbolically to the 'door of the year', the opening of the wet season and the farming year. Likewise, the two gable walls, the stable wall and the fireplace wall, receive two opposing meanings depending on which of their sides is being considered: to the external north corresponds the south (and summer) of the inside, that is, the part of the house in front of and to the right of a person who enters facing the loom; to the external south corresponds the internal north (and winter), that is, the stable, which is behind and to the left of someone going from the door towards the fire. The division of the house into a dark part (the west and north sides) and a bright part (east and south) corresponds to the division of the year into a wet season and a dry season. In short, to each external face of the wall (*essur*) corresponds a region of the internal space (called *tharkunt*, meaning, roughly, a side) which has a symmetrical but opposite meaning in the system of internal oppositions. Each of the two spaces can thus be derived from the other by means of half-rotation on the axis of the threshold. The importance and symbolic value of the threshold within the system cannot be fully understood unless it is seen that it owes its function as a magical boundary to the fact that it is the site of a meeting of contraries as well as of a logical inversion and that, as the necessary meeting-point and crossing-

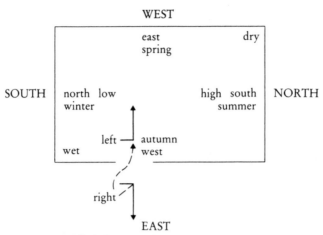

Figure 2 The dual spatial orientation of the house (the bold angles represent the positions of the subject's body)

point between the two spaces, defined in terms of socially qualified body movements,[17] it is the place where the world is reversed.[18]

Thus, each of the two universes has its own east, and the two movements most charged with magical significance and consequences – movement from the threshold to the hearth, which should bring fullness and is performed or ritually controlled by woman, and movement from the threshold to the outside world, which, by virtue of its inaugural value, contains all that the future will bring, especially the future of farming work – can each be performed in accordance with the beneficent orientation, that is, from west to east.[19] The dual orientation of the space of the house means that one is able both to go in and to go out on the right foot (in both senses), with all the magical benefit attached to this observance, without any break in the relationship linking the right-hand side to the high, the bright and the good. The half-rotation of space around the threshold thus ensures, so to speak, the maximization of magical profit, since both centripetal movement and centrifugal movement are performed in a space so organized that one enters it facing the light and also comes out of it facing the light.[20]

These two symmetrical and opposite spaces are not interchangeable but hierarchized. The orientation of the house is primordially defined from outside, from the standpoint of men and, as it were, by men and for men, as the place men come out of. ('Men look at things from outdoors, women look at things from indoors'; 'A house prospers through woman; its outside is beautiful through man.') The house is a world within a world, but one that always remains subordinate, because, even when it displays all the properties and relationships that define the archetypal world, it remains an inverted reflexion, a world in reverse. 'Man is the lamp of the outside, woman the lamp of the inside.' The apparent symmetry must not mislead us: the lamp of day is apparently defined in relation to the lamp of night. In fact the nocturnal light, the female male, remains subordinate to the diurnal light, the lamp of day, that is, the light of the sun. 'Man trusts in God, woman looks to man for everything.' 'Woman', it is also said, 'is twisted like a sickle'; and so even the straightest of these warped natures is never more than straightened up. Once married, woman too finds her east, within the house of man, but her east is only the inversion of a west: for 'the maiden is the west'. The supremacy given to movement outwards, in which man affirms his manliness by turning his back on the house in order to face other men, is merely a form of the categorical refusal of nature, the inevitable origin of man's movement away from nature.

Notes

Preface

The author and publishers are grateful to the Executors of the James Joyce Estate and to The Bodley Head for permission to reproduce the epigraph taken from *Ulysses* by James Joyce.

1 A note on the history of this text: *Esquisse d'une théorie de la pratique* (Droz, 1972) was explicitly conceived and presented as a provisional publication which was to be replaced (with the agreement of the publisher, who undertook to withdraw it from sale at the appropriate time) by a more complete work. The English translation, *Outline of a Theory of Practice*, is already a different book, intermediate between the *Esquisse* and *Le Sens pratique* (*The Logic of Practice*). For the English (and German) versions of the *Esquisse* I made many additions to and corrections of the original text. *The Logic of Practice* is the outcome of much reworking of the material and the manuscript of the *Outline*, resulting in, I believe, comprehensive and fundamental transformations of a text which for a time I regarded as definitive.

2 My one contribution (1968) to discourse on structuralism (the superabundance and style of which have probably played a large part in discouraging me from acknowledging my debt) arose from an endeavour to make explicit and thereby make better use of the logic of this relational and transformational mode of thought, to identify the specific obstacles it encounters in the case of the social sciences, and above all to specify the conditions in which it may be extended beyond cultural systems to social relations themselves, i.e. to sociology.

3 The contents of Mircea Éliade's *Traité d'histoire des religions* (1953) gives a fairly accurate idea of the themes which have guided most collections of data on ritual in Algeria (e.g. the moon, woman and the snake; sacred stones; the earth, woman and fertility; sacrifice and regeneration; the dead and sowing; agrarian and funeral deities, etc.). The same thematic inspiration is found in the work of the Cambridge school (e.g. Cornford 1957; Gaster 1961; Harrison 1963).

4 Jean-Pierre Vernant (1972) similarly shows that a break with Frazerian-style interpretations (which, for example, see Adonis as an embodiment of the 'spirit of vegetation') and a refusal of a 'generalized comparativism, proceeding by direct assimilation, without taking account of the specificities of each cultural system', are the precondition for an adequate reading of the cycles of Greek legends and a correct decoding of the mythic elements, defined by their relative positions within a particular system.

5 The conditions for a genuine science of ethnology and colonial sociology will be fulfilled when it is possible to relate analysis of the content of works to the

social characteristics of the producers (as established, for example, in the work of Victor Karady), in particular their positions in the field of production (and more especially in the colonial sub-field).

6 'When a girl suffers from *djennaba* – a curse which prevents her from marrying and keeps her alone by the hearth – it is the blacksmith who gives her water from *Lbilu*, the quenching tank, with which she washes, naked, before sunrise, at the fountain in a market-place, or at a crossroads or in the village square. This is the water which gives fertility to tools reddened by fire.' Servier (1962: 246) relates this ritual, without further comment, as an example of the blacksmith's role in certain fertility rites (which he explains by invoking the resources of comparative mythology – with the theme of the theft of fire, which is associated with the theft of seed-corn from the threshing floor, as practised among the Bambaras, where it is said to symbolize death and resurrection – and also the blacksmith's role in making the ploughshare and in the start of ploughing). A very similar rite is described by Devulder (1951): to free a girl from *elbur* (fallowness, forced virginity), the *qibla* ('midwife') places a pot full of water overnight on a tree, then uses it to wash the girl who stands on a wheat-cake dish on which there is a piece of iron. Finally, she lights the lamp, the symbol of man, and then goes and pours away the water in the market-place, 'where men pass and at the spot where the butchers slaughter beasts.' These different rites seem to be variants of the rite practised on the eve of marriage, when the *qibla* washes the bride, who stands in a large dish, between two lighted lamps, before applying henna to her. This ritual is designated, in the magic formulae which accompany it, as intended to take away *tucherka*, literally, 'association', i.e. ill-luck and all forms of inability to procreate. (For the sake of simplicity the most common and most economical system of transcription has been adopted. The principle is described in detail in Bourdieu and Sayad 1964: 181–5).

7 While it is clearly not part of the thinking of Claude Lévi-Strauss, who has always taken care to point out the discrepancies between the different aspects of social reality (myth, ritual or art and morphology or economy), this panlogicism is undoubtedly an integral part of the social image of structuralism and of its social effects.

8 'The loom is to the cloth that is created on it as the field to the harvest it bears. All the time that the seed is in it, the field lives with a wonderful life of which the crop is the product. This life sprouts with the seed, grows with the ears of corn, swells with them, and withdraws at the moment when they fall under the harvester's sickle. The field then lies as if dead. It would die completely if the ploughman's skill were not able to restore to it a fragment of that life, so that it can be reborn the following year and lend its strength to the seed. The beliefs are analogous and the rites are very similar. There is a striking analogy between the ceremony of detaching the finished carpet and that of the harvest. In each case there is the same religious respect for the life that is going to be cut off, with all the precautions needed to ensure that it can be reborn. Just as, in the case of weaving, the woman who is the senior weaver plays the principal role, so the first sheaf must be cut by the master of the field or the senior harvester, who bears the title *raïs*, or *agellid* (king) among the Berbers. Just as iron is prescribed for cutting the woollen threads, so the first ears of corn are gathered by hand. Special chants are sung – and the *phrases are the same* in both cases. The weavers have adopted the harvest formulae without changing a word. Nothing more clearly shows the deep sense of the similarity of the two operations' (H. Basset 1922: 157–8).

9 In more cases than one (e.g. in the orientation of the house and its internal space or in the use of the loom), practical logic achieves reconciliations between constraints that we would tend to call technical and constraints that we would call ritual, which may appear miraculous to a mind trained to dissociate them.

10 The corpus on which the philologist or anthropologist works is itself partly the product of the struggles between native interpreters which Mouloud Mammeri so well describes (see Mammeri and Bourdieu 1978) and which my mistrust of the error (symbolized by the work of Griaule) of adopting native theories had led me to underestimate (in favour of a Durkheimian representation of cultural production as collective and impersonal, in short, without producers).

11 The fact that the anthropologist, as an outside observer, is necessarily relegated to externality is in no way a privilege, especially since nothing prevents the native from occupying such a position in relation to his own traditions, so long as he is able to appropriate the instruments of objectification and (though it is not necessarily a corollary) is willing to accept the cost of the exclusion that objectification presupposes and generates. Hence the importance of the development of an ethnology of Algeria by Algerians. I am thinking of the research conducted within the C.R.A.P.E., led by Mouloud Mammeri, whose excellent work on oral 'literature' is well known. (See, for example, Bassagna and Sayad 1974).

12 It cannot of course be denied, and Jack Goody deserves credit for pointing this out, that the different social formations are separated by considerable differences in terms of the techniques of objectification (starting with writing and everything that 'graphic reason' makes possible) and therefore in the generic conditions of access to the logic which relies on these techniques.

13 'They bade the just take the way to the right upwards through the sky, first binding on them in front tokens of the judgement passed upon them. The unjust were commanded to take the downward road to the left, and these bore evidence of all their deeds fastened on their backs' (Plato, *The Republic*, X, 614 c–d). It can be seen in passing that, if Greece has been much exploited, especially in the ethnology of North Africa, to produce 'humanist' effects (in all senses), one can also use a knowledge of an 'ethnologized' (rather than glorified) Greece to understand illiterate societies (and vice versa), and especially everything concerned with cultural production.

14 Pierre Gourou, who brings to light all the inconsistencies of Books XIV to XVII of Montesquieu's *Spirit of the Laws* but without grasping the mythical principle that gives this apparently incoherent discourse its real coherence, rightly points out that 'It was interesting to observe these views of Montesquieu's because they slumber in us, ready to be awakened, as they lived in him. We too think, whatever contradictions are supplied by more accurate observation than in Montesquieu's day, that the people of the North are taller, calmer, more hard-working, more honest, more enterprising, more trustworthy, more disinterested than those of the south' (Gourou 1963).

15 Rather than argue at length for the liberatory functions that sociology can fulfil by providing the means for a reappropriation of schemes of perception and appreciation which are often at the root of a specifically social deprivation, I shall simply refer the reader to Abdelmayak Sayad's article 'Les enfants illégitimes' (1979) and all his research on Algerian emigrants.

BOOK I CRITIQUE OF THEORETICAL REASON

Introduction

1 It is the self-evidence and self-transparence of experience reflecting itself (that of the cogito) that the phenomenologists (e.g. Sartre in *The Psychology of Imagination*) contrasted as the 'certain' to the 'probable' of objective knowledge: 'It is necessary to repeat at this point what has been known since Descartes: that a reflective consciousness gives us knowledge of absolute certainty; that he who becomes aware of "having an image" by an act of reflection cannot deceive himself . . . What has come to be known as an "image" occurs immediately as such to reflection . . . If this consciousness is immediately distinguishable from all others, it is because it presents itself to reflection with certain traits, certain characteristics, which at once determine the judgment "I have an image". The act of reflection thus has a content of immediate certainty which we shall call the *essence* of the image' (Sartre 1971: 1).

2 Through a description of 'practical' intellectuals, Plato identifies two of the most important properties of practice, which is described as a 'race for life' (*peri psychès o dromos*): the pressure of temporal urgency ('the ebbing water of the clepsydra hurrying them on . . .') which makes it impossible to linger over interesting problems, to approach them several times, to go back, and the existence of practical, sometimes life-and-death stakes (*Theaetetus* 172c–173b).

3 A producer of discourse on the objects of the social world who fails to objectify the viewpoint from which he produces this discourse is very likely to convey nothing more than this very viewpoint. This is seen in all the discourses about the 'populace' (*le peuple*) which speak not so much of the 'people' as of the author's relation to them or, quite simply, the social position from which he speaks of them.

Chapter 1 Objectification objectified

1 It is significant, for example, that with the exception of Sapir, who was predisposed by his dual training as linguist and ethnologist to raise the problem of the relationship between culture and language, no anthropologist has tried to bring out all the implications of the homology (which Leslie White is virtually alone in formulating explicitly) between the oppositions which are at the basis of cultural (or structural) anthropology and linguistics: *langue/parole* and culture/conduct.

2 One can extend to the relationship between culture and conduct everything that Saussure says about the relationship between language and speech which is a dimension of it. Just as Saussure posits that the medium of communication is not discourse but language, so cultural anthropology (or iconology, in Panofsky's sense) posits that scientific interpretation treats the sensible properties of practices or works as signs or 'cultural symptoms' which yield their full meaning only to a reading armed with a cultural code transcending its actualizations (implying that the 'objective meaning' of a work or a practice is irreducible either to the will and consciousness of the author or to the felt experiences of the observer).

3 It is no accident that the Sophists (I am thinking in particular of Protagoras and Plato's *Gorgias*), who, unlike the pure grammarians, aimed to secure and transmit practical mastery of a language of action, were the first to raise the question of

kairos, the right moment and the right words for the moment. As rhetoricians they were predisposed to make a philosophy of the practice of language as *strategy*. (It is significant that the original meaning of the word *kairos*, 'vital (and therefore deadly) point', and 'point aimed at, target', is also present in a number of everyday expressions: to strike home, hit the nail on the head, a shaft of wit, etc.).

4 The social implications of the language of execution become clearer when one knows that the debate over the primacy of meaning or execution, of the idea or the material and the manner ('technique', or as Caravaggio called it, *manifattura*) is at the centre of the history of art and the 'emancipation' of the artist and also at the centre of methodological debates among art historians (cf. Lee 1967; Bologna 1972, 1979).

5 The anthropologist's situation is not so different from that of the philologist and his dead letters. Not only is he forced to rely on quasi-texts – the official discourses of his informants, who are inclined to put forward the most codified aspect of the tradition, but, in his analysis of myths and rites for example, he often has to resort to tests established by others, often in ill-defined conditions. The very fact of recording constitutes a myth or rite as an object of analysis by isolating it from its concrete referents (such as the names of places, groups, land, persons, etc.), from the situations in which it functions and the individuals who make it function in relation to practical functions (e.g. to legitimize hierarchies or distributions of properties or powers). As Bateson (1958) shows, mythological culture can become the tool, and in some cases the object, of extremely complex strategies (and this explains, *inter alia*, why agents undertake the immense mnemonic effort needed to acquire mastery of it), even in societies which do not have a highly developed and differentiated religious apparatus. It follows that it is impossible to account fully for the structure of the mythical corpus and the transformations it undergoes in the course of time, by means of a strictly internal analysis ignoring the functions that the corpus fulfils in the relations of competition or conflict for economic or symbolic power.

6 To show that theoretical or theoreticist triumphalism is part of the very air breathed by all those who claim the status of an intellectual, one would have to cite the innumerable declarations of contempt for the incapacity of the 'vulgar' to rise to a thought worthy of the name (and not only those most openly flaunted, such as remarks like 'No one meditates!' and 'Stupidity isn't my strong point' heard from straw-hatted intellectuals in the style of Valéry's Monsieur Teste) scattered through philosophy and literature.

7 'Mythological analysis has not, and cannot have, as its aim to show how men think . . . I therefore claim to show, not how men think in myths, but how myths operate in men's minds without their being aware of the fact' (Lévi-Strauss 1970: 12). Although, taken literally, this text perfectly justifies my reading of Lévi-Strauss's final theory of mythic reason, I have to say – especially at a time when semi-automatic writing, diagonal reading and the critique of suspicion are much in vogue – that in this formualation, which is too elegant to be safe from metaphysical misreadings, one could also find a warning against the temptation of mystical participation and even a valuable contribution to a theory of the practical relation to myth. (Lévi-Strauss is correct in pointing out that, in the production of myth as in the production of discourse, awareness of the rules may be only partial and intermittent because 'an individual who conscientiously applied phonological and grammatical rules in his speech, supposing he possessed the necessary knowledge and virtuosity to do so, would

nevertheless lose the thread of his ideas almost immediately' [1970: 11].)
8 By postulating the existence of a group or class 'collective consciousness' and
  crediting groups with dispositions which can only be constituted in an individual
  consciousness, even when they are the product of collective conditions, such as
  the awakening of consciousness of class interests, the personification of collectives
  removes the need to analyse these conditions, in particular those determining
  the degree of objective and subjective homogeneity of the group in question and
  the degree of consciousness of its members.

Chapter 2 The imaginary anthropology of subjectivism

1 Sartre himself makes the connection between the freedom of the subject as he
  conceives it and divine freedom according to Descartes in a work published at
  much the same time as *Being and Nothingness*: 'If Descartes conceived divine
  freedom as exactly like his own freedom, then he is talking about his own
  freedom, as he would have conceived it without the constraints of Catholicism
  and dogmatism, when he describes the freedom of God. This is a clear case of
  sublimation and transposition. Now, Descartes' God is the freest of the Gods
  forged by human thought; he is the only creating God' (1946: 44–5). And
  further on: 'It took two centuries of crisis – a crisis of faith and a crisis of
  science – for man to recover this creative freedom that Descartes placed in God
  and for this truth, the essential basis of humanism, to be suspected: Man is the
  being whose appearance causes a world to exist. But we should not blame
  Descartes for giving to God what specifically belongs to us: we should rather
  admire him for having laid the bases of democracy, in an authoritarian period,
  for having followed through the demands of the idea of *autonomy* and for
  having understood, long before the Heidegger of *Vom Wesen des Grundes*, that
  the sole foundation of being is freedom' (1946: 51–2).
2 The problem of social classes is one of the sites *par excellence* of the opposition
  between objectivism and subjectivism, which locks research into a series of
  fictitious alternatives.
3 'There is no inertia in consciousness' (Sartre 1957: 89). And elsewhere: 'Descartes
  understood . . . that a free act was an absolutely new production, the germ of
  which could not be contained in a previous state of the world' (Sartre 1946:
  47).
4 Paradoxically, the 'rational actor' theory (in its intellectualist version) can
  therefore relate the differences recorded in practices only to the objective
  conditions.
5 Jon Elster reveals the true nature of an ethical undertaking aimed at using the
  will to make up for the weaknesses of the will, when, discussing the theme,
  which recurs in classical philosophy, of passion fought by passion, he contrasts
  the 'analytic' project with the 'strategic' project of modifying behaviour by
  rational decision: 'The analytical purpose would be to determine to which
  extent the passions actually tend to neutralize each other *in men as they are*.
  The manipulative and the strategic approaches would set passion against passion
  in order to modify the behaviour – the behaviour of others in the manipulative
  cases and the behaviour of self in the strategic case' (1979: 55, Elster's italics).
  Thus the 'coherent and complete attitudes at any point in time' which specifically
  define the 'rational actor' are the product of a 'strategic attitude' aimed at
  controlling them rationally, i.e. a rational ethic.

6 It is significant that Jon Elster, who excludes dispositional concepts from his theory, attributes Descartes's 'preference for the unsupported decision that is rigidly adhered to once taken' to 'an *aristocratic distaste* for calculations of any sort and . . . an *equally aristocratic predilection* for absolute firmness of character, however eccentric' (1979: 59–60, my italics).

7 Paradox spotters would find another fascinating specimen in the 'decision' to love, or no longer to love (like Alidor in Corneille's *La Place royale* who breaks off with the woman he loves simply to prove to himself that he is free).

8 As I have argued elsewhere (Bourdieu 1984: esp. pp. 55–6), the conditions most favouring this illusion arise when the main influence of the material conditions of existence is, paradoxically, exerted negatively, by default, through neutralization of the most direct and harsh economic constraints; and it is expressed and reinforced in an exemplary way by all forms of anti-genetic thought (the most radical of which is provided, once again, by Sartre, with the notion of the 'original project').

9 Effective preferences are defined in the relationship between the set of possibilities and impossibilities that are offered and the system of dispositions; every change in the set of possibilities determines a change in preferences that are subordinated to the logic of the *habitus* (see Bourdieu 1984: 208ff.).

10 When one breaks away from economism in order to describe the universe of possible economies, one escapes from the spurious choice between purely material, narrowly economic interest, and disinterestedness; and one is able to satisfy the principle of sufficient reason according to which there is no action without a *raison d'être*, i.e. without interest, or, to put it another way, without investment in a game and a stake, *illusio*, involvement.

11 The existence of invariant principles of the logic of fields allows a use of common concepts which is quite different from the simple analogical transfer of the concepts of economics that is sometimes seen.

Chapter 3 Structures, *habitus*, practices

1 Ideally, one would like to be able completely to avoid talking about concepts for their own sake and so running the risk of being both schematic and formal. Like all dispositional concepts, the concept of the *habitus*, which is predisposed by its range of historical uses to designate a system of acquired, permanent, generative dispositions, is justified above all by the false problems and false solutions that it eliminates, the questions it enables one to formulate better or to resolve, and the specifically scientific difficulties to which it gives rise.

2 The notion of the *structural relief* of the attributes of an object, i.e. the character that causes an attribute (e.g. colour or shape) 'to be more easily taken into account in any semantic treatment of the signified which contains it' (Le Ny 1979: 190ff.), like the Weberian notion of 'average chances' which is its equivalent in another context, is an abstraction, since relief varies according to dispositions. However, it enables one to escape from pure subjectivism by taking note of the existence of objective determinations of perceptions. The illusion of the free creation of the properties of a situation and, therefore, of the ends of action, no doubt finds an apparent justification in the circle, characteristic of all conditional stimulation, whereby the *habitus* can produce the response objectively inscribed in its 'formula' only to the extent that it confers a triggering efficacy on the situation by constituting it according to its own principles, i.e. making it exist as a pertinent question in terms of a particular way of questioning reality.

3 In social formations in which the reproduction of relations of domination (and economic or cultural capital) is not performed by objective mechanisms, the endless work required to maintain relations of personal dependence would be condemned to failure if it could not count on the permanence of *habitus*, socially constituted and constantly reinforced by individual or collective sanctions. In this case, the social order rests mainly on the order that reigns in people's minds, and the *habitus*, i.e. the organism as appropriated by the group and attuned to the demands of the group, functions as the materialization of the collective memory, reproducing the acquisitions of the predecessors in the successors. The group's resulting tendency to persist in its being works at a much deeper level than that of 'family traditions', the permanence of which presupposes a consciously maintained loyalty and also guardians. These traditions therefore have a rigidity alien to the strategies of the *habitus*, which, in new situations, can invent new ways of fulfilling the old functions. It is also deeper than the conscious strategies through which agents seek expressly to act on their future and shape it in the image of the past, such as testaments, or even explicit norms, which are simple calls to order, i.e. to the probable, which they make doubly potent.

4 'We call this subjective, variable probability – which sometimes excludes doubt and engenders a certainty *sui generis* and which at other times appears as no more than a vague glimmer – *philosophical probability*, because it refers to the exercise of the higher faculty whereby we comprehend the order and the rationality of things. All reasonable men have a confused notion of similar probabilities: this then determines, or at least justifies, those unshakeable beliefs we call *common sense*' (Cournot 1922: 70).

5 One of the virtues of subjectivism and of the 'moralism of consciousness' (or the examination of conscience) which it often disguises is that, in the analyses that condemn actions subject to the pressures of the world as 'inauthentic' (cf. Heidegger on everyday existence and 'das Man' or Sartre on 'serious-mindedness'), it shows, *per absurdum*, the impossibility of the 'authentic' existence that would absorb all pre-given meanings and objective determinations in a project of freedom. The purely ethical pursuit of 'authenticity' is the privilege of those who have the leisure to think and can afford to dispense with the economy of thought that 'inauthentic' conduct allows.

6 Contrary to all forms of the occasionalist illusion which inclines one to relate practices directly to properties inscribed in the situation, it has to be pointed out that 'interpersonal' relations are only apparently person-to-person relations and that the truth of the interaction never lies entirely in the interaction. This is forgotten when the objective structure of the relationship between the assembled individuals or the groups they belong to – that is, distances and hierarchies – is reduced to the momentary structure of their interaction in a particular situation and group, and when everything that occurs in an experimental situation is explained in terms of the experimentally controlled characteristics of the situation, such as relative positions in space or the nature of the channels used.

7 Thus ignorance of the surest but best-hidden basis of the integration of groups or classes can lead some people to deny the unity of the dominant class with no other proof than the impossibility of empirically establishing that the members of the dominant class have an explicit policy, expressly imposed by concertation or even conspiracy; while it can lead others to see the only possible basis for the unity of the dominated class in the awakening of consciousness, a kind of revolutionary cogito that is supposed to bring the working class into

existence by constituting it as a 'class in itself'.

8 It can be understood why dancing, a particular and spectacular case of synchronization of the homogeneous and orchestration of the heterogeneous, is everywhere predisposed to symbolize and reinforce group integration.

9 It is easy to see that the infinite possible combinations of the variables associated with the trajectories of each individual and of the lineages from which he comes can account for the infinity of individual differences.

10 The most profitable strategies are usually those produced, without any calculation, and in the illusion of the most absolute 'sincerity', by a *habitus* objectively fitted to the objective structures. These strategies without strategic calculation procure an important secondary advantage for those who can scarcely be called their authors: the social approval accruing to apparent disinterestedness.

11 Generation conflicts oppose not age-classes separated by natural properties, but *habitus* which have been produced by different modes of generation, that is, by conditions of existence which, by imposing different definitions of the impossible, the possible and the probable, cause one group to experience practices or aspirations that another group finds unthinkable or scandalous as natural or reasonable, and vice versa.

12 Emotion, the extreme case of such anticipation, is a hallucinatory 'presenting' of the impending future, which, as bodily reactions identical to those of the real situation bear witness, leads a person to live a still suspended future as already present, or even already past, and therefore necessary and inevitable – 'I'm a dead man', 'I'm done for'.

Chapter 4   Belief and the body

1 The term *obsequium* used by Spinoza to denote the 'constant will' produced by the conditioning through which 'the State fashions us for its own use and which enables it to survive' (Matheron 1969: 349) could be used to designate the public testimonies of recognition that every group requires of its members (especially at moments of co-option), i.e. the symbolic tributes due from individuals in the exchanges that are set up in every group between the individuals and the group. Because, as in gift exchange, the exchange is an end in itself, the tribute demanded by the group generally comes down to a matter of trifles, that is, symbolic rituals (rites of passage, the ceremonials of etiquette, etc.), formalities and formalisms which 'cost nothing' to perform and seem such 'natural' things to demand ('It's the least one can do . . .', 'it wouldn't cost him anything to . . .') that abstention amounts to a challenge.

2 The anthropologist would speak much more effectively about the beliefs and rites of others if he started by making himself the master and possessor of his own rites and beliefs, both those that are buried in the folds of his own body and in his turns of phrase and those that run through his scientific practice itself, his prophylactic notes, his propitiatory prefaces or his exorcizing references, not to mention his cult of the founding fathers and other eponymous ancestors. It would at least become apparent to him that stakes which, from the outside, are perfectly derisory can in some conditions become questions of life and death.

3 'What need is there', Leibniz asked elsewhere, 'always to know what one is doing? Do salts, metals, plants, animals, and a thousand other animate or inanimate bodies know how they do what they do, and do they need to know?

Does a drop of oil or grease need to understand geometry in order to become round on the surface of water?' (Leibniz 1866d: 401).

4 Thus, practical mastery of the rules of politeness and, in particular, the art of adjusting each of the available formulae (e.g. at the end of a letter) to the various classes of possible recipients presupposes implicit mastery, and therefore recognition, of a set of oppositions constituting the implicit axiomatics of a given political order: oppositions between men and women, between younger and older, between the personal, or private, and the impersonal (administrative or business letters), between superiors, equals and inferiors.

5 This does not rule out the possibility that specifically biological determinations of sexual identity may help to determine social position (e.g. by favouring dispositions more or less close to the established definition of excellence which, in a class society, are more or less favourable to social mobility).

6 Like hysteria which, according to Freud, 'takes expressions literally, really feeling the heart-rending or the smack in the face which a speaker refers to metaphorically'.

7 The opposition between the sexes can also be organized on the basis of the opposition, which is used intensively in gestural or verbal insults, between the front (of the body), the site of sexual difference, and the behind, which is sexually undifferentiated, feminine and submissive.

8 As well as all the social verdicts, charged with all the arbitrary violence of naturalized arbitrariness, directly applied to one's own or other people's bodies, which constitute the body as destiny ('She's too tall for a girl' or 'It [a scar] doesn't matter much for a boy'), all the schemes and all the realizations of the schemes in social classifications or objects (tools, ornaments, etc.) divided into rich (luxury) or poor, etc., speak directly to the body, sometimes simply through the physique or posture that is required for their appropriate use, thus shaping the relation to the body and even experience of the body. Thus, in a universe that makes the opposition between the big (physically, but also socially) and the small the fundamental principle of the difference between the sexes, it is not surprising that, as Seymour Fisher observes, men tend to be dissatisfied with parts of their body that they see as 'too small', whereas women tend to worry about parts of their body that they see as 'too big'.

9 If non-literate societies seem to have a particular bent for the structural games which fascinate the anthropologist, their purpose is often mnemonic. The remarkable homology to be observed in Kabylia between the structure of the distribution of the families in the village and the distribution of graves in the cemetery (at Aït Hichem or Tizi Hibel) clearly makes it easier to locate the traditionally anonymous graves (with expressly transmitted landmarks added to the structural principles).

10 Thus, in the game of *qochra*, which the children play in early spring (at Aïn Aghbel), the cork ball (the *qochra*) which is fought for, passed and defended, is the practical equivalent of woman. In the course of the game the players must both defend themselves against it and, once possessing it, defend it against those trying to take it away. At the start of the match, the leader of the game repeatedly asks, 'Whose daughter is she?' but no one will volunteer to be her father and protect her; a daughter is always a liability for men. And so lots have to be drawn for her, and the unlucky player who gets her must accept his fate. He now has to protect the ball against the attacks of all the others, while at the same time trying to pass it on to another player; but he can only do so in an honourable, approved way. A player whom the 'father' manages

to touch with his stick, telling him 'She's your daughter now', has to acknowledge defeat, like a man temporarily obliged to a socially inferior family from whom he has taken a wife. For the suitors the temptation is to take the prestigious course of abduction, whereas the father wants a marriage that will free him from guardianship and allow him to re-enter the game. The loser of the game is excluded from the world of men; the ball is tied under his shirt so that he looks like a girl who has been got pregnant.

11 This principle belongs as much to magic as to morality. For example, it is said: '*Leftar n-esbah' d-esbuh' n-erbah'*', breakfast in the morning is the first meeting that augurs well' (*erbah'*, to succeed, to prosper).

12 One of the effects of the ritualization of practices is precisely that of assigning them a time – i.e. a moment, a tempo and a duration – which is relatively independent of external necessities, those of climate, technology or economy, thereby giving them the kind of arbitrary necessity that specifically defines cultural arbitrariness.

13 The opposition between male wheat and female barley seems very generally attested. For example, a riddle reported by Genevois: 'I sowed something green, behind the mountain. I don't know if it will be wheat or barley' – answer, the child in the mother's womb.

14 This means to say that the 'learning by doing' hypothesis, associated with the name of Arrow (1962), is a particular case of a very general law: every made product – not least, symbolic products, such as works of art, games, myths, etc. – exerts by its very functioning, particularly by the use made of it, an educative effect which helps to make it easier to acquire the dispositions required for its adequate use.

15 Erikson's observations on the Yoruk (1943) might be interpreted in the same light.

Chapter 5 The logic of practice

1 Populism achieves a more unexpected combination, since it tends to imagine the 'populace' as the bourgeois sees himself.

2 The logic of practice owes a number of its properties to the fact that what logic calls the universe of discourse remains there in the practical state.

3 It can be seen, incidentally, that the points of view adopted on the house are opposed in accordance with the same logic (male/female) that they apply. This reduplication, the basis of which lies in the correspondence between the social divisions and the logical divisions, and the circular reinforcement that results from it, no doubt play a part in locking agents into a closed, finite world and a doxic experience of that world.

4 To get an idea of how these verbal assemblages work, one might consider the role played, in the judgements of ordinary existence, by couples of adjectives, which give body to the unjustifiable verdicts of taste.

5 The fact that practical sense cannot (without special training) 'run in neutral', disengaged from any concrete situation, condemns to unreality all surveys by questionnaire that record the responses induced by the abstract stimuli of the survey situation as if they were authentic products of the *habitus*. In fact they are laboratory artefacts, which stand in the same relation to reactions in real situations as folklorized rites, performed for the benefit of tourists (or anthropologists), to the rites imposed by the imperatives of a living tradition or the urgency of a critical situation. This is seen most clearly in all surveys

which ask the subjects to become their own sociologist and say what class they think they belong to, or whether they think social classes exist, and if so, how many; in such an artificial context and with such artificial questions, these surveys have no difficulty in disorienting the sense of one's place in the social space which enables one to situate oneself and other people practically, in the ordinary situations of life.

6 There are acts that a *habitus* will never produce if it does not encounter a situation in which it can actualize its potentialities. We know, for example, that the extreme situations of times of crisis give some people the opportunity to reveal potentialities unknown to themselves and to others. This interdependence of *habitus* and situation is exploited by film directors when they bring together a *habitus* (chosen, intuitively, as a principle generating a particular style of words, gestures, etc.) and an artificial situation designed to trigger it off, thus creating the conditions for the production of practices (which may be completely improvized) complying with their expectations.

7 These schemes can only be grasped in the objective coherence of the ritual actions that they engender – although they can sometimes be apprehended, almost directly, in discourse, when, for no apparent reason, an informant 'associates' two ritual practices that have nothing in common except a scheme.

8 Breaking with the 'mentalism' of most descriptions of religion, George Duby (1976: 18) points out that the religion of the knights 'came down entirely to a matter of rites, gestures and formulae', and he emphasizes the practical, bodily character of ritual practices: 'When a warrior took an oath, what counted most in his eyes was not the commitment of his soul but a *bodily posture*, the contact that his hand, laid on the cross, the Scriptures or a bag of relics, had with the sacred. When he stepped forward to become the liege man of a lord, it was again an *attitude*, a *position of the hands*, a ritual sequence of words, which only had to be uttered in order to bind the contract' (1976: 62–3, my italics).

9 The extreme form of what constitutes the inclination inherent in the role of the interpreter is represented by the speculations of theologians. Always tending to project their own states of mind into the analysis of the religious, they have moved on without difficulty, through a reconversion homologous with that of the analysts of literature, to a spiritualized form of semiology in which Heidegger or Congar rub shoulders with Lévi-Strauss or Lacan or even Baudrillard.

10 The antigenetic prejudice leading to unconscious or overt refusal to seek the genesis of objective structures and internalized structures in individual or collective history combines with the antifunctionalist prejudice, which refuses to take account of the practical functions that symbolic systems perform; and together they reinforce the tendency of structuralist anthropology to credit symbolic systems with more coherence than they have or need to have in order to function. In reality, these systems are products of history which, like culture as described by Lowie, remain 'things of shreds and patches', even if the patches that the necessities of practice force on agents are constantly undergoing restructurings and reworkings tending to integrate them into the system.

11 The history of perspective proposed by Panofsky (1924–5) is an exemplary contribution to a social history of conventional modes of cognition and expression – so long as one breaks radically with the idealist tradition of 'symbolic forms' and endeavours to relate historical forms of perception and representation systematically to the social conditions in which they are produced and reproduced (by express or diffuse education), i.e. to the structure of the groups producing and reproducing them and to the positions of those groups in the social structure.

12 The propensity to conceive the magical economy along the lines of political economy is seen, for example, whenever the principle of reciprocity intervenes to determine sacrifice, seen as the exchange of one life for another. A typical case is the sacrifice of a sheep at the end of treading-out, on the grounds that a good harvest must be paid for by the loss of a member of the family, with the sheep serving as a substitute.

13 Similarly, the difficulty of steering a course between class racism and populism, between unfavourable prejudice and favourable prejudice, which is another form of condescension, leads some people to conceive the relation to the dominated classes in terms of the old Platonic opposition between separation (*chorismos*) and participation (*methexis*).

14 For example, to understand how the curse, the extreme form of performative speech through which the elders constantly exercise their power, can work, one has to bear in mind the whole set of social conditions that have to be fulfilled in order for performative magic to operate in this case: in particular, profound poverty, both material and mental (not least that which is produced by belief in magic, the fear of others, the word of others, group opinion, of which belief in the evil eye is no doubt simply the limiting case), and also the power given to the utterance of common sense, and to the person who utters it, when it has on its side the whole social order, the whole of past experience; and all this in a situation of deep insecurity, in which, as in times of catastrophe, people avoid challenging fate.

15 Griaule's mystical reading of Dogon myths and Heidegger's inspired exegesis of the Pre-Socratics are two paradigmatic variants of the same effect, separated only by the 'nobility' of their pretext and of their references.

16 It scarcely needs to be pointed out that here the 'primitives' (as elsewhere the working class) are only a pretext for ideological battles in which what is really at stake lies in the present interests of the ideologues. It would probably be no more difficult to show this apropos of the noisy, facile denunciations of colonial anthropology which are now fashionable than apropos of the enchanted vision of archaic or peasant societies which, in other times, accompanied mandarin denunciation of the 'disenchantment of the world'.

17 Here one has to quote Arnold van Gennep, who points out that ancient narratives were enacted in a kind of total drama, and not simply recited: 'So-called popular literary production is a useful activity, necessary for the maintenance and functioning of social organization, by virtue of its link with other, material, activities. Especially in its early stages, it is an organic element, and not, as used to be thought, a superfluous aesthetic activity, a luxury' (van Gennep 1913: 8). Pursuing the same logic, Mouloud Mammeri brings to light the practical functions of Kabyle wisdom and of the poets who are its guardians (Mammeri and Bourdieu 1978).

18 I shall try to show that, at the level of functions, ritual expresses the state of the productive forces, which determine it negatively through uncertainty and insecurity in the form of a kind of immense effort to perpetuate natural and human life that is always threatened and suspended, while, at the level of structures, it retranslates the opposition between labour time and production time into the opposition between two types of rites, the legitimizing and euphemizing rites associated with ploughing and harvesting and the propitiatory rites of the periods of gestation and waiting. The opposition, which dominates the whole of agrarian life, between labour time (that which depends on man)

and production time (that which depends on nature alone) is conceived in the same terms as the division of labour between the sexes, with on the one hand the brief, violent, discontinuous, unnatural interventions of man in production (ploughing or harvesting) and reproduction and on the other the long, slow gestation, the nurturing, maintenance and defence of life, which is the work of women.

Chapter 6 The work of time

1 'Don't be offended at me for making this offer . . . I am so thoroughly conscious of counting for nothing in your eyes, that you can even take money from me. You can't take offence at a gift from me' (Dostoyevsky 1966: 44).
2 A gift always contains a more or less disguised challenge. 'He has put him to shame', the Moroccan Berbers used to say, according to Marcy (1941), apropos of the challenge-gift (*thawsa*) which marked the great occasions. It can be seen that the logic of challenge and riposte is the limit towards which gift exchange moves when generous exchange tends towards an 'overwhelming' generosity.
3 Though presented here in deductive form, these propositions were not produced by deduction, as can be seen from the successive versions of the analysis (the first, published in 1965, was still very close to the native, i.e. official, representation; the second, published in 1972, was based on a series of case-studies and presented the model put forward here, but in a less economical form.
4 Rites of possession or exorcism and all magical struggles show, through this limiting case, that magical acts are 'logical' operations performed in situations of life-and-death urgency. The 'magical stereotyping' that Weber refers to is probably due in part to the fact that mistakes have grave consequences.
5 The statements contained in the customary law of a particular clan or village represent only a very small proportion of the universe of possible acts of jurisprudence, and if one adds to them the statements produced from the principles to be found in the customs of other groups, this still gives only a limited idea of the full possibilities.
6 The *qanun* of each clan (or village) essentially consists of a list of specific misdemeanours each followed by the corresponding fine. The principles from which these consecrated acts of jurisprudence are produced are left implicit. For example, the *qanun* of Agouni-n-Tesellent, a village of the Ath Akbil tribe, includes, in a total of 249 clauses, 219 'repressive laws' (in Durkheim's sense), i.e. 88 per cent, as against 25 'restitutory' laws, i.e. 10 per cent, and only 5 clauses concerning the foundations of the political system.
7 All sorts of examples of this will be seen in the analyses below, such as *elbahadla*, excessive humiliation, in the exchanges of honour, or marriage with the parallel cousin in matrimonial exchanges.
8 The verb *qabel*, which several informants offer as a kind of concentrated expression of all the values of honour, in fact brings all these levels together, since it designates all at once bodily postures (standing up straight, facing up to someone, looking him in the eyes), recognized virtues (like the art of receiving an honoured guest, or knowing how to confront others, for better or worse, by looking them straight in the face), and mythico-ritual categories (facing the east, the light, the future).
9 If practice is content with a partial or discontinuous logic and a 'satisficing or

limited rationality', this is not because, as has been noted, recourse to empirical procedures or tried and tested decision-making principles enables it to save the costs of information gathering and analysis (cf. Simon 1954). It is also because the saving in logic resulting from intuitive, rule-of-thumb decisions implies a saving in time, which, even in economic choices, is no small matter when one remembers that the characteristic of practice is that it operates in emergency conditions and that the best decision in the world is worthless when it comes too late, after the opportunity or the ritual moment. (Analysts and experimenters forget this when they proceed as if an agent involved in the action could pause to decipher without risking the practical sanction of his delay.)

10 Sayings that exalt generosity, the supreme virtue of the man of honour, coexist with proverbs betraying the temptation to calculate: 'A gift is a misfortune', says one of them, and another: 'A present is a chicken and the recompense a camel.' Playing on the word *lehna*, which means both 'present' and 'peace', and on *elahdya* which means 'present', the Kabyles also say: 'You who bring us peace (a present), leave us in peace', 'Leave us in peace (*lahna*) with your present (*elahdya*)', or 'The best present is peace'.

11 This is true, for example, of all research on the cult of art and culture. The sociology that brings to light the 'objective' truth must expect to see the self-evidences that it supplies (I am thinking, for example, of the relationship between educational level and visits to art galleries established in *L'Amour de l'art* [Bourdieu 1966]) countered by a denial (in Freud's sense) which is only the defensive form of ordinary gainsaying. This must lead it to integrate into its theoretical construction the illusion, that is, the belief, that it has had to combat, and the objectification of the conditions of its production and functioning. (This is what I have tried to do in my work subsequent to *L'Amour de l'art* on the conditions of production of the belief in the value of the work of art.)

12 The effect of symbolic imposition that official representation intrinsically exerts is intensified by a deeper effect when semi-learned grammar, a normative description, is (differentially) taught by a specific institution and so becomes the basis of a cultivated *habitus*. Thus, in a class society, the legitimate linguistic *habitus* presupposes objectification (more precisely, thesaurization and formalization by grammarians) and inculcation, by the family and the educational system, of the system of rules (the grammar) resulting from this objectification. In this case, as in the field of art and, more generally, of learned ['high' – trans.] culture, it is the semi-learned ['middle-brow'] norm (grammar, scholastic categories of perception, appreciation and expression, etc.) which, incorporated (in the form of 'culture'), becomes the principle of the production and understanding of practices and discourses. It follows that relations to high culture (and formal language) are objectively defined by the degree of incorporation of the legitimate norm. The ease of those who, with a precocious and deep command of the learned grammar of practices and discourses, are so manifestly in line with its demands that they can allow themselves the liberties with the rule that define excellence, is opposed to the tension and pretension of those whose strict conformity to the rule reveals that they are limited to execution of the rule; not to mention those who, whatever they do, cannot fall into line with rules that are made against them.

13 Those who are designated to speak about the group on behalf of the group, the authorized spokesmen to whom the anthropologist is first referred (men rather than women, respected middle-aged or old men rather than young or

marginal men), offer a discourse in line with the view that the group wants to give and have of itself, emphasizing (especially to an outsider) values (e.g. those of honour) rather than interests, rules rather than strategies, etc.

14 Between the agent whom the 'excellence' of practice naturally complying with the official rule predisposes to serve as a delegate and spokesman and the agent who, not content with breaking the rules of the game, does nothing to hide or extenuate his transgressions, there is a recognized place for the agent who, by offering the appearances or the intention of conformity, i.e. recognition, to the rule he can neither observe nor refuse, contributes to the official existence of the rule.

15 Competition for official power is restricted to men; women can only compete for a power that always remains unofficial. Men have the whole social order and the whole official institution working for them, starting with mythico-ritual and genealogical structures, which, by reducing the opposition between the official and the private to the opposition between the outside and the inside, and therefore between the male and the female, establish a systematic hierarchization assigning female interventions to a shadowy, clandestine or, at best, unofficial existence. Even when women hold the real power, as is often the case, at least in matrimonial matters, they can only exercise it fully so long as they leave the appearances, the official manifestation, of power to men. Women can have a degree of power only if they are willing to make do with the unofficial power of the *éminence grise*, a dominated power which can only be exerted by proxy, covered by an official authority, so that it still serves the authority it makes use of.

Chapter 7   Symbolic capital

1 To convince oneself this is so, one only has to remember the tradition of 'confraternity' within the medical profession. No doctor ever pays a fellow doctor a fee. Instead, he has to find him a present, without necessarily knowing what he wants or needs, not worth too much more or too much less than the price of the consultation, but also not coming too close, because that would amount to stating the price of the service, thereby giving away the self-interested fiction that it was free.

2 'You've saved me from having to sell' is what a man says in such cases to the lender who prevents land falling into the hands of a stranger, by means of a sort of fictitious sale (he gives the money while allowing the owner the continued use of his land).

3 The reluctance to use formal guarantees increases with the social proximity of the parties and with the solemnity of the guarantees invoked. Similarly, the share of the loss that the partners agree to bear when an animal suffers an accident varies greatly depending on the relationship between them. A man who has lent an animal to a very close relative will minimize his partner's responsibility.

4 This distinction (like the related distinction that Marx makes between labour time – here, the time devoted to ploughing and harvesting – and production time – which, as well as the labour time, includes the nine months between ploughing and sowing) has been imposed by the effects of the economic domination linked to colonization and more especially by the generalization of monetary exchange. The awareness of unemployment, measured by the discrepancy between the fact of declaring oneself 'in work' and the real activity

in the days preceding the survey, varies with the degree of penetration of the capitalist economy and the associated dispositions (see Bourdieu 1979: 57).

5 Since the price of time rises as productivity rises (and with it the quantity of goods offered for consumption, and hence consumption itself, which also takes time), time becomes scarcer as the scarcity of goods declines. Squandering of goods can even become the only way of saving time which is now more valuable than the goods that could be saved if time were devoted to maintenance, repair, etc. (see Becker 1965). This is no doubt one of the bases of the contrast in attitudes to time that has often been observed.

6 It has to be borne in mind that the distinction between economic capital and symbolic capital is the product of the application of a principle of differentiation alien to the universe to which it is applied and that it can only grasp the undifferentiatedness of these two states of capital in the form of their perfect convertibility.

7 A man who seeks to belie his reputation as a 'house man' (*argaz ukhamis* – as opposed to the 'market man') is put in his place with: 'Since you're only a *thakwath* man, stay a *thakwath* man!' (*thakwath* designates the alcove in the wall of the house, used to hide the small, typically feminine objects which must not be left on view, spoons, rags, weaving tools, etc.).

8 Proof that what is at stake in marriage strategies is not reducible to the bridewealth alone is provided by history, which, here too, has dissociated the symbolic and the material aspects of transactions. In being reduced to its purely monetary value, the bridewealth has been dispossessed, even in the agents' own eyes, of its significance as a symbolic rating, and the debates that used to take place about it, having been reduced to the level of haggling, come to be seen as shameful.

Chapter 8 Modes of domination

1 Although he draws no real conclusions from it, Bertrand Russell (1938: 12–14) expresses very well an intuition of the analogy between energy and power which could serve as the basis for a unification of social science: 'Like energy, power has many forms, such as wealth, armaments, civil authority, influence or opinion. No one of these can be regarded as subordinate to any other, and there is no one form from which the others are derivative. The attempt to treat one form of power, say wealth, in isolation, can only be partially successful, just as the study of one form of energy will be defective at certain points, unless other forms are taken into account. Wealth may result from military power or from influence over opinion, just as either of these may result from wealth.' And he goes on to define the programme for a science of the conversions of the different forms of social energy: 'Power, like energy, must be regarded as continually moving from any one of its forms into any other, and it should be the business of social science to seek the laws of such transformations.'

2 'The less social power the medium of exchange possesses (and at this stage it is still closely bound to the nature of the direct product of labour and the direct needs of the partners in exchange) the greater must be the power of the community which binds the individuals together, the patriarchal relation, the community of antiquity, feudalism and the guild system. Each individual possesses social power in the form of a thing. Rob the thing of this social power and you must give it to persons to exercise over persons. *Relations of*

personal dependence (entirely spontaneous at the outset) are the first social forms, in which human productive capacity develops only to a slight extent and at isolated points. *Personal independence founded on objective [sachlicher] dependence* is the second great form, in which a system of general social metabolism, of universal relations, of all-round needs and universal capacities is formed for the first time' (Marx 1973: 157–8, my italics).

3 The belief, often observed in gnostic religions, that knowledge may be transmitted by various forms of magical contact – most typically, a kiss – can be seen as an effort to transcend the limits of this mode of conservation: 'Whatever it is that the practitioner learns, he learns from anothr *dukun*, who is his *guru* (teacher); and whatever he learns, he and others call his *ilmu* (science). *Ilmu* is generally considered to be a kind of abstract knowledge or supernormal skill, but by the more concrete-minded and "old-fashioned", it is sometimes viewed as a kind of substantive magical power, in which case its transmission may be more direct than through teaching' (Geertz 1960: 88).

4 'The poet is the incarnate book of the oral people' (Notopoulos 1938: 469). In a very fine article, William C. Greene (1951) shows how a change in the mode of accumulation, circulation and reproduction of culture results in a change in the function it is made to perform, together with a change in the structure of cultural products. Eric A. Havelock (1963) similarly shows that cultural resources are transformed, even in their content, by change in 'the technology of preserved communication' and in particular by the shift from mimesis – a practical reactivation which mobilizes all the resources of a 'pattern of organized actions' with a mnemonic function (music, rhythm, words) in an act of affective identification – to the written word which, because it exists as a text, is repeatable, reversible, detached from the situation and predisposed by its permanence to become an object of analysis, control, comparison and reflexion.

5 Wealth, a gift God makes to man so that he can relieve the poverty of others, chiefly implies duties. The belief in immanent justice, which governs a number of practices (such as collective oath-taking), no doubt helps to turn generosity into a sacrifice that will merit in return the blessing of generosity. 'A generous man is a friend of God' ('the two worlds belong to him'); 'Eat, you who are used to feeding others'; 'Lord, give unto me that I may give' (only a saint can give without owning).

6 Usurers are universally despised and some of them, fearing ostracism, prefer to grant their debtors extra time (e.g. until the next olive harvest) rather than force them to sell land in order to pay.

7 Archaic societies devote more time and effort to 'form', because their refusal to recognize self-evidences such as the 'business is business' or 'time is money' on which the unaesthetic life-style of the 'harried leisure classes' in so-called advanced societies is based, imposes a stronger censorship of personal interest. So it is understandable why these societies offer connoisseurs of beautiful forms the enchanting spectacle of a life-style conducted as art for art's sake.

8 Benveniste's history of the vocabulary of Indo-European institutions charts the linguistic milestones in the process of unveiling and disenchantment which leads from physical or symbolic violence to 'economic' law, from ransom (of a prisoner) to purchase, from the prize (for a notable action) to wages, from moral recognition to the recognition of debts, from worthiness to credit-worthiness, and from moral obligation to the court order (Benveniste 1973: 159–84).

9 The question of the relative value of the different modes of domination – a

question raised, at least implicitly, by Rousseauistic evocations of primitive paradises or Americanocentric disquisitions on 'modernization' – is totally meaningless and can only give rise to necessarily interminable debates on the advantages and disadvantages of 'before' and 'after', the only interest of which lies in the revelation of the writer's own social fantasies, i.e. his unanalysed relationship to his own society. As in all comparisons of one system with another, it is possible *ad infinitum* to contrast partial representations of the two systems (e.g. enchantment versus disenchantment) differing in their affective colouring and ethical connotations depending on which of them is taken as a standpoint. The only legitimate object of comparison is each system considered as a system, and this precludes any evaluation other than that implied *in fact* in the immanent logic of its evolution.

10 A man who fails to 'give others the time he owes them' is reproached in terms like these: 'You've only just arrived, and now you're off again.' 'Are you leaving us? We've only just sat down . . . We've hardly spoken.'

11 The marabouts are in a different position, because they wield an institutionally delegated authority as members of a respected body of 'religious officials' and because they maintian a separate status for themselvse. They do this by practising fairly strict endogamy and a whole set of traditions specific to themselves, such as confining their women to the house. The fact remains that these men who, as the saying goes, 'like mountain torrents, grow great in stormy times', cannot derive profit from their quasi-institutionalized role as mediators unless their knowledge of the traditions and of the persons involved gives the means of exerting a symbolic authority which only exists by virtue of direct delegation by the group. The marabouts are most often simply the loophole, the 'door', as the Kabyles say, that enables groups in conflict to compromise without losing face.

12 Thinking in terms of 'instances' owes its almost inevitable social success to the fact that, as is shown by the most elementary analysis of usages, it makes it possible to mobilize all the reassuring symbolism of architecture for classificatory and apparently explanatory purposes, with 'structure' of course, and therefore 'infrastructure' and 'superstructure', but also 'base', 'basis', 'ground', 'foundations', not forgetting Gurvitch's inimitable 'floors' (*paliers*) (in depth . . .).

13 The analogy with Descartes's theory of continuous creation is perfect. And when Leibniz criticized a conception of God condemned to move the world 'as a carpenter moves his axe or as a miller drives his millstone by diverting water towards the wheel' (1939c: 92), and put forward, in place of the Cartesian universe, which cannot subsist without unremitting divine attention, a physical world endowed with a *vis propria*, he was initiating the critique – which did not find full expression until much later (in Hegel's Introduction to the *Philosophy of Right*) – of all forms of the refusal to acknowledge that the social world has a 'nature', that is, an immanent necessity.

14 The existence of mechanisms capable of ensuring the reproduction of the political order, without any express intervention, in turn induces acceptance of a restricted definition of politics and of the practices oriented towards acquisition or conservation of power, which tacitly excludes the competition for control over the mechanisms of reproduction. Thus, when social science takes as its main object the sphere of legitimate politics, as what is called 'political science' now does, it uncritically accepts the pre-constructed object that reality imposes on it.

15 It has often been pointed out that the logic that makes the redistribution of

goods the *sine qua non* of the perpetuation of power tends to slow down or prevent the primitive accumulation of economic capital and the emergence of division into classes (see for example Wolf 1959: 216).

16 A social history of the notion of the 'title', of which the title of nobility or the educational qualification (*titre scolaire*) are particular cases, would have to show the social conditions and the effects of the shift from personal authority (e.g. the *gratia* – esteem, influence – of the Romans) to the institutionalized title, in other words from honour to *jus honorum*. Thus, in Rome, the use of titles (such as *eques Romanus*) defining a *dignitas*, an officially recognized position within the State (as distinct from a purely personal quality) was, like the use of *insignia*, progressively subjected to detailed control by custom or law (see Nicolet 1966: 236–41).

17 Educational qualifications, a measure of rank, indicating an agent's position in the structure of the distribution of cultural capital, are socially perceived as guaranteeing possession of a particular quantity of cultural capital.

18 In the ideological struggle among the groups (age groups, the sexes, etc.) or the social classes for the power to define reality, symbolic violence, a misrecognized and thus recognized violence, is held in check by the awakening of awareness of arbitrariness ('consciousness-raising'), which deprives the dominant of part of their symbolic strength by sweeping away misrecognition.

19 It was not a sociologist but a group of American businessmen who conceived the 'bank-account theory' of public relations: 'It necessitates making regular and frequent deposits in the Bank of Public Good-Will, so that valid checks can be drawn on this account when it is desirable' (quoted by MacKean 1944). See also Gable (1953: 262) on the different ways in which the National Association of Manufacturers tries to influence the general public, teachers, churchmen, women's club leaders, farmers' leaders, etc., and H. A. Turner (1958) on the way in which 'an organization elevates itself in the esteem of the general public and conditions their attitudes so that a state of public opinion will be created in which the public will almost automatically respond with favor to the programs desired by the group'.

Chapter 9   The objectivity of the subjective

1 It goes without saying that this indispensable distinction is somewhat fictitious. To grasp reality, the social scientists has to apply logical instruments of classification and perform in a conscious and controlled way the equivalent of the classifying operations that are performed in ordinary practice. Those who insist on the critique of individual representations as the precondition for access to an 'objective' reality quite inaccessible to common experience ('We believe it a fruitful idea', said Durkheim [1982b: 171], 'that social life must be explained not by the conception of it formed by those who participate in it, but by the profound causes which escape their consciousness') are no doubt willing to acknowledge, like Durkheim himself, that one cannot 'know' this reality without applying logical instruments. The fact remains that there is an undeniable affinity between physicalism and the positivist inclination to see classifications either as arbitrary, 'operational' divisions (like age groups or income brackets), or as the simple recording of 'objective' separations grasped in the form of discontinuities in distributions or bends in curves.

2 Apart from the existential questionings of bourgeois adolescence (Am I upper-middle or lower-middle class? Where does the *petite bourgeoisie* end and the

grande bourgeoisie begin?) and the strategic calculations of those who intend to count (or discount) friends or adversaries, to 'count' or 'catalogue' themselves (a good translation, all in all, of *kathègoresthai*), the question of the 'real' limits between groups is almost always, in social practice, a question of administrative politics. The administrator knows (better than sociologists) that membership of classes, even the most formal statistical categories, such as age-brackets, is accompanied by 'advantages' or obligations, such as the right to retire or conscription for military service; and that the frontiers between the groups thus delimited are the stakes in struggles (e.g. for retirement at sixty or the assimilation of a category of casual workers into the class of permanent staff) and that the classifications establishing these frontiers are instruments of power.

3 Then there is a quite separate group who start out from the standpoint of social physics and use the objective continuity of most of the distributions as an argument for refusing any reality to social classes other than as heuristic concepts or as statistical categories arbitrarily imposed by the social scientist, whom they see as solely responsible for the discontinuity introduced into a continuous reality.

4 One could equally well take as an example any of the sub-universes of the field of cultural production, such as the universe of painting, where the value of each artist is defined in a similar interplay of infinitely reflected judgements. A perfect knowledge of the 'game' (which has 'rules' only for those who are excluded from it, and for that very reason) – the conduct to follow with critics, dealers, other artists, remarks to make to the same, people to frequent or to avoid, places (for exhibitions, in particular) to be seen in or to shun, the ever narrower groups one needs to have been part of – is here also one of the most absolute conditions for accumulation of the fiduciary value that constitutes notoriety.

5 The view of the social world that interactionism presents corresponds to a social universe with a very low degree of institutionalization of symbolic capital, that of the urban middle clasess, where the hierarchies are multiple, blurred (as is the case with 'middle-rank' educational qualifications) and fluid, and where the objective uncertainty is reinforced, for the ordinary consciousness, by the low degree of mutual acquaintance and the corresponding lack of even minimal knowledge of the most 'objective' economic and social characteristics.

6 Individual and collective perception, or, more precisely, individual perception oriented by collective representations, tends to generate contrasting representations, each group tending to define the values with which it associates its value by opposition to the values of other groups that are (perceived as being) higher, and more especially, lower than itself. The (mental) representations that the various groups form of the (theatrical) representations that (intentionally or not) other groups give them, appear to the observer as systems of oppositions which reproduce the real differences between life-styles in a sharper, simpler (sometimes even caricatural) form, and which help both to produce the divisions and to legitimate them by presenting them as grounded in nature.

BOOK II   PRACTICAL LOGICS

Chapter 1   Land and matrimonial strategies

1 This chapter is a much revised version of Bourdieu 1972.
2 The errors inherent in legalistic thinking are most clearly seen in the works of historians of law and custom. The whole way in which they have been trained to think, and also the nature of the evidence they study (such as notarial documents, which represent a combination of the legal precautions introduced by the notaries – the conservators of a learned tradition – and the procedures actually envisaged by their clients), incline these historians to consecrate inheritance and marriage strategies as strict rules.
3 Because the agents possess *complete* genealogical information at the level of marriage possibilities (which presupposes constant mobilization and updating of their competence), bluff is virtually excluded ('B. is very grand, but at his family's home, near A., everything is very small'), since every individual can be brought down at any time to his objective truth, that is, the social value (in terms of the native criteria) of his entire kin over several generations. This is not true in the case of a distant marriage: 'He who marries afar', the saying goes, either cheats or is cheated [on the value of what he is gettng].'
4 There are strong reasons to think that the innumerable protective clauses surrounding the *adot* in the marriage contract, designed to ensure its 'inalienability, imprescriptibility and unseizability' (guarantees, hierarchy of creditors, etc.), are products of the legal imagination. Thus, separation of the spouses, one of the instances of dissolution of marriage which, according to the contracts, entails restitution of the dowry, is almost unknown in peasant society.
5 The head of the 'house' had the monopoly of outside contacts, particularly the important transactions negotiated in the market-place. He thus had authority over the financial resources of the family, and hence over its entire economic life. The younger son, who was generally confined to the family estate (which further reduced his chances of marriage) could acquire a modicum of economic independence only if he were able to put away a small nest-egg of his own (savings from a war pension, for example), for which he was envied and respected.
6 The *relative* autonomy of political rights with respect to property rights is convincingly shown by the ways in which the *adot* was managed. Although the wife remained theoretically the owner of the *adot* (since the obligation to return its equivalent in quantity and value could come into effect at any time), the husband was entitled to the income and, once there were offspring, he could use it to endow the younger children (his rights were naturally more limited in the case of real estate, especially land). For her part, the heiress had the same rights over her husband's dotal property as a man over his wife's dowry, so that her parents received the income from the assets their son-in-law had brought into the marriage and managed them so long as they lived.
7 Marriage provided peasant families with one of their most important opportunities to perform monetary as well as symbolic exchanges which asserted the positions of the two families in the social hierarchy and, by the same token, reasserted that hierarchy. Since it could entail the enhancement, conservation

or dissipation of material and symbolic capital, it was probably at the heart of the dynamics and statics of the whole social structure, within the limits of the permanence of the mode of production.

8 One of the most widely used subterfuges to favour a child consisted in handing over to him, long before his marriage, two or three head of cattle, which were held under a *gasalhes* arrangement and brought in good profits. (*Gasalhes* was an informal contract by which one entrusted a reliable friend with the care of one or more head of cattle, having first estimated their value. Proceeds from the products, as well as gains and losses from the sale of the meat, were shared by both partners.)

9 The end of the story is no less edifying: 'After a lot of quarrelling, the whole dowry had to be returned to the widow, who went back to her family. Shortly after the marriage of the eldest son, about 1910, one of the daughters had been married, also with a dowry of 2,000 francs. When the war came, the family brought back the daughter who had married into the S. family (on one of the neighbouring properties) to take the place of the son. The other daughters, who lived further away, were very upset about this decision. But the father chose the daughter who was married to a neighbour because this was the way to increase his patrimony.'

10 Occasionally, an important family who could afford the additional burden might keep one of the daughters at home. 'Marie, the eldest daughter of the L.'s of D., could have married. She was turned into a younger daughter, and like all younger daughters, she became an unpaid servant for life. They dulled her wits. Very little was done to find her a husband. That way they kept the dowry, they kept everything. Now she looks after the parents.'

11 The chances of the lineage dying out due to the celibacy of the eldest son were virtually nil in the heyday of the system.

12 The *adot*, normally paid to the father or mother of the bridegroom and only exceptionally (i.e. if his parents were deceased) to the heir himself, was meant to become part of the patrimony of the family resulting from the marriage. If the marriage was dissolved or if one of the spouses died, it went to the children, if any, although the surviving spouse continued to have use of the income. If there were no children, it reverted to the family of the spouse who had brought it into the marriage. Some marriage contracts stipulated that in the event of separation, the father-in-law only had to pay the interest on the *adot* brought in by the son-in-law, thus giving the latter the possibility of returning to the family after reconciliation.

Chapter 2 The social uses of kinship

1 On the deductive relationship between kinship names and attitudes to kinship, see Radcliffe-Brown (1952: 62; 1960: 25) and Lévi-Strauss (1958: 46). On the term 'jural' and the use that Radcliffe-Brown makes of it, see Dumont (1971: 41): 'jural' relationships are those 'which are subject to precise, binding prescriptions, whether concerning people or things'.

2 The majority of earlier investigators accepted the native explanation that endogamous marriage had the function of keeping the property in the family, advancing as evidence – and with some reason – the closeness of the relationship between marriage and inheritance practices. Against this explanation Murphy and Kasdan quite rightly object that the Koranic law that gives a woman half of a son's share is rarely observed, and that the family can in any case count

on the inheritance contributed by in-marrying women (see Granqvist 1931; Rosenfield 1957).

3 'It has long been known that societies which advocate marriage between certain types of kin adhere to the norm only in a small number of cases, as demonstrated by Kunstadter and his team through the use of computer simulations. Fertility and reproduction rates, the demographic balance of the sexes and the age pyramid never show the perfect harmony necessary for every individual, when the time comes for him to marry, to be assured of finding a suitable spouse in the prescribed degree, even if the kinship nomenclature is broad enough to confuse degrees of the same type but unequally distant, often so much so that the notion of a common descent becomes merely theoretical' (Lévi-Strauss 1969: xxx).

4 Murphy and Kasdan say the same thing, but without drawing out the conclusions when they remark that genealogies and the manipulation of genealogies have as their main function the encouragement of the vertical integration of social units which parallel-cousin marriage tends to divide and close in upon themselves.

5 The most rigorously checked genealogies do indeed contain systematic lacunae. Since the strength of the group's memory of an individual depends on the value they attach to him or her at the moment when data are collected, genealogies are better at recording men (and men's marriages), especially when they have produced numerous male descendants, than women (except, of course, women who marry within the lineage); they record close marriages better than distant marriages, single marriages better than the complete series of all the marriages of the same individual (polygamy, multiple remarriages after divorce or death of the spouse). There is in fact every reason to think that informants may fail to mention whole lineages when their last representative has died without male descendants (thus confirming the native theory that sees all birth as a resurrection and the individual without male descendants as a person whom no one will 'call up' – as spirits are called up – and so resurrect).

6 Thus, the apparently most ritualized acts of matrimonial negotiation and of the ceremonies accompanying the wedding – which, by their greater or lesser solemnity, have the secondary function of declaring the social significance of the marriage (broadly speaking, the higher the families are in the social hierarchy, and the more distant they are in genealogical space, the more solemn will be the ceremony) – are opportunities to deploy strategies aimed at manipulating the objective meaning of a relationship that is never entirely univocal, either by making a virtue of necessity and scrupulously observing the proprieties or by masking the objective significance under the ritual intended to celebrate it.

7 Physical and mental deformities present an extremely difficult problem for a group which rigorously denies social status to a woman without a husband or even to a man without a wife (even a widower is obliged to remarry quickly) – especially when these infirmities are seen and interpreted through the mythico-ritual categories. One can imagine the sacrifice it represents – in a universe in which a wife can be repudiated because she has a reputation for bringing bad luck – to marry a woman who is left-handed, one-eyed, lame or hunchbacked (this deformity representing an inversion of pregnancy), or who is simply sick and weak, all of these being omens of barrenness and wickedness.

8 'You give wheat, you bring back barley.' 'You give wheat to bad teeth.' 'Make your offering out of clay, if you don't get a cooking-pot you will get a couscous steamer.' Among the eulogies of parallel-cousin marriage I have collected, the following are particularly representative: 'She won't ask you for much for herself, and there's no need to spend much on the wedding.' 'He may do what

he will with his brother's daughter, and no evil will come from her. And then he will live in greater unity with his brother, doing as their father recommended for the sake of brotherhood (*thaymats*): "Do not listen to your women!"'; 'A woman who is a stranger will despise you, she will be an insult to your ancestors, believing that her own are more noble than your own. Whereas, with the daughter of your *âamm*, your grandfather and hers are one and the same; she will never say "A curse on your father's father!"'; 'The daughter of your *âamm* will not abandon you. If you have no tea, she will not demand any from you, and even if she should die of hunger in your house, she will bear it all and never complain about you.'

9 Jurists' fascination with the vestiges of matrilineal kinship has led them to take an interest in the case of the *awrith*, which they see, to use their own terminology, as a 'contract for the adoption of an adult male' (for Algeria, see Bousquet 1934; Lefèvre 1939; for Morocco, Marcy 1930, 1941; Bendaoud 1935; Turbet 1935).

10 Here is a particularly significant testimony: 'As soon as she had her first son, Fatima set about looking for his future wife. She considered several possibilities, keeping her eyes open on all occasions, in her neighbours' houses, among her own stock, in the village, when visiting friends, at weddings, on pilgrimages, at the fountain, in her travels, and even when she had to go and present her condolences. So it was that she married off all her children almost without noticing it' (Yamina 1960).

11 If the mythical idealization (blood, purity, the inside, etc.) and the ethical exaltation (honour, virtue, etc.) which surround purely agnatic marriage are set aside, then ordinary marriages are spoken of no differently than parallel-cousin marriage. For example, marriage with the father's sister's daughter is regarded as capable of ensuring harmony between the women and the wife's respect for her husband's parents (her *khal* and *khalt*) as successfully as parallel-cousin marriage – and at less cost, since the tension created by the rivalry implicitly unleashed by any marriage between different groups over the status and living conditions offered to the bride has no reason to arise, at this degree of familiarity.

12 These extra-ordinary marriages escape the constraints and proprieties that bear on ordinary marriages (particularly because they have no 'sequels'). Apart from the case in which a defeated group (clan or tribe) gave a woman to the victorious group and the two groups, to indicate that there were no winners or losers, then exchanged women, it could also happen that the victorious group would give a woman to the other group without taking anything in return. The marriage would then bring together not the most powerful families, but a small family of the victorious group and a great family of the defeated group.

13 'Marriage afar is exile', 'Marriage outside, marriage into exile (*azwaj ibarra, azwaj elghurba*)', a mother often says when her daughter has been given to a another group in which she has no acquaintances (*thamusni*), still less even remote kin. It is also the song of the bride married into exile: 'O mountain, open your door to the exile. Let her see her native land. Foreign soil is the sister of death. For man as for woman.'

14 This is part of the explanation for early marriage: an unmarried girl is the very incarnation of the vulnerability of the group. Her father's chief concern is to liquidate this threat as soon as possible by placing her under the protection of another man.

15 Chelhod (1965), who reports that 'in the low language of Aleppo, prostitutes

are called "daughters of the maternal aunt"', also quotes a Syrian proverb which expresses the same disapproval of marriage with the mother's sister's daughter: 'Because of his impure character, he married his maternal aunt's daughter.' Similarly, in Kabylia, to express the total lack of any genealogical link, men will say, 'What are you to me? Not even my mother's sister's daughter's son – *mis illis khalti.*

16 An indirect confirmation of the significance given to parallel-cousin marriage may be seen in the fact that the person responsible for the solemn opening of ploughing, an action homologous with inaugural marriage, had no political role and that his duty was purely honorary or, one might say, symbolic, that is, at once undemanding and respected. This figure is referred to by the names *amezwar* (the first), *aneflus* (the man of trust), or *aqdhim* (the elder), *amghar* (the old man), *amasâud* (the man of luck), or, more precisely, *amezwar, aneflus, amghar nat-yuga* (the first, the man of trust, the old man of the yoke of oxen or the plough). The most significant term, because it explicitly states the ploughing–marriage homology, is *bulâaras*, the man of the wedding (see Laoust 1920).

17 In such a system, the misfirings of the mechanisms of reproduction – matrimonial misalliance, sterility entailing the disappearance of the lineage, the break-up of undivided ownership – are no doubt the main factors in the transformations of the economic and social hierarchy.

18 The customary laws, which all, without exception, provide for sanctions against the person who murders a man from whom he is to inherit, are evidence that overt conflicts were frequent: 'If a man kills a kinsman (whose heir he is) unjustly and so as to inherit from him, the *djemaa* shall take all the murderer's goods' (*qanun* of the Iouadhien tribe, quoted by Hanoteau and Letourneux 1873: vol. 3, 432; see also pp. 356, 358, 368, etc.).

19 The weakening of the cohesive forces (correlative with the slump in symbolic values) and the strengthening of the disruptive forces (linked to the appearance of sources of monetary income and the ensuring crisis of the peasant economy) lead to refusal of the elders' authority and of the austere, frugal aspects of peasant existence. The younger generation demand the right to dispose of the profit of their labour, in order to spend it on consumer goods rather than on the symbolic goods which would enhance the family's prestige and influence.

20 Without speculating as to the causal link between these facts, it may be noted that 'illnesses of bitter jealousy' receive great attention from relatives, especially mothers, who deploy a whole arsenal of curative and prophylactic rites. (To express an insurmountable hatred, reference is made to the feeling of the little boy who is suddenly deprived of his mother's affection by the arrival of a new baby and grows thin and pale like someone moribund or 'constipated'.).

21 It is significant that customary law, which only exceptionally intervenes in domestic life, explicitly favours undivided ownership (*thidukli bukham* or *zeddi*); 'People living in a family association pay no fine if they fight. If they separate, they pay like other people' (Hanoteau and Letourneux 1873: vol. 3, 423).

22 Here is a typical account of how this sort of marriage is arranged: 'Before he had learned to walk, his father found him a bride. One evening, after supper, Arab went and called on his elder brother (*dadda*). They chatted. His brother's wife had her daughter on her lap. The little girl stretched out her arms towards her uncle, who picked her up, saying, "May God make her Idir's wife! That's so, isn't it, *dadda*? You won't say no?" Arab's brother replied: 'What does a

blind man want? Light! If you relieve me of the care she gives me, may God take your cares from you. I give her to you, with her grain and her chaff, for nothing!"' (Yamina 1960: 10).

23 Whether through their control over inheritance, which lends itself to all sorts of strategic manipulations, ranging from sheer delay in the effective transmission of powers to the threat of disinheritance, or through the various strategic uses to which they can put their officially recognized monopoly of matrimonial negotiations, the elders have the means of taking advantage of the socially recognized limits of youth. (For an analysis of the strategies used by the heads of noble houses to keep their heirs in a subordinate position, forcing them to go out on dangerous adventures far from home, see Duby 1973: 213–15, and esp. p. 219.).

24 As Chelhod (1965) rightly points out, all observations confirm that the tendency to marry endogamously, which is more marked in nomadic tribes in a constant state of war than in settled tribes, tends to reappear or intensify when there are threats of war or conflict. Likewise, in Kabylia, those who perpetuate undivided ownership – or the appearances of it – often invoke the danger of separating so long as rival families remain united.

25 By means of secret negotiations, the 'old woman' (*thamgharth*) sometimes manages to interfere in a marriage being arranged entirely by the men, and to make *thislith* promise to leave her complete authority in the house, warning her that otherwise she will prevent the marriage. The sons have some grounds for suspecting their mothers of giving them for wives only girls that the mothers will be able to dominate without difficulty.

26 The marriages of the poor (especially those poor in symbolic capital) are to the marriages of the rich, *mutatis mutandis*, as female marriages are to male marriages. The poor cannot afford to be too demanding in matters of honour. 'The only thing a poor man can do is show he is jealous.' This means that, like women, the poor are less concerned with the symbolic and political functions of a marriage than with its practical functions, attaching, for example, much more importance to the personal qualities of the spouses.

27 A girl's value on the marriage market is in a sense a direct projection of the value socially attributed to the two lineages of which she is the product. This is seen clearly when the father has had children by several marriages: whereas the sons' value is unrelated to their mothers' value, the daughters' value depends on the social status of their mothers' lineages and the strength of their mothers' positions in the family.

28 Likewise, when two sisters follow each other closely, the family will avoid marrying off the younger one until the elder is married or already promised, except in cases of *force majeure* (infirmity, illness, etc.).

Chapter 3   Irresistible analogy

1 Many observers (Lévi-Provençal 1918; Laoust 1920; Hassler 1942; Galand-Pernet 1958) have brought to light the uncertainties of all calendar references which result from the fact that many agrarian rites and practices have been superficially Islamized; the marabouts are often appealed to as experts and often intervene in agrarian rites such as rainmaking. Hassler is, so far as I am aware, the only observer to note the variations from one place to another and one

informant to another: 'The calendar as presented here gives an overall view of the Kabyle year, but, *depending on the tribe*, and often depending on the person questioned, the details differ or are unknown' (Hassler 1942, my italics).

2 The narrative present is used here systematically to describe practices that were present in the informants' memories at a given moment though they may have more or less completely fallen into disuse for a greater or longer time.

3 The sine-wave diagram seemed essential because it alone makes it possible to highlight the turning-points or thresholds (spring, autumn) while presenting the marked moments of the agrarian year both as the ordered points of a linear, oriented sequence (running from autumn to summer, i.e. from west to east, from evening to morning) and as the points of a circle which can be obtained by folding the diagram along the X–Y axis.

4 In view of the purpose of this presentation, it did not seem useful to associate each legend, symbol, saying or proverb with a (necessarily incomplete) list of the authors who mention it, and so to carry out the kind of philological critique that would be needed to determine to what extent the different observations totally or partially overlap (either through borrowing – overt or otherwise – or through separate collection, in the same place or different places), or complement or contradict one another, etc. I shall simply give here a list of the books or articles in which some of the information (limited to the Kabyle regions) used in this reconstruction appears and reappears (there is of course considerable duplication), followed by a list of the books and articles, among those consulted for comparative purposes, on the basis of the hypothesis of cultural unity, that contain useful information or interpretations: Anon. *BEI* 1934; Anon. FDB 1954; Balfet 1955; Boulifa 1913; Calvet 1957; Chantréaux 1941–2; Dallet 1953; Devulder 1951, 1957; Genevois 1955a, 1955b, 1962, 1967, 1969, 1972; Hassler 1942; Hénine 1942; Lanfry 1947a, 1947b; Laoust 1918b, 1920, 1921; Sister Louis de Vincennes 1953; Marchand 1939; Maury 1939; Ouakli 1933a, 1933b; Picard 1958; Rahmani 1933, 1935, 1936, 1938, 1939a, 1939b; Rolland 1912; Servier 1962, 1964; Schœn 1960; Yamina Aït Amar ou Saïd 1952. For comparative purposes: H. Basset 1922; Ben Cheneb 1905–7; Biarnay 1909, 1924; Bourrilly 1932; Destaing 1907, 1911; Galand-Pernet 1958, 1969; Gaudry 1929; Laoust 1912, 1918a; Lévi-Provençal 1918; Marçais and Guiga 1925; Menouillard 1910; Monchicourt 1915; Tillion 1938; Westermarck 1911, 1926.

5 More generally, the complicity that the anthropologist so readily obtains when he shows an interest in the most fundamental cultural themes results from the fact that the intellectual activity that his inquiries provoke in his informants may appear to them as identical with the intellectual activity in which they spontaneously indulge, from which most of the cultural productions they offer him – proverbs, sayings, enigmas, gnomic poems, etc. – have sprung.

6 Cf. the use of the cauris, a symbol of the vulva, as an instrument of homoeopathic prophylaxis against the evil eye. The sight of the vulva is thought to bring bad luck (among women it is an insult to lift one's dress, *chemmer*). Menstrual blood is reputed to have destructive power. This is one of the foundations of the fear of women.

7 Ritual defloration as practised in some societies should probably be understood in terms of the same logic.

8 The *qibla*, an old woman who shares the blacksmith's power to confront the dangers of the crossing of contraries, sits on the lower beam of the loom to keep it in place when the cloth is rolled on the upper beam.

9 As has been seen, the duality of woman is translated into the logic of kin relations as the opposition between the patrilateral and the matrilateral cross cousin.

10 Russet and red – especially in the form of henna – are associated with virility (cf. the application of henna on the eve of the great ceremonies of manhood: circumcision and marriage). The sacrificial ox (expected to bring rain) must not be russet.

11 'Every day they strut around, and they have the good couscous. Women get coarse couscous (*abelbul*)' (Picard 1958: 139). Women's chants, especially the laments that accompany the milling of grain, are full of such declarations. But women's resistance to male domination is mainly expressed in magic, the weapon of the dominated, which remains subject to the dominant categories ('The enemy of woman is man'; 'Women's rivalry killed him without him ever being ill'). For example, to reduce a man to the state of a donkey (*aghiul*, a taboo word replaced by a euphemism borrowed from Arabic), i.e. the state of a slave deprived of will, women used a dried donkey's heart, salted and ground as a magic potion.

12 The wet season is the time for oral instruction, when the group memory is formed. In the dry season, this memory is acted out and enriched by participation in the acts and ceremonies which confirm the unity of the group. Summer is when the boys learn practically their future tasks as peasants and their obligations as men of honour.

13 The fundamental operators, uniting and separating, are the practical equivalent of filling and emptying: to marry is *âammar*, to be full. The crossroads, the point of intersection of the four cardinal directions and of those who come or go in those directions, is the symbol of the male-full, company (*elwans*), which is opposed on the one hand to the emptiness of the fields and the forest (*lakhla*), solitude, fear, the 'wilderness' (*elwah'ch*), and on the other hand to the female-full (*laâmara*), the village or the house. For this reason it plays a role in some rites designed to secure female fertility.

14 *Ehdjeb* is to protect, mask, hide, confine (women); hence *leh'djubeya*, confinement of women (Genevois 1968: vol. II, 73).

15 'The boar mates in *eliali*', but '*ah'gan* is when the boar's flanks shiver'; or else it is in *en-natah*', sometimes called 'the days of the shivering boar'.

16 According to Westermarck, the 17th of May is called *el mut-el ardh*, the death of the land. Westermarck relates a whole series of traditions all of which indicate the dessicating character of that day (for example, a man who sleeps then, loses his affection for his wife), and he also notes that the scarifications performed then are particularly efficacious.

17 A woman who is obliged in exceptional circumstances to perform these essentially male actions must take special ritual precautions. According to Servier (1962: 1243), a woman who was forced to plough wore a dagger in her girdle and put *arkasen* on her feet; and according to Biarnay (1924: 47), in Morocco, women who were forced to sacrifice an animal, another action forbidden to a woman, had to put a spoon – a phallic symbol – between their thighs, underneath their clothes.

18 The child's hair used to be placed in one pan of a pair of scales and the equivalent in money in the other. This sum was then used to buy meat, or kept as a nest-egg for the boy to use to buy meat on his first visit to the market. Elsewhere, the father would cut off the ear-tip of a goat; the animal, together with its offspring, became the boy's property. The women of the

neighbourhood brought eggs and his mother would make egg pancakes. It was a family festivity, as big or as small as the family chose to make it.

19 *Azegzaw* designates blue, green and grey. It can qualify fruit (green), meat (raw), corn (unripe), a grey rainy sky (it is often applied to the sky in the chants accompanying rain-making rites – Picard 1958: 302), grey like the ox of the autumn sacrifice (Servier 1962: 74, 368). *Azegzaw* brings good fortune: a gift of something green, especially in the morning, brings good luck.

20 A proof of the link between ritual and sacrilegious transgression can be seen, *a contrario*, in the fact that a number of activities are performed with very little ritual accompaniment. These include all *gathering* activities (e.g. picking figs and olives), in the broadest sense (hoeing and gardening, sheep-shearing, planting fig trees, treading out, and churning milk). Thus the rites concerned with trees are very few in number, very variable and very 'transparent': for example, to cure the 'sadness' of the olive trees, their trunks are daubed with henna 'to make them happy', an ass's head is hung in their branches, etc.

21 Circumcision and tree pruning, like scarification and tattooing, partake of the logic of purification, in which the instruments made with fire have a beneficent function, like the *insla* fires, rather than the logic of murder.

22 The family responsible for inaugurating the ploughing occupies a position no less ambiguous than that of the blacksmith (*elfal* is never mentioned in relation to it), and its role as a magic screen does not entitle it to a high place in the hierarchy of prestige and honour.

23 In spite of a well-founded distrust of comparisons between elements dissociated from the historical systems from which they derive their value, one is struck by the similarity between these invocations, in which the field or the grain is asked to be an accomplice in its own sacrifice, and all the ritual precautions with which the Ancient Greeks sought to obtain some sign from the sacrificial ox that it assented to its own murder, which was thus denied (cf. Détienne and Vernant 1979: esp. p. 18).

24 The frequency of large- and small-scale fighting in the fig season led early observers, encouraged by native remarks (an over-excited person is said to have 'eaten too many figs' and a thoughtless person is said to 'rub figs on his head'), to speculate that the source of the ebullience reigning at that time of year lay in the figs themselves: 'There is one season in particular when it really seems that men's mind are more heated than at any other time . . . When they speak of the fig season, which they call *kherrif*, autumn, it seems to be agreed that everyone shall be agitated at that time, just as it is customary to be merry at carnival times' (Devaux 1859: 85–6).

25 Corresponding, in the spatial order, to this purely male time of violence and the point of honour, is the forge, an entirely male house. In it, 'the hearth' (*elkanun*), a raised part, with the actual fire on one side and the bellows on the other (separated by a low wall under which the tubes run to the bellows), is opposed to 'the anvil', the lower part of the forge, close to the door, where one also finds the tubs of water used to quench the heated, beaten iron (Boulifa 1913: 225–6).

26 Separation from the maternal world is also separation from the maternal kin. This ceremony is therefore likely to vary depending on the material and symbolic power relation between the two lineages. The different variants of the ritual would need to be analysed in a similar way to that applied to variations in marriage ritual (and in particular they would have to be related to the history of the power relations between the groups concerned).

27 The relative autonomy of the logic of ritual, which is confirmed by the constant features that are observed throughout the Maghreb, in spite of climatic and economic differences, does not rule out variations. These probably derive first from variations in economic conditions, and in particular, limits on working time, linked to the climate and the corresponding type of cultivation, with, for example, the opposition between the farmers and tree-growers of the uplands and the cereal-growers of the plains (a number of ritual jokes among the lowland people deride the highlandrs for sowing or reaping so late). Secondly, they are due to the particular history of each self-enclosed local unit (as Germaine Tillion pointed out, even units of measurement varied from one village to another). As with the customs recorded in the *qanun*, or carpet and pottery decorations, these local histories fix and perpetuate different products of the same schemes in particularities which are often sustained by the pursuit of distinction (vis-à-vis another clan or village).

28 It is probably no accident that sanctioning (*lah'lal*) and taboo (*h'aram*) are explicitly mentioned in the cases of ploughing and marriage. To start ploughing before the licit (*lah'lal*) moment is regarded as a *h'aram* act that can only result in a *h'aram* product. An informant said of the day in autumn called *yum chendul*, when various divination rites are centred on the wind (Calvet 1957: 19), that a wise man called Chendul refused to plough, despite abundant rain, because the omens which are only revealed on that day, the 33rd day of autumn, warned that it would be a bad year. In what is called *el h'aq* (e.g. *el h'aq lakhrif*, the ban on fig harvesting), the magical dimension is again present, since the assembly which determines it calls downs curses on those who infringe it; but the fact that transgression is sanctioned by a fine (also called *el h'aq*) makes clear the social-convention aspect of the taboo. In the case of marriage, although the term *lah'lal* is only used to designate the sum of money that the bridegroom gives to his bride before the consummation of the marriage (in addition to the bridewealth and presents), the sanctioning function of the wedding ceremony is underlined by a number of features (e.g. *imensi lah'lal*). Thus, as has been seen, the wedding season was inaugurated by a marriage between parallel cousins, which was predisposed to fulfil this role by its conformity to the principles of the mythic world-view.

29 Here too, practical symbolism is not without ambiguity. A mother of twins may be blessed, but she is also suspected of magic. Twins suggest the idea of hatred. Even more than *inulban*, children close to each other in age who compete for their mother's breast, twins (*akniwan*) are jealous and hostile to each other, like co-wives, called *thakniwin* (singular, *thakna*), 'twin sisters'.

30 The relationship between the fork and the main beam is that of woman and man (a riddle: 'the woman supports the man'; 'grandmother supports grandfather', etc.), slave and master (a riddle: 'the slave strangles his master'), earth and sky (Genevois 1955a, and 1963: 21–1). The strangling theme should probably be related to the saying 'The enemy of man is woman'. The squared beam which forms the ridgepole of the roof and rests on the two forks is identified with the honour of the master of the house (the carrying of the main beam gives rise to a ceremony bringing together all the men of the village, like the bearing of the corpse in a funeral).

31 For a number of reasons (including the fact that oil is unequivocally associated with the dry, the hot and the male), one has to set aside the native theory, probably of learned origin (it is also found in other traditions), of the correspondence between the threefold division of the lamp and the threefold

division of the human being, with the clay representing the body, the oil the sentient soul, *nefs*, and the flame the subtle soul, *ruh'* (Servier 1964: 71–2).

32 In songs, the man is often referred to as 'the rifle of the house'. A woman who only has daughters is told, 'Poor woman, I pity you, may a rifle soon be hung on your loom wall' (*tasga*). *Thamazgulth*, used of an animal which is sterile or has miscarried, comes from the root *zgel*, to miss the target. When his marriage is consummated, the bridegroom comes out of the bridal chamber firing a rifle.

33 I say 'practically treated as' to avoid putting into the consciousness of the agents (with expressions like 'experienced as' or 'seen as') the representation which has to be constructed in order to understand the practices objectively oriented by the practical scheme and to communicate this understanding.

34 This dialectic of death and resurrection is expressed in the saying (often used nowadays in another sense when speaking of generation conflicts): 'From life they draw death, from death they draw life' (a scheme that reappears in the riddle: 'Something dead out of something living' – an egg. 'Something living out of something dead' – a chick).

35 The 'grave of the stranger' or of the man without male descendants is one of the sites to which evil is transferred. Almost every village has one, covered with shards, vases and dishes that have been used to 'fix the evil'. In some villages (Sidi Aïch), there is no stranger's grave but a spot called 'Sidi Ali Aghrib' fulfils the same function; elsewhere, the chosen site is called 'the last grave'. Women who want to get rid of an evil (especially a baby's illness) bring a jar of water and an egg, eat the egg, and leave behind the shell and the jar: 'The evil does not come back, just as the stranger did not go home.' To 'put a child to sleep in its mother's womb', a 'stone' from the hearth is picked up and turned seven times one way, then seven times the other way, around the pregnant woman's waist, before being buried in the stranger's grave. Similarly, to avoid pregnancy, a woman takes a hank of combed wool and places it under her pillow overnight; the next day, she gets up early and, with her hands behind her back, steps seven times over her sleeping husband; at each stride, she ties a knot in the wool, and then, without looking back, goes and buries the wool in the stranger's grave.

36 The term *ajedjig* is also used to refer to this group of fast-growing, prolific plants – wheat, broad beans, chick-peas – which are predisposed to express wishes of happiness and prosperity ('so they will flower', 'so they will multiply and reproduce').

37 This function is sometimes explicitly formulated. It is said, for example, that when cereals, a soft food, are being sown, one must 'eat soft'.

38 The separation between the sexes is marked from early childhood. Among the public signs of the social value set on a boy, the most typical are the cries of 'you-you' which mark his birth and all the rites of passage: 'If I can be driven out of my house by a stranger, why did my mother shout "you-you" [for my birth]?' (Boulifa 1913: 167). Male privilege is marked in food, clothing and games. A boy eats with the man as soon as he starts to walk and go to the fields. When he is old enough to watch over the grazing goats, he is entitled to the afternoon snack (milk and a handful of figs). Boys' games are competitive and modelled on combat; girls' games are a 'make-believe' imitation of their adult tasks (a boy who is sickly or puny, or surrounded by many sisters, and who plays at girls' games, is called 'the girls' boy' or 'Mohand of his mother'. A boy is outside, with his goats, or with the men, working or in the assembly

(as soon as he can walk, the women send him out, saying 'Go outside and you'll become a man'); the woman who takes the men their meal is accompanied by her son, even when he is very small, as if he were a substitute for her husband (many men use their sons to keep watch on their wives). Girls stay indoors, sweeping, cooking or looking after the infants.

39 For example, depending on the needs and occasions of ritual practice, birth, as an opening and a beginning, can be linked either to the birth of the year – itself situated at different moments according to the occasion – or to the birth of spring, in the order of the year, or again, to dawn, in the order of the day, or to the appearance of the new moon, or to the sprouting of the corn, in the order of the grain cycle. None of these relationships prevents death, to which birth is opposed, from being identified either with the harvest, within the cycle of the life of the field, or with fecundation treated as resurrection, that is, with the birth of the year, within the grain cycle, etc.

40 Granet (1929: 304–9) gives some striking examples of the would-be impeccable, but merely fantastic, constructions produced by the effort to resolve the contradictions arising from the hopeless ambition of giving an intentionally systematized form to the objectively systematic products of analogical reason. For example, the theory of the five elements, a scholarly elaboration (second to third centuries BC) of the mythical system, establishes homologies between the cardinal points (plus the centre), the seasons, the substances (earth, fire, wood, metal) and the musical notes.

41 This meaning is clearly indicated by the rope game (Laoust 1920: 146–7), a sort of tug-of-war between the men and the women, in which the rope is suddenly cut and the women fall on their backs, inviting the sky to rain its fertilizing seed upon their wombs.

42 Magic, a product of anxiety and distress, produces anxiety and distress. Thus, the unremitting vigilance applied to speech is partly due to the fact that, very often, only the situation can determine the meaning of words (or acts) which, depending on the circumstances, will produce either themselves (e.g. dryness) or their opposite.

43 The familiarity with this mode of thought that is acquired in scientific practice itself can give one a (still very abstract) idea of the subjective sense of necessity that it gives to those whom it possesses. This elastic logic of overdetermined, 'fuzzy' relationships, protected from contradiction or error by its very weakness, can never encounter within itself an obstacle or a resistance capable of inducing reflexive examination or questioning. It can therefore only acquire a history from outside, through the contradictions arising from synchronization (favoured by literacy) and from the systematizing intention that it expresses and makes possible.

44 For contrary reasons, the analysis of the internal space of the house is reserved for an appendix. Although it retains its value as proof, it still relies on the logic of structuralism in its mode of exposition.

Appendix

1 This text is a slightly modified version of an article first published in 1970 (Bourdieu 1970). Although the principles of subsequent analyses are already present in it (as is shown by the attention given to the movements and displacements of the body), this interpretation of the space inside the Kabyle

house remains within the limits of structuralist thought. I have none the less chosen to reproduce it here, as an appendix, because of the status of the house as an inverted microcosm: the reduced image of the world that if offers could serve as an introduction to the more complete and more complex analyses elsewhere in this book. As well as providing additional evidence to support them, it gives an idea of the objectivist reconstruction of the system of relationships that was a necessary stage in moving to the final interpretation, which itself sometimes seems close to intuitionist apprehension.

2 Even the most precise and methodical descriptions of the Berber house (Laoust 1912: 12–15; 1920, 50–53; Maunier 1930: 120–77; Genevois 1955a) present, in their very meticulousness, systematic lacunae which had to be made good by direct inquiry.

3 With this one exception, the walls are given different names, according to whether they are considered from the inside or the outside. The outside is plastered over with a trowel by the men, whereas the inside is whitewashed and hand-decorated by the women. This opposition between the two points of view is, as will be seen, a fundamental one.

4 The transporting of beams, which are identified with the master of the house, is also called *thaârichth*, like the loft and like the stretcher used to carry a corpse or a wounded animal which will be slain far from the house. It gives rise to a social ceremony the meaning of which is exactly similar to that of burial. By virtue of its imperative character, the ceremonial form it assumes and the extent of the group that it mobilizes, this collective task (*thiwizi*) has no equivalent other than burial. As much merit (*h'assana*) accrues from taking part in the carrying of the beams, an act of piety always performed without remuneration, as from taking part in the collective activities connected with funerals (digging the grave, extracting or transporting the stone slabs, helping to bear the coffin or attending the burial).

5 Among the Arabs, to perform the magic rite intended to render women unfit for sexual relations, the betrothed girl is made to step through the slackened warp on the loom, from the outside inwards, that is, from the middle of the room towards the wall before which the weavers sit and work. The same operation, performed in the opposite direction, undoes the charm (Marçais and Guiga 1925: 395).

6 House building, which always takes place when a son is married and which symbolizes the birth of a new family, is forbidden in May, as is marriage (Maunier 1930).

7 The duality of rhythm linked to the division between the dry season and the wet season is manifested, *inter alia*, in the domestic order. Thus in summer the opposition between the lower part and the higher part of the house takes the form of the opposition between the house proper, where the women and children retire to bed and where the stores are kept, and the courtyard where hearth and hand-mill are set up, meals are eaten, and feasts and ceremonies take place.

8 The opposition between the house and the assembly (*thajmaâth*) is seen clearly in the different designs of the two buildings. Whereas the house is entered by the door in its front wall, the assembly building is designed as a long covered passage, completely open at the two gables, which one can walk right through.

9 The blacksmith is the man who, like women, spends his days indoors, beside the fire.

10 The hearth is the site of a number of rites and the object of taboos that make

it the opposite of the dark part of the house. For example, it is forbidden to touch the ashes during the night, to spit into the fireplace, to spill water or to weep tears there (Maunier 1930). Likewise, those rites that aim to bring about a change in the weather and are based on an inversion, make use of the opposition between the wet part and the dry part of the house. Thus, to change the weather from wet to dry, a wool-packing comb (an object made with fire and associated with weaving) and a glowing ember are left on the threshold overnight; conversely, to change from dry to wet weather, the wool-packing and carding combs are sprinkled with water on the threshold during the night.

11 Conversely, the bringing of new fireplace stones into the house, on inaugural dates, is a filling-up, an input of goodness and prosperity. The divinations performed at such times are therefore concerned with prosperity and fertility. If a cockchafer grub is found under one of the stones, there will be a birth in the course of the year; a green plant means a good harvest; ants, a bigger flock; a woodlouse, more cattle.

12 The bereaved are told, to console them, 'He will leave you *baraka*', if an adult has died, or '*Baraka* has not gone out of the house', in the case of a baby. The corpse is placed near the door with the head turned towards the outside. Water is heated on the stable side and the washing of the corpse is done near the stable; the embers and ashes of this fire are scattered outside the house; the board used in washing the corpse is left in front of the door for three days.

13 Various objects are hung over the door. Their common feature is that they manifest the dual function of the threshold, a selective barrier which must keep out emptiness and evil while letting in fullness and goodness.

14 A newborn girl is wrapped in the softness of a silk scarf; a boy is swathed in the dry, rough bindings that are used to tie sheaves.

15 It goes without saying that the opposite arrangement (as in a mirror image of the ground-plan of the house) is possible, though rare. It is explicitly said that all that comes from the west brings misfortune, and a door facing that way can only receive darkness and sterility. In fact, if the inversion of the 'ideal' ground-plan is rare, this is firstly because when secondary houses are set at right angles around the courtyard, they are often simply lodging rooms, without kitchen or cowshed, and the courtyard is often closed off, on the side opposite the front of the main house, by the back of a neighbouring house, which itself faces east.

16 The two *s'uffs*, political and martial factions which were mobilized as soon as any incident occurred (and which were related in variable ways to the kinship-based social units, ranging from superimposition to complete separation), were named *s'uff* of the upper part (*ufella*) and *s'uff* of the lower part (*buadda*), or *s'uff* of the right (*ayafus*) and *s'uff* of the left (*azelmadh*), or *s'uff* of the east (*acherqui*) and *s'uff* of the west (*aghurbi*). The last pair of terms was less common but was kept to designate the two sides in ritual games (from which the traditional battles between the two *s'uffs* derived their logic); it still survives nowadays in the language of children's games.

17 In some regions of Kabylia, two people in a liminal situation – the young bride, and a boy circumcised at the time of the same celebration – must cross paths on the same threshold.

18 This explains why the threshold is directly or indirectly associated with the rites intended to bring about a reversal of the course of events by carrying out a reversal of the basic oppositions: the rites to obtain rain or fine weather, for instance, or those performed at the turning-points of the year (e.g. the night

before *en-nayer*, the first day of the solar year, when charms are buried at the threshold).

19 The correspondence between the four corners of the house and the four cardinal points is expressed clearly in some propitiatory rites observed in the Aures. When the fireplace is renewed, on new year's day, the Chaouia woman cooks some fritters, breaks the first one cooked into four pieces, and throws them towards the four corners of the house. She does the same thing with the ritual dish prepared on the first day of spring (Gaudry 1929: 58–9).

20 To show that this is probably an instance of a very general form of magical thought, one further, very similar, example will suffice. The Arabs of the Maghreb considered it a good sign, Ben Cheneb (1905–7: 312) relates, for a horse to have its front right foot white and its rear left foot white. The master of such a horse cannot fail to be happy, since he mounts towards white and dismounts towards white (Arab horsemen mount on the right and dismount on the left).

Bibliography

ABBREVIATIONS

ARSS = *Actes de la recherche en sciences sociales*
BEI = *Bulletin de l'enseignement des indigènes*
FDB = Fichier de documentation berbère (published at Fort-National)
RA = *Revue africaine*

Anon. (n.d.): Démarches matrimoniales. FDB.
Anon. 1934: L'Aïd S'Ghir en Kabylie. *BEI*, Jan.–Dec.
Anon. 1954: L'immolation. FDB.
Anon. 1964: Valeur du sang, rites et pratiques à l'intention sacrificielle. FDB, no. 84.
Arrow, K. J. 1962: The economic implications of learning by doing. *Review of Economic Studies*, 39, 155–73.
Attneave, F. 1953: Psychological probability as a function of experienced frequency. *Journal of Experimental Psychology*, 46, 81–6.
Bachelard, G. 1969: *The Poetics of Space*. Boston, Mass.: Beacon Press.
Balfet, H. 1955: La poterie des Aïd Smail du Djurdjura: éléments d'étude esthétique. *RA*, 99, 289–340.
Bally, C. 1965: *Le Langage et la vie*, Geneva: Droz.
Bassagana, R. and Sayad, A. 1974: *Habitat traditionnel et structures familiales en Kabylie*. Algiers: Mémoires du C.R.A.P.E.
Barth, F. 1953: Principles of social organization in southern Kurdistan. *Universitets Ethnografiske Museum Bulletin* (Oslo), 7.
Basset, A. 1963: *Textes berbères du Maroc (parler des Aït Sadden)*. Paris: Imprimerie nationale.
Basset, H. 1922: Les rites du travail de la laine à Rabat. *Hesperis*, 2, 139–60.
Bateson, G. 1958: *Naven*. Stanford, Calif.: Stanford University Press (1st edn 1936).
Becker, G. S. 1965: A theory of the allocation of time. *Economic Journal*, 75, 493–517.
Ben Cheneb, M. 1905–7: *Proverbes arabes d'Alger et du Maghreb*. Paris: Leroux.
Bendaoud, Capitaine 1935: L'adoption des adultes par contrat mixte de mariage et de travail chez les Beni Mguild. *Revue marocaine de législation, doctrine, jurisprudence chérifiennes*, 2, 34–40.

Benet, F. 1957: Explosive markets: the Berber highlands. In K. Polanyi, C. M. Arensberg and H. W. Pearson (eds), *Trade and Market in the Early Empires*, New York: Free Press.

Benveniste, E. 1973: *Indo-European Language and Society*. London: Faber.

Berelson, B. and Steiner, G. A. 1964: *Human Behavior*. New York: Harcourt, Brace & World.

Berque, J. 1954: Qu'est-ce qu'une tribu nord-africaine? In *Hommage à Lucien Febvre*, Paris.

——1955: *Les Structures sociales du Haut Atlas*. Paris: PUF.

——1956: Cent vingt-cinq ans de sociologie maghrébine. *Annales*.

Biarnay, S. 1909: *Études sur le dialecte berbère d'Ouargla*. Paris.

——1915: Notes sur les chants populaires du Rif. *Archives berbères*. 1, 23ff.

——1924: *Notes d'ethnographie et de linguistique nord-africaines*. Paris: Leroux.

Bologna, F. 1972: *Dalle arti minori all'industrial design. Storia di una ideologia*. Bari: Laterza.

——1979: I metodi di studio dell'arte italiana e il problema metodologico oggi. In *Storia dell'arte italiana, I*, Rome: Einaudi, 165–273.

Boudon, R. 1977: *Effets pervers et ordre social. Paris: PUF.* (Trans. *The Unintended Consequences of Social Action*, London: Macmillan, 1982.)

Boulifa, S. 1913: *Méthode de langue kabyle. Étude linguistique et sociologique sur la Kabylie du Djurdjura*. Algiers: Jourdan.

Bourdieu, P. 1958: *Sociologie de l'Algérie*. Paris: PUF. For English translation see 1962c.

——1961: Révolution dans la révolution. *Esprit*, 1, 27–40.

——1962a: De la guerre révolutionnaire à la révolution. In F. Perroux (ed.), *L'Algérie de demain*, Paris: PUF, 5–13.

——1962b: Célibat et condition paysanne. *Études rurales*, 5–6, 32–136.

——1962c: *The Algerians*. Boston, Mass.: Beacon Press.

——1963: *Travail et travailleurs en Algérie*. Paris/The Hague: Mouton.

——1964a: *Le Déracinement: la crise de l'agriculture traditionnelle en Algérie*. Paris: Éditions de Minuit.

——1964b: The attitude of the Algerian peasant towards time. In J. Pitt-Rivers (ed.), *Mediterranean Countrymen*, Paris/The Hague: Mouton, 55–72.

——1965: The sentiment of honour in Kabyle society. In J. Peristiany (ed.), *Honour and Shame*, London: Weidenfeld & Nicolson, 191–241.

——1966: *L'Amour de l'art*. Paris: Éditions de Minuit (to be published in translation by Polity Press, 1990).

——1968: Structuralism and theory of sociological knowledge. *Social Research*, 35 (4), 681–706.

——1970: La maison kabyle ou le monde renversé. In J. Pouillon and P. Maranda (eds), *Échanges et communications. Mélanges offerts à Claude Lévi-Strauss à l'occasion de son 60ᵉ anniversaire*, Paris/The Hague: Mouton, 739–58.

——1971: Genèse et structure du champ religieux. *Revue française de sociologie*, 12, 295–334.

——1972: Les stratégies matrimoniales dans le système des stratégies de repro-duction. *Annales*, 4–5, 1105–27.

——1975a: L'ontologie politique de Martin Heidegger. *ARSS*, 5–6, 109–56.

——1975b: Le langage autorisé. Note sur les conditions sociales de l'efficacité du discours rituel. *ARSS*, 5–6, 183–90.

——1976: Les conditions sociales de la production sociologique: sociologie coloniale et décolonisation de la sociologie. In *Le Mal de voir*, Paris: Union Générale d'Éditions, Cahiers Jussieu 2, 416–27.

——1979: The sense of honour. In *Algeria 1960*, Cambridge: Cambridge University Press and Paris: Éditions de la Maison des Sciences de l'Homme.

——1984: *Distinction: A Social Critique of the Judgement of Taste*. London: Routledge & Kegan Paul and Cambridge, Mass.: Harvard University Press (original French edn 1979).

Bourdieu, P. and Delsaut, Y. 1975: Le couturier et sa griffe, contribution à une théorie de la magie. *ARSS*, 1, 7–36.

Bourdieu, P. and Saint-Martin, M. de 1975: Les catégories de l'entendement professoral. *ARSS*, 3, 69–93.

Bourdieu, P. and Sayad, A. 1964: *Le Déracinement: la crise de l'agriculture traditionnelle en Algérie*. Paris: Éditions de Minuit.

Bourrilly, J. 1932: *Éléments d'ethnographie marocaine*. Ed. E. Laoust. Paris: Librairie coloniale et orientaliste Larose.

Bousquet, G. H. 1934: Note sur le mariage mechrouth dans la région de Gouraya. *Revue algérienne*. Jan.–Feb., 9–11.

Brunswik, E. 1949: Systematic and representative design of psychological experiments. In J. Neymen (ed.), *Proceedings of the Berkeley Symposium on Mathematical Statistics and Probability*. Berkeley, Calif.: University of California Press, 143–202.

Calvet, L. 1957: Rites agraires en Kabylie. *Algeria* (Algiers), new series, 51, 18–23.

Chantréaux, G. 1941–2. Le tissage sur métier de haute-lisse à Aït Hichem et dans le Haut-Sebaou. *RA*, 85, 78–116 and 212–29; and 86, 261–313.

Chastaing, M. 1951: *La Philosophie de Virginia Woolf*. Paris: PUF.

Chelhod, J. 1965: Le mariage avec la cousine parallèle dans le système arabe. *L'Homme*, 5 (3–4), 113–73.

Chomsky, N. 1967: General properties of language. In I. L. Daley (ed.), *Brain Mechanisms Underlying Speech and Language*, New York/London: Grune & Straton, 73–88.

Cornford, F. M. 1957: *From Religion to Philosophy: A Study in the Origins of Western Speculation*. New York and Evanston, Ill.: Harper & Row (1st edn 1914).

Cournot, A. 1922: *Essai sur les fondements de la connaissance et sur les caractères de la critique philosophique*. Paris: Hachette (1st edn 1851).

Cuisenier, J. 1962: Endogamie et exogamie dans le mariage arabe. *L'Homme*, 2 (2), 80–105.

Dallet, J.-M. 1949: Les i'assassen. FDB.

——1953: Le verbe kabyle. FDB.

Destaing, E. 1907: *Fêtes et coutumes saisonnières chez les Beni Snous*. Algiers: Jourdan.

——1911: *Études sur le dialecte berbère des Beni Snous*. Paris: Leroux.

——n.d.?: Interdictions de vocabulaire en berbère. In *Mélanges René Basset*.

Détienne, M. and Vernant, J. P. 1979: *La Cuisine du sacrifice en pays grec*. Paris: Gallimard.

Devaux, C. 1859: *Les Kébaïles du Djerdjera. Études nouvelles sur les pays vulgairement appelés la Grande Kabylie*. Marseilles: Camion and Paris: Challamel.

Devulder, M. 1951: Peintures murales et pratiques magiques dans la tribu des Ouadhias. *RA*, 95.

———1957: Rituel magique des femmes kabyles, tribu des Ouadhias. *RA*, 101, 299–362.

Dostoyevsky, F. 1966: The gambler. In *The Gambler, Bobok, A Nasty Story*. Harmondsworth: Penguin.

Doutté (ed.): *Magie et religion dans l'Afrique du Nord*. Algiers.

Dubin, R. and Dubin, E. R. 1965: Children's social perceptions: a review of research. *Child Development*, 38 (3).

Duby, G. 1973: *Hommes et structures du Moyen Age*. Paris/The Hague: Mouton.

———1976: *Le Temps des cathédrales: l'art et la société de 980 à 1420*. Paris: Gallimard.

Duhem, P. *The Aim and Structure of Physical Theory*. New York: Atheneum. (2nd French edn 1914.)

Dumont, L. 1971: *Introduction à deux théories d'anthropologie sociale*. Paris: Mouton.

Durkheim, E. 1956: *Education and Sociology*. New York: Free Press.

———1960: *Montequieu and Rousseau: Forerunners of Sociology*. Ann Arbor, Mich.: University of Chicago Press.

———1976: *The Elementary Forms of the Religious Life*. London: Allen & Unwin. (1st French edn 1912.)

———1977: *The Evolution of Educational Thought*. London: Routledge & Kegan Paul. (*L'Évolution pédagogique en France*. 1938.)

———1982a: *The Rules of Sociological Method*. New York: Free Press. (1st French edn 1895.)

———1982b: The materialist conception of history. In 1982a, 167–74.

Elster, J. 1979: *Ulysses and the Sirens*. Cambridge: Cambridge University Press.

Emmerich, W. 1959: Young children's discriminations of parents and child roles. *Child Development*, 30, 403–19.

———1961: Family role concepts of children ages six to ten. *Child Development*, 32, 609–24.

Erikson, E. H. 1943: Observations on the Yurok: childhood and world image. *University of California Publications in American Archaeology and Ethnology*, 35, 257–302.

———1945: Childhood and tradition in two American Indian tribes. In *The Psychoanalytic Study of the Child*, New York: International Universities Press, vol. I.

Favret, J. 1966: La segmentarité au maghreb. *L'Homme*, 6 (2), 105–11.

———1968: Relations de dépendance et manipulation de la violence en Kabylie. *L'Homme*, 8 (4), 18–44.

Finley, M. I. 1953: Land debt and the man of property in classical Athens. *Political Science Quarterly*, 68, 249–68.

———1965a: Technical innovation and economic progress in the ancient world. *Economic History Review*, 18, 29–45.

———1965b: La servitude pour dettes. *Revue d'histoire du droit français et étranger*, 4th series, 43, 159–84.

Frazer, J. G. 1912: The spirits of the corn and the wild. In *The Golden Bough*, London: Macmillan (3rd edn), vol. I, part 5, ch. 7, 214–69.

Freud, S. 1961: Negation. In *Complete Psychological Works*, London: Hogarth Press.

Gable, R. W. 1953: N.A.M.: Influential lobby or kiss of death? *Journal of Politics*, 15 (2).

Galand-Pernet, P. 1958: La vieille et la légende des jours d'emprunt au Maroc. *Hesperis*, 29–94.

——1969: Un 'schème-grille' de la poésie berbère, étude du motif des métamorphoses dans les poèmes chleuhs. *Word*, 25, 120–30.

Garfinkel, H. 1967: *Studies in Ethnomethodology*. Englewood Cliffs, NJ: Prentice-Hall.

Gaster, T. H. 1961: *Thespis: Ritual, Myth and Drama in the Ancient Near East*. New York: Doubleday.

Gaudry, M. 1929: *La Femme chaouia de l'Aurès. Études de sociologie berbère*. Paris: Geuthner.

Geertz, C. 1960: *The Religion of Java*. New York: Free Press and London: Collier-Macmillan.

Genevois, H. 1955a: L'habitation kabyle. FDB, no. 46.

——1955b: Ayt-Embarek, Notes d'enquête linguistique sur un village des Beni-Smaïl de Kerrata. FDB, no. 49.

——1962: Tawrirt n'At Mangellat. FDB.

——1963: Trois cent cinquante énigmes kabyles. FDB.

——1967: Sut-Tadut, la laine et le rituel des tisseuses. FDB.

——1968: Superstition, recours des femmes kabyles. FDB, nos 97 and 100.

——1969: La femme kabyle: les travaux et les jours. FDB.

——1972: La terre pour le Kabyle, ses bienfaits, ses mystères. FDB.

Gluckman, M. 1961: Ethnographic data in British social anthropology. *Sociological Review*, 9, 5–17.

Goody, J. 1977: *The Domestication of the Savage Mind*. Cambridge: Cambridge University Press.

Goody, J. (ed.) 1968: *Literacy in Traditional Societies*. Cambridge: Cambridge University Press.

Goody, J. and Watt, I. 1962–3. The consequences of literacy. *Comparative Studies in Society and History*, 5.

Gourou, P. 1963: Le déterminisme physique dans l'Esprit des lois. *L'Homme*, 3 (4), 5–11.

Granet, M. 1929: *La Civilisation chinoise*. Paris: Armand Colin.

Granqvist, H. 1931. Marriage conditions in a Palestinian village. *Commentationes Humanarum Societas Fennica*, 3.

Greene, W. C. 1951: The spoken and the written word. *Harvard Studies in Classical Philology*, 9, 24–58.

Hanoteau, A. 1867: *Poésies populaires de la Kabylie du Djurdjura*. Paris: Imprimerie nationale.

Hanoteau, A. and Letourneux, A. 1873: *La Kabylie et les coutumes kabyles*. Paris: Imprimerie nationale.

Harris, M. 1964: *The Nature of Cultural Things*. New York: Random House.

Harrison, J. 1963: *Themis: A Study of the Social Origins of Greek Religion*. London: Merlin Press (1st edn 1912).

Hartley, R. E. 1960. Children's concept of male and female roles. *Merril-Palmer Quarterly*, 6, 83–91.

Hassler, A. 1942: Calendrier agricole. FDB.

Havelock, E. A. 1963: *Preface to Plato*. Cambridge, Mass.: Harvard University Press.

Hénine, 1942: Préjugés locaux et coutumes agricoles locales. *L'Éducation algérienne*, 3, 19–26.

Hocart, A. M. 1970: *Kings and Councillors*. Chicago: University of Chicago Press (first pub. 1936).

Husserl, E. 1931: *Ideas: General Introduction to Pure Phenomenology*. London: Allen & Unwin.

Jakobson, R. 1956: *Fundamentals of Language*. The Hague: Mouton.

Klein, M. 1948: *Contributions to Psychoanalysis*. London: Hogarth.

Kohlberg, L. 1967. A cognitive-developmental analysis of children's sex-role concepts and attitudes. In E. Maccoby (ed.), *The Development of Sex Differences*, London: Tavistock.

Lacoste, C. 1962: *Bibliographie ethnographique de la Grande Kabylie*. Paris: Mouton.

Lacoste-Dujardin, C. 1970: *Le Conte kabyle. Étude ethnologique*. Paris: Maspero.

Lanfry, J. 1947a: Dialogue entre l'homme et l'hiver. FDB, no. 19.

——1947b: La vie féminine en Kabylie, *lembarba*, abandon par l'épouse du domicile conjugal. FDB.

Laoust, E. 1912: *Études sur le dialecte berbère du Chenoua*. Paris: Leroux.

——1918a: *Étude sur le dialecte berbère des Ntifa*. Paris.

——1918b: Le nom de la charrue et de ses accessoires chez les Berbères. *Archives berbères*, 3, 1–30.

——1920: *Mots et choses berbères: notes de linguistique et d'ethnographie*. Paris: Challamel.

——1921: Noms et cérémonies de feux de joie chez les Berbères du Haut et de l'Anti-Atlas. *Hesperis*.

Leach, E. 1962: On certain unconsidered aspects of double descent systems. *Man*, 62.

Le Ny, J. F. 1979: *La Sémantique psychologique*. Paris: PUF.

Lee, R. W. 1967: *Ut Pictura Poesis*. New York: Norton.

Lefébure, C. 1978: Linguistique et technologie culturelle, l'exemple du métier à tisser vertical berbère. *Techniques et culture*, Bulletin de l'équipe de recherche 191, no. 3, 84–148.

Lefèvre, L. 1939. *Recherches sur la condition de la femme kabyle*. Algiers: Carbonel.

Leibniz, G. W. 1866a. *Œuvres philosophiques*. Ed. P. Janet. Paris: Ladrange.

——1866b: *Nouveaux essais*. In Leibniz 1866a, tome I.

——1866c: *Second éclaircissement du système de la communication des substances* (first pub. 1696). In Leibniz 1866a, tome II.

——1866d: *Théodicée*. In Leibniz 1866a, tome I.

——1939a: *Opuscula Philosophica Selecta*. Paris: Boivin.

——1939b: *Meditationes de cognitione, veritate et ideis*. In Leibniz 1939a.

——1939c: *De ipsa natura*. In Leibniz 1939a.

Leiris, M. 1934. *L'Afrique fantôme*. Paris: Gallimard.

Lévi-Provençal, E. 1918: Pratiques agricoles et fêtes saisonnières des tribus Djebalah de la vallée moyenne de l'Ourargla. *Archives berbères*, 3.

Lévi-Strauss, C. 1947: La sociologie française. In G. Gurvich and W. E. Moore (eds), *La Sociologie au XXᵉ siècle*, Paris: PUF, vol. II.

——1951: Language and the analysis of social laws. *American Anthropologist*, April–June.

——1952: *Race and History*. Paris: UNESCO.

——1958: La geste d'Asdiwal. École pratique des hautes études, Section des sciences religieuses, Annuaire 1958–1959. (Trans. as 'The story of Asdiwal', in *Structural Antrhopology*, vol. II, London: Allen Lane, 1977, pp. 146–97.)

——1959: Le problème des relations de parenté. In J. Berque (ed.). *Systèmes de parenté*, Paris: École pratique des hautes études.

——1966: *The Savage Mind*. London: Weidenfeld & Nicolson. (1st French edn 1964.)

——1968: *Structural Anthropology*. London: Allen Lane. (1st French edn 1958.)

——1969: *The Elementary Structures of Kinship*. Revised edition. London: Social Science Paperbacks. (1st French edn 1967.)

——1970: *The Raw and the Cooked*. Trans. J. and D. Weightman. London: Cape. (1st French edn 1964.)

——1987: *Introduction to the Work of Marcel Mauss*. Trans. F. Baker. London: Routledge & Kegan Paul. (1st French edn 1950.)

Lord, A. B. 1960: *The Singer of the Tales*. Cambridge, Mass.: Harvard University Press.

Sister Louis de Vincennes 1953: Les At Mengellat. FDB.

——n.d.: Les quatre saisons. FDB.

MacKean, D. 1944: *Party and Pressure Politics*. New York: Houghton Mifflin.

Mammeri, M. and Bourdieu, P. 1978: Dialogue sur la poésie orale en Kabylie. *ARSS*, 23, 51–66.

Marçais, W. and Guiga, A. 1925: *Textes arabes de Takrouna*. Paris: Leroux.

Marchand, H.-F. 1939: Masques carnavalesques et carnaval en Kabylie. In *4ᵉ Congrès de la Fédération des sociétés savantes de l'Afrique du Nord (Rabat, 1938)*, Algiers, 805–14.

Marcy, G. 1930: Le mariage en droit coutumier zemmour. *Revue algérienne, tunisienne et marocaine de législation et jurisprudence*, July.

——1941: Les vestiges de la parente maternelle en droit coutumier berbère et le régime des successions touarègues. *RA*, 85, 187–211.

Marx, K. 1956: The time of production. In *Capital*, Moscow: Progress Publishers, vol. II, part 2, ch. 13, 242–51.

——1973: *Grundrisse*. Harmondsworth: Penguin.

——1975: *Economic and Philosophic Manuscripts of 1844*. In K. Marx, *Early Writings*, Harmondsworth: Penguin.

Matheron, A. 1969: *Individu et société chez Spinoza*. Paris: Éditions de Minuit.

Maunier, R. 1930: *Mélanges de sociologie nord-africaine*. Paris: Alcan.

Maury, M. 1939: Coutumes et croyances se rapportant à la vie agricole à Makouda, commune mixte de la Mizrana. *BEI*, 37–47.

Mauss, M. 1966: *The Gift*. London: Cohen & West.

Mead, G. H. 1962: *Mind, Self and Society*. Chicago: University of Chicago Press.

Menouillard, 1910: Pratiques pour solliciter la pluie. *Revue tunisienne*.

Monchicourt, C. 1915: Mœurs indigènes: les rogations pour la pluie (Thlob en nô). *Revue tunisienne*, 65–81.

Mott, M. 1954: Concept of mother: a study of four- and five-year old children. *Child Development*, 23, 92–104.

Murphy, R. F. and Kasdan, L. 1959: The structure of parallel cousin marriage. *American Anthropologist*, 61, 17–29.

Needham, R. 1958: The formal analysis of prescriptive patrilateral cross-cousin marriage. *Southwestern Journal of Anthropology*, 14, 199–219.

Nicod, J. 1961: *La Géometrie dans le monde sensible*. Paris: PUF.

Nicolet, C. 1966: *L'Ordre équestre à l'époque républicaire*, vol. I, Paris.

Nietzsche, F. 1954: *Twilight of the Idols*. In *The Portable Nietzsche*, ed. W. Kaufmann, New York: Viking Press.

——1966: *Beyond Good and Evil*. Trans. W. Kaufman. New York: Vintage Books.

——1969: *On the Genealogy of Morals*. Trans. W. Kaufmann and R. J. Hollingdale. New York: Vintage Books.

Notopoulos, J. A. 1938: Mnemosyme in oral literature. *Transactions and Proceedings of the American Philological Association*, 69, 465–93.

Nouschi, A. 1961: *Enquête sur le niveau de vie des populations rurales constantinoises de la conquête jusqu'en 1919. Essai d'histoire économique et sociale* Paris: PUF.

——1962: *La Naissance du nationalisme algérien*. Paris: Éditions de Minuit.

Ouakli, S. 1933a: Légendes kabyles sur les temps et les saisons. *BEI*, 112–14.

——1933b: Le calendrier agricole en Kabylie. *BEI*, 25–8.

——1935: Aïn-Sla (légende kabyle). *BEI*, 14–16.

Panofsky, E. 1924–5: Die Perspektive als 'symbolische Form'. *Vorträge der Bibliothek Warburg*, Leipzig/Berlin, 258–330.

Parfit, D. 1973. Later selves and moral principles. In A. Montefiore (ed.), *Philosophy and Personal Relations*, London: Routledge & Kegan Paul, 137–69.

Pascal, B. 1966: *Pensées*. Trans. A. J. Krailsheimer. Harmondsworth: Penguin.

Peters, E. L. 1967. Some structural aspects of the feud among the camel-herding Bedouin of Cyrenaica. *Africa*, 37, 261–82.

Picard, 1958. *Textes berbères dans le parler des Irjen*. Algiers, typolithograph.

Polanyi, K. 1944: *The Great Transformation*. New York: Rinehart.

——1968: *Primitive, Archaic and Modern Economics*. New York: Doubleday.

Preston, M.G. and Baratta, P. 1948: An experimental study of the action-value of an uncertain income. *American Journal of Psychology*, 61, 183–93.

Proust, M. 1976. *Swann's Way*. London: Chatto & Windus.

Quine, W. V. 1972: Methodological reflections on current linguistic theory. In D. Harman and G. Davidson (eds), *Semantics of Natural Language*, Dordrecht: D. Reidel, 442–54.

Radcliffe-Brown, A. R. 1952: *Structure and Function in Primitive Society*, London: Cohen & West.

——1960: *African Systems of Kinship and Marriage*. London: Oxford University Press.

Rahmani, S. 1933: Les trois premiers jours des labours chez les Beni Amrous. *BEI*, no. 292.

——1935: Le mois de mai chez les Kabyles. *RA*, 2ᵉ & 3ᵉ trim., 361–6.

——1936: Rites relatifs à la vache et au lait. In *2ᵉ Congrès de la Fédération des sociétés savantes de l'Afrique du Nord (Tlemcen, 1936)*, Algiers, 791–809; also *RA*, 2ᵉ et 3ᵉ trim., 1936, 791–809.

——1938: La grossesse. *In 3ᵉ Congrès de la Fédération des sociétés savantes de l'Afrique du Nord (Constantine, 1937)*, Algiers, 217–46.

——1939a: L'enfant chez les Kabyles jusqu'à la circoncision. *RA*, 1ᵉʳ trim., 65–120.

——1939b: Coutumes kabyles du Cap Oakas. *RA*, 1ᵉʳ trim.

——1949: Le tir à la cible et le nif en Kabylie. *RA*, 93, 1ᵉʳ & 2ᵉ trim., 126–32.

Rolland, C. 1912: L'enseignement indigène et son orientation vers l'agriculture. *BEI*, April.

Rosenfield, H. 1957: An analysis of marriage statistics for a Moslem and Christian Arab village. *International Archives of Ethnography*, 48, 32–62.

Russell, B. 1938: *Power: A New Social Analysis*. London: Allen & Unwin.

Ruyer, R. 1966: *Paradoxes de la conscience et limites de l'automatisme*. Paris: Albin Michel.

Sahlins, D. D. 1960: Political power and the economy in primitive society. In G. E. Dole and R. L. Carneiro (eds), *Essays in the Science of Culture*, New York: Crowell, 390–415.

——1962–3: Poor man, rich man, big man, chief: political types in Melanesia. *Comparative Studies in Society and History*, 5, 285–303.

——1965: On the sociology of primitive exchange. In M. Banton (ed.), *The Relevance of Models for Social Anthropology*, London: Tavistock, 139–236.

Sister Saint-François and Sister Louis de Vincennes 1952. Politesse féminine kabyle. FDB, April.

Samuelson, P. 1951: *Economics*. New York/London: McGraw-Hill.

Sartre, J.-P. 1946: *Descartes*. Geneva/Paris: Éditions des Trois Collines.

——1953: Réponse à Lefort. *Les Temps modernes*, 89, 1571–1629.

——1957: *Being and Nothingness*. London: Methuen. (First pub. 1943, *L'Etre et le néant*, Paris: Gallimard.)

——1960: *Critique de la raison dialectique*. Paris: Gallimard.

——1972: *The Psychology of Imagination*. London: Methuen. (First pub. 1940, *L'Imaginaire*, Paris: Gallimard.)

Saussure, F. de 1974: *Course in General Linguistics*, London: Fontana.

Sayad, A. 1979: Les enfants illégitimes. *ARSS* 25, 61–82; and 26, 68–83.

Schœn, P. 1960: Les travaux et les jours du paysan kabyle. *Liens*, 12, 1–63.

Schutz, A. 1962: *Collected Papers, I: The Problem of Social Reality*. The Hague: Martinus Nijhoff.

Servier, J. 1962: *Les Portes de l'année*. Paris: Laffont.

——1964: *L'Homme et l'invisible*. Paris. Laffont.

Simon, H. 1954: A behavioral theory of rational choice. *Quarterly Journal of Economics*, 69, 99–118.

Tillion, G. 1938: Les sociétés berbères de l'Aurès méridional. *Africa*.

Turbet, Capitaine 1935: L'adoption des adultes chez les Ighezrane. *Revue marocaine de législation, doctrine, jurisprudence chérifiennes*, nos 2 & 3.

Turner, H. A. 1958: How pressure groups operate. *Annals of the American Academy of Political and Social Science*, 319, 63–72.

Turner, V. 1967: *The Forest of Symbols*. Ithaca, NY and London: Cornell University Press.

Valéry, P. 1960: Tel Quel. In *Œuvres*, vol. II, Paris: Gallimard.

Van Gennep, A. 1911: Études d'ethnographie algérienne. *Revue d'ethnologie et de sociologie*, 1–103.

——1913: *La Formation des légendes*. Paris: Flammarion.

——1960: *The Rites of Passage*. London: Routledge & Kegan Paul. (First French edn 1909.)

Van Velsen, J. 1964: *The Politics of Kinship: A Study in Social Manipulation among the Lakeside Tonga*. Manchester: Manchester University Press.

Vernant, J. 1972: Introduction to M. Détienne, *Les Jardins d'Adonis*, Paris: Gallimard.

Weber, M. 1922: *Gesammelte Aufsätze zur Wissenschaftslehre*. Tübingen: J. C. Mohr.

——1968: *Economy and Society*, vol. I. New York: Bedminster.

Weiszacker, C. C. von 1971: Notes on endogenous theory of change. *Journal of Economic Theory*, 3, 345–72.

Westermarck, E. 1911: The popular rituals of the great feasts in Morocco. *Folklore*.

——1926: *Ritual and Belief in Morocco*. London: Macmillan.

Whiting, J. M. W. 1941: *Becoming a Kwoma*. New Haven, Conn.: Yale University Press.

Williams, B. A. O. 1973: Deciding to believe. In *Problems of the Self*, Cambridge: Cambridge University Press, 136–51.

Wittgenstein, L. 1963: *Philosophical Investigations*. Oxford: Basil Blackwell.

——1979: *Remarks on Frazer's Golden Bough*. Retford: Brynmill.

Wolf, E. 1959: *Sons of the Shaking Earth*. Chicago: Chicago University Press.

Yamina (Aït Amar ou Saïd) 1952: Tarurirt Uzal (chez les Aït Mangellet) FDB.

——1960: Le mariage en Kabylie. Trans. by Sr Louis de Vincennes. *C.E.B.F.* no. 25, Fort-National (first pub. 1953).

Zellal, B. 1964: Le roman de chacal, contes d'animaux. FDB, no. 81.

Ziff, P. 1960: *Semantic Analysis*. New York: Cornell University Press.

Index

DISCARDED